University of Dublin,

TRINITY COLLEGE.

~~~~~~~~~

WAR LIST,

FEBRUARY, 1922

DUBLIN:

HODGES, FIGGIS, & CO.,

BOOKSELLERS TO THE UNIVERSITY,

20 NASSAU STREET.

University of Dublin,

TRINITY COLLEGE.

WAR LIST.

University of Dublin,

TRINITY COLLEGE.

WAR LIST.

THE War List of Trinity College, Dublin, is divided into the following parts:—

A. Members of Trinity College, containing 3,042 names, pp. 1–224.

B. Members of the Dublin University Officers' Training Corps who were not Members of Trinity College, containing 450 names, pp. 225–252.

C. Employés of Trinity College, containing 26 names, pp. 253–4.

D. Employés of Trinity College Printing House, containing 11 names, p. 255.

$$
\begin{aligned}
&A— 3,042 \\
&B— \quad 450 \\
&C— \quad \ \ 26 \\
&D— \quad \ \ 11 \\
&\overline{}
\end{aligned}
$$

Total, 3,529

The first List A attempts to record the Naval and Military services of Trinity men in the Great War. The intention is to give the month and year of the first appointment, and to record promotions, distinctions, casualties, and the fronts on which men served. In order to recognize the work done by the Dublin University Officers' Training Corps, those who were members of the

Corps are distinguished by an asterisk (*) placed in front of their names. In giving military appointments, honors, and names of regiments, the contractions used in the Army List have been adopted. Also the following abbreviations have been used :—" Ent. 1914 " denotes that a man entered Trinity College in 1914 ; and " Med. School 1914 " denotes that a man matriculated in the Medical School in 1914, but did not enter Trinity College.

This main List A of 3,042 names may be analysed as follows :—

454 were killed in action or died on service.

In addition, it has been noted that 343 other men were wounded ; but this number does not pretend to be adequate.

869 were Undergraduates, who gave up their College Course to serve in the Great War.

993 served on the Medical side, and, with few exceptions, were members of the Dublin University School of Physic.

231 were Graduates of the Dublin University School of Engineering.

193 were Chaplains.

27 were Women.

293 obtained the Military Cross, with 37 Bars.

102 were given the D.S.O., with 9 Bars.

It has been noted that 390 were mentioned in despatches ; but the number does not profess to be complete.

The list also contains the names of 96 persons who entered Trinity College after the completion of their service.

The following additional honors have been noted :—

V.C. 1 ; G.C.B. 1 ; K.C.B. 3 ; C.B. 22 ; K.C.M.G. 6 ; C.M.G. 31 ; K.C.I.E. 1 ; C.I.E. 4 ; G.C.V.O. 1 ; K.B.E. 6 ;

C.B.E. 21 ; O.B.E. 43 ; M.B.E. 16 ; Legion of Honor (France), 16 ; Croix de Guerre (France and Belgium), 82.

Order of :—The Crown (Italy and Belgium), 9 ; St. Anne (Russia), 2 ; White Eagle (Serbia), 3; St. Sava (Serbia), 5 ; Nile (Egypt), 2 ; Aviz (Portugal), 4 ; Leopold (Belgium), 1 ; King George (Greece), 2 ; St. George (Greece), 1 ; St. Stanislas (Russia), 1 ; St. Maurice and St. Lazarus (Italy), 1 ; Knight of Grace of St. John of Jerusalem, 1.

Knights, 2 ; C.H. 1 ; D.F.C. 1 ; Bronze Medal for Valour (Italy), 2 ; American D.S.M. 3 ; D.C.M. 1 ; M.S.M. 1 ; Certificates for Bravery, 3 ; Italian Silver Medal, 2 ; Royal Red Cross Decoration, 1 ; Greek Medal for Military Merit, 1 ; D.M.S. Italy, 1 ; Médaille d'Honneur, 1.

This record, although incomplete and inadequate, shows the splendid part played by the sons of the University of Dublin in the Great War. The record is incomplete because details of service can be supplied only by the men themselves or their friends. It is inadequate because no attempt is made to relate the sacrifices made by men in order to fight for the Empire. Many gave up good appointments ; and many came back from Australia, from Canada, from South Africa, and from the utmost bounds of the Empire to quit themselves like men in the great fight for freedom.

The record of services of Medical Graduates and Undergraduates has been compiled mainly by Dr. A. F. Dixon ; and in that department the War List of Sir Patrick Dun's Hospital, edited by Dr. H. C. Drury, has given much assistance. Also the record of the Engineering School, edited by Mr. J. T. Jackson, has been of great value, so that the names of no past or present members of the

School who served in the War have been omitted from this list.

In estimating the services rendered by members of the University of Dublin, it is right to bear in mind that there was no conscription in Ireland, so that, for the most part, these services were voluntary.

This list, by the kindness of the *Irish Times* newspaper, was published to date in twenty-six instalments in 1916 ; and a first edition was published in October of that year. Thus the fact that Trinity College was compiling such a list was given great publicity, and, accordingly, if any names are omitted, or if any records are incomplete, the editor cannot accept the whole responsibility.

In this list the names of those who worked at munitions are not given ; and the names of women are inserted only when they served in hospitals abroad, or in such positions that, had they been men, they would have been given military rank.

OFFICERS' TRAINING CORPS.

List B contains 450 names, which, together with 1,040 from List A, give a total of 1,490 men trained by the Corps. In trying to follow out the appointments of the men in List B, the editor found that 36 had been killed in action. This number does not profess to be exhaustive.

Of those in List C, 1 College Porter ; and of those in List D, 2 employés of the Printing House were killed or died on service.

M. W. J. FRY,
39 Trinity College,
Editor.

February, 1922.

University of Dublin,

TRINITY COLLEGE.

WAR LIST.

MEMBERS OF TRINITY COLLEGE.

A

Abbott, Vivian Hartley Church ;
Ent. 1898 ; Pte. 29 Canadian Infantry, June 1916 ; wounded at Lens, 21 Aug. 1917 ; missing, believed killed, 22 Aug. 1917.

Abraham, James Johnston ;
M.B. 1900; M.D. 1908 ; Surg. Serbian Army, Oct. 1914 to Apr. 1915 ; Lt. R.A.M.C., Apr. 1915 ; Capt. 1915 ; Maj. 1916 ; A/Lt.-Col. and A.D.M.S., H. Q., lines of communication, 1917 ; D.S.O., Apr. 1918 ; despatches, June 1918, Jan. 1919 ; C.B.E. (Mil.), June 1919.

*****Acheson, James Alexander ;**
B.A. 1915 ; Temp. 2 Lt. R.F.A., Dec. 1915 ; 2 Lt. R.H. and R.F.A., June 1917 ; Lt. 1917 ; wounded.

Acheson, Malcolm King ;
M.B. 1906; M.D. 1910; Lt. R.A.M.C., Oct. 1914 ; Capt. 1915 ; M.C. Nov. 1916 ; wounded, Oct. 1918.

*****Acheson, Richard William ;**
M.B. 1915 ; Lt. R.A.M.C., July 1915 ; Capt. 1916.

Acton, Rev. Armar Edward ;
B.A. 1910 ; Army Chaplain, 4 Cl., Mar. 1916 ; att. Border R. ; died of wounds, 4 Nov. 1917.

*****Acton, Owen Henry ;**
Ent. 1909 ; 2 Lt. 5 Conn. Rang., Oct. 1914 ; Lt. 1915 ; wounded, Kut El Amara, Jan. 1916.

*Adam, Alfred Chalmers ;
> Ent. 1915; 2 Lt. R.G.A., Aug. 1915; A/Capt. 1916; Lt. 1917 ; gassed, May 1918.

Adam, James MacCormac ;
> B.A.I. 1910 ; Ceylon Volunteers; Acting Censor, 1914–17.

Adam, Walter Eustace ;
> M.B. 1911 ; M.D. 1913 ; Lt. R.A.M.C., Dec. 1914 ; Temp. Capt. 1915 ; M.C. Dec. 1916 ; Capt. 1918; despatches, June 1919 ; A/Maj. 1919.

Adams, Charles ;
> M.B. 1880 ; Lt.-Col. I.M.S., Apr. 1901.

Adams, George Chatterton ;
> B.A. 1900 ; 2 Lt. 2 R. Innis. Fus., June 1901 ; Capt. 1915 ; Dardanelles; Serbia; commanding 5 Bn., Sept. 1915; M.C. ; Temp. Lt.-Col. commanding 6 Bn., Aug. 1917.

*Adderley, Alfred Herbert ;
> Ent. 1910; 2 Lt. 3 Ches. R., Oct. 1914 ; Lt. 1915 ; 2 Lt. 1, 2 Ches. R., 1916 ; Lt. 1917.

Adderley, Charles Joseph ;
> B.A.I., 1907 ; 2 Lt. R.G.A., Dec. 1916 ; Lt. 1918.

Adderley, Rev. Robert Archibald ;
> B.A. 1899; M.A. 1904 ; Army Chaplain, 4 Cl., Oct. 1915 ; France, 1915.

Alcock, Richard Evans ;
> Ent. 1910 ; 2 Lt. R.G.A., Aug. 1914 ; Capt. 1916 ; died in hospital, Malta, 1 March 1917.

Alderdice, Gerald Leslie ;
> Ent. 1908 ; Driver H.A.C., Sept. 1914 ; Egypt 1915 ; 2 Lt. R.G.A., Oct. 1916 ; wounded, Aug. 1917.

Alexander, Rev. Alfred Gahagan ;
> M.B. and M.D. 1906; Lt. R.A.M.C., Jan. 1916 ; Capt. 1917.

Alexander, John Donald ;
> M.B. 1889 ; Lt. Col. R.A.M.C., Aug. 1914 ; despatches, Jan. 1917, May 1917; D.S.O., June 1917; Officer, Order of Leopold, Sept. 1917 ; Croix de Guerre, Mar. 1918; despatches, 1919 ; C.B E., June 1919.

Alison, Douglas Smyth ;
> Ent. 1907 ; Pte. 3 Sea. Highrs. 1914 ; 2 Lt. 15 London R., Oct. 1917.

*Allardyce, George Gilmour.
> Ent. 1912; Australian A.M.C., Apr. 1915 ; wounded, Dardanelles ; died at Oxford of wounds received in France, 18 May 1918.

*Allardyce, William Swirles;
Ent. 1914; Surg. Prob. R.N.V.R., Oct. 1916; H. M. S.
"Negro"; lost in collision, N. Sea, 21 Dec. 1916.

Allen, Atwell Harold;
Ent. 1910; 2 Lt. 13 R. Ir. Rif., Sept. 1914; Lt. 1915.

Allen, George Henry Loftus;
Ent. 1910: Lt. 13 Conn. Rang., Sept. 1914; Lt. Empld. Recg.
Duties, May 1915.

Allen, George Leverstone;
Assistant Registrar, School of Physic; Major R.A.M.C., March
1916.

*Allen, Harold Gower;
Ent. 1910: 2 Lt. A.S.C., Oct. 1914; Lt. 1917.

Allen, Theodore Wright;
M.B. 1914; Lt. R.A.M.C., T. F., June 1915; Capt. 1915;
France 1916.

Allen, Wellesley Roe;
M.B. 1909; Lt. R.A.M.C., July 1915; invalided with dysentery
from Helles to Alexandria, Dec. 1915; Capt. 1916; Ghaza Campaign, Egypt; S.M.O. to Egyptian Hospital, Cairo; died, Cairo,
of typhus, 11 March 1919.

*Allen, Wentworth;
B.A.I. 1915; Cadet R.E., May, 1916; 2 Lt. Aug. 1916; Lt.
1918; France; Italy; despatches.

Allen, William;
Ent. 1914; Pte. D Co. 7 R. Dub. Fus., Nov. 1914; wounded,
Gallipoli, Aug. 1915; 2 Lt. 15 L'pool R., Dec. 1915.

Allen, William Hamilton;
M.B. 1883; M.D. 1889; Lt. R.A.M.C., March 1915; Capt. 1916.

*Alley, George Oliver Fairlough;
M.B. 1915; Temp. Lt. R.A.M.C., July 1915; Temp. Capt. 1916;
M.C., June 1917; Bar to M.C., Sept. 1918; 2nd Bar, Feb. 1919;
Capt. R.A.M.C., Feb. 1919.

Allman, Rev. William Brown;
B.A. 1901; M.A. 1905; Army Chaplain, 4 Cl., June 1918.

Allman-Smith, Edward Percival;
M.B. 1910; Lt. R.A.M.C., Jan. 1912; Captain 1915; M.C.
Aug. 1917; O.B.E. 1919.

*Allman-Smith, Henry Vincent Lees;
Ent. 1914; 2 Lt. 12 R. Innis. Fus., Aug. 1915; wounded, Sept.
1916.

4 WAR LIST, TRINITY COLLEGE, DUBLIN.

Allworthy, Samuel William ;
M.A and M.D. 1890; Temp. Capt. R.A.M.C., May 1917 ;
Major; France.

*Alton, Ernest Henry, F.T.C.D. ;
B.A. 1896; M.A. 1899 ; Fellow 1905; Lt. T.F., O.T.C.,
Unattached List, June 1914 ; Capt. 1915 ; M.C., Jan. 1917.

Ambrose, Alexander ;
M.B. and M.D. 1883 ; Lt. R.A.M.C., Sept. 1914 ; att. 5 London
R. ; Capt. 1915.

Anderson, Frederick Alexander ;
M.B. 1909 ; M.D. 1912 ; Lt. R.A.M.C., May 1915 ; Capt. 1916.

Anderson, Robert Alexander ;
M.B. 1914 ; Lt. R.A.M.C., Nov. 1914 ; Capt. 1915.

Anderson, Rev. Samuel Robert ;
B.A. 1894 ; M.A. 1908 ; Chaplain R.N., Dec. 1902.

Anderson, Walter Graham Moore ;
M.B. 1902; Staff Surgeon R.N.; lost in the "Clan McNaughton,"
3 Feb. 1915.

Anderson, Wilfred Harpur ;
Ent. 1919 ; 2 Lt. R.G.A., July 1916 ; Lt. 1918.

*Andrews, Harold Edward ;
Ent. 1896; Lt. Prob. R.A.M.C., Aug. 1914 ; Surg. Prob.
R.N., H.M.S. "Mentor," Feb. 1915 ; wounded.

Annesley, Charles Dudley Joynt ;
Ent. 1906 ; 2 Lt. 3 R. Muns. Fus., July 1915 ; Pte. 11 R.
Highrs., April, 1916.

Archdale, Rev. Mervyn ;
B.A. 1890 ; Hon. Chaplain to Forces, 3 Cl., Aug. 1914 ; O.B.E.
1919.

Archer, Arthur Montfort ;
M.B. 1881 ; M.D. 1885 ; 2 War Hosp. Birmingham.

*Archer, Ernest Thomas James ;
Ent. 1919 ; Cadet D.U.O.T.C. 1918 ; volunteered and accepted.

Archer, George Johnston Stoney ;
M.B. 1897 ; Lt. R.A.M.C., July 1898 ; France, 1914 ; Lt. Col.
1915.

Ardill, George Hubert,
Ent. 1914 ; Pte. 5 E. Kent R., May 1915 ; 2 Lt. W. Kent R.
Jan. 1916 ; Lt. 1917.

*Armstrong, Arthur Patrick;
Ent. 1916; Rhyll, Sept. 1918; demob., Jan. 1919, and gazetted
2 Lt. R. Ir. Fus.

Armstrong, Rev. Aylmer Richard;
B.A. 1912; Pte. A.S.C., Nov. 1915; Salonika, 1915–17; 2 Lt.
R.G.A., S.R., Sept. 1917; Sheerness, 1917–18; Bere Island,
1918–19.

Armstrong, Charles Martin;
Ent. 1913; Pte. D. Comp., 7 R. Dub. Fus.; Gallipoli; invalided;
2 Lt. 10 R. Dub. Fus., Jan. 1916; France; killed in action, Beaumont Hamel, 8 Feb. 1917.

Armstrong, Claude Blakeley;
B.A. 1911; M.A. 1914; 2 Lt. O.T.C., T.F. Unattached List,
Nov. 1914.

*Armstrong, Gordon;
Ent. 1916; R. A. Cadet School, July 1917; 2 Lt. R.G.A., Dec.
1917.

Armstrong, Henrietta;
Ent. 1920; Inspector Munitions, 1916; Motor Despatch Rider
R.A.F., 1917–18; home.

Armstrong, James Noble;
M.B. 1914; Lt. R.A.M.C., Aug. 1914; Capt. 1915; att.
2 D.L.I.; killed, France, 22 Aug. 1915.

Armstrong, James Septimus;
Ent. 1912; Pte. R.A.M.C., July 1915; France, Sept. 1915, to
March 1917; 2 Lt. 6 R. Dub. Fus., Nov. 1917; France; M.C.,
1918.

Armstrong, William Edward Macaulay;
M.B. 1907; M.D. 1910; Lt. R.A.M.C., Sept. 1914; Capt. 1915.

*Arnold, William John;
Ent. 1912; 2 Lt. 6 R. Dub. Fus., Aug. 1914; Capt. 1915; 2-Lt.
(R.), June 1916.

Arundel, Robert James;
M.B. and M.D. 1895; on Hosp. Ship "Asturias," Oct. 1914;
Lt. R.A.M.C., June 1916; Capt. 1917.

Ashbee, Henry Guy Neville;
B.A. 1914; 2 Lt. A.S.C., July 1915; Lt. I.A. 1917.

Ashley, Maurice;
Ent. 1914; Sandhurst, Aug. 1916; 2 Lt. 1, 2 R. Ir. Fus., May
1917; killed in action, 23 Nov. 1917.

Ashworth, Albert Edwin ;
> Ent. 1911 ; Pte. 7 R. Dub. Fus., Aug. 1914 ; 2 Lt. A.S.C., May 1915 ; Capt. 1917.

Askins, John Hawkins ;
> M.B. 1904 ; Lt. R.A.M.C., Mar. 1915 ; Capt. 1916 ; wounded, Jan. 1917.

Askins, Robert Arthur ;
> M.B. 1907 ; M.D. 1913 ; Lt. R.A.M.C., Dec. 1915 ; Capt. 1916 ; despatches, Aug. 1919.

Aston, Herbert Reid ;
> B.A.I. 1907 ; 2 Lt. I.A. res. of offs., Jan. 1918 ; Lt. 1919 ; att. R.E. ; A/Major ; Mesopotamia.

Atkins, Robert Humphreys ;
> M.B. 1901 ; Staff Surg. R.N., June 1910 ; Surg. Cr., 1916 ; H. M. S. " Bristol," 1918 ; " Dido," 1919.

*Atkins, Robert Ringrose Gelston ;
> M.B. 1914 ; Lt. R.A.M.C., Aug. 1914 ; Capt. 1915 ; despatches, Jan, 1916 ; wounded, July 1917 ; M.C., Oct. 1917.

*Atkins, William Ringrose Gelston ;
> Sc.D. 1914 ; 2 Lt. R. Flying Corps, June 1916 ; temp. Capt. 1916 ; Egypt, 1916 ; Maj. 1918.

Atkinson, Rev. Charles Vereker Chester ;
> B.A. 1890 ; M.A. 1906 ; Army Chaplain, May, 1915.

Atkinson, Edward William ;
> B.A. 1894 ; 2 Lt. 1 R. Innis. Fus., Aug. 1896 ; Maj. 1915 ; D.S.O. May 1915 ; despatches.

Atkinson, Hon. Hector John ;
> Ent. 1897 ; 2 Lt. R. Ir. Fus., March 1900 ; France, 1914 ; Capt. 4 Bn. 1915 ; home duty, 1915 ; died, 26 May 1917.

Atkinson, John Noel ;
> Ent. 1919 ; A/Staff Sergt. R.A.M.C. ; wounded, June 1916.

*Atkinson, Matthew William ;
> Ent. 1910 ; 2 Lt. R.G.A., Oct. 1914 ; Adjt. Temp. Lt. 1916 ; A/Capt. 1917 ; despatches.

*Atkinson, Thomas John Day ;
> B.A. 1903 ; Capt. 5 R. Ir. Fus., Oct. 1914 ; Staff Captain, Jan. 1915 ; wounded, Dardanelles, Aug. 1915.

Atkinson, Thomas Joyce ;
> B.A. 1898 ; M.A. and LL.B. 1910 ; Capt. 9 R. Ir. Fus , Sept. 1914 ; Maj. 1915 ; missing, believed killed, 1 July 1916.

*Atkinson, William Herbert ;
> B.A. 1898 ; 2 Lt. 7 R. Dub. Fus., Feb. 1916.

Atkinson-Fleming, Frederick Charles;
> M.B. 1914 ; Lt. R.A.M.C., Aug. 1914; Capt. 1915; M.C. June 1916.

*Atock, Arthur George ;
> Ent. 1915; Pte. 11 Black Watch, March 1916 ; twice awarded Parchment Certificate for bravery in the field ; 2 Lt. R. Dub. Fus., Dec. 1916; trsf. R. E. Dec. 1917 ; M.C. Sept. 1918 ; 155 Fd. Coy. ; killed in action, 13 Sept. 1918.

Attridge, Richard John ;
> M.B. 1908 ; M.D. 1913; Lt. R.A.M.C., July 1915 ; Capt. 1916 ; Egypt; Palestine.

*Austin, James;
> B.A. 1910 ; M.A. 1914 ; 2 Lt. 14 Manch. R., Mar. 1915 ; died of wounds received in action, 21 June 1917.

Aykroyd, Wallace Ruddell ;
> Ent. 1919 ; Flight Cadet R.A.F., May 1918.

Aylward, Gerald Francis ;
> Ent. 1909 ; Capt. 50 Canadian Infantry.

B

Babington, Oscar John Gilmore ;
> B.A.I. 1901 ; Lt. Royal Marines, Oct. 1918.

Badham, Robert Armstrong Alexander ;
> Ent. 1916 ; 2 Lt. 61 King George's Own Pioneers, India, Dec. 1917 ; Mesopotamia, 1918 ; A/Capt. 1918; Lt. 1918.

*Baile, George Frederick Cecil ;
> B.A. 1915 ; 2 Lt. R.E., Dec. 1914 ; Lt. 1915 ; wounded, France, Dec. 1915 ; died of wounds, 9 Nov. 1917.

Baile, Robert Carlyle ;
> B.A.I. 1911 ; 2 Lt. R.E., Nov. 1914 ; killed in action, France, 16 Oct. 1915

*Bailey, Kenneth Claude;
> Ent. 1914 ; Pte. R.A.M.C.

Baillie, George ;
> M.B. 1900 ; Lt. R.A.M.C., June 1900 ; Maj. 1912.

*Baillie, George Richard Launcelot ;
> Ent. 1914; Temp. 2 Lt. 4 R. Innis. Fus., June 1915 ; 2 Lt. 1, 2 Bns., March 1916 ; Temp. Lt. 1917 ; killed in action, 3 Oct. 1918.

Baillie, John Robert ;
> B.A. 1881 ; Hon. Lt. Col. Donegal Artillery Militia ; retired ;
> Maj. R.A., Nov. 1914.

*Baillie, William Kingsley ;
> Ent. 1916 ; Quetta, July 1917 ; 2 Lt. 3 R. Innis. Fus., May
> 1918.

Baker, Arthur Lancelot;
> Ent. 1912 ; 2 Lt. 5 R. Dub. Fus., Aug. 1914 ; Lt. 1915.

*Baker, Arthur Wyndowe Willert ;
> M.B. 1875 ; M.D. 1887 ; M. Dent. Sc. 1904 ; Lt. R.A.M.C.
> (T. F.), Jan. 1916 ; A/Capt., 1916 ; despatches, Jan. 1917.

Baker, John Cotter ;
> M.B. 1908 ; Trooper, Nth. Bengal Mounted Rifles.

Baker, Richard John ;
> B.A. 1880 ; M.D. 1888 ; Lt. I.M.S., Apr. 1881 ; Lt. Col. 1901 ;
> retd. 1910 ; Commandant Indian Fld. Amb. C., Sept 1914.

Baker, Walter Henry ;
> Ent. 1912 ; Pte. R.A.M.C , Lance Corp., 1915 ; 2 Lt. M.G.C.,
> Aug. 1917 ; died of wounds, 20 Oct. 1918.

Ball, Annie Muriel Kift ;
> B.A. 1912 ; V.A.D., France 1916–19 ; despatches.

Ball, Sir Charles Arthur Kinahan, Bart. ;
> M.B. 1900 ; M.D. 1902 ; King George V Hospital, Dublin ;
> Major R.A.M.C., Jan. 1918 ; 83 (Dub.) Gen. Hosp., France,
> 1918.

Ball, Sir Charles Bent, Bart. ;
> M.Ch. 1872 ; M.D. 1875 ; Regius Prof. of Surgery in the
> University of Dublin ; Lt. Col. R.A.M.C., Nov. 1914 ; died, 17
> March 1916.

Ball, Charles Preston ;
> M.B. 1900 ; M.D. 1903 ; Temp. Major R.A.M.C., July 1917.

*Ball, Nigel Gresley ;
> B.A. 1914 ; 2 Lt. 8 R. Dub. Fus., Nov. 1914 ; Lt. 1915 ;
> wounded, France, Sept. 1916.

*Ball, Robert Gordon ;
> M.B. 1911 ; West Africa Med. S., 1914 ; Temp. Lt. R.A.M.C.
> with B.E.F. in Togoland and the Cameroons ; since dead.

*Ball, William Ormsby Wyndham ;
> M.B. 1912 ; Lt. R.A.M.C., Jan. 1913 ; killed in action, near
> the Aisne, 26 Sept. 1914.

Ballard, Robert;
> Ent. 1900; Pte. 1 L'pool R., Aug. 1915; killed in action, Neuve Chapelle, 10 March 1915.

*Ballentine, George Cecil ;
> Ent. 1911; Lt. 5 R. Innis. Fus., Nov. 1914; wounded Dardanelles, Aug. 1915; Capt. 1915; wounded, Sept. 1916.

*Ballentine, John Stevenson ;
> Ent. 1915; Saudhurst, Oct. 1915; Lt. I.A., Aug. 1917.

Banks, Harry ;
> L.M. 1917; M.B. 1918: Temp. Surg.-Lt. R.N., July, 1917; Grand Fleet, Destroyers, 1917, 1918.

*Bantry-White, Henry Ernest ;
> M.B. 1913; Lt. R.A.M.C., Aug. 1914; Capt. 1915; M.C. Aug. 1918; wounded Sept. 1918.

Barbor, John Hamilton ;
> B.A. 1911; 2 Lt. A.S.C., Sept. 1911; Capt. 1914; despatches, Jan. 1917 and May 1918; M.C. Jan. 1918.

Barbor, Richard Dawson ;
> B.A. 1900; Lt. A.S.C. 1901; despatches, 1916; Lt.-Col. and Assistant Qr. Master Gen., 1916.

Barker, Cecil Massy Arbuthnot;
> Ent. 1912; 2 Lt. 6 R. Ir. Fus., Sept. 1914; killed in action, Dardanelles, 17 Aug. 1915.

Barker, Rev. Ernest Lindsey-Bucknall ;
> B.A. 1907; M.A. 1913; Army Chaplain, 4 Cl., July 1915–19.

Barlas, Alexander Richard ;
> M.B. 1917; Temp. Lt. R.A.M.C., Oct. 1917; Temp. Capt. 1918; Lt. R.A.M.C., April 1919.

Barney, Richard William Durbin ;
> B.A. 1909; 2 Lt. 6 R. Muns. Fus., Mar. 1915; Lt. 1917.

*Barrett, Ernest Albert;
> Ent. 1915; No. 3 R.G.A. Cadet School, May 1917.

*Barrett, Hamilton Beresford ;
> Ent. 1914; 2 Lt. 10 R. Dub. Fus., July 1916; wounded.

*Barrett, Robert Andrew Cecil;
> Ent. 1912; 2 Lt. R.G.A., Oct. 1914; Lt. 1917.

*Barrett, William Wagner ;
> Ent. 1912; 2 Lt. 9 R. War. R., May 1915; M.C; Temp. Capt. 1916; 2 Lt. M.G.C., Oct. 1916; Lt. 1916; Bar to M.C.

Barrington, Sir Charles Burton, Bart. ;
> B.A. 1870 ; M.A. 1877 ; Driver of his own Motor Ambulance, France, 1915.

Barrington, Henry Gordon ;
> Ent. 1913 ; 2 Lt. R.G.A. (T.F.), July 1915; Lt. 1916.

Barrington, John Beatty ;
> B.A. 1882; In charge of a fleet of ambulances, France, 1915 ; Croix de Guerre, 1915.

*Barron, Harrie ;
> B.A.I. 1912; 2 Lt. R.G.A., Oct. 1914 ; wounded, France, March 1916 : Temp. Lt. 1916.

Barry, Alfred Martin Harte ;
> Ent. 1884 ; Pte. 1914, Botha's Campaign ; S. A. Infantry ; Serg. ; killed in action, German E. Africa, 9-10 May, 1916.

Barry, Edward Cecil Joseph ;
> Ent. 1913 ; 2 Lt. R.G.A., Apr. 1915 ; Lt. 1917 ; French Croix de Guerre, March 1919 ; Order of King George 1, 4 cl., Oct. 1919.

*Bartley, Thomas Douglas Murray ;
> Ent. 1910 ; 2 Lt. 6 Lan. Fus., Aug. 1914; wounded, Dardanelles, June, 1915 ; Capt. 1916.

*Bate, Alfred Francis ;
> B.A. 1913; 2 Lt. 4 R. Dub. Fus., Aug. 1914; attchd. 2 Leins. R.; killed in action, France, 14 March 1915.

Bate, Edwin Beresford ;
> M.B. 1909 ; Lt. R.A.M.C., Aug. 1918.

*Bateman, Arthur Cyril ;
> M.B. 1914; Lt. R.A.M.C. Aug. 1914; Capt. 1915 ; France 1915 ; att. 7 Cam. Highrs. ; M.C. Sept. 1917 ; missing, 28 March 1918.

*Bateman, Charles Herbert Gerald ;
> Ent. 1916 ; 7 Cadet Bn., Jan. 1917 ; 2 Lt. 3 R. Mun. Fus., April 1917.

Bateman, Edgar Noel ;
> M.B. 1913 ; Capt. Australian A.M.C., Jan. 1916 ; Maj. 1919.

*Bateman, Godfrey ;
> M.B. 1915; Lt. R.A.M.C., Oct. 1915 ; France, 1916, 1917 ; Capt. 1916.

Bateman, Reginald John Godfrey ;
> B.A. 1906; M.A. 1909 ; Prof. of English, Saskachewan University ; Platoon Sergt., 28 Bn. 6 Canadian Inf. Bge. ; France 1915 ; Lt. Univ. Bn., 1916 : Major 1916 ; relinquished rank to get to France, 1917 ; wounded, Aug. 1917 ; A/Capt. 1918 ; killed in action, 3 Sept. 1918, buried near Dury, Hindenburg Line.

*Bates, Hubert Tunstall ;
> M.B. 1912 ; Lt. R.A.M.C., Oct. 1914 ; Capt. 1915 ; despatches, Jan. 1916 ; A/Maj. 1918 ; O. B. E. June, 1919.

*Bates, Richard Sydney Patrick ;
> Ent. 1915 ; Pte. R. Dub. Fus., Mar. 1916 ; 2 Lt. I.A., June 1917 ; Lt. 1918.

Battersby, Augustus Wolfe ;
> B.A. 1909 ; Lt. 4 Conn. Rang., Dec. 1914 ; att. 2 Nigerian R.; died of fever, West Africa, 8 June, 1915.

*Battersby, Francis John Gerrard ;
> Ent. 1911 ; 2 Lt. 4 R. Ir. Fus., Aug. 1914 ; wounded, France, Aug. 1915 ; Capt. 1916.

Battersby, John ;
> M.B. 1879 ; Lt. R.A.M.C., Feb. 1881 : Lt. Col. 1901 ; ret. 1910 ; re-emp. Aug. 1914 as Inspector of Recruits, Irish Command, till Feb. 1918 ; died 8 Apr. 1919.

*Baxter, Elliott Esmond ;
> Ent. 1913 ; 2 Lt. R.E., O.T.C., T.F., Unattached List, April 1916 : 2 Lt. R.E., June 1916 ; France ; trsf. I. Sappers and Miners.

*Baxter, Gerald Dorritt ;
> Ent. 1913 ; 2 Lt. R.E., Aug. 1915 ; India ; Mesopotamia ; Palestine.

*Beard, Alan Stephen ;
> Ent. 1911 ; 2 Lt. Conn. Rang. S.R., Dec. 1912 ; Lt. 1 Conn. Rang., Nov. 1914 ; wounded, Flanders, Oct. 1914 and May 1915 ; Capt. 1917.

Beard, Frederick Gerald Vesey ;
> B.A. 1914 ; 2 Lt. 9 Worc. R., Nov. 1914 ; Lt. 1915 : attd. 4 Bn.

Beare, George ;
> M.B. 1892 : Med. Offr. S. African E.F. against German S.W. Africa.

Beasley, James Joyce ;
> Ent. 1912 ; 2 Lt. 6 R. Ir. Fus., Sept. 1914 ; killed in action, Dardanelles, 9 Aug. 1915.

Beater, Leslie Orlando ;
> B.A. 1903 ; M.A. 1907 ; Pte. A.S.C., 1914 ; Staff Sergt.-Maj., June 1915.

*Beater, Orlando Lennox ;
> Ent. 1906 ; 2 Lt. 9 R. Dub. Fus., Sept. 1914 ; Lt. 1915 ; Capt. 1916.

Beattie, Andrew Ernest;
    Ent. 1899; Hon. 2 Lt. A.S.C., Oct. 1900 ; Maj. 1914.

Beattie, John Osborne ;
    B.A. 1906; 2 Lt. I. A., 16 Rajputs, Jan. 1906; Capt. 1915.

*Beattie, Sidney Herbert ;
    B.A. 1911; 2 Lt. 2 North'n R., Feb. 1912; France, 1914;
    Capt. 1915 ; wounded, France, Aug. 1915 ; wounded Sept. 1916 ;
    wounded July 1917; temp. Lt.-Col. 1917 ; M.C. Aug 1917.

Beatty, Ada Violet ;
    Ent. 1912 ; Military Hosp., Malta.

*Beatty, Desmond ;
    Ent. 1912; Lt. 8 R. Dub. Fus., Dec. 1914; A/Capt. 1917 ;
    Capt. 1918.

*Beatty, Eric Edge ;
    Ent. 1911; 2 Lt. 6 Conn. Rang., Sept. 1914; Lt. 1915 ; killed,
    France, 29 Apr. 1916.

Beatty, Frederick George ;
    M.B. 1913 ; Lt. R.A.M.C., May 1915; Capt. 1918.

Beatty, Henry ;
    B.A. 1914 ; 2 Lt. 15 Lancers, I.A., Sept. 1917 ; Temp. Capt.
    1917.

*Beatty, Ivan Wakefield ;
    Ent. 1914; R.N. Aux. Sick Berth Reserve, Feb. 1916; 2 Cav.
    C. S. July 1917; 2 Lt. I.A., Apr. 1918.

Beatty, James ;
    M.B. 1895; M.D. 1896 : Lt. R.A.M.C., Sept. 1915 ; Capt.
    1916.

*Beatty, John Edge ;
    Ent. 1914 ; 2 Lt. R.F.A., Feb. 1918 ; wounded, France, Sept.
    1918; Lt. 1919.

Beatty, John Colley Pounden ;
    M.B. 1906; Lt. R.A.M.C., Sept. 1915.

Beatty, Rev. John ;
    B.A. 1895 ; M.A. 1898; Chaplain R.N., Mar. 1901.

*Beatty, Thomas Edward Bellingham ;
    L.M. and L.Ch., 1915 : Lt. R.A.M.C. (S.R.), Dec. 1915 ; Capt.
    1916 ; France, 1916–1919; Capt. R.A.M.C., Aug. 1919.

Beatty, William Dawson ;
    B.A.I. 1908 ; 2 Lt. R.E., Oct. 1915 ; Egypt ; Palestine ; Syria ;
    despatches ; Capt.

*Beaufort, James Morris ;
    Ent. 1910 ; 2 Lt. A.S.C., Sept., 1914 ; Capt. 1915 ; Capt. R.A.F.,
    1917.

Beaumont, Rev. Henry Foxton ;
    B.A. 1913 ; Army Chaplain, 4 Cl., Dec. 1915 ; France.

*Becher, John Hedges ;
    B.A.I. 1911 ; 2 Lt. R.E., Jan. 1915 ; A/Capt. 1916 ; despatches.

Becher, William Stewart ;
    B.A.I. 1892 ; Pte., Sportsman's Bn., 24 R. Fus , Nov. 1914 ;
    wounded, Bernafay Wood, 28 July 1916 ; died of wounds 30 July
    1916.

Beckerson, Robert Ernest ;
    Ent. 1905 ; 1st Canadian Contingent ; 2 Lt. 8 Norf. Reg., Feb.
    1915 ; Capt. 1916 ; M.C. Apr. 1917 ; Bar to M.C. Jan. 1918 ; Lt.
    I.A., 1918.

*Beckerson, Rev. William Townley ;
    B.A. 1912 ; B.D. 1916 ; Temp. Army Chaplain, 4 Cl., Sept.
    1916–19 ; France, 1916 ; Croix de Guerre (Belgian), Jan. 1919 ;
    Chaplain to Forces, 4 Cl. 1919.

*Beckett, Alfred John ;
    Ent. 1911 ; Lt. A.V.C., Aug. 1914 ; Capt. 1915.

Beckett, Gerald Gordon Paul ;
    M.B. 1911 ; Lt. R.A.M.C., June 1916 ; Egypt ; Salonica ;
    German East Africa.

Beckett, James ;
    M.B. 1911 ; M.D. 1912 ; Lt. R.A.M.C., July 1915 ; Tem. Hon.
    Capt. 1918.

Beckett, Osborne ;
    B.A. 1910 ; 2 Lt. 6 R. Dub. Fus., Jan. 1915.

Beers, Edward St. John ;
    Ent. 1884 ; Lt. Australian Contingent ; Capt. 1916.

Beeston, Hon. Joseph Lievisley ;
    Med. School 1879 : Col. Australian A.M.C. ; Gallipoli ; C.M.G.
    Nov. 1915 ; despatches, Nov. 1915.

Belhomme, Richard Michel ;
    B.A.I. 1892 ; mobilized in French Army.

Bell, Cecil William James ;
    Ent. 1916 ; Pte. R.A.M.C., 1916 ; Corporal ; missing, believed
    drowned, 15 Apr. 1917.

Bell, Louis MacSherry ;
    Ent. 1917 ; Sub-Lt. R.N.V.R.

Bell, Theodore ;
  M.B. 1887 ; M.D. 1891 ; Lt. R.A.M.C., June 1915 ; Capt. 1916.

Bellamy, George Cuming ;
  B.A. 1891 ; M.A. 1897 ; National Reserve ; late Colonial Civil
  Service.

*Bellingham, Arthur Stuart ;
  Ent. 1912 ; 2 Lt. R.F.A., Dec. 1913 ; France, 1914 ; Comdg.
  a Batt., Battle of Loos ; Lt. 1915 ; A.D.C. 1915 ; wounded, 1915 ;
  gassed, 1916 ; Capt. 1917 ; A/Major 1918.

Bennet, Rev. Edward Armstrong ;
  B.A. 1910 ; M.A. 1919 ; Army Chaplin, 4 Cl., Nov. 1914-19 ;
  France 1915 ; M.C. Sept. 1916 ; Snr. Chaplain 18 I. Div. Mesopo-
  tamia, 1917 ; 3 Cl., 1919.

Bennet, John Leslie ;
  Ent. 1905 ; B.A. 1920 ; 2 Lt. 5 R. Ir. Fus., Nov. 1914 ; A/Capt.
  1915 ; Gallipoli ; wounded and invalided out, Nov. 1916.

*Bennett, John Harvey ;
  Ent. 1914 ; Pte. A.S.C. Mechanical Transport.

Bennett, Lionel Vaughan ;
  B.A.I. 1894 ; Lt. A.S.C., Jan. 1915 ; Capt. Feb. 1915 ; M.C.
  Nov. 1916 ; France.

Bennett, Richard Galwey ;
  Ent. 1899 ; Corporal, Rhodesian Platoon, 3 K. R. Rifle Corps ;
  France 1915.

Bennett, Vere Raymond ;
  M.A. 1911 ; 2 Lt. 3 Notts & Derby R., June 1915 ; Lt. 1916 ;
  M.G.C., 1916 ; killed in action, 10 Apr. 1917.

Benson, Charles Molyneux ;
  M.B. 1902 ; M.D. 1904 ; Temp. Major R.A.M.C., Nov. 1917 ;
  83 (Dub.) Gen. Hosp., France, 1917.

*Benson, Ernest Edmondson ;
  Ent. 1915 ; Cpl. A.S.C. (M.T.), Sept. 1916 ; wounded, 1917.

*Benson, Geoffrey ;
  Ent. 1914 ; 2 Lt. 1, 2 R. Ir. Rif., Apr. 1916 ; Lt. 1917 ;
  wounded, 1917.

*Benson, Robert Hulme ;
  Ent. 1913 ; 2 Lt. 3, 2 R. Ir. Regt., Aug. 1915.

Benson, Wallace ;
  M.B. 1902 ; Lt. R.A.M.C., July 1905 ; Maj. 1915 ; despatches,
  Jan. 1916 ; D.S.O. Feb. 1917 ; Bt. Lt.-Col. 1918 ; British E. A.

*Bergin, Charles Joseph ;
  B.A.I. 1916 ; Cadet R.E., Oct. 1916 ; 2 Lt. 10 R. Dub. Fus., Aug.
  1917 ; France ; M.C.

Bernard, Henry William ;
    M.B., 1897; Lt. R.A.M.C., Dec. 1916; Capt. 1917.

Bernard, William Sidney Hamilton ;
    Ent. 1907; Sergt. Canadian Contingent Oct. 1914; Sub. Lt.
    R.N. Div., Nov. 1915; Assist. Paymaster R.N.R., 1916.; Pay-
    master, 1918.

Berry, Rev. Robert Seymour Brendon Sterling ;
    B.A. 1907; M.A. 1911; Army Chaplain, 4 Cl., Oct. 1914;
    O.B.E. 1919.

Berry, Winslow Seymour Sterling ;
    M.B. 1904; Lt. R.A.M.C., Oct. 1914; Capt. 1915; A/Maj.
    1918; O.B.E. June 1919; Croix de Guerre; despatches 1919;
    M.C.

*Best, Francis Olphert;
    Ent. 1915; D.U.O.T.C.; volunteered and accepted, May 1918.

*Best, George Kenneth ;
    Ent. 1912; Pte. R.E.

*Best, James Cecil Corbett ;
    Ent. 1914; 7 Officers' Cadet Bn., Apr. 1916; 2 Lt. M.G.C.,
    Aug. 1916; Lt. 1918.

Best, Victor Greer ;
    M.B. 1911; M.D. 1911; Lt. R.A.M.C., June 1917.

Bevis, Clotilda Bain ;
    M.B. 1916; Resident M.O., Warren War Hosp., Gilford, Surrey.

*Bewley, Arthur Geoffrey ;
    Ent. 1912; Motor Cyclist Sect. R.E., 1914; 2 Lt. R.F.A., Aug.
    1915; wounded, 1917; gassed; despatches.

Bewley, Harold de Beauvoir ;
    B.A. 1909; Lt. att. Nigerian Regt. July 1917; German East
    Africa.

Bewley, Henry Theodore ;
    M.B. 1883; M.D. 1888; Lecturer in Medical Jurisprudence;
    Physician, Dublin Red Cross Hospital.

Bible, Noel Harding ;
    Ent. 1915; 2 Lt. 3 R. Ir. Fus., Aug. 1915; wounded, Sept. 1916;
    Lt. 1917.

Biddulph, Richard Edmund ;
    M.B. 1877; Dep. Inspector-General of Hospitals and Fleets
    R.N. Apr. 1907; retired.

Biddulph, Robert Wallis ;
    M.B. 1870; Fleet Surgeon, R.N. Oct. 1893; retired.

Biggs, James Richard ;
B.A.I. 1909 ; Capt. Canadian Engineers, France, 1915–19.

*Birch. Alfred Granville ;
B.A. 1908 ; Lt. A.S.C., Jan. 1915 ; Capt. 1915 ; Major 1916 ;
despatches, Jan. 1917.

*Birch, Edward Noble Warburton ;
B.A. 1913 ; 2 Lt. A.S.C., Aug. 1913 ; Temp. Capt. 1914 ;
Lt. 1915 ; Capt. 1917 ; Major 1918.

Bird, Elliott Beverley ;
Ent. 1898 ; Maj. R.A.M.C., Sept. 1914 ; France ; despatches ;
despatches and D.S.O. Jan. 1917 ; Croix de Guerre.

Bird, George Armitage ;
Ent. 1919 ; R.N.A.S., Aug. 1917 ; Lt. R.A F., 1918 ; served
as pilot till Armistice ; Administrative off. at Demobilisation.

*Bird, Harold Theodore ;
Ent. 1919 ; R.G.A., O.C.B., Uckfield, Feb. 1917 ; 2 Lt. R.G.A.,
S.R., June 1917 ; France.

Bird, Jason Grant ;
M.B. 1918 ; Lt. R.A.M.C., 1917 ; Capt. R.F.C., M.S. 1918.

Bird, Joseph Godfrey ;
M.B. 1916 ; Lt. I.M.S., Jan. 1917 ; Temp. Capt. 1918.

Bird, Percy James Sandys ;
M.B. and M.D. 1900 ; Capt. Canadian A.M.C. 1916 ; Maj. 1919.

Bird, Rev. Richard ;
B.A. 1904 ; Army Chaplain, 4 Cl. Apr. 1915 ; Sen. Chaplain,
1916 ; France 1915–18 ; despatches (twice), D.S.O., Jan. 1918 ;
Prisoner of War, 1918.

*Birney, Herbert ;
Ent. 1913 ; 2 Lt. 7 Leins. R., Dec. 1915 ; Lt. 125 Napier's Rifles,
I.A., Nov. 1917 ; Palestine ; wounded, Sept. 1918.

Black, Cecil ;
Ent. 1914 ; R.N. Div.; killed in action.

*Black, Desmond Gerard ;
Ent. 1917 ; R.F.C. Farnboro', Apr. 1917 ; Fermoy, Sept. 1918.

Black, Gibson ;
B.A. 1899 ; Acting Paymaster, Army Pay Dept.

*Black, Thomas Samuel Cuthbert ;
Ent. 1910 ; Pte. 7 R. Dub. Fus.; wounded, Gallipoli ; died
Alexandria, Aug. 1915.

Blackhall, Henry William Butler;
> B.A. 1911; L.L.B. 1912; Pte. S.Ir.H. June 1916; France and Flanders, 1916, 1917; 2 Lt. 3 Ches. R., Mar. 1918; att. R.A.F., Aug. 1918.

Blackham, Olive Gertrude;
> M.B. 1917; M.D. 1921; A/R.A.M.C., Mil. Hosp., Alexandria.

Blackley, Frederick John;
> M.B. 1902; M.D. 1904; Lt. R.A.M.C., April 1915; France; despatches, June 1916.

Blackley, Humphrey Lewis;
> M.B. 1911; Lt. R.A.M.C., Mar. 1917.

Blackmore, Rev. Alfred Thomas Gardner;
> B.A. 1909; M.A. 1912; Army Chaplain, 4 Cl., May 1918.

Blackwell, Charles;
> B.A. 1906; Pte. H.A.C., Aug. 1914; 2 Lt. 16 R. Fus., May 1915; killed in action, 20 July 1916.

Blair, Rev. John Collins;
> Med. School, 1916; B.A., R.U.I.; Volunteer Worker, Y.M.C.A., France.

Blair, Ribton Gore.
> B.A. 1913; F.R.C.S.I.; Lt. R.A.M.C., March 1914; France 1915; Capt. 1916; M. C. 1918.

*Blair-White, Arthur;
> B.A. 1915; 2 Lt. R.F.A., Nov. 1914; France, 1915; Lt. 1916; Croix de Guerre, Sept. 1918.

*Blair-White, John Henry;
> Ent. 1912; 2 Lt. 9 R. Dub. Fus., Sept. 1914; 2 Lt. New Armies, Trench Mortar Bat., 1916; Temp. Capt. 1916; Lt. 1917.

Blake, Harold Morton Joseph;
> Ent. 1910; 2 Lt. 3, 2 R. Muns. Fus., Aug. 1915; Lt. 1916; died of wounds, 20 Nov. 1917.

Blake, Valentine Charles Joseph;
> Ent. 1906; D.I., R.I.C.; Capt. 1 I. Gds., Oct. 1914; killed in action, France, 28 Jan. 1916.

Blood, Horace FitzGerald;
> Ent. 1902; L.R.C.P. & S.I.; Lt. R.A.M.C., Mar. 1915; Capt. 1916.

*Bluett, Augustus Sterling;
> Ent. 1910; Pte. R.A.M.C., Mar. 1916; trsf. Gunner R.G.A., May 1916; rejoined R.A.M.C., Dec. 1916; Egypt and Palestine, July 1917–March 1919.

c

*Bluett, Douglas ;
Ent. 1915 ; Pte. R.A.M.C., July 1915 ; Salonika, 1915–18 ;
Corpl. Welsh R. 1917 ; Cadet C. 1917.

*Blunden, Eric Overington ;
B.A.I. 1915 ; 2 Lt. R.E., Sept. 1915 ; France; Lt. 1916 ; Capt. ;
despatches.

Boles, William Samuel ;
M.B. 1883 ; Lt. R.A.M.C., 1885 ; Maj. 1899 ; Med. charge of
Troops, Kinsale.

Bolster, Francis ;
M.B. 1896 ; M.D. 1905 ; Fleet-Surg. R.N., Nov. 1913 ; Surg.
Comdr. 1911 ; C.M.G. Aug.1917 ; Gold Medal of W. London Med.
Chir. Soc. for the best work done under the most difficult and
dangerous conditions from the beginning of the war to the end of
1916, in H.M. Navy.

Bolster, George William Corless ;
Ent. 1914 ; 2 Lt. 2 R. Dub. Fus., Aug. 1915 ; Lt. 1916 ; att.
R. Innis. Fus.

*Bolton, Reginald Rainsbury ;
Ent. 1913 ; 2 Lt. R.F.A., June 1915 ; Lt. 1917 ; M.C. ;
Salonika ; Egypt.

Bolton, Samuel Henry ;
Ent. 1981 : Lt. A.S.C., Aug. 1914 ; France 1915 : Capt. 1916.

Booth, Ernest Brabazon ;
M.B. 1902 ; M.D. 1904 : Lt. R.A.M.C., Jan. 1905 ; Capt. 1908 ;
Maj. 1915 ; D.S.O., Jan. 1916 ; despatches, June 1916 ; Cameroons.

*Booth, Henry Slator ;
Ent. 1916; attested May 1918 ; discharged as Sergt. D.U.O.T.C.,
Mar. 1919.

Bond, Henry Wilfrid Dudley ;
B.A.I. 1910 : Lt. R.E., 1916–7 ; att. Egyptian E.F.

Bond, Robert Patrick ;
Ent. 1901; Div. Test. 1908 ; Army Chaplain, 4 Cl., July 1916.

*Bor, Norman Loftus ;
Ent. 1911 ; 2 Lt. 6 Conn. Rang., Sept. 1914 ; Lt. 1916 ;
wounded, France, Sept. 1916 ; Capt. 1917.

Bourchier, Rev. Wilfrid La Rive ;
B.A. 1907 ; M.A. 1913 ; Army Chaplain, 4 Cl. Aug. 1914.

Bouchier-Hayes, Henry ;
Med. School, 1885 ; L.R.C.P. & S.I. ; Lt. R.A.M.C., Feb. 1916 ;
Capt. 1917.

Boudren, Christopher Dominic ;
Ent. 1914 ; 2 Lt. 3 R. Muns. Fus., July 1915.

Bourke, Ernest Albert ;
Med. School ; L.R.C.P. & S.I. ; Lt. R.A.M.C., Jan. 1898 ;
Lt.-Col. 1915 ; despatches, Oct. 1914 ; D.S.O.

Bourke, Robert Gascoyne ;
Ent. 1918 ; 2 Lt. 2 R. Dub. Fus., June 1916 ; Gallipoli ; France ;
Egypt ; l.t. 1917.

Bowles, John de Vere ;
Ent. 1895 ; 2 Lt. R.A., 1900 ; France 1914 ; despatches, Jan.
1915 ; Brigade Maj., 1915 ; D.S.O.

Bowles, Ludlow Tonson ;
Ent. 1877 ; 2 Lt. E. Surr. R., 1880 ; Lt.-Col. commanding
1 Bn. Channel Islands Militia, March 1913.

Boxwell, Ambrose ;
Ent. 1894 ; 2 Lt. R. War. R., May 1899 ; Capt. 1908 ; Capt.
I.A. 119. Inf., 1909.

Boxwell, John ;
Ent. 1897 ; B.E.F. in German E. Africa.

Boxwell, William ;
M.B. 1903 ; M.D. 1912 ; Capt. R.A.M.C., France, 1917.

*Boyce, Norman M'Connell ;
M.B. 1915 ; Lt. R.A.M.C., July 1915 ; Capt. 1916 ; despatches,
1917.

Boyd, Alfred Ernest ;
M.B., 1896 ; Capt. R.A.M.C., Jan. 1918.

Boyd, Cecil Anderson ;
M.B. and M.D. 1905 ; Lt. R.A.M.C., Dec. 1914 ; France 1915 ;
Capt. 1915 ; despatches, Jan. 1916 and July 1917 ; Salonika ; M.C.
Sept. 1918.

*Boyd, Donald William Parker ;
Ent. 1916 ; 2 Lt. R.A.F., Sept. 1918 ; France, 1918 ; Germany.

Boyd, Henry Alexander ;
B.A. 1900 ; 2 Lt. R.F.A., Mar. 1900 ; Maj. 1914 ; despatches,
June 1915.

*Boyd, Robert ;
B.A. 1913 ; 2 Lt. 7 R. Dub. Fus., Oct. 1915 ; France ; Capt.
1917 ; Prisoner of War, March 1918.

*Boyd, Rev. Robert McNeill ;
B.A. 1912 ; Army Chaplain, 4 Cl., Feb. 1915 ; M.C. 1917 ;
despatches.

Boyd, Shepherd McCormick;
Med. School 1883 ; F.R.C.S.I. ; Surg. Capt. R.F.A., Sept. 1899. wounded, 1918.

Boyd, William Gaston ;
Ent. 1904 ; Canadian Contingent ; France 1915 ; died of wounds, 13 Oct. 1916.

*****Boyers, Edwin ;**
M.B 1915 ; Lt. R.A.M.C., Oct. 1915 ; 2 years in France ; Capt. 1916 ; despatches, Dec. 1917 ; died of pneumonia, 25 Oct. 1918.

*Boyers, Hedley ;
M.B. 1913 ; Lt. R.A.M.C., Aug. 1914 ; Capt. 1915 ; M.C. Jan. 1917.

Boyle, James Caird Carson ;
Ent. 1919 ; 2 Lt. 7/8 R. Innis Fus., Feb. 1918 ; France 1918 ; gassed 1918 ; Lt. 1919.

*****Brabazon, Alan ;**
Ent. 1914 ; Pte. R. Dub. Fus. 1914 ; 2 Lt. 6 Leins. R., Jan. 1915 ; Lt. 1915 ; Gallipoli ; Salonika ; Palestine ; despatches ; Capt. 1917 ; died of wounds received in action, 8 March 1918.

*****Braddell, Edward Terence ;**
Ent. 1912 ; 2 Lt. R.E., Sept. 1914 ; invalided from France, 1915 ; France, 1916 ; died of wounds, Gaza, 27 March 1917.

Braddell, John Waller ;
Ent. 1911 ; 2 Lt. 5 R. Ir. Fus., May 1915 ; Mach. G. C., March 1916 ; wounded, Oct. 1916.

Braddell, Monckton O'Dell ;
M.B. 1883 ; Lt. R.A.M.C., Feb. 1884 ; Lt.-Col., 1914 ; C.B.E. June 1919.

Bradford, Rev. Samuel ;
M.A. 1888 ; Offg. Min. R.N. Holyhead, 1915-6.

Bradlaw, Albert Stanley ;
Ent. 1916 ; Surg. Prob. R.N.V.R., Oct. 1918 ; H.M.S. "Coreopsis."

*****Bradley, John M'Donald ;**
Ent. 1908 ; 2 Lt. 7 R. Dub. Fus., Jan. 1916 ; Lt. 1917 ; died of wounds received in action, 30 Sept. 1918.

Bradshaw, John Russell ;
Ent. 1912 ; Cadet 20 O.C.B.

Bradshaw, Samuel John M'Clean ;
M.B. 1895; M.D. 1899 ; Capt. (Local Rank) R.A.M.C.,
Cameroons Expedit. Force; Lt. R.A.M.C., Oct. 1916 ; died of
disease contracted on active service, Aug. 1920.

Bradshaw, Thomas Robert ;
M.B. and M.D. 1882; Maj. R.A.M.C., July 1908; 1 Western
Gen. Hosp., Liverpool.

*Bradstreet, Gerald Edmund ;
B.A.I. 1913 ; 2 Lt. R.E., Aug. 1914 ; Capt. 1915 : wounded,
Gallipoli, Aug. 1915 ; despatches ; killed in action, Gallipoli, 7 Dec.
1915.

*Brady, Cecil Francis Clarke ;
M.B. 1915 ; Lt. R.A.M.C., July 1915 ; France, 1916-18 ; Capt.
1916 ; wounded, Sept. 1916 ; despatches, Apr. 1918.

Brady, Henry John ;
M.B. 1902 ; Capt. S.A.M.C.

Brady, John Banks ;
B.A. 1907 ; M.A. 1908 ; Capt. 3 K. R. Rif. C., Nov. 1914 ;
France 1915.

Brazier-Creagh, George Washington ;
L.M. and L.Ch. 1880 ; Lt. R.A.M.C., July 1881 ; C.M.G. 1901 ;
Lt.-Col. 1901 ; France 1914 ; despatches, Feb. 1915, Jan. 1917,
May 1917, Dec. 1918 ; C.B. June 1917 ; Col. 1919.

Bredin, Rev. Edward Robert ;
B.A. 1905 ; Chapl. R.N., Feb. 1911, H.M.S. " Warrior."

*Bredin, Waldene Edgar ;
Ent. 1910 ; 2 Lt. 2 R. Ir. Regt., Sept. 1914 ; Lt. 1914 ; Temp.
Capt. 1918.

*Breen, Ian ;
Ent. 1914 ; 2 Lt. 1, 2 R. Ir. Regt., Aug. 1915; R.F.C. 1915.

*Breen, Thomas Francis Pennifather ;
M.B. 1912; Lt. R.A.M.C., Jan. 1914 ; Capt. 1915 ; A/Maj.
1918; att. 142 F.A. : killed in action, 18 Sept. 1918.

Brennan, John Henry ;
Ent. 1887 ; 2 Lt. Volunteer Bn. R. Welsh Fus., 1901 ; Capt.
3 Bn. June 1903 ; killed near Zonnebeke, Belgium, 19 Oct. 1914.

Brennan, Joseph Rowland ;
M.B. 1917 ; Surg. R.N., Feb. 1917.

*Brereton-Barry, Ralph ;
Ent. 1916 ; Sandhurst, Dec. 1917.

*Brereton-Barry, William Roche ;
> Ent. 1915 ; 2 Lt. 10 R. Dub. Fus., Feb. 1916 ; Irish Rebell. 1916 ; went to front 1917 ; wounded 16 Aug. 1917 ; officially presumed killed, 16 Aug. 1917 ; Certificate for " gallant conduct and devotion to duty."

Brett, Charles Anthony ;
> Ent. 1914 ; 2 Lt. 3 Conn. Rang., Oct. 1914 ; Lt. 1915 ; wounded, Jan. 1917 ; M.C.

Brew, Cecil ;
> M.B. 1894 ; Hon. rank R.A.M.C., St. John's Hospital, France.

Brewer, James Angus ;
> Ent. 1912 ; Pte. 7 Lond. R., Oct. 1914 ; 2 Lt. 9 S. Lan. R., Dec. 1914 ; France ; Salonika 1915 ; A/Capt. 1916 ; Lt. and A/Capt. 1917 ; Capt. 1917 ; despatches, March 1918, and Oct. 1918 (Salonika) ; died of wounds received in action, 18 Sept. 1918.

*Bridge, Allman Vizer ;
> Ent. 1913 ; 2 Lt. 6 R. Ir. Regt., Sept. 1914 ; wounded, Aug. 1916, March 1918, and Nov. 1918 ; Lt. 1916 ; Temp. Capt. 1917 ; M.C. Feb. 1919 ; Bar to M.C. March 1919.

Bridge, George Allman ;
> M.B. 1914 ; Lt. R.A.M.C., Aug. 1914 ; Capt. 1915 ; M.C. Sept. 1918.

*Bridge, Maurice Frederick ;
> Ent. 1912 ; 2 Lt. A.S.C., Sept. 1914 ; Capt. 1915 ; R.F.C. 1917 ; wounded, March 1918.

Bridge, Richard Edwin Athol ;
> Ent. 1900 ; 2 Lt. R.G.A., 1904 ; Lt. I.A. 94 Russell's Native Inf., 1907 ; Capt. I.A., S. & T. Corps, June 1913 ; France 1914 ; D.S.O. Aug. 1917 ; A/Maj., Bagdad, 1918.

Bridge, William Purefoy ;
> B.A. 1903 ; Pte., D. Co., 7 R. Dub. Fus., Sept. 1914 ; died of wounds, Dardanelles, 10 Aug., 1915.

Brien, Frederick George ;
> B.A. 1904 ; 2 Lt. 9 R. Innis. Fus., Oct. 1914 ; wounded, France, July 1916 ; 2 Lt. R.F.A., July 1917 ; Italy, 1917 ; France, 1918 ; killed in action, 20 Apr. 1918.

Brindley, Louis Kirwan ;
> B.A.I. 1907 ; Zanzibar Defence Force ; M.B.E.

Britton, William Kerr Magill ;
> B.A.I. 1913 ; 2 Lt. R. Muns. Fus., Apr. 1916 ; attchd. R. Flying C. 1916 ; wounded, Dec. 1916 ; killed, Yatesbury, Wilts, 23 May, 1917.

Brock-Hollinshead, Laurence ;
Ent. 1875 ; 2 Lt. R. W. Kent R., Aug. 1879 ; Maj. 1894 ; retd. 1904 ; re-empld. 1914.

*Broderick, Thomas Joseph ;
Ent. 1910 : Lt. 6 R. Ir. Regt., Nov. 1914 ; killed in action, 15 April, 1916.

Brook, Rev. Thomas ;
B.D. 1897 ; LL. D. 1901 ; M.B. and M.D. 1912 ; Army Chaplain, 3 Class, Sept. 1911 ; despatches, Jan. 1916 ; B.E.F. 1914–5 ; Med. E.F. 1916–7.

Brooks, Basil George ;
M.B. 1906 ; M.D. 1906 ; Lt. R.A.M.C. 1918.

Brooks, Ralph Terence St. John ;
M.B. 1909 ; M.D. 1913 ; Temp. Lt. R.A.M.C., July 1917 Capt. 1918.

Broughton, Rev. Arthur Hardwick ;
B.A. 1904 ; M.A. 1908 ; Army Chaplain, 4 Cl., Apr. 1915.

Brown, Ernest ;
Ent. 1879 ; Pte. Driscoll's Scouts.

*Brown, John Barry ;
B.A. 1906 ; 2 Lt. 4 Conn. Rang., Apr. 1915 ; att. 15 R. Ir. Rif. 1916 ; Lt. 1918.

Brown, Thomas Gerard Loudon ;
Ent. 1900 ; Lt. 4 Conn. Rang., Feb. 1915 ; Capt. 1915 ; wounded, France, March 1916 ; M.C. Sept. 1916.

Brown, William ;
B.A. 1899 ; 2 Lt. A.S.C., May 1900 ; Capt. 1909 ; I.A. 1912 ; France 1914 ; Mesopotamia 1915.

Browne, Charles Robert ;
M.B. 1890 ; M.D. 1893 ; Maj. R.A.M.C. (T.F.), Jan. 1914 ; Bt. Lt.-Col. Aug. 1917.

Browne, Cyril Edward ;
Ent. 1911 ; 2 Lt. A.S.C., Oct. 1914 ; Temp. Capt. 1916 ; M.C. Jan. 1918.

Browne, Rev. Geoffrey Edward ;
B.A. 1899 ; Army Chaplain, 4 Cl., Oct. 1914 ; M.C. 1916.

Browne, Rev. Harold Bailey ;
Ent. 1906 ; 2 Lt. A.S.C., April 1915 ; Capt. 1918.

Browne, Hawtrey William ;
M.B. 1914 ; Lt. R.A.M.C., Sept. 1914 ; Capt. 1915 ; M.C. Dec. 1916 ; bar to M.C. Sept. 1918.

*Browne, Percival Hugh ;
> B.A. 1910 ; LL.B. 1912 ; 2 Lt. Army Cyc.C., Aug. 1915 ; Lt.
> 1916 ; wounded, Somme, Aug., 1916; despatches, Jan. 1917 ;
> M.C. Jan. 1918.

*Browne, Robert Francis ;
> B.A. 1911 ; LL.B. 1912 ; 2 Lt. A.S.C., Sept. 1915; France
> 1915 ; Egypt 1916 ; France 1916–9 ; Lt. 1917 ; att. Labour Corps,
> 1917 ; Capt. and Adjt. 1918; att. E. Surr. R., 1918.

*Browne, Walter FitzGerald ;
> Ent. 1914 ; 2 Lt. R.F.A., Nov. 1915 ; Lt. 1917.

Brownell, Thomas Charles ;
> Ent. 1912 ; 2 Lt. Audit Staff, Oct. 1915.

Brownrigg, Rev. Ernest Graham ;
> B.A. 1897 ; M.A. 1901 ; Army Chap, 3 Cl., Aug. 1917 ; Med.
> E. F., 1916–9 ; M.B.E.

Brownrigg, Henry John ;
> M.B. 1897 ; M.D. 1897 ; Capt. R.A.M.C·, June 1915.

Bruce, George Evans ;
> Ent. 1885 ; 2 Lt. Norf. R., Aug. 1888 ; Maj. 1908 ; retired,
> 1911 ; Maj. 3. R. Dub. Fus. 1915.

Brunner, Basil Leonard ;
> Ent. 1916 ; Pte. Middlesex R., Feb. 1917 ; Sergt. ; France ;
> Flanders.

*Brunskill, Gerald ;
> Ent. 1914 ; 2 Lt. 5 R. Suss. R., Sept. 1914 ; Temp. Lt. 1915 ;
> Lt. 1917.

Brunskill, John Handfield ;
> M.B. 1900 ; Lt. R A.M.C., Nov. 1900 ; Maj. 1912 : prisoner,
> Sept. 1914 ; released, July 1915 ; despatches, Feb. 1915, June
> 1916, Jan. 1917, April 1919 ; Lt. Col. 1916 ; D.S.O. Jan. 1917 ;
> O.B.E. Jan. 1919.

Bryan, John Northridge Lewis ;
> B.A. 1914 ; 2 Lt. 8 L'pool R., Dec. 1914 ; Capt. 1915.

Bryan, Rev. Richard Booth ;
> B.A. 1890 ; M.B. and M.D. 1907 ; Lt. R.A.M.C., Apr. 1916 ;
> Capt. 1917.

Bryan, William Jacob ;
> B.A. 1913 : 2 Lt. 15 R. Fus., Sept. 1914 ; died from illness
> contracted while on service, 18 Nov. 1916.

*Buchanan, George ;
> M.B. 1914 ; Lt. R.A.M.C., July 1915 ; Capt. 1916.

Buchanan, Harry Cyril Dudley;
    Ent. 1914; Pte. Leeds Pals Bn., W. York R., Dec. 1914;
    2 Lt. 27 Midd'x. R., July 1915; wounded, France, 28 Oct., died
    12 Nov. 1916.

Buchanan, John Blacker Whitla ;
    M.B. 1884 ; Lt. R.A.M.C., Jan. 1886 ; Lt.-Col. 1914 ; brought
    t₁ notice of Secretary of State for valuable services rendered in
    connexion with the war, Feb. 1917.

Buchanan, Walter James Thompson ;
    M.B. 1887; M.D. 1903; Capt. I.M.S., Oct. 1887; Lt. Col. 1907;
    C.I.E. 1913; K.B.E. 1918; K.C.I.E. 1918.

*Buchanan, William Oliver ;
    Ent. 1913; 2 Lt. R.G.A, April 1917 ; invalided, July 1917 ;
    2 Lt. Labour C., Aug. 1917 ; France, 1917–19 ; Lt. 1918.

*Buckley, Charles Dudley Maybury ;
    M.B. 1914 ; Lt. R.A.M.C. (S.R.), Aug. 1914 ; Capt. (S.R.) 1915;
    despatches, Jan. 1917; Capt. R.A.M.C., Feb. 1918 ; M.C. Jan.
    1918.

Buckley, Charles Edward ;
    Ent. 1915 ; Pte. M.T., Oct. 1916 ; Pte. Bedford R.; wounded,
    Sept. 1918.

*Buckley, Frederick Arthur ;
    B.A.I. 1911 ; Trooper British East African Mounted Pioneers,
    Oct. 1915; 2 Lt. African Railway Corps, Aug. 1916.

Bulfin, Edward Stanislaus ;
    Ent. 1881 ; Lt. York R., Nov. 1884 ; C.V.O. 1910; C.B. 1913 ;
    Maj.-Gen. 1914 ; wounded, Ypres, Nov. 1914 ; commanding 28 Div.,
    Dec. 1914; despatches, Feb. 1915, Jan. 1916 ; K.C.B. Jan. 1918 ;
    Lt.-Gen., Jan. 1919 ; despatches 8 times; Palestine.

Bull, Frederick Hilary Penrose ;
    Ent. 1905 ; Canadian Gordon Highrs.; 2 Lt. 12 R. Innis. Fus.,
    Nov. 1915; Lt. 1917.

*Bullen, Walter Alexander ;
    Ent. 1910; Motor Despatch Rider, Aug. 1914 ; 2 Lt. A.S.C.,
    Sept. 1914 ; 2 Lt. R. Ir. Fus. 1914 ; Lt. 1916 ; Macedonia.

Burgess, John Buchanan ;
    M.B. 1910 ; M.D. 1911 ; Lt R.A.M.C., Aug. 1914 ; Capt. 1915 ;
    Mesopotamia 1916.

*Burgess, Richard Llewellyn ;
    Ent. 1917 ; Fermoy, Sept. 1918.

Burgess, Robert Balderston ;
    B.A. 1913 ; 2 Lt. A.S.C., Nov. 1914 ; Capt. R.E., Jan. 1915 ;
    died of wounds, France, 9-10 Dec. 1915.

Burke, Joseph Birmingham ;
> B.A. 1888 ; LL.B. and M.A. 1891 ; Pte. R.A.M.C., Aug. 1915.

Burke, Osborne Samuel ;
> Ent. 1912 ; 2 Lt. R.F.A., Oct. 1914 ; killed in action, 25 Sept. 1916.

Burke, William Henry ;
> M.B. 1882 ; Maj. I.M.S., Sept. 1894 ; Lt. Col. 1902 ; retired ; temp. empld. 1915.

Burkitt, Rev. Francis Hassard ;
> B.A. 1910 ; Chaplain, R.N., June 1913 ; H.M.S. "Superb" 1913–16 ; "Glory" 1916 ; "Victory" 1917–18 ; "Terrible" 1918–19.

Burnell, Rev. Cyril Joseph :
> B.A. 1908 ; M.A. 1915 ; Afmy Chaplain, 4th Class, May 1915–19.

*Burns, Arthur Strong ;
> Ent. 1915 ; R.A.F., Oct. 1918.

Burns, John William ;
> M.B. 1905 ; M.D. 1907 ; Lt. R.A.M.C., Oct. 1915 ; Capt. 1916 ; Surg. Spec. No. 5 Gen. Hosp. ; France : Salonika.

Burns, Percival Fossy Tackaberry ;
> Ent. 1913 ; 2 Lt. 15 L'pool R., Sept. 1915 ; France, 1916 ; died of wounds, 21 March 1917.

Burrell, Arthur Ambrose ;
> M.B. 1902 ; Temp. Capt. R.A.M.C., Dec. 1915.

Burrows, Charles Selss ;
> B.A.I. 1907 ; 2 Lt. 14 North'd Fus., Jan. 1915 ; Capt 1916 ; M.C. ; killed in action, Trigny, Champagne, 28 May 1918.

Burrows, Oswald Vincent ;
> M.B. 1912 ; Lt. R.A M.C., Dec. 1915 ; Capt. 1916 ; M.C. Oct. 1917 ; bar to M.C.

Burtchaell, Charles Henry ;
> M.B. 1889 ; Lt. R.A.M.C., Apr. 1891 ; Col. 1915 ; C.M.G. 1915 ; despatches, Feb. 1915, June 1915, Jan. 1916 ; Croix D'Officier, Legion d'honneur, Feb. 1916 ; despatches, Jan. 1917, May 1917, and Dec. 1917 ; C.B. 1917 ; despatches May 1918, Dec. 1918 and July 1919 ; Belgian Order of the Crown ; Belgian War Cross ; Knight of Grace, Order of Hospital St. John of Jerusalem. Dec. 1918 ; Temp. Lt.-Gen. 1918 ; Hon. Surg. to the King 1918 ; K.C.B. 1919 ; Lt.-Gen. 1919 ; American D.S.M. 1919 ; Commandeur, Legion of Honour Oct. 1919 ; Croix de Guerre, Nov. 1920 ; Dir.-Gen. Med. Services, B.E.F., France.

Bushe, Charles Kendal ;
> M.B. 1900 : M.D. 1901 ; Staff Surgeon R.N., Dec 1908 ; Surg. Comr. 1918 ; C.B.E. 1919.

Butler, Richard Bolger ;
> B.A. 1906 ; 2 Lt. 30 Lancers, June 1906 ; Capt. 1914 : Adj. Governor's Body-Guard, Madras ; M.C. ; despatches (twice).

Butler, William Bibbie ;
> Ent. 1913 ; 2 Lt. 3 Bord. R., Oct. 1914 ; attd. Welsh R.; Lt. 1916 ; Capt. 1917 ; M.C.

*Butt, John Gillis ;
> M.B. 1914 ; Lt. R.A.M.C., July 1914 ; Capt. 1915 ; last seen attending a wounded Colonel under fire, France, presumed killed, 29 Oct. 1914.

*Byrn, William Andrew ;
> Ent. 1911 ; Surg.-Prob. R.N., Sept. 1915 ; H.M.S. " Lawford," 1915 ; "Laforey" 1916 ; Medit. and N. Sea.

Byrne, Harold Edward ;
> B.A.I. 1898 ; Staff Capt. Ord. Dept. Apr. 1917 ; Capt. R.E., Oct. 1917 ; France 1916-19 ; A/Maj.

Byrne, Henry Stanhope ;
> B.A.I. 1908 ; 2 Lt. R.E., March 1915 ; Lt. 1916 ; Capt. 1918.

C

Caddell, Ernest Duncan ;
> M.B. 1906 ; Lt. R.A.M.C., July, 1906 ; Capt. 1910 ; despatches, Oct. 1914 ; M.C. Jan. 1915 ; Temp. Maj. 1916 ; A/Lt.-Col. 1917 ; despatches, May and Dec. 1917.

Caddell, Henry Mortimer ;
> B.A. 1896 ; 2 Lt. A.S.C. May 1900 ; Temp. Lt. Col., Assistant Director of Transport, 1915 ; on Staff, France and Belgium 1914-17 ; D.S.O. ; despatches Feb. 1915, June 1918, and Jan. 1918 ; Bt. Lt.-Col. ; C.M.G.

Caddell, Walter Buckingham ;
> Ent. 1897 ; 2 Lt. R.G.A., May 1900 ; Maj. 1915 ; Deputy Assistant Director of Military Aeronautics, 1915 ; Order of St. Anne 3 Cl., from Czar of Russia, 1916 : Croix de Chevalier, Legion of Honour, 1917 ; Bt. Lt.-Col.

Cahill, Bernard Staunton ;
> Ent. 1896 ; Serg. R.A.M.C. ; France ; D.C.M. 1918.

Caldwell, Alexander Francis Somerville ;
>B.A. 1895; 2 Lt. 1 Volunteer Bn. North'n R., Feb. 1903;
Capt. 8 N. Lan. R., 1914; Maj. 1915; France; Lt.-Col. 1917;
despatches (twice); wounded; D.S.O. 1918.

Caley, Rev. William Leonard Bertram ;
>B.A. 1918; M.A. 1920; B.E.F., France, with Y.M.C.A., 1915;
Army Chaplain, 4 Cl., May, 1916; at front about Ypres. 1917;
wounded, July 1917; relinquished Commission, 1918.

*Callaghan, Arthur Nickson ;
>B.A. & LL.B., 1913; 2 Lt. 14 L'pool R., Nov. 1914; France;
Salonika, 1915; despatches; Lt. 1917; killed in action, Salonika,
30 Aug. 1917.

Callaghan, Eugene Owen Cruess ;
>Ent. 1915; 2 Lt. R.F.C., March 1916; flew with his squadron
to the front, July 1916; killed with six of his squadron during a
torrential downpour of rain, 27 Aug. 1916.

*Callaghan, Leslie Wilfrid ;
>Ent. 1909; Lt. 8 W. York R., April 1915; Lt. 1915; Temp.
Capt.; killed in action, France, 9 Oct. 1917.

*Callaghan, Robert William Hatfield ;
>Ent. 1912; 2 Lt. 7 R. Dub. Fus., Jan. 1915; Gallipoli 1915;
Servian Front and subsequent retreat 1915: Salonika 1916;
wounded, Oct. 1916, in attack on Bulgar positions at Tenikoj,
whilst in charge of A. Co. 7 R. Dub. Fus.; retired Apr. 1917 as
Capt. on account of loss of sight.

Callaghan, Thomas Edmonds ;
>Ent. 1916; Sapper R.E. : trsf. Tank Corps.

Campbell, Arthur Alexander ;
>L. Dent. Sc. 1909 : Surgeon Dentist, Lt. R.A.M.C., March, 1915 ;
Capt. 1916.

*Campbell, David ;
>Ent. 1913; 2 Lt. 6 R. Ir. Rif., Aug. 1914; Lt. 1915; wounded,
Dardanelles, Sept. 1915; Temp. Capt. 1916; Salonika; M.C.;
Capt. 1917; despatches.

Campbell, Rev. Edward Gordon ;
>B.A. 1910 ; Army Chaplain, 4 Cl., Nov. 1915.

Campbell, Rev. Edward FitzHardinge ;
>B.A. 1903 ; Army Chaplain, 4 Class, May 1906 ; Deputy Assist.
Chap.-Gen.; despatches, Dec. 1917; D.S.O. Jan. 1918; B.E.F.
1914–18.

Campbell, Rev. Ernest Henry FitzGerald ;
  B.A. 1911; Army Chaplain, Oct. 1914-Feb. 1915 ; June 1918-
  1919.

Campbell, Francis Ernest Archer ;
  Ent. 1897 ; 2 Lt. Jan. 1916 : Assist. Dep. Censor, France 1916 :
  Staff Lt. 1916; France 1916-19; 2nd in command, Prisoners of
  War Section, G.H.Q., 1916-17 ; Capt. 1917 ; Offr. Instr. Lond.
  Distr. 1919; att. H.Q. Lond. Distr. 1919-20 : area Ed. Offr. 1920 ;
  Major Army Ed. C. (Regular Com.) Nov. 1920 ; H.Q. Lond. Distr.
  1920-21 ; despatches (twice) ; O.B.E. March 1919.

Campbell, John Yeaman ;
  B.A. 1911 ; 2 Lt. A.S.C., March, 1915; Lt. Dec. 1915 ; Temp.
  Capt. 1917 ; Lt. Lab. C. 1917.

Campbell, Philip Sydney ;
  Ent. 1911 ; Sub-Lt Drake Bn. R.N. Div., Sept. 1914 ; Antwerp ;
  Lt.-Comdr. ; wounded Gallipoli ; despatches, Dec. 1915 ; France,
  1916 ; killed in action, Beaumont Hamel, 13 Nov. 1916.

Campbell, Robert Morris ;
  Ent. 1901 ; 2 Lt. A.S.C., July 1903 ; Maj. 1914 ; Dep. Assistant
  Director of Supplies and Transport, 1915 ; Bt. Lt-Col. for distin-
  guished services in Italy, 1918 ; despatches, 1918.

Campbell, Walter Islay Hamilton ;
  B.A.I. 1909 ; Lt. empld. Inland Water Transport, Oct. 1916.

*Campbell, William ;
  B.A. 1911 ; M.A. 1914 ; 2 Lt. R.F.A., Jan. 1916 ; attd. R.F.C. ;
  killed in action, 6 July 1917.

*Campbell, William ;
  Ent. 1914 ; 2 Lt. A.S.C., Oct. 1915.

Campion, Henry Stephen ;
  M.B. 1917 ; Lt. R.A.M.C., Oct. 1917 ; Capt. 1918.

Canning, Charles Colquhoun ;
  Ent. 1912 ; 2 Lt. 11 R. Ir. Rif., Sept. 1914 ; Lt. 1915 ; Capt.
  and Adj. 1916 ; empld. R. Ir. Fus., 1918.

*Cardew, William Gordon ;
  Ent. 1904 ; 2 Lt. A.C.C., Apr. 1915 ; empld. 15 Hamps. R.,
  1915 ; Lt. 1917.

*Carew, Desmond ;
  Ent. 1916 ; O.T.C. Aug. 1916 ; Quetta ; 2 Lt. I.A.

*Carey, Cecil William Victor ;
  B.A. 1908 ; Ll.B. 1910 ; 2 Lt. A.S.C., Oct. 1915.

Carey, Thomas Augustus;
B.A. 1905 ; 2 Lt. Ir. Gds., Aug. 1917 ; killed in action, 5 Dec. 1917.

Cargin, Eleanor Macpherson ;
Ent. 1912 ; Stobart Relief Expedition, Serbia, 1915.

*Carolin, Charles George Sinclair ;
B.A.I. 1915 ; 2 Lt. A.S.C. (M.T.), July 1915 ; 2 Lt. R.E., Sept. 1917 ; Lt. 1917 ; France ; wounded, Oct. 1918 ; M.C. June 1919.

*Carpenter, George Kingsford ;
Ent. 1914 ; Y.M.C.A. Huts, July 1918.

Carpenter, Rev. Thomas Lionel ;
B.A. and M.A. 1919 ; Army Chaplain, 4 Cl., Oct. 1918 ; att. 9 Essex R.

Carr, Charles Henry ;
M.B. and M.D. 1898 ; Lt. R.A.M.C., May, 1900 ; Maj. 1912 ; Lt.-Col. 1918 ; despatches, March 1918.

Carroll, Frederick FitzGerald ;
M.B. 1897 ; Lt. R.A.M.C., Jan. 1898 ; Lt.-Col. 1915 ; Soudan despatches, Oct. 1916, June 1919 ; D.S.O., Jan. 1917 : Order of the Nile, Oct., 1916 ; P.M.O. Egyptian Army.

Carroll, Henry Arthur;
Ent. 1891 ; 2 Lt. R. Muns. Fus., March 1897 ; Maj. 1914 ; Mesopotamia 1915 ; Temp. Lt.-Col. 1916 ; relief of Kut ; despatches (twice); died of illness contracted on active service, 31 Oct. 1918.

Carroll, Henry Frederick ;
B.A.I. 1909 ; 2 Lt. R.E., Aug. 1915 ; Lt. 1916 ; Capt. 1917 ; despatches ; M.C.

Carson, Walter Peter ;
M.B. 1878 ; Lt.-Col. I.M.S. ; despatches, Sept. 1917.

Carter, Rev. Anthony Basil ;
B.A. 1907 ; M.A. 1910 ; Army Chaplain, 4 Cl., Jan. 1916.

Carter, Ernest FitzWilliam ;
Ent. 1914 ; 2 Lt. 4 R. Innis. Fus., Aug. 1914 ; Lt. 1915 ; wounded.

Carter, Gerald Bailey ;
M.B. 1896 ; Lt. R.A.M.C., May 1900 ; Maj. 1909 ; ret. 1911 ; re-empld. Aug. 1914.

Carter, Herbert St. Maur ;
M.B. and M.D. 1904 ; Lt. R.A.M.C., July 1904 ; Maj. 1915 ; despatches, Feb. and May 1915 ; D.S.O., June 1915 ; A/Lt.-Col. 1915 ; despatches, May 1917.

Carter, James Edward ;
M.B. 1889 ; Lt. R.A.M.C., Jan. 1891 ; Maj. 1905 ; D.A.D.M.S., 1915 ; A/Lt.-Col. 1918.

Carter, William Bellingham ;
B A.I. 1896 ; Capt. R.E., May 1915 ; France, 1915–19.

*Cary, Falkland Litton;
Ent. 1915 ; R. N. Aux. Sick Berth Res., Jan. 1916.

Casement, Edgar Reginald ;
B.A.I. 1908 ; Lt. R. E., June 1915 ; East Africa.

Casement, Francis ;
M.B. 1906 ; Lt. R.A.M.C., Jan. 1907 ; Capt. 1910 ; Deputy Assistant Director Med. Serv. ; Croix de Chevalier, Legion d'honneur, Feb. 1916 ; D.S.O. June 1917 ; despatches, Jan. 1918 ; Bar to D.S.O. ; A/Lt.-Col. 1918.

Casey, William Francis ;
B.A. 1916 ; Inns of Court O.T.C., Aug. 1918.

*Cathcart, William Blacker ;
M.B. 1915 ; Lt. R.A.M.C., Aug. 1914 ; Capt. 1915 ; Maj. 1918 ; M.C. Jan. 1919.

Chadwick, Ven. Walter ;
B.A. 1897 ; Army Chaplain ; died of Blackwater Fever, 2 Oct. 1917.

*Chaloner, John Cole ;
B.A. 1911 ; 2 Lt. A.S.C., May 1915 ; Lt. 1915.

Chambers, Charles Perceval ;
M.B. 1917 ; Temp. Lt. R.A.M.C., Feb. 1918 ; Capt. 1919 ; permanent Com. ; Palestine, 1921.

Chambers, Frederick William ;
Ent. 1915 ; B.A. 1919 ; Pte. Nov. 1916 ; 2 Lt. R.F.C., May 1917 ; Lt. R.A.F., Aug. 1918 ; discharged unfit, 1918.

Chambers, Joseph ;
M.B. 1887 ; Fleet Surgeon R.N., Feb. 1905 ; Operating Surg. R.N. Hosp., Chatham, 1915-19 ; C.M.G. June 1919 ; Surg. Rr. Ad. 1920.

Chambre, John ;
M.B. and M.D. 1905 ; Lt. R.A.M.C., Jan. 1917 ; Capt. 1918.

Chance, Sir Arthur ;
Ent. 1883 ; Tem. Lt.-Col. Sept. 1917 ; C.B.E. June 1919.

Chance, Arthur ;
M.B. and M.D. 1912 ; M.Ch. 1915 ; Lt. R.A.M.C., Dec. 1915 ; Capt. 1916.

Chance, Norman ;
      B.A.I. 1908 ; Cadet R.E., May 1916 ; 2 Lt. R.E., July 1916 ;
      Lt. 1918 ; France ; Flanders ; despatches ; Major 1919 whilst Road
      Control Offr.

Chance, Percival Vincent ;
      B A.I. 1908 : Punjab Light Horse ; Mesopotamia ; Capt. May
      1918 whilst Assist. Irrig. Off.

*Chandler, Harold Morgan ;
      B.A.I. 1913 ; 2 Lt. R.E., Jan. 1914 ; Lt. 1915 ; Temp. Capt.
      1916 ; Capt. 1917.

Chapman, Marjorie Greer Fawcett ;
      M.B. 1913 ; Woolwich Arsenal, 1917.

Chapman, Robert Sturgeon ;
      Ent. 1914 ; Surg. Prob. R.N.V.R.

*Chapman, Robert William ;
      M.B. 1914 ; Lt. R A.M.C., March 1916 ; Capt. 1917.

Chapman, Thomas Paul ;
      M.B. 1917 ; Lt. R.A.M.C.; May 1917 ; Capt. 1918.

Charles, Samuel Francis Allen ;
      M.B. 1908 ; M.D. 1911 ; Lt. R.A.M.C., Nov. 1915 ; Trench
      fever, 1916 ; returned home, 1916 ; died Oct. 1918.

*Charlton, Frederick Johnston ;
      Ent. 1912 ; 2 Lt 5 Conn. Rang., Sept. 1914 ; Lt. 1915 ; wounded,
      Dardanelles, Aug. 1915, Suvla Bay, Sept. 1915 ; Lt. I.A. 1918.

Chatterton, Bernard Robert ;
      M.B. 1891 ; M.D. 1895 ; M.Ch. 1896 ; Lt. I.M.S. 1893 ; Lt.
      Col. 1913 ; despatches, N.W. Frontier, July 1916.

*Chatterton, Robert Charles Dickson ;
      Ent. 1911 ; Despatch Rider, Aug. 1914 ; Temp. 2 Lt. A.S.C.
      (M.T.) Jan. 1915 ; 2 Lt. A.S.C. Feb. 1916 ; Lt. 1917.

Cherry, Richard Theodore ;
      Ent. 1919 ; 2 Lt. 9 Rif. Brig., Nov. 1914 ; France 1915 ;
      wounded, May 1916 ; Lt. 1917 ; wounded, Dec. 1917 ; Instructor
      11 O.C.B., 1918.

Chester-Walsh, James Henry ;
      B.A.I. 1910 ; 2 Lt. A.S.C., Nov. 1914 ; Attchd. R. Flying C.
      1915 ; 2 Lt. R.F.C., March 1916 ; France ; Lt. A.S.C., 1917.

*Chestnutt-Chesney, Frederick ;
      Ent. 1909 ; 2 Lt. 6 Lan. Fus., Aug. 1914 ; Temp. Maj. 1915 ;
      Capt. 1916 ; wounded March 1918.

Chetwode-Crawley, Francis Hubert M'Carthy ;
M.B. 1896 ; M.D. 1897 ; Capt. R.A.M.C., Apr. 1917 ; Ophth.
Surg. 83 (Dub.) Gen. Hosp., France, 1917.

*Cheyne, John Donald Edmund ;
Ent. 1915 ; 2 Lt. R.G.A., Sept. 1915 ; Lt. 1916.

*Christie, Cedric Pasche ;
Ent. 1912 ; 2 Lt. 15 L'pool R., Nov. 1914 ; died of wounds,
France, 16 December 1915.

Clampett, Reginald Wilton Trevor ;
M.B. 1903 ; Lt. R.A.M.C., Apr. 1915 ; Capt. 1916 ; Tem. Maj.
Malta.

Clancy, Aubrey John Joseph ;
Ent. 1920 ; 2 Lt. 11 R. Dub. Fus., Feb. 1916 ; France and
Flanders ; wounded, June 1917 ; Lt. 1917 ; Capt., Mil. Police
Corps, Aldershot, 1918–20.

*Clancy, George Davis Louis ;
Ent. 1913 ; 2 Lt. 4 R. Ir. Rif., Oct. 1914 ; attchd. 1 Leins. R.,
1915 ; France, 1915 ; Salonika, 1915 ; Lt. 1916 ; missing, believed
drowned, 4 May 1917, on the torpedoed transport H.M.S.
" Transylvania."

Clarendon, Rev. William Randall Slacke ;
B.A. 1904 ; 2 Lt. 12 R. Innis. Fus., Apr. 1915 ; Capt. 1915.

*Clarke, Edward Rupert ;
Ent. 1911 ; Pte. ; France ; 2 Lt. 4 London R., Sept. 1916 ; att.
9 K. R. Rif. C. ; killed in action, 9 Apr. 1917.

Clarke, Rev. Henry Jessop St. John ;
B.A. 1913 ; M.A. 1921 ; Army Chaplain, 4 Cl., Apr. 1916 ;
Egyptian E. F. 1916-9; wounded, Palestine, Aug. 1917; despatches
Feb. 1919.

Clarke, Ina Marion ;
Demonstrator in Anatomy, T.C.D. ; F.R.C.S.I. ; Ulster Volunteer Hosp., Pau, France.

Clarke, James William ;
Ent. 1913 ; 2 Lt. R.E., Nov. 1914 ; enteric, Suvla Bay,
Nov. 1915; wounded, France, 16 July, 1916 ; Lt. 1916 ; A/Capt.
1918.

Clarke, Maurice Noble ;
Ent. 1910 ; 2 Lt. A.S.C., Jan. 1915 ; Capt. 1915 ; A/Major
1919.

Clarke, Reginald Arthur George ;
Ent. 1911 ; Temp. 2 Lt. A.S.C., Dec. 1914 ; 2 Lt. A.S.C.,
Nov. 1915 ; Lt. 1917 ; att. Infantry, 1917 ; empld. Min. of Lab.
1919.

D

Clarke, Sydney Alfred ;
>M.B. 1917; Lt. R.A.F., Med. Serv., Sept. 1918; Capt. 1919.

Clarke, Thomas Henry Matthew ;
>M.B. 1895 ; Lt. R.A.M.C., Jan. 1897; D.S.O. 1899; C.M.G. 1903; Lt. Col. 1915; despatches, Jan. 1916 ; C.B.E. Jan. 1919.

Clarke, Rev. William Harrington McCann ;
>B.A. 1895 ; B.D. 1900 ; Army Chaplain, 4 Cl., May 1917-19.

Classon, Eric Carter ;
>Ent. 1917 ; 2 Lt. R.A.F.; France.

*Clay, Horace Frederick Samuel ;
>Ent. 1910 ; 2 Lt. A.S.C., Dec. 1914 ; Capt. 1915.

*Clegg, Richard Bagnall ;
>B.A.I. 1914 ; 2 Lt. R.E., Aug. 1915; 15 Field Co. ; killed in action, Somme, 18 July, 1916.

Clements, Shuckburgh Upton Lucas ;
>B.A.I. 1909 ; Hon. Capt. 4 R. Ir. Fus., June 1904 ; Lt. Nigeria R., Sept. 1915 ; Major 4 R. Ir. Fus., 1916 ; Cameroons, France ; D.S.O. ; despatches.

Clements, Rev. William Dudley ;
>B.A. 1906; Chaplain, R.N., Sept. 1911.

Clery, James Albert ;
>M.B. 1870 ; C.B. 1901 ; Surg.-Gen. A.M.S., 1902 ; retired ; temp. employed, July 1915.

Clesham, Thomas Henry ;
>B.A. 1906 ; Natal Light Horse, 1914-5 ; 2 Lt. Manch. R., July 1915 ; killed in action, 1 July, 1916.

Clibborn, John ;
>B.A. and L.C.E. 1868 ; 2 Lt. July 1869 ; Lt.-Col. I.A. 1895 ; C.I.E.

*Clinch, Andrew Daniel ;
>M.B. and M.D. 1898 ; Lt. R.A.M.C., unattached, Sept. 1914 ; Capt. 1915.

Close, Wills Burleigh ;
>B.A.I. 1909; 2 Lt. R.E., July, 1917 ; 2 Lt. R.A.F. (Eng. Branch) Apr. 1918 ; A/Capt. 1919.

*Clouston, Noel Stuart ;
>B.A.I. 1909 ; 2 Lt. R.E., Jan. 1916 ; France ; Capt. and Adj. 1918 ; O.B.E.

Cluffe, William Ashley Graves ;
> M.B. and M.D. 1902 ; Lt. R A.M.C.. May 1915.

Cochrane, Edward Webber Warren ;
> M.B. 1895 ; Lt. R.A.M.C., July 1896 ; Lt.-Col. 1915 ; D.S.O.,
> Jan. 1918 ; despatches, June 1919 (Mesopotamia).

Cochrane, Hugh Carew ;
> B.A.I. 1906 ; Cpl. R.E. ; 2 Lt. R.E., March 1917 ; Lt.
> Tunnelling Co. R.E., Sept. 1918 ; France.

Cochrane, John Ernest Charles James ;
> B.A. 1893 ; Hon. Maj. Donegal Mil. Nov. 1900 ; D.S.O. 1900 ;
> Res. of Offrs. 1905 ; Maj. R.F.A., 1914 ; Temp. Lt. Col. attchd.
> New Zealand Artillery, 1915 ; France 1916.

Cochrane, John Stewart ;
> Ent. 1914 ; 2 Lt. 18 R. Ir. Rif., Feb. 1915 ; Lt. 1917.

Cochrane, Sir Stanley Herbert, Bart.;
> B.A. 1902 ; M.A. 1912 ; Lt. 7 R. Dub. Fus., Nov. 1914.

Coffee, Francis Warren.
> Ent. 1906 ; 2 Lt. R. Ir. Rif., Oct. 1915 ; at front 1916 ; att.
> 14 R. Ir. Rif. ; killed in action, 16 Aug. 1917.

Coffey, Joseph Patrick ;
> Ent. 1907 ; Pte. 7 R. Dub. Fus. ; wounded, Suvla Bay,
> 1 Sept. 1915.

Coghlan, Thomas ;
> B.A. 1909 ; Corporal I. Gds.

*Cole, David Henry ;
> B.A. 1910 ; M.A. 1913 ; 2 Lt. A.S.C., Nov. 1914 ; Lt. 1915 ;
> temp. Capt. 1916 ; Capt. 1918.

Cole, Fleetwood John ;
> B.A.I. 1916 ; 2 Lt. A.S.C., M.T., 1917-19 ; France.

Colgan, John ;
> M.B. 1912 ; Lt. R.A.M.C., Jan. 1916 ; Capt. 1917 ; Hospital
> Ship "Wandilla," Mediterranean, 1916-7 ; France, 1917-9 ;
> wounded, May 1918.

*Colhoun, William Albert ;
> Ent. 1910 ; 2 Lt. 4 R. Ir. Fus., Aug. 1914 ; France 1915 ; Capt.
> 1915 ; Salonika 1915 ; despatches, Jan. 1916 ; M.C., Jan. 1916 ;
> France 1917 ; wounded, Apr. 1917 ; Bar to M.C., May 1917 ;
> India 1918 ; Lt. I.A. June 1918 ; Capt. 1919 ; despatches, 1919
> (India).

Collen, George Denbigh ;
> M.B. 1893 ; M.D. 1897 ; Capt. R.A.M.C., T.F., Dec. 1909 ;
> att. 7 Lond. R. 1914.

*Collins, Eugene Finbarre ;
Ent. 1915 ; 2 Lt. 9 R. Muns. Fus., Sept. 1914 ; Lt. 1915.

*Collins, Frederick Richard ;
Ent. 1910 ; 2 Lt. 3 R. Dub. Fus., Aug. 1914 ; Capt. 1915.

*Collins, Herbert Stratford ;
Ent. 1909 ; M.B. 1918 ; 2 Lt. A.S.C., Sept. 1914 ; France 1914-1918 ; Capt. 1915 ; Major 1917 ; despatches, Apr. 1918.

Collins, John Cornelius ;
Ent. 1919 ; A/Lt. R.G.A. ; Mons 1914.

Collins, John Rupert ;
M.B. 1901 ; M.D. 1903 ; Capt. R.A.M.C., Dec. 1915.

*Collins, Maurice ;
B.A1. 1914 ; 2 Lt. R.G.A., Aug. 1915 ; Lt. 1917 ; 305 S.B. ; killed in action, 11 Sept. 1918.

*Collins, William Tenison ;
Ent. 1912 ; Pte. R.A.M.C., Sept. 1915 ; 2 Lt. R.G.A., Oct. 1915 ; Lt. 1917.

*Collis, William Henry ;
Ent. 1911 ; 2 Lt. 7 R. Innis. Fus., Sept. 1914 ; Capt. 1916 ; killed in action, 9 May 1917.

Collis, William Stewart ;
B.A. 1883 ; M.A. 1890 ; served 6 months on 1st British Ambulance Unit to Italy.

Colquhoun, Jane Frances ;
M.B. 1913 ; Women's Hospital, Royal Arsenal, Woolwich.

Comerford, Charles Henry ;
M.B. 1916 ; Lt. R.A.M.C., July 1916 ; Capt. 1917.

Condon, de Vere ;
M.B. 1897 ; M.D. 1906 ; Lt. I.M.S., Jan. 1898 ; Maj. 1909 ; Lt.-Col. 1917.

Condon, Edmund Charles Hill ;
B.A.I. 1901 ; M.A.I. 1907 ; Capt. 1. Defence Force.

*Conlin, Bernard Francis ;
B.A. 1915 ; 2 Lt. R.F.A., Aug. 1916 ; died of wounds received in action at the battle of the Somme, 9 Oct. 1916.

*Conlin, John Francis ;
Ent. 1913 ; 2 Lt. R.F.A., Oct. 1914 ; France 1915 ; Lt. 1916 ; wounded, June 1917 ; Capt. 1917 ; M.C. June 1919, for services in Italy.

Connell, Richard Aldworth ;
M.B. 1906 ; Staff-Surgeon R.N., May 1914 ; Sg. Cr. 1918.

Conner, Henry Longfield ;
>B.A. 1910 ; 2 Lt. R. Flying Corps, Oct. 1915 ; Assist. Equip.
Offr. 1916.

Conyngham, Cecil Taylour ;
>M.B. 1906 ; Capt. R.A.M.C.; killed, East Africa, 4 Nov. 1914.

*Cooke, George Henry ;
>Ent. 1913 ; 2 Lt. R.G.A., Aug. 1915 ; Lt. 1917 ; A/Major 1918 ;
M.C. Jan. 1918.

Cooke, John Hamilton ;
>M.B. 1889 ; Surg. Capt. Antigua Defence Force, B. W. India
Sept. 1908 ; Lt. R.A.M.C., Jan. 1916 ; Capt. 1916.

*Cooke, John Harbourne ;
>B.A. 1912 ; 2 Lt. R.G.A., S.R. Oct. 1914 ; Lt. 1916 ; 2 Lt.
R.G.A., Aug. 1916 ; M.C.

Cooke, Rev. Richard Hans de Brabant ;
>B.A. 1909 ; 2 Lt. A.S.C., Nov. 1914 ; Lt. 1915.

Cooney, Arthur Cuthbert ;
>B.A. 1911 ; Lt. R. G. A.; Sept. 1914 ; Capt. 1917.

Cooper, Edward Joshua ;
>Ent. 1912 ; 2 Lt. 1 E. Surr. R., Feb. 1915 ; Lt. 1916 ; Assist.
Instr. M.G.C., 1916.

*Cooper, William Campion ;
>B.A. 1912 ; Lt. I.A. 53 Sikhs, Dec. 1913 ; drowned in S.S.
" Persia," Jan. 1916.

*Cope, George Ivan ;
>B.A.I. 1915 ; 2 Lt. R.E., Sept. 1915 ; France ; Italy;
Capt. 1919 ; M.C.

*Cope, Joseph Victor ;
>M.B. 1915 ; Lt. R.A.M.C., July 1915 ; Capt. 1916 ; wounded,
Dec. 1917 ; M.C. Jan. 1918.

Coppinger, Charles Joseph ;
>M.B. 1904 ; Lt. I.M.S., Feb. 1905 ; Capt. R.A.M.C., Mar.
1911 ; wounded, Flanders, Nov. 1914 ; Major 1915.

Coppinger, Francis Romney ;
>M.B. 1906 ; Lt. I.M.S., Feb. 1908 ; Capt. R.A.M.C., July 1914;
despatches, Aden, July 1916 ; O.B.E. June 1919.

Coppinger, Walter Valentine ;
>M.B. 1897 ; M.D. 1899 ; Lt. I.M.S., June 1900 ; Maj. 1911 ;
Mesopotamia ; despatches, 1918 ; D.S.O. Sept. 1918.

Corbally, William Lewis ;
> Ent. 1894 ; Capt. R.F.A., Sept. 1914 ; died of wounds, 6 May 1915.

*Corbet, Robert Henry Joseph Mulhall;
> Ent. 1915 ; M.B. 1921 ; Surg. Prob. R.N.V.R., Sept. 1917 ; H.M.S. " Raider," Grand Fleet.

Corbett, Daniel Maurice ;
> M.B. 1905; Lt. R.A.M.C., July 1906; Capt. 1910; Prisoner of War, Oct. 1914–July 1915; Bt. Major 1917; Salonika; despatches, July 1917 ; St. Sava, 4 cl. Jan. 1918 ; despatches, 1919 ; O.B.E. June 1919.

Corbett, Rev. Frederick St. John ;
> B.A. 1884 ; M.A. 1887 ; Chaplain to Forces, 3 Cl. T.F., att. 3 Lond. R., May 1912 ; died 14 March 1919.

Corbett, William Edward Manderson ;
> Med. School 1881 ; L.R.C.P.& S.I.; Capt. 5 Devon R., March 1903 ; Major R.A.M.C., June 1916.

*Corkey, Isaac Whitla ;
> M.B. 1915; Lt. R.A.M.C., July 1915; M. C., June 1916; Capt. 1916.

Corlett, Rev. Edwin Joseph ;
> B.A. 1890 ; M.A. 1902 ; Army Chap. 4 Cl. June 1916–17.

Corley, Anthony Purdon Hagarty ;
> M.B. and M.D. 1902 ; Capt. 11 Infantry Bn., 1 Australian Div.; killed in action, Dardanelles, 30 Sept. 1915.

Corley, Henry Cecil;
> B.A. 1900 ; Pte. B. Co. 2 Bn. 12 London R., Feb. 1915.

Corley, Henry Hagarty ;
> Ent. 1897 ; 2 Lt. 11 Manch. R., Dec. 1914.

*Cormac-Walshe, Edward Joseph ;
> B.A. 1912 ; 2 Lt. 2 Leins. R., Feb. 1912 ; Capt. ; wounded, Flanders, Oct. 1914 ; died of wounds, 5 Nov. 1914.

*Cormac-Walshe, Henry ;
> B.A. 1912; 2 Lt. R.H.A., Dec. 1913 ; Lt. 1915 ; Temp. Capt. ; 29 Bde. ; died of wounds, 7 Nov. 1917.

Corscadden, Francis Theodore George ;
> Ent. 1907 ; 2 Lt. 14 R. Ir. Rif., Jan. 1915 ; died of wounds, Thiepval, 18 June, 1916.

Cosbie, Maurice Hastings ;
> Ent. 1920 ; Pte. R.A.F., 1918 ; 3rd Mechanic Rigger ; Home.

Cosgrave, Alexander Kirkpatrick ;
>M.B. 1909 ; Lt. R.A.M.C., Dec. 1914 ; Capt., Jan. 1916 ;
>France ; M.C. Jan. 1918.

Cosgrave, Ephraim M'Dowell ;
>M.B. 1876; M.D. 1878 ; Pres. R.C.P.I.; Physician, Dublin
>Castle Red Cross Hosp.

Costello, Charles Fleming ;
>Ent. 1920 ; 2 Lt. R.F.A., Oct. 1914 ; Capt. 1917.

*Costello, John Walter ;
>Ent. 1917; Quetta, July 1917 ; 2 Lt. I.A., Aug. 1918.

*Costeloe, Francis Herbert John ;
>Ent. 1912 ; 2 Lt. R.G.A., Nov. 1916; Lt. 1918.

Cotes, Digby Charles Bathe ;
>Ent. 1914 ; 2 Lt. 7 N. Staff. R., Sept. 1914 ; wounded, Dar-
>danelles, Aug. 1915 ; Lt. 1915 ; Capt. 1917 ; died of wounds
>received in action, 15 Oct. 1918.

Cotter, Rev. John Beresford ;
>B.A. 1912 ; Army Chap., 4 Cl., Feb. 1918-19.

Coulter, Francis Clements ;
>B.A. 1912 ; 2 Lt. 9 S. Wales Bord., Nov. 1914; Lt. 1917 ;
>empld. Min. of Labour.

Coulter, John ;
>Ent. 1911 ; Pte. Canadian A.M.C., 2 Canadian Contingent,
>Aug. 1914.

*Coursey, Edward Bartholomew ;
>Ent. 1912 ; 2 Lt. R.G.A., S.R. Oct. 1915 ; Lt. 1917 ; M.C. ;
>Capt. ; Chevalier de l'Ordre de la Couronne ; Croix de Guerre
>(Belge.)

Cowan, Philip Chalmers ;
>Ent. 1912 ; 2 Lt. 8 Manch. R., Aug. 1914 ; Lt. 1915 : Temp.
>Capt. 1916 ; R. Flying C., Oct. 1916 ; missing, 8 Nov. 1917,
>presumed killed.

*Cowan, Sidney Edward ;
>Ent. 1914 ; 2 Lt. R. Flying Corps, Oct. 1915 ; M.C. May 1916 ;
>bar to M.C. Oct. 1916 ; second bar, Nov. 1916 ; Flight Comdr. 1916 ;
>killed in an air combat, 17 Nov. 1916.

Cowdy, Henry Lloyd ;
>B.A. 1901 ; 2 Lt. R.G.A., Sept. 1918.

Cox, Edward Orme ;
> B.A.I. 1907 ; Capt. I.A. Res. of Offs. ; att. R.E., Mesopotamia ; despatches (4 times) ; M.B.E.

*Cox, John Francis ;
> Ent. 1911 ; Pte., D Co., 7 R. Dub. Fus. ; invalided ; 2 Lt., 10 Bn., Sept. 1915 ; wounded, Nov. 1916, France ; M.C. Jan. 1917 ; Lt. 1917 ; empld. Min. of Labour.

Cox, Samuel ;
> Ent. 1911 ; 2 Lt. 11 N. Lan. R., Feb. 1915 ; Capt. 1916.

Cox, Stafford Mouritz ;
> M.B. 1888 ; M.D. 1895 ; Maj. R.A.M.C., Apr. 1915 ; Malta.

Craddock, Cecil Graham ;
> Ent. 1911 ; Pte. 10 R. Dub. Fus., Nov. 1915 ; 2 Lt. 1, 2 R. Dub. Fus., March 1917 ; att. 2 R. Muns. Fus. ; Lt. 1918.

*Craig, Arthur Brent ;
> B.A. 1911 ; 2 Lt. 16 Midd'x. R., Sept. 1914 ; 2 Lt. A. Cyclist C., 1914 ; Lt. 1916 ; Capt. 9 Worc. R., March 1917.

*Craig, Eric William ;
> M.B. 1915 ; Lt. R.A.M.C., Sept. 1915 ; Capt. 1916 ; despatches, May 1917 ; M.C. Aug. 1917.

Craig, George Daly ;
> B.A. 1912 ; Pte. 6 Black Watch, May 1915 ; 2 Lt. 3 R. Ir. Fus., Aug. 1915 ; Lt. 1917.

Craig, George Eric Gwynn ;
> Ent. 1908 ; 2 Lt. 39 Canadian Infantry, 1914 ; Lt. May 1915 ; Capt. 1918.

Craig, George Ernest ;
> M.B. 1909 ; Lt. R.A.M.C.

*Craig, Isaac Murray ;
> B.A.I. 1914 ; 2 Lt. R.E., Oct. 1914 ; Lt. 1915 : A/Capt. ; Gallipoli ; Balkans ; Palestine ; killed in action, Palestine, 22 Aug. 1918.

Craig, James ;
> M.B. 1885 ; M.D. 1891 ; King's Prof. of Medicine, 1910 ; Physician, Castle Red Cross Hosp., Dublin, 1915.

Craig, John Russell ;
> Ent. 1916 ; Surg. Sub-Lt. R.N.V.R. ; H.M.S. " Red Gauntlet," Harwich Patrol.

*Craig, Malcolm Thomas ;
>B.A.I. 1916 ; Cadet R.E., May 1916 ; 2 Lt. R.E., Nov. 1916 ;
>Lt. 1918 ; India ; Mesopotamia ; Egypt.

Craig, Newman Lombard ;
>B.A. 1905 ; LL.D. 1911 ; 2 Lt. I.A., Jan. 1906 ; 2 Lt. A.S.C.,
>1909 ; Capt. 1914 ; Temp. Maj. 1914 ; despatches, Jan. 1917,
>May 1917 and July 1919 ; D.S.O. ; Assist. Q.M.G. 1918 ;
>Belgian Order of the Crown, 5 Cl. ; Belgian War Cross with palm ;
>Chevalier, Legion of Honour ; O.B.E. ; Inter Allied Mil. Com-
>mission in Hungary.

*Craig, Thomas Patrick ;
>Ent. 1913 ; 2 Lt. 7 Leins. R., Sept. 1914 ; Lt. 1917 ; killed in
>action, 22 March 1918.

*Craig, William Hedley ;
>B.A. 1913 ; Despatch Rider, Sept. 1914 ; 2 Lt. R.E., Jan. 1916 ;
>Mesopotamia, 1916 ; att. R.F.C., Jan. 1917 ; killed in action,
>15 April 1917.

*Craig-McFeely, William Norman ;
>Ent. 1920 ; 7 Cadet Bn. May 1916 ; 2 Lt. 5 R. Muns. Fus., Sept.
>1916 ; Lt. 1918.

Crane, James Henry ;
>M.B. 1909 ; M.D. 1912 ; M.O., Duke of Lancaster's Own
>Yeomanry, Jan. 1913 ; Capt. att. R.A.M.C. (T.F.). Apr. 1915 ;
>M.B.E., June 1919.

*Crawford, Edward Sydney Atkinson ;
>Ent. 1917 ; Sandhurst, Sept. 1918.

Crawford, Frederick Alexander Ferrier ;
>B.A. 1908 ; Lt. 5 R. Sc. Fus., Sept. 1914 ; A/Capt. 1914 ;
>Capt. 1915.

Crawford, George Brown ;
>Med. School 1885 ; M.D., M.Ch. (R.U.I.) ; Hon. Lt. R.A.M.C.,
>Oct. 1899 ; Lt. 1915 ; Capt. 1916.

Crawford, Herbert de Lisle ;
>M.B. 1910 ; Hon. Lt. R.A.M.C., June 1915 ; Lt. Feb. 1916 ;
>Capt. 1917 ; Etaples, 1915-6 ; Popperinghe, 1916-7 ; Irish Counties'
>War Hospital, 1917-9.

Crawford, John ;
>Ent. 1914 ; 2 Lt. 17 R. Ir. Rif., Oct. 1915 ; wounded, France,
>Aug. 1917 ; Lt. 1917.

Crawford, John Jones ;
>M.B. 1897 ; M.D. •1901 ; Lt. R.A.M.C., May 1915 ; Civil
>Surgeon, Malta ; Capt. 1916.

Crawford, Mabel Alice Dobbin ;
  M.B. 1913 ; M.A.O. 1917 ; Area Medical Controller, Q.M.A.A.C.
  Irish Command, 1918.

Crawford, Robert ;
  Ent. 1915 ; 2 Lt. 14 R. Ir. Rif., Aug. 1915.

Crawford, Thomas Maitland ;
  Ent. 1901; Temp. Lt. R.A.M.C., Oct. 1915; Temp. Capt. 1916;
  M.C. Feb. 1918.

*Crealock, William Etienne Wyse ;
  B.A.I. 1912; 2 Lt. I.A. Res. of Offs. Feb. 1915; att. S. & T.
  Corps. I. E. F. to N. W. Frontier, 1915 ; Turkish Arabia, 1916 ;
  Capt. 1918 ; despatches (twice).

Creaser, Thomas ;
  M.B. 1904; M.D. 1907; Staff Surgeon R.N., Nov. 1914 ;
  H.M.S. " Boadicea," Feb. 1916 ; Sg. Cr. 1918.

Cree, Robert Ewart ;
  M.B. & M.D. 1902; Lt. R.A.M.C., Sept. 1914; Capt. 1915;
  despatches, June 1915, Jan. 1916; M.C. Jan. 1916; France;
  Mesopotamia ; Maj. 81 Fld. Amb., 1918 ; Salonika.

Creery, William Foster ;
  Ent. 1909; B.Sc., Manchester : 2 Lt. 7 Manch. R., May 1914 ;
  Capt. 1915 ; Lt. 1 Conn. Rang., Apr. 1915 ; Soudan and Egypt,
  1914-1915; Gallipoli, 1915 ; France, 1915 ; Mesopotamia, 1915 ;
  Temp. Capt. 1918.

Crichton, Alec Godfrey ;
  B.A.I. 1911; 2 Lt. 7 R. Dub. Fus., March 1915; killed in
  action, Suvla Bay, 16 Aug. 1915.

Crichton, Brian Dodwell ;
  M.B. 1912; M.D. 1915; Lt. R.A.M.C., March 1915; Capt.
  1916; France, 1916 ; India, 1917-9.

Crichton, Eric Cuthbert ;
  M.B. 1912; Capt. R.A.M.C., Aug. 1915 ; Palestine, 1916, 1917 ;
  Egypt, 1918-9 ; despatches, Jan. 1918.

*Crofton, Patrick George ;
  Ent. 1917 ; O. Cadet Bn. (Oxford), June 1918.

Crofton, Richard Marsh ;
  B.A. 1913; 2 Lt. 36 Jacob's Horse.

Crofton, Thomas Horsfall ;
  B.A.I. 1912 ; Pte. Canadian Sea. Highrs.; 2 Lt. 5 Conn. Rang.,
  Jan. 1915 ; Capt 1915 ; M.C. and Parchment ; killed in action
  near Roussoy, France, 21 March 1918.

*Croker, William Pennefather ;
> M.B. 1912; Lt. R.A.M.C., Jan. 1913; Prisoner of war, Oct. 1914–July 1915 ; Capt. 1915; France 1916 ; Legion of Honour, Croix de Guerre, Nov. 1918.

Croly, Arthur England Johnson ;
> B.A. 1898; M.A. 1899; Col. R.A.M.C., ret., temp. empld., Feb. 1915 ; Col. A.D.M.S. Aug. 1918.

Croly, Arthur England Johnson ;
> Ent. 1899; Capt. 11 Bn. Australian E. F. Aug. 1914 ; severely wounded, Dardanelles; despatches ; Temp. Maj. 1917.

Croly, Henry ;
> M.B. 1891; M.D. 1895; Lt. R.A.M.C., July 1915 ; Mediterranean E. F. 1915 ; Capt. 1916.

Cronin, Richard Thomas.
> Ent. 1920 ; 2 Lt. 4 Conn. Rang., Jan. 1916; att. M.G.C.; Lt. 1917; att. Tank C. ; A/Capt., 1918; B.E.F. France ; wounded, Nov. 1917.

Cronyn, John George ;
> B.A. 1880; Lt. R.A.M.C., Sept. 1915; R. Herbert Hosp. Woolwich ; Capt. 1916.

*Crookshank, Arthur Chichester ;
> Ent. 1912 ; Pte. D. Comp., 7 R. Dub. Fus., Sept., 1914; missing since 16 Aug. 1915, reported killed in action, Suvla Bay, 1915.

*Crookshank, Henry;
> Ent. 1910; Pte. D. Co., 7 R. Dub. Fus., Sept. 1914; wounded, Dardanelles ; 2 Lt. R.E., Dec. 1915 ; Lt. 1917; Egypt; Palestine ; France ; despatches.

*Crosbie, Francis ;
> M.B. 1911; M.D. 1912; Lt. R.A.M.C., Aug. 1914; Capt. 1915; despatches, Salonica, Dec. 1916.

*Crosbie, Herbert ;
> Ent. 1911 ; Pte. 10 Western Canadian R., 1 Canadian Contgt. ; wounded, Flanders, May 1915 ; 2 Lt. 3 R. Dub. Fus., June 1915.

*Crosbie, John Henry Breuell ;
> Ent. 1914; M.B. 1920; Surg. Prob. R.N.V.R., Sept. 1916 ; H.M.S. "Oak."

Cross, Charles Garsted ;
> B.A. 1901 ; 2 Lt. 6, 2 Norf. R., Oct 1915 ; Lt. 1917; Brig. Musk. Off. 1917; M.B.E. 1917.

Cross, Philip Frederick ;
> Ent. 1911 ; Pte. London Irish.

Crosslé, Francis Clements ;
>M.B. 1911 ; Australian A.M.C.

Crosslé, Howard ;
>M.B. 1901 ; M.D. 1904; Lt. I.M.S., July 1902; Maj. 1914.

Crosthwait, Herbert Leland ;
>B.A.I. 1889; 2 Lt. R.E., March 1890; Maj. 1910; Lt.-Col.
>1918.

Crosthwait, Rev. William Frederick ;
>B.A. 1912 ; M.A. 1916 ; Army Chap., 4 Cl., June 1916 : M.C.
>Feb. 1919.

Crosthwait, William Sylvester ;
>Med. School 1889 ; L.R.C.P.& S.I ; Lt. R.A.M.C., June 1900 ;
>Maj. 1912 ; despatches, Sept. 1918.

*Crowe, Henry George ;
>Ent. 1914 ; 2 Lt. R. Ir. Regt., July 1916 ; R. F. C. Nov.
>1917 ; Lt. 1918 ; M.C. June 1918.

Crowe, Lewis Wright ;
>M.B. 1894 ; M.D. 1895 ; Lt. R.A.M.C., Oct. 1915 ; Capt. 1916.

Crowley, Thomas William ;
>M.B. 1902 ; M.D. 1903 ; Lt. R.A.M.C. Dec. 1914 ; Capt. 1915 ;
>despatches, Jan. 1916.

Crozier, Francis Rawdon Moira ;
>B.A. 1897 ; Capt. 6 R. Ir. Fus., Dec. 1914 ; wounded, Darda-
>nelles, Aug. 1915 ; wounded, Oct. 1916 ; Lt.-Col., empld. Min.
>of Lab. 1918.

Crozier, Gerard Irvine ; .
>Ent. 1903 ; Pte. 7 Leins. R. 1915 ; 2 Lt. 6 Bn., Jan. 1916 ; Lt.
>1917 ; died of malaria, Mudros, 1919.

Crozier, Herbert Charles ;
>Ent. 1898 ; 2 Lt. 1 R. Dub. Fus., Jan. 1902 ; Capt. 1913 ;
>M. C., July 1915 ; Maj. 1917.

Crozier, Rev. John Winthrop ;
>B.A. 1902 ; M.A. 1906 ; Army Chaplain, 4 Cl., Feb. 1915 ;
>France, 1915. ; despatches.

*Crozier, William Magee ;
>B.A. 1897 ; 2 Lt. 9 R. Innis. Fus., Sept. 1914 ; Lt. 1914 ;
>wounded and missing, France ; reported killed in action, 1 Aug.
>1916.

*Cullen, James Arthur William ;
>Ent. 1909 ; M.B. 1917 ; Lt. R.A.M.C., Aug. 1914 ; Capt. 1917 ;
>A/Maj. 1918.

Cullinan, Frederick John Fitz James ;
Ent. 1914 ; 2 Lt. 9 W. Rid. R., Sept. 1914; Capt. 1915;
M. C. 31 March 1916 ; 2 Lt. 1, 2 L'pool R., Feb. 1916 ; att. 9 W.
Rid. R.; Lt. 1917 ; A/Capt. 1918.

Cullinan, George Critchley ;
Ent. 1903 ; R.G.A. Feb. 1919.

*Cullinan, Robert Hornidge ;
B.A. 1903; 2 Lt. 7 R. Muns. Fus., Nov. 1914; Capt. 1915 ;
killed in action, Dardanelles, 8 Aug. 1915.

Cullum, Sidney John ;
M.B. 1901; M.D.1905; Lt. R.A.M.C., Nov. 1914; Capt. 1915.

Culverwell, George Hugh ;
M.B. 1913; M.D. 1914 ; Lt. R.A.M.C., Apr. 1915 ; Capt. 1917;
Macedonia, 1918.

*Culverwell, Rev. Oliver Gerald ;
Ent. 1910; 2 Lt. A.S.C., Dec. 1914 ; Lt. 1915.

Cummings, Basil Stewart Johnson ;
Ent. 1919 ; Pte. 17 Lond. R.

Cummins, David Patrick ;
Ent. 1920 ; 2 Lt. M.G.C. Dec. 1916; Lt. 1918.

Cummins, William Ashley ;
B.A. and LL.B. 1908 ; 2 Lt. Bucks Bn., Oxf. and Bucks
L.I., Sept. 1914; Capt. 1916.

Cunningham, John ;
M.B. 1904 ; M.D. 1906 ; Lt. I.M.S , Feb. 1905 ; Capt. 1908 ;
despatches, N. W. Frontier, July 1916 ; Maj. 1917.

*Cunningham, William Anthony ;
Ent. 1917; R.A.F. June 1918.

Curtis, Douglas Charles Middleton ;
Ent. 1909 ; Qr. M. Sergt., 7 R. Dub. Fus.; 2 Lt. 1 Garr. Bn.
Hamp. R., Sept. 1916 ; Lt. 1918.

Curtis, Rev. John ;
B.A. 1902 ; B.D. 1905 ; Army Chaplain, 4 Cl., March 1916 ;
Mediterranean E. F.

*Cusack, James Joseph ;
Ent. 1920 ; 2 Lt. 4 Conn. Rang., July 1918 ; B.E.F., France.

*Cusack, Ralph Smith Oliver ;
Ent. 1892 ; Lt. A.S.C., Nov. 1915 ; Capt. 1917; A/Maj. 1917 ;
despatches.

*Cusack, Reginald Ernest ;
    Ent. 1913; 2 Lt. 4 R. Dub. Fus.. Nov. 1914 ; died of pneumonia
at Sittingbourne, 15 April, 1915.

D

*Dagg, Thomas William ;
    Ent. 1916; Garr. O.C.B., July 1917; 2 Lt. 3 Garr. Bn. R. Ir.
Fus., Sept. 1917 ; France ; Flanders.

*Dale, John Francis ;
    Ent. 1912 ; 2 Lt. 12 R. Welsh Fus., Aug. 1915 ; Lt. 1917.

*D'Alton, Melfort Campbell ;
    Ent. 1883; 2nd Lt. 8 N. Lan. R., Nov. 1914; relinquished
Commission, ill-health.

Daly, Charles Calthorp De Burgh ;
    M.B. 1883; Lt. R.A.M.C., Apr., 1915 ; Capt. 1916 ; brought to
notice of Secretary of State for valuable services rendered in
connexion with the war, Feb. 1917 ; O.B.E. Dec. 1919.

*Daly, Charles Patrick ;
    Ent. 1905 ; 7 O. Cadet Bn., Nov. 1917.

*Daly, Hubert Dean ;
    B.A.I. 1910; Inns of Court O.T.C., January 1916 ; 2 Lt.
R.F.A., Sept. 1916 ; Lt. 1918 ; France.

*Daly, Oscar Bedford ;
    B.A. 1903 ; 2 Lt. 15 Welsh R., Sept. 1915 , Lt. 1917 (spl. appt.) ;
M.B.E.

*Daly, Richard St. George Hercules Langrishe ;
    Ent. 1904 ; Corp. 13 Hussars ; attd. 11 Hussars; wounded and
missing while rescuing an officer, Messines, 31 Oct., 1914.

Dalzell, Rev. Henry ;
    B.A. 1891 ; M.A. 1895 ; Chaplain R.N., Nov., 1897.

*Daniel, Herbert M'Williams ;
    M.B. 1915 ; Lt. R.A.M.C., Feb. 1916 ; Capt. 1917.

*D'Arcy, Henry Lewis Norman ;
    Ent. 1913 ; 2 Lt. 4 E. Surr. R., Aug. 1914; Lt. 1915.

D'Arcy, Richard John Peacock ;
    Ent. 1905 ; Assistant Paymaster, R. N. Reserve, Aug. 1914.

*Darling, Owen Richard ;
    Ent. 1914 ; 2 Lt. 10, 1 R. Ir. Fus., Nov. 1915 ; Lt. 1917 ;
Lt. I.A., 1918.

Davidson, Andrew Hope ;
>M.B. 1917; Lt. R.A.M.C., 1917; Egyptian E.F. ; Syria and Asia Minor.

Davidson-Houston, James Hamilton ;
>B.A. 1889; M.A. 1893; Capt. R. Fus. (ret. pay), June, 1903 ; Hon. Maj., Staff Appointment, Aug. 1914.

Davies, Alfred Lewis ;
>Ent. 1908; Lt. 4 R. Welsh Fus., Oct. 1912; Lt. 1918.

*Davies, Arthur Cecil ;
>B.A 1911; Chota Nagpur Light Horse.

*Davies, Emlyn Berkeley ;
>B.A. 1913 ; 2 Lt. 4 W.York. R., Oct. 1914 ; Capt. 18 Welsh R., 1916.

Davies, George Harold William ;
>B.A. 1909 ; Calcutta Light Horse.

Davis, Charles Frederick Fellowes ;
>Ent. 1903; Capt. 6 R. Innis. Fus., Oct. 1914; Salonika.

*Davis, George Hall ;
>Ent. 1913 : 2 Lt. 7 R. Muns. Fus., Sept. 1914 ; Capt. 1915 ; Despatches, Jan. 1916 ; Dardanelles ; Salonika.

*Davis, Harold Percy Whitton ;
>Ent. 1912 ; 2 Lt. 12 S. Lan. R., Jan. 1915 ; Lt. 1915.

*Davis, James Seymour ;
>Ent. 1918; volunteered and accepted, Aug. 1918.

Davis, Richard Christopher ;
>Ent. 1914 ; 2 Lt. 3 Manch. R., Oct. 1914; att. 1 Bn. ; killed in action, relief to Kut, 8 March 1916.

Davoren, Alfred John ;
>M.B. 1891; Lt. R.A.M.C., May 1915 ; Capt. 1916.

*Davoren, Vesey Alfred :
>B.A. 1914 ; 2 Lt. 7 Suff. R., Aug. 1914 ; Lt. 1915 ; Capt. 1918 ; Education Off.

Davys, Gerard Irvine ;
>M.B. 1901 ; M.D. 1911 ; Lt. I.M.S., July 1902 ; Maj. 1914.

Dawson, Lionel Edward ;
>B.A.I. 1908 ; M.A.I. 1920 ; Lt. Mesopotamia Rys., Feb. 1918 ; Capt. 1919 ; Mesopotamia, 1918-20.

*Dawson, William James Eric ;
>Ent. 1915 ; 2 Lt. R.F.A., Jan. 1916 ; Lt. 1917.

Dawson, William Richard ;
>M.B. 1890 ; M.D. 1891 : Maj. R.A.M.C., Sept. 1915 ; despatches,
>Sept. 1917 ; Temp. Hon. Lt.-Col. 1917 ; O.B E. June 1919.

Day, Rev. Edward Rouviere ;
>B.A. 1891 ; M.A. 1896; Army Chaplain, Feb. 1893 ; 1 Cl. 1912 ;
>France, 1914–8; Assist. Chap.-Gen. 1917–8 ; Principal Chap.,
>Egyptian E.F. 1918; C.M.G. Jan. 1916; despatches, Jan. 1917 ;
>C.B.E. June 1919 ; Mons Star (with rosette) ; General Service and
>Victory Medals.

*Day, James William ;
>Ent. 1912 ; 7 Cadet Bn., July 1916 ; 2 Lt. 12 London R., July
>1916 ; Lt. 1918.

*Day, John Edward ;
>Ent. 1913 ; 2 Lt. 6 R. Ir. Regt.,.Aug. 1914 ; Capt. 1916;
>wounded, Apr. 1916 ; died of wounds, 6 Apr. 1917.

Day, John Marshall ;
>M.B. 1895 ; M.D. 1899 ; R.A.M.C., Oct. 1917.

Day-Lewis, Rev. Frank Cecil ;
>B.A. 1900 ; Army Chaplain, 4 Cl., Dec. 1915–17 ; Hon. Chaplain,
>1918.

Deacon, Charles Henry ;
>Ent. 1911 ; 2 Lt. 17 R. Ir. Rif., May 1915; Lt. 1917.

Deakin , Herbe rt Andrew ;
>Ent. 1914 ; 2 Lt. 9 S. Staff. R., Sept. 1914 ; trsf. to 23 Div.
>Cyclist Co. May 1915; France 1915 ; 2 Lt. 1 & 2 S. Staff. R.,
>June 1915 ; Lt. 1916 ; R.A.F., 1918; France, 1918; slightly
>wounded, May 1918 ; 2 Lt. R.A.F., May 1918.

*Deale, Eric William Swain ;
>B.A. 1915 ; 2 Lt. R.F.A., Dec. 1915 ; gassed, June 1917 ; Lt.
>1917.

Deale, Violet Mabel ;
>M.B. 1916 ; Hospital Staff, Malta, 1916.

Deane, Rev. Charles Beresford ;
>B.A. 1905 ; M.A. 1919 ; Army Chaplain, 4 Cl., Jan. 1916–19 ;
>M.C. 1917 ; Temp. 3 Cl. 1918.

*Deane, Edward Newenham ;
>B.A. 1914 ; 2 Lt. R.E., Aug. 1914 ; Lt. 1915 ; Capt. 917.

Deane, Joseph Eugene ;
Ent. 1915: Pte. 10 R. Dub. Fus., Jan. 1916 ; Surg. Prob. 1918 ;
despatches, Oct. 1918.

*Deane, Thomas Alexander David ;
Ent. 1913; 2 Lt. Royal Marine L. I., Sept. 1914 ; Portsmouth
Bn., Gallipoli, 1915 ; killed in action, Dardanelles, 3 May, 1915.

Deane-Oliver, Margaret Esther Silver ;
Ent. 1921 ; V.A.D. Irish Counties' Hosp. and 1 W. Gen. Hosp.,
Wallasley, 1917–19.

Deane-Oliver, Richard Edward ;
B.A.I. 1915 ; 2 Lt. R.E., Aug. 1915 ; killed in action, France,
7-8 Sept. 1916.

*Deanesly, Geoffrey Richard ;
Ent. 1915 ; Pte. 3 Conn. Rang., Aug. 1917 ; M.G.C., Aug. 1918 ;
wounded, Le Cateau, Oct. 1918 ; left arm amputated ; discharged,
Nov. 1919.

de Burgh, Ulick George Campbell ;
B.A. 1875 ; First Comn., Sept. 1876 ; Col. 1900 ; C.B. ; retd.
from Staff, 1908 ; Dept. of Prisoners of War, 1915.

de Courcy, Thomas Louis ;
M.B. and M.D. 1906 ; Lt. R.A.M.C., T.F., Nov. 1914 ; Capt.
1915.

*Delmege, James O'Grady ;
Ent. 1910 ; 2 Lt. 4 D. Gds., Aug., 1914; Lt.; died of gas
poisoning, France, 7 June, 1915.

de Montmorency, Rev. Arthur Hervé Alberic Bouchard ;
B.A. 1907 ; M.A. 1912; Army Chaplain, 4 Cl., Sept. 1915.

Dempsey, Rev. John Cunningham ;
B.A. 1904 ; M.A. 1907 ; Army Chaplain, 4 Cl. ; died from
exposure through his ship being lost, Aug. 1917.

Dench, Reginald Arthur ;
Ent. 1915 ; 2 Lt. 7 Leins. R., Jan. 1916 ; France 1916-18 ; Lt.
1917 ; M.C. March 1917 ; Bar to M.C. Oct. 1917 ; despatches
(3 times) ; A/Capt. 1917 ; Capt. 1918.

Denham, Charles Holmes ;
M.B. 1911 ; Lt. R.A.M.C., Aug. 1914 : Capt. 1915.

Denham, William Knox ;
Ent. 1905 ; S. African Campaign, with Botha ; Flight Lt., R.N.
Air S., Apr. 1916.

Dennard, Leslie David ;
Ent. 1919 ; Pte. R.A.M.C., Feb. 1915 ; Dardanelles ; India ;
E. Africa ; S. Africa.

E

Denning, Frederick Arthur Vere ;
> Ent. 1907 ; M.B. Edin.; Surg. Lt. R.N., May 1915.

*Denning, Reginald Ernest Vere ;
> Ent. 1910 ; 2 Lt. 3 R. Dub. Fus., July 1913 ; Capt. 1915.

Denroche, Charles Thursby ;
> B.A. 1913 ; 2 Lt. 7 Leins. R., Sept. 1914 ; Capt. M.G.C., Sept. 1915 ; Maj. 1918.

*Denroche, Ivan George ;
> Ent. 1909 ; 2 Lt. 10 N. Staff. R., Nov. 1914 ; wounded, Gallipoli, Aug. 1915 ; Capt. Labour C., 1918.

De Renzy, Annesley St. George ;
> B.A. 1891 ; French Medical Service.

*Despard, Ernest Richard ;
> Ent. 1907 ; 2 Lt. M.G.C., Sept. 1916 ; 2 Lt. Tank Corps, Oct. 1916 ; Lt. 1917 ; died of wounds, 26 Sept. 1917.

Devenish, John Graham ;
> Ent. 1896 ; Lt. R. Innis. Fus., 1899 ; retired ; New Zealand E. F.

Devenish, Rev. Robert Cecil Sylvester ;
> B.A. 1911 ; Army Chaplain, 4 Cl., March 1915-19.

*Deverell, William Berenger Statter ;
> Ent. 1910 ; Temp. Lt. A.S.C., Dec. 1914 ; Tempt. Capt. 1915 ; 2 Lt. A.S.C. (R.), May 1915 ; A/Capt. 1916 ; Adj. 1916-1919 ; Suvla Bay, Salonika, Serbia 1915 ; Egypt 1916 ; Palestine 1917-18 ; Syria 1918.

Devereux, Robert Meade Daly ;
> M.B. 1918 ; Lt. R.A.M.C., Aug. 1918.

Devine, James Arthur ;
> M.B. and M.D. 1897 ; D.S.O. 1902 ; Major R.A.M.C., March, 1915 ; despatches, March 1918 ; O.B.E. June 1919.

Devlin, Charles Joseph ;
> Ent. 1919 ; A.B., R.N.

Dickie, Robert Kelso ;
> Ent. 1919 ; 2 Lt. R.A.F., Sept. 1918 ; Italy.

Dickie, Thomas Wallace ;
> B.A. 1909 ; 2 Lt. 4 R. Dub. Fus., 1907 ; Capt. 1912 ; Staff Offr., 1914 ; Bt. Maj. 1918.

Dickinson, Cyril Henry ;
> Ent. 1895 ; Motor Service.

Dickinson, Frank Selwyn ;
> Ent. 1895 ; 2 Lt. A.S.C. Dec. 1915.

Dickinson, Harold Evory ;
Ent. 1893 ; Capt., Military Landing Offr., Sept. 1915.

Dickinson, William Michael Kington ;
B.A. 1908 ; 2 Lt. unatt. Feb. 1908 ; Lt. I.A., 20 Deccan Horse,
1910.

Dickson, James Alfred Nicholson ;
Ent. 1914 ; 2 Lt. 3 R. Innis. Fus., Apr. 1915; Lt. 1916 ;
Lt. M.G.C., 1916 ; wounded, Sept. 1916.

Dickson, William Arthur ;
Ent. 1920 ; 2 Lt. R. Ir. Regt. June 1915 ; wounded, France, 1916 ;
Lt. 1917 ; empld. Min. of Lab.; A/Capt. and Adjt. 1918.

Digges La Touche, Rev. Everard;
B.A. 1904 ; M.A. 1908 ; Litt.D. 1910; Australian Expeditionary
Force; killed, Suvla Bay, 7 Aug. 1915.

*Dillon, Edward Alfred Tandy ;
B.A.1. 1909 ; Lt. R.E., Feb. 1915 ; France ; A/Maj. 1917 ;
M.C. 1919.

Dillon, Henry de Courcy ;
M.B. 1907 ; Lt. R.A.M.C., Aug. 1914; wounded, Flanders,
Oct. 1914 ; Capt. 1915.

Dillon, Henry Vere Shirley ;
B.A.I. 1905 ; 2 Lt. I.A. Res. of Offs. Aug. 1918 ; att. 3 Sappers
and Miners.

*Dillon, John Joseph ;
Ent. 1914 ; 2 Lt. 4 Conn. Rang., Jan. 1915; Lt. 1916 ; M.C.

Dillon, Leopold Magregor ;
Ent. 1912 ; 2 Lt. R.G.A., Jan. 1916; Lt. 1917.

*Dillon, William Ambrose ;
B.A. 1913 ; Commn. in Intelligence Dept., June 1916.

Dilworth, Claude Stanley ;
Ent. 1918 ; 2 Lt. R.A.F.

*Dilworth, Robert Kildahl ;
Ent. 1915; 2 Lt. 1, 2 R. Muns. Fus., Apr. 1916 ; killed in action,
28 Dec. 1916.

*Dimond, Francis Robert ;
Ent. 1914 ; 2 Lt. 15 L'pool R., March 1915; 13 Bn. 1916 ;
France, 1916 ; killed in action, France, 31 July 1917.

Dinsmore, Gerald Telford ;
Ent. 1917 ; volunteered and accepted.

*Disney, Thomas Brabazon Lambert ;
> Ent. 1912; Motor Desp. Rider, Aug. 1914; despatches, Feb. 1915 ; 2 Lt. R.E., Sept. 1915 ; 2 Lt. Ox. and Bucks. L. I., June 1916 ; (empld. R.E.) ; Lt. 1916 ; A/Capt. 1918 ; M.C.

Disney, Rev. William ;
> B.A. 1885; M.A. 1912; Army Chaplain, 4 Cl., July 1915–16 and 1917–19.

Diver, Walter Stewart ;
> Ent. 1919 ; Fight Cadet, R.A.F.

*Dixon, Frederick Ernest Reginald ;
> Ent. 1913 ; 2 Lt. A.S.C., Nov. 1914 ; France, 1915 ; Lt. 1915 ; 2 Lt. R.E., Dec. 1915 ; Lt. 1917 ; M.C.

Dixon, Geoffrey Francis ;
> B.A. 1914 ; 2 Lt. Supply and Transport Corps, I.A., 1915 ; Lt. I.A. Res. of Offs., Camel Corps ; died of pneumonia, on active service in Persia, 1 Aug. 1918.

*Dixon, Henry Bryan Frost ;
> M.B. 1913; Lt. R.A.M.C., Aug. 1914; Capt. 1915; despatches, Jan. 1916; Flanders ; M.C. Nov. 1916 ; bar to M.C. July 1918.

Dixon, Joseph Francis ;
> M.B. 1899 : M.D. 1904 ; Lt. R.A.M.C., Nov. 1913 ; Maj. 1915.

*Dixon, Patrick Kerr ;
> Ent. 1916 ; No. 2 R.G.A. Cadet School, May 1917 ; 2 Lt. R.G.A., Sept. 1917 ; Flanders and France, 1917 ; despatches, June 1919 ; Lt. 1919.

*Dixon, Reginald Malyn ;
> B.A.I. 1914 ; 2 Lt. R.E., Oct. 1914 ; Flanders ; Lt. 1915 ; M.C. Jan. 1917 ; Croix de Guerre, Aug. 1918 ; Capt. 1918.

*Dixon, Roland Vickers ;
> Ent. 1911 ; 2 Lt. 2 K.O. Sco. Bord., Jan. 1914 ; Lt. 1914 ; wounded; Flanders ; Capt. 1918.

Dixon, Stephen Mitchell ;
> B.A.I. 1891 ; Capt. R.E. Ry. Troop, France, 1917–19.

*Dobbin, George Frederick ;
> Ent. 1912 ; 2 Lt. 6 R. Ir. Fus., Sept. 1914 ; killed, Dardanelles, 16 Aug. 1915.

Dobbin, Roy Samuel ;
> M.B. and M.D. 1899 ; Mil. War Hospital, Cairo, 1915 ; Capt. R.A.M.C., Apr. 1917 ; Surg. Specialist, B.E.F., France, 1917 ; Allied Army of Black Sea, 1919 ; despatches, 1919 ; O.B.E. June 1919.

*Dobbs, Cathcart Eric Stewart ;
Ent. 1913 ; 2 Lt. A.S C., Jan. 1914 ; despatches and Military
Cross, June 1915 ; Capt. 1916 ; Adj. 1919.

Dobbs, Rev. Henry Ballina Carrig ;
B.A. 1900 ; M.A. 1912 : Army Chaplain, 4 Cl., March 1917–19.

*Dobbs, Kildare Dixon Borrowes ;
Ent. 1917 ; O.T.C., Apr. 1918 ; volunteered and accepted.

Dobbs, Richard Conway ;
Ent. 1897 ; 2 Lt. 2 R. Ir. Fus. Apr. 1900 ; Maj. 1915 ; D.S.O. ;
Temp. Lt.-Col. 1916 ; A/Lt.-Col. 1917 ; Temp. Lt.-Col. 1918 ;
Comdg. Serv. Bn. Oxford and Bucks L. I. 1917 ; Serv. Bn. S.
Wales Bord. 1917–18 ; Bt. Lt-Col. 1919.

*Dobbyn, Alexander Lee ;
Ent. 1914 ; 2 Lt. 5 R. Ir. Fus., Oct. 1915 ; M.C. Oct. 1916 ;
Lt. 1917 ; Bar to M.C. ; despatches ; wounded.

*Dobbyn, William Augustus Nelson ;
Ent. 1914 ; 2 Lt. 16 L'pool R., Oct. 1915 ; attd. 15 Lan. Fus. ;
killed in action, France, 4 Jan. 1917.

Dobson, George Magill ;
M.B. 1883 ; Maj. Res. of Officers, March 1897 ; Maj. R.A.M.C.,
Aug. 1914.

*Dobson, James Robinson ;
Ent. 1907 ; Pte. 1 R. Scots, Mar. 1914 ; 2 Lt. 8 R. Ir. Fus.,
Feb. 1916 ; died of wounds received in action, 19 Feb. 1917.

Dockrell, George Shannon ;
Ent. 1906 ; 2 Lt. 9 Rifle Brig., Dec. 1914 ; Lt. 1915 ; wounded,
France, Aug. 1915 ; Staff Capt. 1917 ; Maj. 1919.

*Dockrell, Kenneth Brooks ;
B.A. 1909 ; Rhyll, Sept. 1918.

Dockrell, Morgan ;
B.A. 1903 ; 2 Lt. I.A., Jan. 1906 ; Capt. 116 Mahrattas, 1914.

*Dockrill, John Stuart ;
M.B. 1914 ; Lt. R.A.M.C., Aug. 1914 ; Capt. 1915 ; despatches,
Jan. 1916.

Dods, John George ;
M.B. 1910 ; M.D. 1912 ; Lt. R.A.M.C., Dec. 1915 ; Capt. 1916.

*Doherty, James Walker ;
B.A. 1897 ; M.A. 1910 ; 2 Lt. A.S.C., May 1915 ; Lt. 1915.

D'Olier, Bertram Isaac ;
M.B. 1893 ; M.D. 1895 ; Lt. R.A.M.C., Sept. 1914 ; Capt. 1915 ;
Dardanelles.

Dollar, Rev. Joseph Bartholomew ;
B.A. 1911 ; 2 Lt. 1 Ir. Gds., June 1915; Lt. 1915; France, 1915-18 ; Capt. 1919; wounded Sept. 1916 and July 1917.

*Donaldson, John Coote ;
Ent. 1913 ; 2 Lt. A.S.C., July 1915 ; Lt. June 1916; transf. Lt. M.G.C., 1917; M.C. Feb. 1919.

Donaldson, John George West ;
Ent. 1898 ; Capt. Ry. Constr. Co., Mesopotamia.

Donnell, Eric Douglas ;
B.A.I. 1911 ; 2 Lt. 3 R.W. Surr. R., Jan. 1915 ; attchd. 2 Yorks L.I.; France, 1915 ; Capt. 1916 ; M.C. June 1918 ; Capt. 8 R. W. Surr. R. 1918.

Donovan, Charles ;
Med. School 1886 ; M.B., R.U.I. Lt. Col. I.M.S., June 1913.

Doran, George William ;
M.B. 1916 ; Lt. R.A.M.C., May 1916 ; Capt. 1917.

Doran, Henry Francis ;
B.A.I. 1910 ; Lt. I.A. Res. of Offs. Nov. 1918 ; Mesopotamia.

*Dorman, Richard Hampden Hobart ;
Ent. 1914 ; 2 Lt. 4 R. Muns. Fus., Aug. 1914 : Lt. 1915 ; att. Tank Corps, 1916 ; Capt. 1917 ; wounded June 1917 at Wychaete ; gassed, April 1918.

Dorman, Thomas Robert Hobart ;
Ent. 1911 ; 2 Lt. 2 R. Muns. Fus., March 1915 ; missing, near Lille, 16 Feb. 1916 ; afterwards reported died of wounds, 21 Feb. 1916.

Dormer, Percival Atkin ;
M.B. 1918 ; Lt. R.A.F., M.S., Aug. 1918.

Dougan, Frederick Robert ;
M.B. 1914 ; Lt. R.A.M.C., Dec. 1914 ; Capt. 1915 ; M.C. 1918.

Dougan, George ;
M.B. 1906 ; M.D. 1907 ; Lt. R.A.M.C., July 1916 ; despatches, Mesopotamia, Nov. 1917.

*Douglas, Archibald Beck ;
B.A. 1911 ; 2 Lt. 6 R. Innis. Fus., Sept. 1914 ; Lt. 1915; wounded, Dardanelles, Aug. 1915 ; Capt. 1917.

*Douglas, Arthur Henry ;
B.A.I. 1913 ; 2 Lt. R.E., Oct. 1914 ; Lt. 1915 ; wounded, 1916 ; M.C. Oct. 1916 ; Capt. 1918.

*Douglas, Hugh Lawford ;
    Ent. 1919 ; M.G.C. Sept. 1917 ; 2 Lt. Tank C. May 1918;
    France.

Douglass, James Henry ;
    M.B. 1901 ; M.D. 1903 ; Lt. R.A.M.C., Dec. 1914 ; Maj. 1916 ;
    O.B.E.

Douglass, William Nicholas Gerald ;
    B.A.I. 1901 ; 2 Lt. R.E., Oct. 1914 ; Capt. 1915.

Dow, Thomas Miller ;
    I.C.S. Student, T.C.D., 1914–5 ; 2 Lt. 36 Sikhs, Aug. 1916 ;
    Lt. 1917.

Dowd, Wilfred Rodney Godfrey ;
    Ent. 1914 ; 2 Lt. R.G.A., Oct. 1915 ; Lt. 1917.

Dowden, Richard ;
    M.B. and M.D. 1898 ; Temp. Lt. R.A.M.C., May 1915.

*Dowley, Edward Joseph ;
    Ent. 1914 ; 2 Lt. 13 Lan. Fus., Jan. 1915 ; 2 Lt. M.G.C. Nov.
    1915 ; Lt. 1916 ; A/Capt. 1918.

Dowley, Thomas Paul ;
    M.B. 1908 ; S. African M. Corps, Brit. E. Africa.

*Dowling, Thomas Michael ;
    Ent. 1910 ; 2 Lt. A.S.C., Oct. 1914 ; Lt. 1916, K. Afr. Rif. ;
    Capt. 1917 (whilst Ry. Traff. Off.).

*Dowling, William James ;
    M.B. 1915 ; Lt. R.A.M.C., Aug. 1914 ; Capt. 1916 ; despatches
    May 1917 and Aug. 1918 ; M.C. Nov. 1918 ; Bar to M.C. Jan.
    1919.

*Dowse, Henry Harvey ;
    Ent. 1912 ; Pte. 7 R. Dub. Fus., Sept. 1914 ; wounded, Dar-
    danelles, Aug. 1915 ; 2 Lt. A.S.C., 1916 ; France, 1916, 1917 ;
    Lt. 1917 ; R.A.F., 1917 ; seriously injured in aeroplane accident,
    Oct. 1917 ; Italy, 1917 ; wounded, Oct. 1918 ; died of influenza at
    Genoa, 10 Nov. 1918.

*Dowse, John Cecil Alexander ;
    M.B. 1914 ; Temp. Lt. R.A.M.C., Aug. 1914 ; Capt. 1915 ;
    despatches and M.C. Jan. 1916 ; Lt. R.A.M.C., Jan. 1917 ; A/Maj.
    1918 ; Bar to M.C. Oct. 1918.

Dowse, Richard Victor ;
    Ent. 1915; Surg. Prob. R.N.V.R., July 1917 ; H.M.S. "Milne,"
    Dover Patrol.

Dowse, William Arthur Clarence ;
Ent. 1913 ; 2 Lt. 11 Ches. R., Nov. 1914 ; Lt. 1915 ; missing, reported killed in action, France, 3 July 1916.

Doyle, Kingsley Dryden ;
B.A.I. 1887 ; M.A. 1895 ; Lt. R.N.V.R., R.N.A.S. ; Capt. R.A.F., Apr. 1918 ; Exp. Armament Off.

*Draper, Arthur Philip ;
M.B. 1912 ; M.D. 1914 ; Lt. R.A.M.C., Jan. 1917 ; wounded, Nov. 1917 ; M.C. 1917 ; Capt. 1918.

Draper, Charles Frederick ;
B.A.I. 1899 ; M.A. 1903 ; Capt. RE., Nov. 1915 ; Egypt ; Palestine ; Chief Engineer and afterwards Bridge Engineer to Palestine Military Railways ; O.B.E. ; despatches (twice).

Drennan, Charles Edward ;
Ent. 1903 ; L.R.C.P.I.; British Red Cross, France, March 1916 ; Temp. Hon. Lt. R.A.M.C., June 1916.

Drennan, Henry Denis ;
M.B. 1906 ; Staff Surgeon R.N., May 1915 ; Surg. Cr. 1919 ; D.S.O. Jan. 1919.

Drew, Desmond ;
M.B. 1909 ; Capt. S.A.M.C. ; German W. Africa, 1917.

Drummond, William Stuart Gordon ;
B.A. 1906 ; Lt. A.S C., Sept. 1914 ; Capt. 1915 ; France and Flanders ; Temp. Maj. 1916 ; despatches (twice) ; D.S.O. Jan. 1918.

Drury, Francis James ;
M.B. 1883 ; Maj. I.M.S., Apr. 1897 ; Col. 1912 ; died 30 Nov. 1915.

Drury, Henry Cooke ;
M.B. 1883 ; M.D. 1894 ; Lt.-Col. R.A.M.C., Oct. 1917 ; 83 (Dub.) Gen. Hosp., France, 1917.

Drury, Rev. John ;
B.A. 1906 ; M.A. 1913 ; served in Army 1917–19.

*Drury, Kenneth Kirkpatrick ;
M.B. 1912 ; M.D. 1914 ; Lt. R.A.M.C., Aug. 1914 ; Capt. 1915 ; France ; M.C. June 1916 ; despatches May 1917 ; A/Maj. 1918 ; D.A.D.M.S., 1919.

*Drury, Noel Edmund ;
Ent. 1901 ; 2 Lt. 6 R. Dub. Fus., Feb. 1915 ; Temp. Capt. 1915 ; Lt. 1915 ; Dardanelles ; Salonika ; Capt. 1918.

Drysdale, Matthew Robert ;
B.A. 1911 ; 2 Lt. R.G.A., March 1915 ; Lt. 1916.

*Duckworth, Henry Launcelot D'Olier ;
    M.B. 1913 ; Surg. R.N., Sept. 1914 ; France.

*Dudgeon, Arthur ;
    B.A.I. 1911 ; 2 Lt. R.G.A., Jan. 1915 ; att. R.E. Field Survey ;
    died in France of pneumonia, 19 Nov. 1918.

Dudgeon, Edward Caufield ;
    Ent. 1919 ; 2 Lt. A.S.C. Nov. 1914 ; Lt. 1915 ; 2 Lt. R.A.F. ;
    wounded.

*Dudgeon, William Christian ;
    B.A.I. 1912 ; 2 Lt. R.G.A., Jan. 1915 ; Lt. 1917 ; France.

Dudley, Harold Benson ;
    B.A. 1908 ; Pte. Malay Rifles.

Dudley, Walter Lionel ;
    B.A. 1908 ; 2 Lt. 4 Welsh R., Feb. 1912 ; Tempt. Capt. 1915 ;
    wounded, Suvla Bay, Aug. 1915 ; Capt. 1916 ; Educational Insr.
    1919.

Duffey, Arthur Cameron ;
    M.B. 1896 ; M.D. 1897 ; Lt. R.A.M.C., Nov. 1900 ; Maj. 1912.

*Duffield, Rev. John ;
    B.A. 1909 ; M.A. 1913 ; Army Chaplain, 4 Cl., Feb. 1915–19.

*Duggan, George Grant ;
    B.A. 1908 ; Lt. O.T.C., T.F., Unattached List, Feb. 1913 ; Capt.
    5 R. Ir. Fus., Oct. 1914 ; died of wounds, Dardanelles, 16 Aug.
    1915.

*Duggan, John Rowswell ;
    Ent. 1911 ; 2 Lt. 5 R. Ir. Regt., Sept. 1914 ; Lt. 1915 ; killed
    in action, Dardanelles, 16 Aug. 1915.

*Dunbar, Thomas Bartholomew O'Connor ;
    Ent. 1909 ; 2 Lt. A.S.C., Aug. 1914 ; wounded, Sept. 1916.

*Duncan, Alan George Douglas ;
    Ent. 1913 ; 2 Lt. 12 R. W. Fus., Nov. 1914 ; wounded, Gallipoli ;
    Lt. Labour C., 1917 ; A/Cap. 1918.

Duncan, Rev. Edward Francis ;
    B.A. 1907 ; M.A. 1910 ; Army Chaplain, 4 Cl., May 1915 ;
    M.C. Dec. 1916 ; despatche, Jan. 1917 ; killed in action, 11 March
    1917.

Duncan, Robert Stephens ;
    Ent. 1916 ; 2 Lt. 9 R. Ir. Fus., July 1918.

Dunlop, Rev. Douglas Lyall Chandlee ;
    B.A. 1904 ; Army Chaplain, I.A., 1918–19.

Dunlop, Rev. Keith Malcolm ;
    B.A. 1904 ; Army Chaplain, 4 Cl., Sept. 1916–18.

Dunn, Frank Jerome;
B.A. 1887; M.B. (R.U.I.); Snr. Assist. Surg. Sup. Med. Dept. I.A., March 1915.

Dunn, Henry Nason;
M.B. 1888; Capt. R.A.M.C., Jan. 1895; Lt. Col. 1914; despatches, June 1916, Jan. 1917, Dec 1917, July 1919; D.S.O. Jan. 1917; C.M.G., March 1918; wounded, Nov. 1918; despatches, 1919.

Dunn, Patrick James Smyth;
M.B. 1909; Temp. Lt. R.A.M.C., Sept. 1917.

Dunn, Robert Edward;
M.B. 1911; Australian E.F., Capt., Gallipoli, 1915.

Dunn, Wilfred James;
M.B. 1907; Lt. R.A.M.C., Feb. 1908; Capt. 1911; A/Lt.-Col. 1916; O.B.E.; despatches (Mesopotamia), June 1919.

Dunphy, Robert Michael Joseph;
B.A.I. 1911; 2 Lt. R.F.C., March 1916; Lt. 1917; France served 1915-19.

Dwyer, Frederic Conway;
M.B. 1883; M.D. 1884; Pres. R.C.S.I.; Surgeon, Dublin Castle Red Cross Hosp.; Lt.-Col. R.A.M.C., July 1917.

E

*Eagar, Frederick Maitland;
Ent. 1912; 2 Lt. 5 R. Ir. Fus., Sept. 1914; wounded, Sept. 1915; Lt. I.A. 1916; wounded, June 1917.

Eagar, Robert James Conway.
Ent. 1892; 2 Lt. 11 R. Ir. Rif., Apr. 1915; France 1915.

Eames, William L'Estrange;
M.B. 1886; C.B. 1901; Lt. Col., Australian A.M.C., Sept. 1914; despatches, June 1915; Bt. Col. 1918; C.B.E. June 1919.

*Earl, John Cecil St. George;
Ent. 1914; Pte. R. Ir. Fus. 1916; prisoner of war, Apr. 1918.

Eckford, George Shields;
Ent. 1892; Temp. Capt. R.E., Nov. 1914.

*Edwards, Geoffrey Dixon;
Ent. 1910; 2 Lt. 3 R. W. Fus., Aug. 1914; Capt. 1915; Observer, R.F.C., 1916; empld. Min. of Lab., 1918.

Egan, Alexander Howard ;
B.A. 1913 ; Pte. Ceylon Planters' Rifles.

Egan, Percy Blackwood ;
M.B. 1906 ; M.D. 1907 ; Surg. R.N., May 1908 ; Surg.-Lt. Cr.
1914 ; H.M.S. "Empress of Asia," 1914 ; H.M S. " Suva," 1915 ;
H.M.S. " Indus " ; H.M.S. " Fisgard iv," 1919.

Egan, Rev. Pierce John ;
B.A. 1888 ; M.A. 1899 ; Army Chaplain, 4 Cl., July 1915 ; died
of dysentery, Alexandria, 6 Apr. 1916.

Egerton, Samuel William ;
Ent. 1896 ; 2 Lt. R.A. March 1900 ; 2 Lt. I.A. 1900 ; Capt. I.A.,
7 Harlana Lancers, March 1909 ; Major 1915.

*Elford, William Philp ;
Ent. 1912 ; Surg. Prob., R.N., H. M. S. " Laverock " ; Surg.
R.N. 1918.

Elgee, Herbert Alcock ;
B.A.I. 1890 ; Temp. Capt. R. E., Aug. 1917-19.

Ellerker, William Thomas ;
Ent. 1914 ; 2 Lt. R.G.A., Feb. 1915 ; Flanders, 1915 ; wounded,
France, March 1916 ; Lt. 1916 ; Capt. 1917.

Elliott, Alfred Charles ;
M.B. 1906 ; Lt. R.A.M.C., Jan. 1907 ; Capt. 1910 ; France,
1914 and 1915 ; despatches, Jan. 1916 ; A/Lt.-Col. 1918.

Elliott, Charles Johnstone ;
Ent. 1899 ; Lt. Australian A.S.C. 1915.

*Elliott, James ;
Ent. 1915 ; R.A. Cadet School, June 1917 ; 2 Lt. R.F.A.
July 1918 ; France ; wounded.

Elliott, James May ;
M.B. 1910 ; Capt. R.A.M.C., Jan. 1915 ; wounded, July 1916 ;
wounded, Oct. 1918.

Elliott, Joseph Haslett ;
M.B. 1907 ; M.D. 1908 ; Lt. R.A.M.C., Aug. 1914 ; Capt. 1915 ;
despatches, May 1917 ; M.C. Jan. 1918.

*Elliott, Robert Andrew George ;
M.B. 1913 ; Lt. R.A.M.C., Nov. 1915 ; Capt. 1916 ; R.A.F.
Dec. 1918 ; Maj.

*Elliott, Thomas Cecil Moore ;
Ent. 1911 ; Pte. 7 R. Dub. Fus., Sept. 1914 ; killed in action,
Dardanelles, 16 Aug. 1915.

Elliott, William Herron ;
M.B. 1914 ; Temp. Lt. R.A.M.C., Nov. 1914 ; Temp. Capt. 1915 ; A/Lt.-Col. ; Capt. R.A.M.C., May 1918 ; M.B.E. Nov.; 1918 ; East Africa ; died, Cologne, 1919.

*Ellis, Charles ;
B.A. 1915 ; 2 Lt. R.F.A., Dec. 1915 ; Lt. 1917 ; A/Capt. 1917.

Ellis, James Graves St. John ;
B.A.I. 1910 ; 2 Lt. R.E., May 1915 ; died of wounds, Dardanelles, 11 Oct. 1915.

Ellison, Francis Charles ;
M.B. and M.D. 1893 ; Lt. R.A.M.C., Aug. 1915.

Ellison, Francis O'Brien ;
M.B. 1906 ; Temp. Lt. R.A.M.C., Sept. 1917 ; Capt. 1918.

Elmes, Julius Paul Jonathan ;
B.A. 1909 ; 2 Lt. attd. 12 Cavalry, I.A., Aug. 1915 ; Mesopotamia, 1916 ; Capt. 1919.

Elmes, Samuel Eyre ;
Ent. 1906 ; Pte., Signalling Section, 144 Bn., Winnipeg, Dec. 1915 ; killed in action, 15 Aug. 1917.

*Elmitt, Austin Joyce ;
Ent. 1914 ; 2 Lt. 17 Welsh R., Aug. 1915 ; M.C. ; Temp. Capt. ; killed in action, 24 Nov. 1917.

*Elvery, William Malcolm Moss ;
Ent. 1914 ; 2 Lt. 5 R. Innis. Fus., Oct. 1915 ; wounded, France, July 1916 ; 2 Lt. R.A.F. Aug. 1918 ; Hon. Lt. 1919.

Emerson, Donald Bomford ;
B.A.I. 1907 ; 2 Lt. I.A. Res., May 1915 ; attchd. 9 Hodson's Horse. ; Capt. 1919.

Emerson, Henry Horace Andrews ;
M.B. 1905 ; Lt. R.A.M.C., July 1905 ; Maj. 1915 ; Deputy Assistant Director of Med. Services, 1915 ; despatches, June 1916, Jan. 1917, July 1919 ; D.S.O. Jan. 1917 ; Croix de Guerre, June 1917.

*English, Joseph Sandys ;
M.B. 1914 ; Lt. R.A.M.C., Dec. 1914 ; Capt. 1916.

English, William Larmour ;
M.B. 1911 ; Lt. R.A.M.C. Aug. 1917 ; Capt. 1918.

Ennis, Rev. Alexander Dallas Lecky ;
B.A. and M.A. 1904 ; Army Chaplain, 1902 ; 3 Cl., 1914 ; served through war ; despatches ; O.B.E. ; 2 Cl. 1919 ; 1 Cl. 1921.

Ensor, Howard ;
    M.B. 1897; Lt. R.A.M.C., July 1899; D.S.O. 1901; Brevet
    Col. 1915; despatches, Oct. 1914, Feb. 1915, June 1915, Jan. 1917,
    May 1917 ; C.M.G. Jan. 1918 ; Bt. Col. 1918.

Erskine, William Francis ;
    M.B. 1901; M.D. 1902 ; Lt. R.A.M.C. June 1917 ; Capt. 1918.

Etlinger, Henry ;
    Ent. 1899; 2 Lt. N. Staff. R., Jan. 1902; Capt. 1911 ; Capt.
    I.A. 9 Bhopal Inf. 1912 ; killed in action, Ypres, 27 Apr. 1915.

Eustace, George Wallace ;
    M.B. 1893; M.D. 1898; Lt. R.A.M.C., Nov. 1914; Capt. 1915;
    M.C. Nov. 1917.

Evans, Charles Leonard ;
    Ent. 1909 ; 2 Lt. Ser. Bns. Durh. L. I. July 1915; D.L.I.
    Bombs, Trench Mortars, and Staff; France ; Mesopotamia ; Staff
    Capt. ; M.C. June 1919.

Evans, Edward ;
    L.M., L.Ch., 1914; Lt. R.A.M.C. Aug. 1916 ; killed in action,
    9 April 1917.

Evans, Fisher Arthur Haslett Freke ;
    Ent. 1912 ; 2 Lt. 6 R. Lanc. R., Aug. 1914 ; wounded, Dar-
    danelles, Aug. 1915; invalided, enteric, Dec. 1915 ; Lt. 1915;
    2 Lt. 1, 2 Bn., Feb. 1916; Temp. Capt. 1916; wounded, Dec.
    1916 ; killed in action, Mesopotamia, 11 Jan. 1917.

Evans, John ;
    M.B. and M.D. 1900 ; Capt. S.A.M.C., Nov. 1915; Maj. 1917;
    British E. Africa ; despatches, July 1917 ; D.S.O. 1919.

*Evans, William Francis ;
    M.B. 1913 ; M.D. 1915; Lt. R.A.M.C., Aug. 1914 ; Capt. 1915.

Evans, William John Percival ;
    Ent. 1906 ; served in R.A.M.C. 1915-19.

Evans, William St. Leger ;
    B.A.I. 1913 ; 2 Lt. 6 R. Innis. Fus., Sept. 1914 ; Lt. 1914.

Evatt, George Joseph Hamilton ;
    Med. School 1863; M.D., Q.U.I.; C.B. 1903 ; Surg. Gen.
    A.M.S., Feb. 1910 ; Maj.-Gen. 1918; K.C.B. 1919.

*Eves, Edmund Lombard ;
    B.A. and LL.B. 1895 ; Lt. A.S.C., Oct. 1914; Capt. 1915.

Eves, Graves William ;
    B.A.I. 1893 ; Capt. 35 Poona Bn., I. Def. Force.

Eves, Thomas Swan;
> M.B. 1907; Lt. R.A.M.C., Feb. 1908; Capt. 1911; A/Lt.-Col. 1916–19; despatches, July 1916, Dec. 1917, Dec. 1918; D.S.O. Jan. 1918; Bar to D.S.O. July 1918.

Ewart, Gerald Valentine;
> B.A. 1906; Lt. A.S.C., Sept. 1914 : Capt. 1915; Maj. 1918.

Exham, Cecil Harmer;
> B.A. 1910; 2 Lt. 4 R. Muns. Fus., Aug. 1914; Capt. 1916; Capt. M.G.C. 1918.

Eyre-Powell, Rev. John William Alcock;
> B.A. 1907; M.A. 1913; Army Chaplain, 4 Cl. Oct. 1917; att. H.Q., 27 Lab. Corps; killed in action, 16 April 1918.

F

*Falkiner, Frederic Baldwin;
> Ent. 1913; Pte. R. Dub. Fus., Sept. 1914; Gallipoli; Corp. and Serg., M.G.C., Serbia; M.G. Instructor, Salonika; 2 Lt. 17 R. Ir. Rif., Dec. 1916; France; Bronze Medal for valour conferred by the King of Italy; M.C.; 2 Lt. R.F.C. July 1917; France; missing, 21 Aug. 1917, reported killed in action.

Falkiner, John M'Intire;
> Med. School 1885; F.R.C.S.I.; Lt. R.A.M.C., Aug. 1914; Capt. I.M.S., Aug. 1915.

Falkiner, Ninian M'Intire;
> M.B. 1884 : M.D. 1900; Lt. R.A.M.C., April 1915; Registrar, Lord Derby's War Hosp.; Capt. 1916; despatches, Sept. 1917.

*Falkner, Francis Stanley George;
> Ent. 1910; R.G.A. Cadet Schl., June 1918.

Falkner, Henry George;
> Med. School 1888; L.R.C.P.& S.I.; Temp. Col. R.A.M.C., Feb. 1915; Assistant Director of Med. Services.

Falls, Charles Fausset;
> B.A. 1882; M.A. 1890; Maj. 11 R. Innis. Fus., Dec. 1914.

*Falvey, Dermot Francis Judge;
> Ent. 1911; 2 Lt. 6 Shrops. L.I., Nov. 1914; France; wounded, Sept. 1916; Lt. 1917.

Fannin, Edward Morgan;
> M.B. 1897; Lt. R.A.M.C., Dec. 1915; Capt. 1916.

Faris, Romney Robinson;
> B.A.I. 1903; 2 Lt. R.E. Dec. 1915; France; Lt. 1917; A/Capt.

Farran, Charles Ernest ;
> B.A.I. 1910 ; 2 Lt. A.S.C., Oct. 1914 ; Capt. 1915 ; Lt. R.E.,
> Feb. 1916 ; Maj. Comm. 8 Ry. Co. R.E. 1918 ; France ; Belgium ;
> Germany.

Farran, Edmond Chomley Lambert ;
> B.A. and LL.B. 1902 ; 2 Lt. 3 R. Ir. Rif. 1914 ; Capt., Jan.
> 1915 ; wounded and missing, presumed killed in action, France,
> 16 June, 1915.

arran, George Philip ;
> B.A. 1899 ; Lt. 22 L'pool R., Apr. 1915.

ausset, Charles Reginald ;
> B A. 1902 ; LL.D. 1907 ; 2 Lt. 3 R. Ir. Regt., Oct. 1914 ;
> killed in action, St. Julien, 3 May, 1915.

Fausset, Herbert John ;
> M.B. 1868 ; M.D. 1878 ; Hon. Surg.-Col. 6 N. Staff. R., July
> 1903.

ausset, Vivian Herbert ;
> B.A. 1912 ; Pte. 7 R. Dub. Fus. : died of wounds, Gallipoli,
> 19 Aug. 1915.

Fawcett, Arthur Edward ;
> B.A.I. 1911 ; 2 Lt. R.E. Aug. 1916 ; Lt. 1918 ; France ; S.
> Persia ; Afghanistan.

awcett, Charles Ernest White-Spunner ;
> M.B. 1904 ; Lt. R.A.M.C., July 1905 ; Maj. 1915.

awcett, Myles O'Dowda ;
> Ent. 1905 ; Pte. 3 Canadian Contingt., Sept. 1914 ; France,
> Feb. 1915 ; killed in action, Wulverghem, France, 20 Dec. 1915.

awcett, William James ;
> M.B. 1870 ; Surg.-Gen. A.M.S., 1903 ; C.B. 1904 ; retired 1908 ;
> re-employed Feb. 1915 ; Maj.-Gen. on Retired List, 1918.

ayle, Harry ;
> M.B. 1887 ; M.D. 1892 ; Capt. S. African Med. Corps ; attchd.
> 6 R. South African Inf., B. East African E.F. ; German East
> Africa, 1916 ; M.C. Feb. 1917 ; died from disease contracted on
> active service, 1920.

Fayle, Oscar ;
> B.A.I. 1909 ; 2 Lt. 4 R. Ir. Rif., Aug. 1914 ; 2 Lt. R.E., Aug.
> 1915 ; Lt. 1916 ; A/Capt. 1916.

Feary, Stephen ;
> Ent. 1909 ; 2 Lt. R.E., Jan. 1915 ; Lt. 1915 ; Adj. 1916 ;
> A/Capt. 1917 ; D.S.O. Sept. 1918 ; despatches, Jan. 1918.

*Featherstone, Albert John ;
    B.A.I. 1914 ; 2 Lt. R.E., Aug. 1914. ; Lt. ; France ; wounded, Ypres.

*Felton, Robert Evan ;
    Ent. 1913 ; 2 Lt. R.F.A., Oct. 1914 ; Temp. Lt. 1916 ; Trench Mortar Batteries ; Lt. 1917.

Ferguson, Arthur Lindo ;
    B.A.I. 1906 ; Lt. R.E. Aug. 1915 ; France, Flanders, 1915–19.

*Ferguson, Augustus Klinger ;
    Ent. 1915 ; 2 Lt. 1, 2 R. Ir. Regt., Oct. 1916 ; Lt. 1918.

Ferguson, Frank M'Gregor ;
    Ent. 1909 ; Surg.-Prob. R.N., H. M. S. " Albatross," later H.M.S. " Llewellyn."

*Ferguson, Horace William Goer ;
    B A.I. 1911 ; 2 Lt. R.E., Oct. 1914 ; Lt. 1915 ; M.C. ; Capt. 1917 ; Adj. 1918 ; Serbia ; E. Macedonia ; Palestine ; Egypt ; despatches.

Ferguson, Hugh Reynolds McKay ;
    M.B. 1910 ; M.D. 1914 ; W. African Med. Serv. ; B.E.F., Cameroons, Aug. 1915 ; Capt., Oct. 1915 ; despatches.

Ferguson, John Christopher ;
    M.B. 1886 ; Fleet Surg. R.N., Feb. 1904 ; Order of St. Stanislas (Russian), June 1917.

Ferguson, Montgomery du Bois ;
    M.B. & M.D. 1905 ; Lt. R.A.M.C., Dec. 1914 ; Capt. 1916 ; O.B.E.

Ferguson, Nicholas Charles ;
    M.B. 1884 ; Maj. R.A.M.C., May 1897 ; C.M.G. 1901 ; Col. 1915 ; D.D.M.S. 1915 ; despatches, Feb. 1915, June 1915 ; A.D.M.S. 1918.

Ferrar, Benjamin Banks ;
    M.B. 1886 ; M.D. 1891 ; Lt. R.A.M.C., April 1915 ; Capt. 1916 ; despatches.

Ferrier, Alexander Herbert Baxton ;
    B.A. 1907 ; M.A. 1910 ; drowned in the " Lusitania," 7 May 1915, on his way home to join the Army.

Fetherstonhaugh, Alfred Hardinge ;
    Ent. 1917 ; Cadet, R.A.F., 1918.

Fetherstonhaugh, Francis Brian ;
    B.A. 1913 ; Corp. 7 Signal Co. R.E. ; 2 Lt. R.E. Dec. 1916 ; Lt. 1918.

Fetherstonhaugh, William Ernest ;
M.B. 1912; Lt. R.A.M.C., Oct. 1914 ; Capt. 1915.

Ffolliott, Charles Henry;
Ent. 1919 ; 2 Lt. 7 R. Innis. Fus., Aug. 1916; Lt. 1918; Lt.
M.G.C. 1918.

Ffolliott, John Hyde Robinson ;
B.A.I. 1916; Assist. Eng., Civilian Ry. Co., France.

Fielding, Rev. Gerald Trueman ;
B.A. 1904 ; M.A. 1911; Chaplain R.N., May, 1911; North Sea,
1914-5 ; Inns of Court O.T.C. 1916 ; Cadet R.A. 1916; 2 Lt.
R.F.A., April 1917; France, 1917; killed in action, 17 April
1918.

Fielding, Thomas Evelyn ;
M.B. 1897 ; Lt. R.A.M.C., Apr. 1900 ; Maj. 1911 ; despatches,
Oct. 1914, June 1915; D.S.O., June 1915; Lt.-Col. 1918; A/Col.
1918.

*Figgis, Douglas Thomas ;
Ent. 1913 ; 2 Lt. 5 R. Ir. Fus., Sept. 1914 ; Lt. 1915; Capt.
1917.

*Figgis, Neville Johnstone ;
Ent. 1910 ; Lt. 6 Leins. R., Jan. 1915 ; killed in action, Dardanelles, 10 Aug. 1915.

Findlater, Alexander ;
M.B. 1885; M.D. 1886; Capt. R.A.M.C., Dec. 1912 ; Dardanelles ; despatches, Jan. 1916 ; D.S.O., Jan. 1916.

Findlater, Charles Arthur ;
Ent. 1889: Pte. D. Co. 7 R. Dub. Fus. ; wounded, Gallipoli,
Aug. 1915 ; killed in action, 13 Nov. 1916.

Findlater, Herbert Snowden ;
B.A. 1895; M.A. 1898; Lance-Corpl. D Co. 7 R. Dub. Fus.,
Sept. 1914 ; wounded and missing, Dardanelles, Aug. 1915 ;
believed killed.

*Findlater, Percival St. George ;
B.A.I. 1905; 2 Lt. A.S.C., Nov. 1914 ; Capt. 1915; France
1915; despatches, Jan. 1917 ; killed in action, France, 28 Mar.
1918.

*Finlay, Robert Alexander ;
Ent. 1910; Lt. 5 R. Dub. Fus., Aug. 1914 ; attchd. 1 R. Ir. Rif. ;
killed in action, France, 19 May 1915.

Finny, Arthur John ;
B.A. 1907 ; 2 Lt. 8 R. Dub. Fus., Oct. 1914 ; Capt., Nov. 1915 ;
War Office, 1917.

F

Finny, Cecil Edward ;
> M.B. 1901 ; M.D. 1902; Visiting Physician and Anæsthetist to the Southwark Mil. Hosp., Dec. 1915.

Finny, Charles Morgan ;
> M.B. 1910 ; Lt. R.A.M.C., Jan. 1911 ; Capt. 1914 ; wounded 1916.

Fishbourne, Charles Edward ;
> Ent. 1886 ; 2 Lt. North'd Fus., Apr. 1892 ; Maj. 1909 ; Lt. Col. in Command 8 Bn. 1914 ; wounded, Dardanelles ; despatches ; wounded 27 Sept., died of wounds 6 Oct. 1916.

*Fishbourne, Derrick Haughton Gardiner ;
> Ent. 1914 ; 2 Lt. R.G.A., Jan. 1916 ; killed in action, Monchy, France, 6 May 1917.

*Fishe, Edward Gordon ;
> M.B. 1915 ; Lt. R.A.M.C., Aug. 1916 ; Capt. 1917 ;

*Fisher, Arthur George ;
> M.B. 1915 ; Lt. R.A.M.C., June 1914 ; Capt. 1916 ; M.C. Feb. 1917.

Fisher, Rev. Oswald Garrow ;
> B.A. 1913 ; Army Chaplain 1918 ; France ; Belgium ; Mesopotamia ; accidentally killed at Hinaidi, near Bagdad, 4 Nov. 1920.

*Fisher, Sydney Walter ;
> M.B. 1915 ; Lt. R.A.M.C., Oct. 1915 ; Capt. 1916.

Fisher, Vicars Madison ;
> M.B. 1910 ; Lt. R.A.M.C., Sept. 1915 ; Capt. 1916.

Fitt, Arthur Percy ;
> B.A. 1892 ; Secretary, American Y.M.C.A., American E. F. ; served in France and Germany, Sept. 1917-April 1919.

*Fitzgerald, Albert Victor Stewart ;
> Ent. 1903 ; Lt. A.S.C., Nov. 1915 ; Egypt, 1916 ; Capt. 1917.

Fitzgerald, Hon. Arthur Southwell ;
> Ent. 1880 ; 2 Lt. 7 R. Fus., Oct. 1900 ; Capt. 3 R. Ir. Regt., Mar. 1915.

*Fitzgerald, Cecil Lancelot ;
> Ent. 1907 ; 2 Lt. 3 Conn. Rang., Apr. 1915 ; Lt. 1916 ; Capt. 1916 ; despatches, Jan. 1917.

*FitzGerald, Edward Martin ;
> Ent. 1903 ; 2 Cav. Cadet Sq., May 1917 ; 2 Lt. 5 Cav., R. Ir. Lancers, Sept. 1917 ; Capt. Spl. List, 1918.

Fitzgerald, Edward William ;
> Ent. 1894 ; 2 Lt. A.S.C., May 1915 ; Capt. 1915 ; M.C. ; Capt. R.E., 1918 ; Staff Capt. for Ry. Transport, 1918.

*Fitzgerald, George Francis ;
> Ent. 1912 ; 2 Lt. 7 Welsh R., Sept. 1914 ; Lt. 1915 ; Capt. 1916 ;
> wounded, 1918 ; M.C. Sept. 1918.

FitzGerald, Gerald James George ;
> Ent. 1908 ; Lt. R.G.A., S. R., Sept. 1914 ; Capt. 1916.

Fitzgerald, Henry Valentine ;
> B.A. 1904 ; Lt. R.A.M.C., Aug. 1915 ; Capt. 1916.

FitzGerald, Herbert David ;
> B.A.I. 1903 ; Lt. Ry. C. R.E., Belgium, 1918–19 ; Lt. R.E.
> as O.C. of an area of German Rys.

Fitzgerald, James Stephens ;
> Ent. 1896 ; 2 Lt. 1, 2 R. Ir. Regt., Feb. 1900 ; Capt. 1908 ;
> prisoner, retreat from Mons, 21 Sept. 1914 ; Maj. 1915.

Fitzgerald, John David ;
> B.A. 1913 ; Staff Lt. (graded as Capt.), Nov. 1914 ; Railway
> Transport Officer ; Staff Capt. 1916 ; Equipment Offr. R.F.C.
> 1917.

Fitzgerald, Maurice Harrington ;
> B.A. 1911 ; 2 Lt. 9 R. Muns. Fus., Mar. 1915 ; Lt. 1915 ; Adj.
> 8 Bn. 1916 ; M.C. Jan. 1917.

Fitzgerald, Richard Desmond ;
> M.B. 1909 ; Lt. R.A.M.C., Feb. 1915 ; Temp. Capt. 1916 ; des-
> patches, June 1916 ; St. Sava, 4 Cl., Jan. 1818 ; M.C.

*FitzGerald, Richard John ;
> Ent. 1916 ; 1 O.C.B. (M.G. Section), Bisley, March 1917 ; 2 Lt.
> M.G.C. June 1917 ; Lt. 1918.

*Fitzgerald, William James ;
> Ent. 1913 ; 2 Lt. 17 Durh. L. I., July 1915 ; 2 Lt. A. Cyclist
> C., 1915 ; twice wounded ; M.C. ; Croix de Guerre ; A/Capt.
> 1917.

*Fitzgerald, William Raymond ;
> B.A.I. 1911 ; 2 Lt. R. E., Aug. 1915 ; Capt. 1918 ; India.

*Fitzgerald, William Wilks ;
> Ent. 1913 ; Mechanic, R.F.C., Mar. 1915 ; 2 Lt. R.F.C., Sept.
> 1916 ; killed in action, near Mesnil St. Pol, 27 July 1917.

FitzGerald-Lombard, Roger Edward ;
> B.A. 1902 ; M.A. 1911 ; B.A.I. 1920 ; Hon. Capt. in Army,
> Oct. 1902 ; Maj. 11 West Rid. R. 1914 ; Maj. 2 Garr. Bn. Linc.
> R. 1916.

*Fitzgibbon, Francis ;
> B.A. 1903 ; Lt. 5 R. Muns. Fus., May 1915 ; Capt., att. R.E.
> 1915 ; A/Maj. 1918 ; Italy ; despatches, Jan. 1919.

Fitz Gibbon, Henry Elliot ;
> B.A.I. 1911 ; Lt. R.E., E.E.F., 1916-19 ; despatches.

Fitzgibbon, Henry Macaulay ;
> B.A. 1877 ; M.A. 1880; Capt. Conn. Rang. ; retired ; Brig.-
> Musketry Staff Offr. Sept. 1914.

*Fitzmaurice, James Gerald ;
> Ent. 1911; 2 Lt. 7, 2 R. Muns. Fus., Sept. 1914 ; wounded,
> Dardanelles, 9 Aug. 1915 ; Lt. 1915 ; despatches, Jan. 1916 ;
> France, 1916 ; Lt. Tank C. 1916 ; att. M.G.C. 1916 ; Staff Capt.
> 1918 ; M.C.

Fitzmaurice, Robert ;
> Ent. 1884 ; Lt. Col. R.A., March 1914 ; Temp. Brig. Gen.,
> 1915 ; despatches, Jan. 1916 ; D.S.O.

*FitzPatrick, Richard William ;
> Ent. 1914; B.A. 1920 ; Pte. A.S.C., June 1916 ; Staff-Serg.
> 1916; 2 Lt. A.S.C., Dec. 1916; wounded, 1917; Lt. 1918 ; de-
> spatches, Mar. 1918.

Fleming, Arthur Harloe Wynne ;
> Ent. 1913 ; 2 Lt. 5 Norf. R., Jan. 1915 ; Temp. Capt. 1916 ;
> Egypt ; 2 Lt. 1, 2 Norf. R., Oct. 1915 ; Lt. 1917 ; Flying Officer,
> R.F.C., 1917.

*Fleming, Geoffrey Montague Mason ;
> M.B. 1913 ; Lt. R A.M.C., Aug. 1914 ; killed in action,
> Givenchy, 16 June, 1915.

*Fleming, Hans ;
> M.B. 1910 ; Lt. R.A.M.C., Dec. 1914.

Fleming, Hugh M'Cutcheon ;
> M.B. and M.D. 1912 ; Temp. Lt. R.A.M.C., Oct. 1917.

Fleming, Robert ;
> B.A. 1912 ; Temp. 2 Lt. Egyptian Labour Corps ; Canal zone,
> 1916.

Fleming, Robert John ;
> M.B. 1903 ; Capt. R.A.M.C., T.F. (Sanitary Sect.), Nov. 1915.

Fletcher, Arnold Lockhart ;
> B.A.I. 1909 ; 2 Lt. 4 Leins. R., April 1915 ; Mach. G.C. 1916 ;
> died 30 April 1917 of wounds received near Wancourt.

*Fletcher, Donald Lockhart ;
> Ent. 1914 ; 2 Lt. 4 Leins. R., May 1915 ; despatches ; died,
> Macedonia, 28 April 1917.

*Fletcher, Gilbert Maxwell ;
> Ent. 1920 ; 7 O. C. Bn. Apr. 1918 ; 2 Lt. 3 Leins. R. Sept.
> 1918.

Fletcher,·James Henry ;
L.M. and L.Ch. 1914 ; Lt. R.A.M.C., Sept. 1914 ; Capt. 1915;
despatches, Jan. 1916 ; M. C. Jan. 1916 ; wounded, March 1916 ;
despatches, June 1916 ; Bar to M.C. Dec. 1916 ; D.S.O. May 1917 ;
D.A. D.M.S. 1917 ; wounded, Nov. 1917 ; despatches, Jan. 1918 ;
Bar to D.S.O. Feb. 1919.

Flewett, Henry Walter ;
B.A. 1915 ; 2 Lt. R.G.A., Nov. 1915 ; Lt. 1917.

*Flinn, William Henry ;
Ent. 1912 ; 2 Lt. 3 R. Ir. Regt., Aug. 1914 ; wounded,
Flanders, Aug. 1914 ; Lt. 1915 ; Staff Lt. 1916 ; Capt. 1916 ;
D.A. Dir. of Ry. Transport, 1918 ; Temp. Maj. 1918.

*Flood, Frederick George ;
M.B. 1914; Lt. R.A.M.C., Aug. 1914 ; Capt. 1915 ; despatches,
Jan. 1916 ; M.C. June 1917 ; wounded, Sept. 1917 ; Bar to M.C.,
July 1919 ; N. Russia.

Flood, John Wellesley ;
Ent. 1904; M.B. 1909 ; Australian A.M.C. ; Col.

Flood, John Wellesley ;
Ent. 1903 ; L.R.C.P. & S.I. ; Lt. R.A.M.C. Oct. 1914 ; Capt.
1915 ; France ; Mesopotamia.

*Flood, Robert Alexander ;
M.B. 1912 ; Lt. R.A.M.C., July 1912 ; Capt. 1915 ; Prisoner of
War, 13 Nov., 1914 ; A/Maj. 1918 ; M.C. Sept. 1918.

*Flood, Walter Bryan ;
B.A. 1913 ; Lt. A.S.C., Sept. 1912 ; Capt. 1914; A/Maj. 1918.

Flower, John James ;
B.A.I. 1909 ; Pte. 24 R. Fus., Dec. 1914 ; 2 Lt. 17 Lan. Fus.,
Feb. 1915; Gallipoli, 1915 ; wounded, France, 24 July and 24 Aug.
1916.

Flynn, Robert Alexander ;
Med. Sch. 1884 ; F.R.C.P. ; Lt. R.A.M.C., Apr. 1915 ; Capt.
1916.

Fogarty, William Joseph ;
Ent. 1912 ; 2 Lt. S. Ir. Horse, Nov. 1914 ; France, 1915 ; Lt.
1916; Capt.; wounded and missing, 21 March 1918; reported
killed in action.

Fogerty, John Frederick ;
Ent. 1885 ; B.E., R.U.I.; Capt. 3 Wessex Brigade, R.F.A., Feb.
1904 ; Lt. Natal Field Force (Artillery), 1914 ; wounded, German
S. W. African Campaign, 1914–5 ; Temp. Maj. Wessex Bde.
R.F.A., Dec. 1915 ; Temp. Maj. 1915 ; Maj. R.H. and R.F.A.,
1916.

Foley, Gerald Robert Edward ;
> B.A. 1909 ; D.I., R.I.C.; Capt. 5 R. Ir. Regt., Jan. 1916 ;
> Maj. 1918.

Foley, Rev. Hubert Francis St. Patrick ;
> B.A. 1912 ; Temp. Chap. R.N. Oct. 1918 ; H.M.S. " Berwick "
> 1918 ; H.M.S. "Caradoc " 1919.

Foley, John Edward ;
> Ent. 1908 ; Lt. R.A.M.C., Oct. 1914 ; Capt. 1915.

Foley, Thomas William Winspeare ;
> B.A. 1905 ; 2 Lt. 3 Leins. R., Apr. 1915 ; Lt. 1916 ; missing,
> reported killed in action, Givenchy, 9 Sept. 1916.

Follis, Canon Charles William ;
> B.A. 1891 ; M.A. 1897 ; Army Chaplain, 4 Cl., Jan. 1916-18.

*Foot, William ;
> M.B. 1914; Temp. Lt. R.A.M.C., Aug. 1914 ; France, 1915;
> Temp. Capt. 1915 ; despatches, Jan. 1, 1916 ; M.C. Jan. 1916 ;
> Bar to M.C., Oct. 1916 ; Lt. Permanent, Nov. 1916 ; Capt. 1918 ;
> A/Maj. 1918.

*Forbes, Rev. Alfred ;
> Ent. 1910 ; Sergt. D Co. 7 R. Dub. Fus., Sept. 1914 ; Salonika,
> 1916.

Forbes, John Mercer ;
> B.A. 1900 ; 2 Lt. 3 Conn. Rang., Sept. 1915 ; Lt. 1917.

Ford, Herbert Roycroft ;
> M.B. 1914 ; Lt. R.A.M.C., Dec. 1914 ; Capt. 1915 ; wounded,
> Dec. 1917.

*Forde, Robert Geoffrey Alexander ;
> Ent. 1912 ; Pte. A.S.C., April 1917 ; Staff. Sergt.

Forrester, Rev. Ernest Edward Samuel ;
> B.A. 1903 ; M.A. 1908 ; Army Chaplain, 4 Cl., Oct. 1914.

Forsayeth, Francis Noel ;
> Ent. 1907 ; Lt. R G.A., Dec. 1914 ; Capt. 1916.

*Forsyth, Victor Thomas ;
> Ent. 1914 ; 2 Lt. 3 R. Ir. Rif., June 1915 ; Lt. 1916 ; Capt.
> 1917.

*Foster, Albert Victor ;
> Ent. 1914 ; 2 Lt. A.S.C., Oct. 1915 ; Lt. 1916.

Foster, John George ;
> M.B. 1896 ; Lt. R.A.M.C., April 1900 ; Maj. 1912 ; despatches,
> Sept. 1915 ; Turkish Arabia ; despatches (Turkish Arabia), Oct.
> 1916 ; Bt. Col. 1916 ; Lt.-Col. 1917 ; O.B.E. June 1919 ; de-
> spatches (Mesopotamia), June 1919.

Foster, Robert Basil Boothby;
    M B. 1900 ; Lt. I.M.S., Jan. 1901; Maj. 1912; Indian Exp.
Force, 1915 ; despatches, Oct. 1916; Bt. Lt.-Col. 1916 ; Egypt;
Mesopotamia.

Foster, Robert Hosford ;
    Ent. 1912 ; Sergt. R.A.M.C. 1915.

*Foster, Thomas Cartret ;
    B.A. 1914 ; 2 Lt. A.S.C., April 1915 ; Lt. 1916 ; Egypt 1915–18.

Fottrell, Brenden Joseph ;
    B.A. 1906 ; 2 Lt. 3 R. Ir. Regt., Aug. 1914; att. 1 Bt. ; killed
in action, France, 15 March, 1915.

Fowler, Rev. Albert Robinson ;
    B.A. 1907 ; Army Chaplain, 4th Cl., Jan. 1918.

Fowler, Herbert Rodney Ross ;
    M.B. 1905; M.D. 1906; Surg.-Maj. 8 R. Worcester R.

Fowler, John Sharman ;
    Ent. 1882 ; Lt. R.E., Jan., 1886 ; Lt.-Col. 1911 ; Dir. of Army
Signals, Temp. Brig.-Gen. 1914 ; C.B. 1915; Brevet-Col. 1916 ;
D.S.O ; despatches, Jan. 1917; K.C.M.G.

Fowler, Richard Samuel Gardiner ;
    B.A.I. 1902 ; 2 Lt. R.E. (Inland Waterways and Docks Section)
July 1917 ; Lt. 1919.

*Fowler, Robert Robinson ;
    Ent. 1901; Lt. Egyptian Labour Corps, Alexandria, 1915 ; Lt.
Labour C., July 1917 ; A/Maj. 1918.

*Fowler, William Phipps ;
    Ent. 1909 ; 2 Lt. 13 Notts and Derby R., May 1915 ; Lt. 1918

Fox, Brabazon Hubert Maine ;
    Ent. 1886 ; 2 Lt. 1 R. Ir. Rif., Dec. 1888 ; Maj. 2 Bn. 1906;
Res. of Offrs. 1908; Maj. 2nd in command, 9 S. Lan. R. 1914 ;
Salonika, 1916 ; Empld. Convalescent Depot, 1917 ; Min. of Lab.,
1918.

Franklin, Frederick Robert;
    Ent. 1916; 2 Cadet Bn., Apr. 1917 ; 2 Lt. 17 R. Ir. Rif.,
Aug. 1917; France 1917; missing, believed killed, 9 Dec. 1917.

* Fraser, Donald James;
    •Ent. 1911 ; 2 Lt. R.H.A., Aug. 1914; Lt. 1915 ; M.C. ; Capt.
1918.

*Freeman, Charles Henry ;
    Ent. 1916 ; 2 Lt. 2 R. Ir. Regt., Oct. 1916; Lt. 1918.

French, Rev. Alan Edward Penrose ;
B.A. 1900; M.A. 1919; Army Chaplain, 4 Cl., Aug. 1918;
France, 1918 ; Germany, 1918.

French, Claude Alexander;
Ent. 1899; 2 Lt. R. Ir. Regt., Jan. 1903 ; Capt. 1909 ;
Flanders, 1914 ; wounded, Oct. 1914 ; died of wounds, France,
1 June, 1915.

*French, Charles Stockley ;
B.A. 1915; 2 Lt. 2 R. Dub. Fus., Aug. 1914; wounded,
Flanders, Dec. 1914 ; killed in action, St. Julien, 25 April, 1915.

French, Riversdale Sampson ;
M.B. 1889 ; Surg. R.N., Aug. 1914.

Fretton, William Hector ;
B.A.I. 1910; 2 Lt. R.E., Dec. 1916 ; Lt. 1918; A/Capt. 259 Ry.
Const. Coy.; France, Belgium (1916–19).

Friel, Alfred Richard ;
M.B. 1894 ; M.D. 1895 ; Capt. S. African M.C. Sept. 1915 ;
S. African Hosp., B.E.F.

Friel, Robert ;
M.B. 1895 : M.D. 1897 ; Capt. S.A.M.C., S.A. Irish Reg.
Expedition to German South-West Africa ; despatches, Sept. 1918 ;
Capt. R.A.M.C.

Frier, William ;
M.B. 1912 ; Lt. R.A.M.C., Aug. 1914 ; Capt. 1915.

Fry, Oliver Campbell ;
Ent. 1908 ; 2 Lt. 7 R. Ir. Fus., Oct. 1914 ; retired, ill health,
1914 ; R.N. Air Service, 1916 ; Capt. R.A.F., Apr. 1918.

Fry, Philip Golding;
B.A. 1911; 2 Lt. 8 R. Ir. Fus., Oct. 1914 ; Lt. 1915 ; wounded,
France, May 1916 ; Lt. M.G.C., 1916 ; Capt. 1917 ; A/Major
1918.

*Fuller, Franklin Bland ;
Ent. 1916 ; R.A. School, Sept. 1917 ; 2 Lt. R.G.A., April 1918.

*Fullerton, Gordon McComas ;
Ent. 1917 ; Sandhurst, Sept. 1918.

Furlong, Gerald O'Dell ;
Ent. 1909 ; 2 Lt. R.F.A., Sp. Res., Aug. 1910 ; empld. Aug.
1914 ; Lt. 1914 ; Capt. 1917.

Furlong, Sydney Joseph Verner ;
 M.B. 1916 ; Lt. R.A.M.C., Oct. 1916 : Capt. 1917 ; Major
 1918 ; despatches, E.A. Campaign, July 1918 ; despatches, Jan.
 1919 ; O.B.E. June 1919.

*Furlonger, Charles Arthur Mackenzie ;
 Ent. 1914 ; 2 Lt. R. Flying C., July 1916 ; prisoner of war.

G

Gage, Rev. Alexander Hugh ;
 B.A. 1894 ; M.A. 1897 ; Chaplain R.N., July 1900 ; ret. 1916 ;
 H.M.S. " Exmouth," 1914-16.

*Gahan, Edward John Beresford ;
 Ent. 1914 ; 2 Lt. A.S.C., Dec. 1914. ; Capt. 1918 ; France.

Galbraith, Samuel Haughton ;
 B.A.I. 1877 ; M.A. 1886 ; Inspector of Works and Hon. Major
 R.E., May 1907.

Gallagher, William Augustine ;
 B.A. 1907 ; 2 Lt. E. Lan. R., Aug. 1907 ; Capt. 1914 ; killed
 in action, Neuve Chapelle, 12 March 1915; despatches, 31 May,
 1915.

Gallagher, William Richard Gorringe.
 Ent. 1917 ; volunteered and accepted, Sept. 1918.

Gallaugher, William ;
 Ent. 1920 ; Pte. 11, 9 R. Innis. Fus., 1915; Sgt. 1916 ; B.E.F.
 France ; M.S.M.; wounded, 1916 and 1918.

*Gallogly, George Henry ;
 Ent. 1914 ; 2 Lt. 6 R. Ir. Fus., Sept. 1914 ; Lt. 1915 ; wounded,
 Dardanelles, Aug. 1915 ; wounded, Salonika, Dec. 1916 ; Capt.
 1918.

*Galvin, Barry St. John ;
 Ent. 1910 ; 2 Lt. 8 R. Ir. Fus., Sept. 1914 ; Capt. 1915 ;
 wounded, Aug. 1916 ; Military Cross.

Galwey, William Rickards ;
 M.B. 1905 ; Lt. R.A.M.C., 1906 ; Capt. 1909 ; despatches,
 Salonika, Dec. 1916 ; M.C. Jan. 1917 ; despatches, Oct. 1917 ;
 St. Sava, 4 cl., Jan. 1918 ; Bt. Maj. 1918 ; O.B.E. Jan. 1919.

*Gamble, George Sidney ;
 Ent. 1916 ; R.F.A. Cadet School, July 1917 ; 2 Lt. Dec. 1917 ;
 France ; Belgium.

Gamble, Richard Maurice Brooks;
 Ent. 1912; 2 Lt. 7 L'pool R., Sept. 1914; killed in action, Festubert, 16 May 1915.

Garde-Browne, William;
 M.B. 1916; Lt. R.A.M.C., Jan. 1917; Capt. 1918.

Gardiner, Rev. William;
 M.A. 1881; A/Chap. to Forces at Devizes, 1897-1919.

*Gardner, Eric;
 B.A.I. 1913; 2 Lt. R.E., March 1915; Lt. 1916; France.

Garner, Cathcart;
 M.B. 1885; Capt. R.A.M.C., July 1886; Lt. Col. 1914; Mediterranean E.F.; despatches, Jan. 1916; A.D.M.S. 1917; Commander, Order of King George I (Greece); Col. A.M.S., Nov. 1918; C.B.E. Jan. 1919; C.M.G. Dec. 1919; despatches (Gen. Allenby), June 1919.

Garvey, Ivan Harold;
 Ent. 1908; 2 Lt. 3 Conn. Rang., Aug. 1914; Capt. 1915; died of wounds received in action, 20 Feb. 1917; M.C. March 1917.

Garvey, John William Frederick;
 B.A. 1878; M.A. 1887; Lt. (acting Commr.) R.N.V.R., May 1915.

Garvin, Laurence Algernon;
 Ent. 1915; Sergt. R.A.M.C., June 1915.

*Gell, James George Anderton;
 Ent. 1913; 2 Cav. Cadet Sq., May 1917.

Gentleman, John Wesley;
 B.A. 1908; Lt. A.S.C., May 1915; Capt. 1915.

Geoghegan, Francis John;
 M.B. and M.D. 1902; Civil Med. Practitioner, Kinmel Mil. Camp, N. Wales, Jan. 1917; died March 1917.

Geoghegan, Herbert Lyne;
 M.B. 1896; M.D. 1898; Fleet Surg. R.N., May 1915; lost in H. M. S. "Black Prince," at Battle of Jutland, 31 May, 1916.

George, Frederick Ralph;
 B.A. 1905; 2 Lt. Conn. Rang., 1906; killed in action, France, 5 Nov. 1914.

*George, Richard Westropp;
 B.A.I. 1904; Inspector of Works, Hon. Lt. R.E., July 1915; Capt. 1918; M.B.E.

George, Theodore Lea;
 Ent. 1914; 2 Lt. 2 Suff. R., Aug. 1914; wounded, Mons, 10 Oct., and a prisoner 26 Oct. 1914; Lt. 1914.

Gerrard, John Denison Wardell ;
B.A. 1900 ; Lt. A.S.C., Jan. 1915.

Gerrard, John Joseph ;
M.B. 1888 ; A.M.S. 1891 ; Maj. R.A.M.C., 1898 ; Lt.-Col. 1906;
Col. A.M.S. 1915 ; A.D.M.S. 1915 ; D.D.M.S. 1916 ; D.M.S. 5th
Army 1916-18 ; despatches (3 times) ; C.B. 1917 ; Maj.-Gen. 1918 ;
despatches 1919 ; Grand Officer, M.C. of Avis (Portugal).

Gerrard, Percy Netterville ;
M.B. 1895, M.D. 1898 ; Colonial Med. Service; Capt. Malay
States Volunteer Rifles ; killed, Singapore, 15 Feb. 1915.

Gibbon, Edward ;
M.B. 1906; Lt. R.A.M.C. 1906; Capt. 1910; attchd. Egyptian
Army, 1910; despatches, Nov. 1916 and Dec. 1919 ; Maj. 1918 ;
Order of the Nile, 3 Cl., Apr. 1917 ; O.B.E., Nov. 1918.

Gibbon, Thomas Frederick ;
Ent. 1912 ; 2 Lt. 8 R. Ir. Fus., Sept. 1914.

Gibbon, Thomas Holroyd ;
M.B. 1903 ; M.D. 1903 ; Lt. R.A.M.C., Jan. 1905 ; Maj. 1915;
wounded, Flanders, Sept. 1914 ; Temp. Lt.-Col. 1916-17 ; A/Lt.-
Col. 1918 ; despatches, Sept. 1917, June 1919 (Italy); O.B.E.,
June 1919.

*Gibson, Alfred James Edward ;
Ent. 1908 ; Pte. Princess Patricia L.I. 1914 ; L.-Cpl. 1915 ;
M.C. ; 2 Lt. 3 R. Ir. Rif., Aug. 1916; Lt. 1918 ; wounded and a
prisoner, Apr. 1918.

Gibson, Herbert Murray ;
Ent. 1910 ; Pte. 9 Canadian Mounted Rifles, 1914 ; L.-Cpl.
Fortgarry Horse, 1915.

*Gibson, Joseph John Loughlin ;
Ent. 1912 ; Lt. 7 R. Innis. Fus., Nov. 1914 ; Adjt. 1914 ; Capt.
1915.

*Gibson, Thomas Dunlap ;
Ent. 1910; 2 Lt. R.G.A., Dec. 1915.

*Gibson, William Frederick Augustus ;
M.B. 1913 ; Lt. R.A.M.C., Dec. 1914 ; Capt. 1915 ; Gallipoli
invalided; France, 1916 ; died 20 Dec. 1920, from injuries
received in the war.

Gildea, John Arthur Knox ;
Ent. 1909 ; Princess Patricia L. I. 1915 ; 2 Lt. 4 R. War. R.,
Dec. 1915 ; killed in action, 11 July, 1916.

Gill, Donat O'Brien ;
B.A.I. 1910 ; 2 Lt. R.E., Jan. 1915 ; Lt. 1915 ; Equipment
Offr. R.F.C., 1917 ; France ; Salonika ; Egypt.

Gill, Frederick ;
  Ent. 1914 ; M.B. 1918 ; Lt. R.F.C. Med. S., July 1918.

*Gill, Owen Daly ;
  Ent. 1912 ; 2 Lt. R.E., Oct. 1914 ; Lt. 1915.

Gill, Roy Anthony Furlong ;
  B.A. 1910 ; 2 Lt. 5 R. Ir. Regt., Dec. 1914 ; Staff Lt. 1916 ;
  Temp. Capt. 1916.

Gillenders, Rev. Robert ;
  B A. 1904 ; M.A. 1907 ; Army Chaplain, 4 Cl., March 1915-19 ;
  M.C. 1917.

Gillespie, Rev. Edward Acheson ;
  B.A. 1899 ; M.A. 1909 ; Army Chap. 4 Cl., Sept. 1915-18 ;
  Chap. R.A.F., 1918-20.

*Gillespie, Frank Sheppard ;
  M.B. 1914 ; M.D. 1918 ; Lt. R.A.M.C., Aug. 1914 ; France,
  1915, 1916 ; Capt. 1915.

*Gillespie, Ivor Ronald ;
  Ent. 1912 ; 2 Lt. 15 R. Ir. Rif., April 1915 ; wounded, Somme,
  July 1916 ; Lt. 1917.

*Gillespie, John ;
  Ent. 1912 ; LL.B. 1919 ; 2 Lt. R.F.A., Nov. 1915 ; wounded,
  March 1917 and June 1917 ; Capt. 1917 ; M.C. Jan. 1918 ; Bar
  to M.C. Oct. 1918.

*Gillespie, Joseph Cecil ;
  Ent. 1914 ; Pte. R.A.M.C., 1915 ; 2 Lt. R.F.A., Nov. 1917 ;
  gassed, May 1918.

Gilligan, William Boyd ;
  Ent. 1912 ; 2 Lt. 4 R. Ir. Rif., Aug. 1915 ; wounded, Oct. 1916 ;
  Lt. I.A., July 1917 ; att. 88 Infantry.

*Gilmore, George Ross ;
  B.A.I. 1913 ; 2 Lt. R.E., June, 1916 ; France ; 2 Lt. 11 R.
  Dub. Fus., July 1917 ; Lt. New Armies, Empld. Ry. Op. Div.,
  1917.

Gilmour, William Alexander ;
  Ent. 1920 ; Pte. Reserve, Apr. 1915 ; Pte. R. Suss. R., Aug.
  1916 ; Staff R.A.S.C., 1916 ; Sergt. 1919 ; despatches, 1918,
  1919.

*Given, Thomas Frederick ;
  Ent. 1912 ; 2 Lt. 9 R. Ir. Fus., Sept. 1914 ; Lt. 1915 ; Capt.
  1915 ; M.C.

*Glasgow, Benjamin George Little ;
  Ent. 1915 ; Cadet D.U.O.T.C. ; volunteered and accepted.

*Gleeson, Daniel Joseph ;
    Ent. 1919; Cav. Cdt. School, Sept. 1917.

*Glen, James Alexander ;
    B.A. 1915 ; 2 Lt. R.G.A., Dec. 1915 ; Lt. 1917.

*Glenn, Cecil William ;
    B.A. & LL.B. 1915 ; 2 Lt. A.S.C., Jan. 1915; France, 1915 ;
    Lt. 1915 ; killed in action, 28 Jan. 1917.

Gloster, Edward ;
    Ent. 1881; Capt. 7 E. Yorks. Regt., Oct. 1891 ; Maj. 1914 ;
    resigned 1915.

Gloster, Gerald Meade ;
    Ent. 1881; Lt. 1 Devon. R., Nov., 1884; Col. 1914 ; Temp.
    Brig. Genl. 1915; Div. Commander 1918.

*Glynn, Patrick ;
    Ent. 1918 ; B. Res. Bde., R.H.A., Sept. 1917 ; 2 Lt. R.F.A.,
    Jan. 1917; wounded, 1917.

*Godfrey, Francis La Touche, F.T.C.D. ;
    B.A. 1912 ; Fellow, 1915 ; Lt. Ordnance Dept., Aug. 1915;
    A/Capt. 1917 ; France, 1916-19 ; Capt. 1919.

*Goff, Ronald Adrian Jeffers ;
    Ent. 1911 ; 2 Lt. R. Dub. Fus., May 1912 ; 2 Lt. A.S.C., Sept.
    1914 ; Capt. 1917.

Goldsmith, Arthur Waller ;
    M.B. 1904 ; M.D. 1909 ; Capt. S. African M.C., Dec. 1915 ;
    Brit. E. African Expn.

Goldsmith, George Mills ;
    M.B. 1898 ; Lt. R.A.M.C., Jan. 1899; Lt.-Col., 1915 ;
    D.A.D.M.S. 1916 ; despatches, Jan. 1917, Sept. 1917, July 1919 ;
    A.D.M.S. 1917; C.B.E. June 1919.

Goligher, Hugh Garvin ;
    B.A. 1895 ; M.A. 1898 ; Financial adviser to the Commander-
    in-Chief, British Army in France, with precedence as Brigadier-
    General, 1915 ; despatches, Nov. 1915, Nov. 1916, Jan. 1916, Jan.
    1917, May 1917, and Dec. 1918 ; C.B.E., Croix d'Officier, Aug.
    1916 ; Aviz (1st Class), Nov. 1918 ; despatches, Apr. 1919 ;
    American D.S.M.

*Good, Frederick Newby ;
    Ent. 1911 ; 2 Lt. R.G.A., Oct. 1914 ; wounded, France, 17
    May, 1915 ; Lt. 1916 ; France; Salonika : Ord. Dept. 1918.

*Good, Walter ;
    B.A. 1913 ; 2 Lt. R.G.A., Nov. 1914 ; Temp. Lt. 1916 ; M.C.
    Jan. 1917 ; A/Capt. 1917.

Good, William Henry ;
> Ent. 1908 ; 2 Lt. 7 R. Muns. Fus., Sept. 1914 ; killed in action, 16 Aug. 1915.

Good, William Jonathan ;
> B.A. 1909 ; Trooper, Calcutta Light Horse; 2 Lt. I.A. Res. of Offs. Feb. 1917 ; Lt. 1918.

Goodbody, Denis ;
> B.A. 1913 ; Friends' Amb., British Red Cross, France, 1914.

Goodbody, Francis Woodcock ;
> M.B. 1894 ; M.D. 1895; Capt. R.A.M.C., Aug. 1914.

*Goodbody, Godfrey Marcus ;
> Ent. 1915 ; 2 Lt. R.F.A., March 1917.

*Goodbody, Henry Edgar ;
> Ent. 1903; Lt. 4, 1 Leins. R., Aug. 1912; Capt. 1915 ; despatches May 1915 ; killed near Ypres, 12 May, 1915.

*Goodbody, Owen Frederick ;
> B.A.I. 1912 ; 2 Lt. R.E., Nov. 1914; died 20 Oct. 1915, Alexandria, of enteric contracted at Gallipoli.

*Goodbody, Philip Marcus ;
> Ent. 1917; Sandhurst, May 1918.

Goode, John Evans ;
> Ent. 1911 ; 2 Lt. 8 North'n R., Apr. 1915 ; A/Capt. 1917; France ; Flanders ; Lt. 1917 ; Lt. 11 Gar. Bn. Ox. & Bucks L. I. 1918.

Goodenough, Charles Douglas ;
> M.B. 1913 ; Temp. Capt. A.M.S., S. A. Labour Corps.

Goodman, Robert Fox ;
> B.A. 1905 ; 2 Lt. North'd Hussars, Nov. 1914 ; Capt. 1918.

Goold, Rev. Oswald Canning ;
> Ent. 1914 ; Army Chaplain, 4 Cl. Nov. 1918.

*Gordon, Guy Montgomery ;
> B.A.I. 1909 ; Lt. R.E., Apr. 1915 ; Gallipoli; Egypt ; Palestine ; France; Belgium ; Germany ; Mesopotamia ; despatches; M.C. ; Capt. 1918.

Gordon, Leonard M'Arthur Rangdale ;
> Ent. 1909; Pte. Australian Vol. Hosp., 1914 ; 2 Lt. 13 Sco. Rif., Feb. 1915 ; Capt. 1915 ; wounded, Sept. 1916.

*Gordon, Rupert Montgomery ;
> M.B. 1916 ; Lt. R.A.M.C., July 1916 ; Capt. 1917.

Gordon, Thomas Eagleson ;
> M.B. 1890; Surg. Castle Red Cross Hospital, Dublin ; Temp. Lt.-Col. R.A.M.C., July 1917; 83 (Dublin) Gen. Hospl., France.

Gore, William Crampton ;
> M.B. 1897 ; British Red Cross, Boulogne, 1915 ; att. R.A.M.C. ;
> Med. Officer H.M.T. "Aquitania," 1915 ; Lt. R.A.M.C., June
> 1916 ; Capt. 1917 ; Malta ; Salonika ; Italy.

Gorman, Robert Swan ;
> Ent. 1905 ; Pte. Motor Transport, 1915.

*Goulding, Hamilton Barrett ;
> M.B. 1914 ; Lt. R.A.M.C., Aug. 1914 ; Capt. 1915 ; wounded,
> France, July, 1916 ; prisoner of war, Dec. 1917.

Graham, George Frederick ;
> M.B. 1907 ; M.D. 1913 ; Lt. I.M.S., 1908 ; Capt., Aug. 1911;
> despatches, Aug. 1915 ; I.E.F., Turkish Arabia ; wounded, E.
> Africa, Aug. 1917.

Graham, John Frederick ;
> B.A. 1901 ; M.A. 1905 ; Temp. Maj. R.A., Nov. 1915 ; Lt. Col.
> Madras. Art. Vols. ; O. C. C Battery, 6 Art. Training School,
> Luton ; 150 Bde. ; killed in action, France, 1 July, 1916.

*Graham, Roland Harris ;
> M.B. 1915 ; Lt. R.A.M.C., Aug. 1914 ; Capt. 1916 ; Mesopotamia
> and E. Persia.

*Graham, Thomas Ottiwell ;
> M.B. 1906 ; M.D. 1908 ; Lt. R.A.M.C., Dec. 1913 ; Capt. 1915 ;
> despatches, Jan. 1916 ; A/Maj. 1918 ; M.C. Dec. 1918 ; Italy.

*Grandy, Richard Edward ;
> M.B. 1912 ; Lt. R.A.M.C., Aug. 1914 ; Capt. 1915.

Grant, Donald St. John Dundas ;
> M.B. 1881 ; Lt. I.M.S., 1881 ; Col., Jan. 1911 ; ret. 1917.

Graves, Alan Percy ;
> B.A. 1912 ; 2 Lt. 10 Rif. Brig., Sept. 1914 ; 2 Lt. 2 Life Gds.,
> July 1915.

Gray, Frederick William Barton ;
> Ent. 1884 ; 2 Lt. R. Berks R., Aug. 1888 ; Ind. Army, 1890 ;
> D.S.O. 1908 ; Lt.-Col. 1914 ; C.M.G. 1915 ; Temp. Brig.-Gen.
> 1916 ; wounded ; despatches, Feb. 1915, July 1917, and Nov.
> 1917 ; Brigade Commander, Bareilly Brigade, 1918 ; Bt. Col.

Gray, Hampton Atkinson ;
> M.B. and M.D. 1893 ; M.O., in charge Depôt, Armagh.

*Gray, Norman ;
> Ent. 1912 ; 2 Lt. A.S.C., Nov. 1914 ; Lt. 1915.

Gray, Robert Alexander ;
> B.A. and LL.B. 1890 ; 2 Lt. 1 R. Ir. Fus., Oct. 1891 ; Maj.
> 1910 ; wounded and a prisoner, Mons, 1914.

Green, Frederick James ;
> M.B. 1890; M.D. 1892; Lt. R.A.M.C., Jan. 1907; Capt. 1911.; despatches, Dardanelles, Jan. 1916, and Egypt, Dec. 1916; M.C. Jan. 1918; Maj. 1919.

*Green, Herbert Richard Crichton ;
> Ent. 1909; Lt. 2 Manch. R., Dec. 1914 ; France ; Temp. Capt. 1915 ; Capt. 1917.

*Green, Isaac ;
> Ent. 1913; 2 Lt. A.S.C., July 1915; Lt. 1916; Lt. R.F.A., June 1918 ; A/Capt. 1918 ; France, 1915 17 and 1918-19.

•Green, William Osmond;
> Ent. 1914 ; 2 Lt. 10 R. Ir. Rif., May 1915 ; killed in action, 1 July 1916.

Greene, Arthur ;
> M.B. and M.D. 1898 ; Lt. R.A.M.C., T.F., July 1915; Capt. 1916 ; Ophth. Specialist to 5th Army, B.E.F.

Greene, David Campbell ;
> Ent. 1909; Lt. A.V.C., Aug. 1914 ; Capt. 1915.

*Greene, Godfrey Robert ;
> Ent. 1913 ; 2Lt. 11 N. Staff. R., Jan. 1915; M.G.C. 1916 ; killed in action, 3 Sept. 1916.

*Greene, Henry ;
> B.A. 1913 ; 2 Lt. I.A., 92 Punjabis, Jan. 1912; Lt. 1914 ; Egypt, 1914 ; despatches, Feb. 1915 ; Gallipoli ; att. 1/6 Gurkhas, 1915 ; killed in action, Gallipoli, 21 Aug. 1915 ; despatches, Sept, 1915.

Greene, James C. Sullivan ;
> M.B. 1883; Lt. A.M.S., 1885 ; Maj. R.A.M.C. 1897 ; Lt.-Col. 1905 ; ret. 1916.

Greene, John Geddes ;
> Ent. 1911 ; Pte. 7 Leinster R., June 1915; 2 Lt. 9 R. Dub. Fus., Aug. 1915 ; France, 1915 ; wounded, Hulluch, Apr. 1916 ; France, 1916 ; Lt. 1917.

Greene, Maurice Cherry ;
> B.A. 1906 ; Nigerian Field Force.

Greene, Thomas Francis Molesworth ;
> Ent. 1908 ; Pte., Motor Transport, 1915 ; Mediterranean E.F. ; 2 Lt. R.A.S.C. (M.T.), June 1917 ; Lt. 1918.

Greer, Donald Alister ;
> Ent. 1913 ; 2 Lt. 1 Conn. Rang., Dec. 1914 ; died of enteric, Amara, Mesopotamia, 12 July, 1916.

*Greer, Eric Robert S.;
> Ent. 1911 ; 2 Lt. 4 R.W. Fus., Aug. 1914 ; Temp. Lt. 1915 ; Capt. 1915 ; despatches, Jan. 1917 ; Lt. I.A., June 1918 ; Capt. 1919.

*Greer, Fergus Ussher Morris ;
Ent. 1910 ; 2 Lt. R.G.A., Oct., 1914 ; France; Lt. 1917 ; Germany.

Greer, Henry Francis Villiers ;
Ent. 1899 ; Capt. R.G.A., Sp. Res., 1908 ; Maj. 1914 ; A.D.C. to the Governor of Ceylon ; empld. 1914.

*Greer, James Crother ;
Ent. 1912 ; Pte. R.E., Chem. Corps, 1915.

*Greer, James Kenneth MacGregor ;
B.A. 1907 ; Trooper, N. Ir. Horse, Aug. 1914 ; France, Aug. 1914 ; 2 Lt. 3 D. Gds., Dec. 1914 ; att. Ir. Gds. Apr. 1915 ; wounded, Festubert, May 1915 ; 2 Lt. 1 Ir. Gds!, Nov. 1915 ; despatches, Jan. 1916 ; M.C. 14 Jan. 1916 ; Lt. 1916 ; died of wounds, Rouen, 3 Oct. 1916.

Greer, Rev. Richard Ussher ;
B.A. 1890 ; M.A. 1893 ; Army Chaplain, Jan. 1915 ; died, 23 June, 1915.

*Greeves, Norman Mellor ;
Ent. 1915 ; Pte. Feb. 1916 ; 6 Cadet Bn., July 1916 ; 2 Lt. 9 L'pool R., Nov. 1916 ; wounded, Ypres, June 1917 ; discharged, Nov. 1917.

*Gregg, Arthur Leslie ;
Ent. 1911 ; M.B. 1918 ; M.D. 1919 ; Lt. 6 R. Ir. Fus., Nov. 1914 ; wounded, Dardanelles, Aug. 1915 ; despatches, Jan. 1916.

Gregg, Richard George Stanhope ;
M.B. 1907 ; Lt. R.A.M.C., 1908 ; Capt., 1911 ; A/Lt.-Col. 1917 ; Maj. 1919.

Gregory, Joseph Richard ;
Ent. 1920 ; Trooper, S. Ir. H., Oct. 1916 ; France, 1917 ; 2 Lt. R. Ir. Fus., June 1918 ; France.

Grene, John Herbert Cecil ;
M.B. 1911 ; Dispenser, R.A.M.C., Aug. 1914.

*Gribbon, John Stewart ;
Ent. 1912 ; 2 Lt. 11 W. Rid. R., Mar. 1915 ; 2 Lt. 7 K.O.Y.L.I., Mar. 1915 ; 2 Lt. 1 Garr. Bn.W. York R. 1916 ; att. 2 Rif. Bde.; missing, reported killed in action, 27 May 1918.

Grier, Blayney ;
B.A. 1907 ; Pte. 1 Co. 2 Bn. H.A.C. May 1915 ; H.B., M.G.C., 1916 ; France, 1917.

Griffin, Rev. Edward Morgan ;
B.A. 1911 ; Army Chaplain, 4 Cl., Nov. 1915–16 and Jan. 1918–19 ; Egypt, 1916.

G

Griffin, Rev. James Jackson ;
.B.A. 1896; Army Chaplain, Jan. 1916–19 ; Hon. Chaplain, 1919.

*Griffin, James John Wahal ;
Ent. 1911 ; 2 Lt. 9 Bedf. R., Apr. 1915 ; killed in action, France, 15 Nov. 1916.

Griffin, Rev. John Wesley Knox ;
B.A. 1902 ; M.A. 1907 ; Army Chaplain, 4 Cl., Aug. 1914–15 ; B.E.F. 1914–19 ; Temp. 2 Cl. 1916 ; Dep. Assist. Chap. Gen. 1918 ; D.S.O.

Griffin, Thomas Francis ;
M.B. and M.D. 1896 ; Lt. R.A.M.C., Feb. 1915 ; Capt. 1916.

Griffith, Harry Rathborne ;
M.B. 1889 ; M.D. 1893 ; Lt. R.A.M.C., Sept. 1915 ; died on service, 21 May 1916.

Griffith, John William ;
B.A.I. 1898 ; Assistant Engineer, Civilian Ry. Co., France.

*Grimbly, Alan Francis ;
B.A. 1915 ; Lt. (on prob.) R.A.M.C., Aug. 1914 ; Surg.-Lt. R.N., Jan. 1917.

Grime, Allan Godfrey ;
Ent. 1916 ; B.A. 1920 ; Pte. A.S.C., July 1916 ; overseas as Mil. Clerk, 1917 ; served 1916–19.

Grimshaw, Cecil Thomas Wrigley ;
B.A. 1895 ; 2 Lt. R. Dub. Fus., May 1897 ; D.S.O. 1902 ; Maj. 1914 ; killed in action, Dardanelles, 26 Apr. 1915.

Grimshaw, Ewing Wrigley ;
B.A. 1890 ; 2 Lt. R. Dub. Fus., Nov. 1888 : Lt. I. A., 1891 ; Lt. Col., Nov. 1914 ; commanding 62 Punjabis ; killed in action, Mesopotamia, 21 Jan. 1916.

Grove-White, Ion Alexander ;
B.A. 1900 ; 2 Lt. 6 R. Dub. Fus., Jan. 1916 ; 2 Lt. 8 R. Ir. Rif., Jan. 1916 ; Lt. 1917 ; Trench Mortar Batteries, 1917 ; M.C. March 1919.

Grove-White, James Herbert ;
M.B. 1912 ; M.D. 1913 ; Lt. R.A.M.C., Oct. 1914 ; Capt. 1915 ; Lt. I.M.S. 1916 ; Capt. 1916.

Grove-White, Robert ;
B.A. 1904 ; Lt. 7 R. Dub. Fus., Jan. 1915 : Lieut. 5 Conn. Rang., Sept. 1915 ; wounded, Serbia, Dec. 1915.

Gubbins, Sir William Launcelotte;
M.B. 1872; M.D. (*Hon. Causâ*) 1912; Lt. A.M.S., 1873;
M.V.O. 1902; Surg.-Gen. R.A.M.C., 1903; Director-General
Army Medical Service, 1910; K.C.B. 1911; despatches, Sept.
1917; selected for reward for distinguished and meritorious
services, 1918.

Guilgault, Demosthéne;
B.A. 1902; Pte. 2 R. Canadian Mounted Rifles, Sept. 1915;
died, 4 March 1919, at Montreal, of heart failure contracted on
active service.

Guinness, Ernest Whitmore;
B.A. 1887; Lt. Eng. Militia, 1889; Maj. R.E., Sept. 1914.

Guinness, Wyndham Malan Grattan;
M.B. and M.D. 1899; Lt. R.A.M.C., Dec. 1916; Capt. 1917.

Gunn, David Drummond;
Ent. 1889; 2 Lt. K.O. Sco. Bord., Dec. 1893; Maj. 1913; Gen.
Staff Offr., Aldershot Training Centre, 1915; Bt. Lt.-Col., War
Office, 1918.

Gunn, Hamilton Bruce Leveson Gower;
Ent. 1898; 2 Lt. R.A., May 1901; Maj. 1915; despatches 31
May, 1915, 1 Jan. 1916; M.C. 14 Jan. 1916; D.S.O.; A/Lt.-Col.
1916.

Gunn, Kearsley Egerton Leveson Gower;
M.B. 1897; M.D. 1899; Anglo-French Red Cross, Bar le Duc,
France, 1915; Temp. Maj. R.A.M.C., May 1917; France, 1917.

*Gwynn, Rev. Robert Malcolm, F.T.C.D.;
B.A. 1898; Fellow, 1906; M.A. 1906; Army Chaplain, O.T.C.,
T.F., Apr. 1911.

H

Hackett, Rev. George Kennedy;
B.A. 1908; Army Chaplain, 4 Cl., May 1915–19; Hon. Chap.
1919.

*Hadden, David Hamilton;
M.B. 1913; Temp. Lt. R.A.M.C., Sept. 1914; Temp. Capt. 1915;
M.C. Jan. 1917; Bar to M.C. Aug. 1917; Capt. R.A.M.C., June
1918.

*Hadden, George Brownrigg;
M.B. 1914; Temp. Lt. R.A.M.C., Sept. 1914; Temp. Capt.
1915; Lt. R.A.M.C., Jan. 1917; Capt. 1918.

Hadden, Henry Arthur ;
    Ent. 1889 ; L.R.C.P. & S. Edin. ; Lt. R.A.M.C., Dec. 1915 ; Capt. 1916 ; died of pleurisy contracted on active service, 30 **Aug.** 1917.

Hadden, Henry John ;
    M.B. 1885 ; Fleet Surg. R.N., Feb. 1902 ; retd. ; re-empld. 1914 ; R.N. Air Station, Hendon.

*Hadden, John Yelverton ;
    Ent. 1913 ; 2 Lt. R.G.A., Sept. 1915 ; 2 Lt. 4 Conn. R., Dec. 1915 ; Lt. M.G.C., 1918.

Hadden, Marie Annette ;
    M.B. 1916 ; att. R.A.M.C. ; Alexandria.

Hadden, Richard Perrott ;
    B.A. 1907 ; Lt. R.A.M.C., May 1915 ; Gallipoli ; Capt. 1916 ; France ; M.C. Feb. 1919.

Haire, Rev. Archibald Matthew ;
    B.A. 1911 ; M.A. 1917 ; Army Chaplain, 4th Cl., April 1917–19 ; B.E.F.

Haire, Rev. Arthur ;
    B.A. 1903 ; M.A. 1915 ; Army Chaplain, 4th Cl., June 1916.

Haire, George ;
    Ent. 1908 ; 2 Lt. 6 Conn. Rang., Sept. 1914 ; Lt. 1915 ; died of wounds received in action, 7 Jan. 1917.

Haire, Robert ;
    Ent. 1895 ; Winnipeg Rifles ; killed, 7 May 1917.

Halahan, Rev. Francis Johnston ;
    B.A. 1892 ; M.A. 1899 ; Army Chaplain 4 Cl., Sept. 1915 ; 3 Cl. 1916 ; despatches, 1917 and 1918 ; M.C. June 1917 ; bar to M.C. Sept. 1917.

Halahan, Thomas Dufour ;
    M.B. 1890 ; Fleet Surg. R.N., Nov. 1907 ; Surg. Cr. ; O.B.E.

Hall, David Henry ;
    M.B. 1915 ; Lt. R.A.M.C., Jan. 1916 ; Capt. 1917 ; died of wounds, 14 May 1918.

*Hall, Henry Mitchell ;
    Ent. 1908 ; Cadet R.F.A., March, 1916 ; 2 Lt. R.G.A., July 1916 ; Lt. 1918 ; A/Capt. 1918.

Hall, Herbert ;
    Ent. 1916 ; Surg. Sub-Lt. R.N.V.R., Nov. 1918 ; H.M.S. " Partridge" Medit.

*Hall, James Beatty;
>Ent. 1911; 2 Lt. A.S.C. Oct. 1914; France, 1915–17; Lt. 1915; Lt. R F.C. 1916; Egypt, 1918–19.

Hall, John Charles;
>M.B. 1904; M.D. 1910; Capt. R.A.M.C., S. R., Sept. 1913; employed Aug. 1914, 5 D. Gds.; France, 1915.

*Hall, John Ramsay FitzGibbon;
>Ent. 1911; 2 Lt. 2 R. Dub. Fus., Jan. 1915; killed in action, 24 May 1915.

Hall, Philip Augustus;
>M.B. 1916; Lt. R.A.M.C., Oct. 1916; Capt. 1917; R.F.C., M.S., 1918.

*Hall, William Aeneas;
>B.A.I. 1911; 2 Lt. I.A. Res. of Offs. Oct. 1915; Capt. 1919.

Hallaran, William;
>M.B. 1884; Capt. R.A.M.C., July 1887; Col. 1915; died on service, at Jabbulpore, India, 23 Jan. 1917.

Hallowes, Arthur Collis;
>M.B. 1910; Lt. R.A.M.C., April 1917; France, 1917; Capt. 1918; M.C. Jan. 1918.

Hallowes, Brabazon Henry Collis;
>B.A.I. 1909; Capt. R.F.A., Sp. Res., June 1905; employed Nov. 1914; Staff Capt. 1918.

Hallowes, Keith Richard Collis;
>M.B. 1904; Lt. R.A.M.C., July 1917; Capt. 1918.

*Hallowes, Paul Collis;
>Ent. 1910; 2 Lt. 3 R. Dub. Fus., Oct. 1914; wounded, Aisne, Nov. 1914; Capt. 1915; attchd. R. Ir. Regt.; gassed, 1915; Maj. 1916; wounded, Sept. 1916.

Hallowes, Richard Collis;
>M.B. 1904; Lt. R.A.M.C., July 1904; Maj. 1915; despatches, June, 1916; Temp. Lt.-Col. 1915; D.S.O. June 1918.

Halpin, William Oswald;
>M.B. and M.D. 1911; Lt. R.A.M.C., Aug. 1914; Capt. 1915; died of wounds, 10 Aug. 1918.

Hamel-Smith, Lionel Frederick;
>Ent. 1910; B.A. 1920; 2 Lt. R.F.A., Aug, 1918.

*Hamilton, Basil Long;
>Ent. 1913; B.A.I. 1920; 2 Lt. R.G.A., Oct. 1914; France, 1915; invalided 1916; Lt. 1917; France, 1918.

*Hamilton, Cecil Claude;
> Ent. 1914; 2 Lt. 3 Conn. Rang., July 1915; killed in action,
> 16 Aug. 1917.

Hamilton, Charles Wolfe;
> M.B. 1883; M.D. 1894; Lt. R.A.M.C., June 1915; Military
> Hospital, Yelverton, Devonport.

*Hamilton, Ernest James;
> Ent. 1910; 2 Lt. 7 R. Dub. Fus., Dec. 1914; Capt. 1915;
> wounded, Dardanelles, 1 Aug. 1915.

*Hamilton, Geoffrey Cecil Monck;
> Ent. 1913; 2 Lt. 8 R. Dub. Fus., June 1915; killed in action,
> 9 Sept. 1916.

*Hamilton, Hector Macdonald;
> Ent. 1916; 7 Cadet Bn., May 1917; 2 Lt. 3 R. Innis. Fus.,
> Aug. 1917; France, 1917; killed in action, 22 Mar. 1918.

Hamilton, James Alexander Greer;
> M.B. 1876; Maj. Australian A.M.C.

*Hamilton, Noble Holton;
> Ent. 1915; 7 Cadet Bn., Jan. 1917; 2 Lt. R. Dub. Fus., Apr.
> 1917.

Hamilton, Thomas William O'Hara;
> M.B. 1881; Lt. A.M.S., Feb. 1883; C.M.G. 1901; Lt.-Col.
> R.A.M.C., temp. empld., 1914; despatches, Sept. 1917.

Hamilton-Johnstone, Millicent;
> M.B. 1916; att. R.A.M.C.; Alexandria.

*Hammick, St. Vincent Charles Farrant;
> Ent. 1914; Sandhurst, Jan. 1917; died at Sandhurst, 6 Mar.
> 1917.

Hanan, Charles Denis;
> M.B. 1910; M.D. 1912; Surg. R.N., March 1915; Surg.-Lt.

*Hancock, John Henry;
> B.A.I. 1915; 2 Lt. R.E., Oct. 1915; France, 1916; Somme;
> Vimy Ridge; Messines; killed in action near Ypres, 9 June 1917.

Hanewinkel, Ernest Eberhard;
> B.A. 1908; Lt. 19 Lond. Regt., Aug. 1914; Capt. 1915; killed
> in action, France, 31 Aug. 1915.

*Hanna, Henry Lyle;
> Ent. 1911; 2 Lt. A.S.C., Oct. 1914; Lt. 1915; Capt. 1916;
> retired, Hon. Capt. 1918.

Hanna, William John ;
Ent. 1914 ; B.A. 1920; Pte. 10 R. Dub. Fus., Nov. 1915; Cpl.
1916 ; France, 1916 ; Sgt. 1916; Sgt. 1 R. Muns. Fus. 1918 ;
wounded, May 1918; Demob. Jan. 1919.

Hannay, Rev. James Owen ;
B.A. 1887 ; M.A. 1896 ; Army Chaplain, 4 Cl., Jan. 1916–17.

Hannay, Robert;
B.A. 1912; Lt. 2 I. Gds., July 1915; wounded, July 1917 ;
A/Capt. 1918.

*Hannon, Norman Leslie ;
Ent. 1913 ; 2 Lt. 7 L'pool Regt., Aug. 1914 ; killed in action,
Festubert, 16 May, 1915.

*Hanretté, Wilfred Edmund ;
Ent. 1916 ; Staff. Serg. D.P.O.S. Dept., A.S.C., June 1917.

Haran, James Augustus ;
M.B. 1891 ; M.D. 1905 ; Col. Serv. ; Maj. while temp. empld. ;
C.M.G.

Hardy, Henry Russell ;
B.A. 1886 ; 2 Lt. R. W. Surr. R., Aug. 1889 ; Capt. 1898 ;
retired ; attchd. Gen. Staff, Southern Command ; Brig. Maj.,
Mar. 1915.

Hare, Rev. Arthur Neville;
B.A. 1909 ; T.C.F. 1918.

Harkness, William Frederick Samuel;
Ent. 1916 ; 2 Lt. R G.A., Oct. 1917.

Harley, Thomas William ;
M.B. 1901 ; Lt. I.M.S., Jan. 1902 ; Maj. 1914.

Harman, Charles Cecil ;
B.A. 1900 ; 2 Lt. 2 Leins. R., May 1900; Maj. 1915; Bt.
Lt.-Col. 1918 ; D.S.O. ; bar to D.S.O., Feb. 1919.

Harnett, William George ;
M.B. 1905; M.D. 1907; M.O., in charge Military Hospital,
Barnet; Temp. Capt. R.A.M.C., Mar. 1917 ; Prisoner of War,
July, 1918.

Harold, James Murphy ;
L.M. and L.Ch. 1905 ; Pte. Rhodesian Rif. 1914 ; Temp. Capt.
with troops Northern Nigeria, Feb. 1915.

*Harper, Edgar Henry ;
B.A. 1903; 2 Lt. 11 S. Staff. R., Apr. 1915 ; killed in action,
10 July, 1916.

*Harper, James ;
    Ent. 1915 ; 2 Lt. R.F.C., Aug. 1916 ; Capt. R.A.F. ; served,
    1916–19 ; France.

Harper, Thomas Gerald ;
    M.B. 1912 ; Capt. N.Z.A.M.C., April 1917.

*Harpur, Edward Perceval ;
    Ent. 1910 ; 2 Lt. 7 Leins. R., Oct. 1914 ; Lt. 7 R. Ir. Fus.,
    1914 ; Bgde. Tranport Officer, 1916 ; killed in action, Somme,
    11 Sept. 1916.

Harpur, Henry Percy ;
    M.B. 1912 ; Lt. R.A.M.C., Jan. 1915 ; Capt. 1916 ; wounded,
    Nov. 1916.

Harpur, James ;
    M.B. 1900 ; S. Rhodesian M.S.

Harrel, William Vesey ;
    Ent. 1884 ; M.V.O. 1903 ; C.B. 1912 ; Commander R.N.V.R.,
    Vice-Admiral's Staff, Queenstown, 1915.

*Harris, Eric Wallace ;
    Ent. 1914 ; 2 Lt. R.G.A., Nov. 1915 ; Lt. 1917 ; died of wounds
    received in action, 4 Nov. 1917.

Harris, Frederick ;
    M.B. 1914 ; Lt. R.A.M.C., Jan. 1915 ; Capt. 1916 ; Dardanelles,
    Egypt ; France, 1916 ; gassed and wounded, May 1917 ; M.C.
    Sept. 1917.

*Harris, George Armour ;
    B.A.I. 1911 ; 2 Lt. R.E., March 1915 ; Lt. 1916 ; despatches,
    June 1916 ; Capt. 1918.

*Harris, George Arthur ;
    B.A. 1902 ; M.A. 1915 ; Maj. O.T.C., Unattached List, T.F ,
    Feb. 1913 ; Acting Adjt. D.U.O.T.C ; despatches, D.S.O. Jan.
    1917 ; H.Q. Staff, Ir. Command, 1916 ; D.A.Q.M.G. Ir. Command,
    1917 ; O.B.E. 1919.

Harris, St. George Eyre ;
    M.B. 1899 ; M.D. 1902 ; Lt. R.A.M.C., Oct. 1915 ; Salonika,
    1916 ; Capt. 1916.

Harrison, Standish Henry ;
    Ent. 1872 ; 2 Lt. The King's R., Dec. 1874 ; Bt. Col. 1902 ;
    Brig. Comdr., Nov 1914 ; Commanded 2 Lancs. Terr. Brig.,
    1914–16, 170 Infantry Brig., 1916–17 ; Hon. Brig.-Gen., 1917 ;
    served in France as Town Major and Area Commandant, 1917–18.

Hart, Henry Percyvall ;
    M.B. 1907 ; Lt. R.A.M.C., July 1907 ; Capt. 1911 ; wounded,
    March 1916 ; Military Cross, May 1916 ; A/Maj. 1918.

Hart, William Hume ;
> M.B. 1910; Lt. R.A.M.C., Feb. 1916; wounded, Aug. 1917;
> Capt. 1917.

Harte, Campbell M'Pherson ;
> Ent. 1917; Despatch Rider; Sapper R.E. (1918–19).

Harte, Thomas Dillon ;
> Ent. 1910; Pte. R.A.M.C.

Hartigan, James Andrew ;
> Med. School, 1897; M.B. (Dunelm.) 1899 ; Lt. R.A.M.C., Dec.
> 1899; Maj. 1911; Deputy Assistant Director of Med. Serv. 1915;
> despatches, Jan. 1916; D.S.O., Jan. 1916; Lt.-Col. 1917; Temp.
> Col. 1918; A.D.M.S. 1918; C.M.G. 1918; despatches, 1919.

Hartley, John Armstrong ;
> M.B. and M.D. 1906; Lt. R.A.M.C. (T.F.), Jan. 1916; Capt.
> 1916; att. Berks Yeomanry.

*Harvey, Beauchamp Bagenal ;
> B.A.I. 1911 ; 2 Lt. R.E., Nov. 1914 ; Capt. 1918 ; Salonika ;
> France.

*Harvey, Ewart S. Francis ;
> Ent. 1910; 2 Lt. 5 Leins. R., Apr. 1915; 2 Lt. 1, 2 Bns., Sept.
> 1916; Lt. M.G.C., 1916; Capt. 1918; empld. Min. of Lab.

Harvey, Rev. James Gerald ;
> B.A. 1905 ; Army Chaplain, 4 Cl., Oct. 1915–18 ; France, 1916.

*Harvey, John Alan ;
> Ent. 1915; 7 Cadet Bn., May 1917.

Harvey, Joseph ;
> M.B. 1913 ; Lt. R.A.M.C., Apr. 1916 ; Capt. 1917.

Harvey, William Geoffrey ;
> M.B. 1903 ; M.D. 1910; Anglo-French Red Cross, Bar le Duc,
> France, 1915; Hon. Maj. R.A.M C. June 1917.

*Haskins, Lancelot William Roe ;
> Ent. 1914; Woolwich, 1916; 2 Lt. R.F.A., Feb. 1917;
> Flanders; gassed, Oct. 1917; Lt. 1918; invalided 1919.

*Haskins, Nicholas Hopkins Henry ;
> M.B. 1914; Lt. R.A.M.C., Aug. 1914 ; wounded. Dardanelles,
> 20 Aug. 1915 ; Capt. 1915; despatches, Dec. 1916 ; Egypt ; M C.
> June 1918 ; A/Maj. 1918.

Hassard, William ;
> M.B. and M.D. 1905; Surg. R.N., Aug. 1914 ; H.M.S " Ceto " ;
> Surg.-Lt.

*Hatch, Robert Pyne ;
> Ent. 1913 ; 2 Lt. 5 R. Ir. Regt., Oct. 1915 ; Lt. 1917 ; Lt. New Armies, 1917 ; A/Capt. Anti-Gas School, 1918.

*Hatte, Edward Stokes ;
> Ent. 1906 ; Ceylon Planters Rifle Corps, War Contgt. ; Egypt ; Suez Canal ; Dardanelles, 1915 ; 2 Lt. 7 R. Ir. Rif. Aug. 1916 ; wounded, France, Sept. 1916 ; killed in action, 16 Aug. 1917.

Hatton, Rev. John Alexander ;
> B.A. 1878 ; M.A. 1881 ; B.D. 1890 ; Army Chaplain, 1890 ; 1 Cl., 1910 ; ret. 1917.

Haughton, Samuel George Steele ;
> M.B. 1906 ; M.D. and M.A.O. 1913 ; Lt. I.M.S., Aug. 1905 ; Capt. 1909 ; Indian E.F., Turkish Arabia, 1915 ; Prisoner of War, Kut El Amara, May, 1916 ; Maj. 1918.

Haughton, William Steele ;
> M.B. 1894 ; M.D. 1901 ; Surg., Castle Red Cross Hospital, Dublin ; Temp. Maj. R.A.M.C. 1917.

Hayden, Denis Henry Gryffydd ;
> Ent. 1919 ; 2 Lt. 6 R. Welsh Fus., Sept. 1915 ; Lt. 1917 ; Lt. M.G.C. 1917 ; France ; Mesopotamia ; Persia.

*Hayes, Cyril Beauchamp ;
> B.A.I. 1915 ; 2 Lt. R.E., Oct. 1915 ; wounded, France, Apr. and Aug., 1916 ; M.C. Aug. 1916 ; France, 1917 ; Lt. 1917 ; Pilot and Instructor R.A.F., 1918–19.

Hayes, Edmund Duncan Tranchell ;
> M.B. 1915 ; M.D. 1921 ; Lt. R.A.M.C., July 1915 ; Capt. 1916 ; France 1916–19 ; Germany 1919 ; wounded, Lombartzyde, and prisoner of war, July 1917 ; wounded, May 1918 ; despatches, 1919.

*Hayes, Patrick Joseph ;
> Ent. 1913 ; Motor Transport Ser., Jan. 1915 ; 2 Lt. 16 L'pool. R., Oct. 1915 ; 2 Lt. R. Suss. R., Aug. 1916 ; Lt. 1918.

Hayes, William Ivon ;
> M.B. Melbourne ; Chief Demonstrator in Anatomy 1919 ; Australian A.M.C. ; France 1918–19.

Hazelton, Percy Orr ;
> B.A. 1892 ; 2 Lt. Linc. R., Aug. 1892 ; Lt. A.S.C., 1895 ; Lt.-Col. 1914 ; Asst. Director of Transport, 1914 ; Bt. Col. 1917 ; Temp. Col. 1918 ; C.B. ; C.M.G.

*Hazley, John Bradley ;
> Ent. 1917 ; Pte. R.A.F. May 1918.

Head, Alfred Joseph ;
Ent. 1919 ; 2 Lt. H.A.C. and Worc. R. ; wounded, Beaumont Hamel, June 1916 ; Lt. 16 Worc. R. Nov. 1917.

Healy, Christopher James ;
M.B. 1887 ; Lt. R.A.M.C., July 1891 ; Maj. 1903.

*Healy, George Ernest;
Ent. 1912 ; 2 Lt. A.S.C., Nov. 1914 ; Gallipoli ; Lt. 1915 ; died of influenza, Dublin, March 1919.

Healy, George Frederick Columb ;
M.B. 1910 ; M.D. 1912 ; Lt. R.A.M.C., Feb. 1916 ; Capt. 1917.

Healy, John Frederick;
Ent. 1915 ; 2 Lt. 3 R. Ir. Rif., Mar. 1915 ; killed in action, France, 1 July, 1916.

Healy, Patrick Joseph ;
Ent. 1915 ; Surg. Sub.-Lt. R.N.V.R., H.M.S. " Marne," July 1917.

Heaney, Francis James Strong ;
M.B. 1901 ; M.D. 1902 ; Surg. R.N.V.R., Aug. 1914 ; Surg. Lt.-Comdr. 1918.

*Heard, John Galloway ;
Ent. 1915 ; 2 Lt. R.G.A., July 1915 ; Lt. R.E. 1917 ; M.C.

Heard, Richard ;
Med. Sch. 1887 ; M.B., R.U.I. ; Capt. I.M.S., Jan. 1896 ; Lt. Col. 1913.

Hearn, Rev. Daniel James Charles ;
B.A. 1909 ; M.A. 1919; Army Chaplain, 4 Cl., Sept. 1918 ; France 1918–19 ; invalided home, March 1919.

Hearn, Lewis Julius Christopher ;
M.B. 1896 ; Lt. R.A.M.C., July 1897 ; Capt. 1908 ; Res. of Offs. 1914–1919.

Hearn, Thomas Edmund ;
Ent. 1912 ; 2 Lt. 6 R. Muns. Fus., Nov. 1914 ; wounded. Suvia Bay, Aug. 1915 ; Lt. 1916 ; 2 Lt. 1, 2 R. Muns. Fus., Aug, 1915.

*Hearn, William Michael ;
Ent. 1916 ; 7 Cadet Bn., Oct. 1916 ; 2 Lt. Ser. Bns. R. Dub. Fus. Feb. 1919.

*Heatley, Robert Arthur ;
Ent. 1919 ; 2 Lt. R.G.A. Apr. 1918 ; Salonika 1919 ; Lt. 1919.

*Heffernan, William Patrick ;
Ent. 1904 ; 2 Lt. 3 R. Ir. Regt., Aug. 1914 ; atthd. 1 Glouc. R. ; killed in action, France, 9 May 1915.

Hegarty, Donal Kevin Joseph ;
Ent. 1912 ;2 Lt. 3 I. Gds., Oct. 1915 ; wounded ; Lt. 1916 ;
A/Capt. 1917 ; M.C. Jan. 1919.

*Hemmingway, Douglas Lennox ;
Ent. 1913 ; 2 Lt. R.G.A., Dec. 1915 ; Lt. 1917 ; Capt.

*Hemphill, Alexander William ;
Ent. 1914 ; 2 Lt. R.F.A., Feb. 1916 ; wounded, Oct. 1916 ; Lt.
1917.

*Hemphill, Richard Patrick ;
Ent. 1912 ; 2 Lt. 6 Leins. R., Dec. 1914 ; France 1915 ;
Salonika 1915 ; Egypt ; R. Flying C. 1917 ; died of injuries
received in an accident, Heliopolis, Egypt, 24 March 1917.

*Hemphill, Robert ;
M.B. 1912 ; Lt. R.A.M.C., Jan. 1913 ; Capt. 1915 ; despatches,
Jan. 1916 ; Temp. Maj. 1916 ; A/Lt.-Col. 1917 ; D.S.O. June 1918.

*Hemsworth, Thomas Garrett Frederick ;
B.A.I. 1913 ; 2 Lt. R.E., Jan. 1916 ; Lt. 1917 ; A/Capt. 1917 ;
Temp. Maj. 1918 ; India ; Mesopotamia.

Hemus, Donald George ;
Ent. 1914 ; 2 Lt. 12 Worc. R., Aug. 1915 ; Lt. 1918 ; killed in
action, 22 March 1918.

*Henchy, Dudley North ;
Ent. 1911 ; 2 Lt. 7 R. Dub. Fus., May 1915 ; wounded,
Wytschaete, 2 June 1917 ; in hospital until discharged unfit for
service, Aug. 1918 ; Assist. Recruiting Officer, 1918.

Henderson, Alexander Victor Simpson ;
Ent. 1919 : Pte. Argyll and Sutherland Highlanders, and W.O.,
R.A.O.C. ; France.

Henderson, George York ;
B.A. 1914 ; Lt. A.S.C., Nov. 1914 ; Capt. and Adjt. 1914 ;
France 1915 ; 2 Lt. 10 R. Ir. Rif., March 1916 ; wounded, Somme,
1 July 1916 ; wounded, Messines, June 1917 ; 2 Lt. 1, 2 R. Ir. Rif.,
1917 ; M.C. 1917 ; killed in action, battle of Cambrai, 22 Nov.
1917.

Henderson, John Alexander ;
B.A.I. 1906 ; 273rd Ry. Constr. Coy. R.E. 1916–19 ; A/Major.

Henley, Ernest Albert William ;
M.B. 1901 ; M.D. 1911 ; New Zealand Med. Corps ; not accepted
for foreign service owing to his health ; Capt. Apr. 1915 ; died 14
Nov. 1918.

Henley, Frederick Louis ;
B.A. 1906 ; M.A. 1912 ; 2 Lt. 13 Notts and Derby R., July 1915 ;
killed in action, 1 Oct. 1916.

*Hennessy, David Roderick ;
M.B. 1916; 2 Lt. 4, 2 R. Ir. Fus., Aug. 1914; Capt. 1915; Salonika; Lt. R.A.M.C., 1916; Capt. 1917 ; despatches, June 1919.

Henry, Alexander John Dawson ;
B.A.I. 1908 ; 2 Lt. R.F.A., Oct. 1915 ; Lt. 1917 ; R.A.F., 1917 ; 2 Lt. R.A.F. Sept. 1918.

Henry, Arnold Kirkpatrick ;
M.B. 1911 ; Surg. to Serbian Military Hosp. 1915 ; Lt. R.A.M C., Apr. 1916 ; Order of St. Sava ; Médicin Aide Maj. 1 erè Classe, Sept. 1917.

Henry, Dorothy Kate Milne ;
M.B. 1912 ; M.D. 1913 ; Surg. to Serbian Military Hosp., 1915 ; Médicin traitant Hospital 115 bis. xviie Région.

Henry, Howard ;
M.B. 1900 ; M.D. 1906 ; Lt. R.A.M.C. (T.F.), Jan. 1907 ; Capt. 1910 ; wounded, Dardanelles, 4 June, 1915; A/Lt.-Col.; 1918 ; M.C. May 1918 ; Maj. 1919.

*Henry, James Campbell ;
Ent. 1907 ; 2 Lt. 6 R. Dub. Fus., Aug. 1914; 2 Lt. 1 R. Ir. Fus., May 1915 ; Temp. Lt. 1915 ; Lt. 1916.

*Henry, James Maxwell, F.T.C.D. ;
B.A. 1909 ; Fellow, 1914 ; M.A. 1914 ; 2 Lt. O.T.C. Unattached List, Jan. 1916.

Henry, Robert Wallace Wesley ;
M.B. 1892 ; M.D. 1895; Maj. R.A.M.C., Aug. 1914 ; 5th Northern Genl. Hosp., Leicester ; despatches, Feb. 1917, Sept. 1917 ; Bt. Lt.-Col. 1919.

*Henry, William Ernest ;
B.A. 1914 ; 2 Lt. 1 R. Dub. Fus., Aug. 1914 ; 2 Lt. 1 R. Ir. Fus., Feb. 1915 ; wounded, France, 8 May, 1915 ; killed in action, 1 May, 1916.

Heron, James Mathews ;
M.B. 1890 ; M.D. 1893 ; Capt. R.A.M.C., Sept. 1915.

Herringham, Sir Wilmot Parker ;
M.D. (hon. causa) 1909 ; F.R.C.P. ; Lt. Col. R.A.M.C., June 1914 ; Temp. Col. A.M.S. 1914 ; C.B. 1915 ; despatches, Jan. 1917 ; Temp. Maj.-Gen. Dec. 1917 ; despatches Dec. 1917; K.C.M.G. 1919 ; despatches, 1919.

*Heuston, Frederick Gibson ;
Ent. 1910 ; 2 Lt. 6 R. Ir. Fus., Sept. 1914 ; wounded ; killed in action, Dardanelles, 15 Aug. 1915 ; despatches, M.C. Jan. 1916.

*Hewat, Cecil Duxbury ;
>   Ent. 1913 ; 2 Lt. R.F.A., Sept. 1915.

*Hewetson-Johnston, Edward Daniel ;
>   Ent. 1911 ; 2 Lt. Cheshire Field Co. R.E., T.F., Aug. 1915 ;
>   Lt. 1916 ; A/Capt. 1918 ; M.C.

Hewitt, Claude Lifford Richard ;
>   .B.A.I. 1911 ; Jnr. Insp. Gun Carriage Factory, Jubbulpore,
>   India.

Hewitt, Eileen Mabel ;
>   M.B. and M.D. 1916 ; Hospital Staff, Woolwich Arsenal, 1916 ;
>   M.B.E.

Hewitt, Robert Morton ;
>   M.B. 1894 ; M.D. 1895 ; Lt. R.A.M.C., Jan. 1916 ; Capt. 1917 ;
>   France.

Hewson, Frank Lloyd ;
>   B.A. 1907 ; 2 Lt. A.S.C., Feb. 1908 ; Capt. 1914.

*Hickman, Poole Henry ;
>   B.A. 1902 ; Lt. 7 R. Dub. Fus., Sept. 1914 ; Capt. Jan. 1915 ;
>   killed, Dardanelles, 15 Aug. 1915.

Hickson, Bertram Evelyn ;
>   B.A. 1908 ; Lt. I.A. 27 Lt. Cavalry, Dec. 1910 ; Capt. 1915.

*Hickson, Samuel ;
>   M.B. 1884 ; Lt. A.M.S. 1885 ; Maj. R.A.M.C., May 1897 ;
>   Col. R.A.M.C., 1914 ; C.B. 1915 ; A.D.M.S. 1914–16 ; D.D.M.S.
>   1916–18 ; Maj.-Gen. 1917 ; K.B.E. ; K.H.S. ; despatches, Oct.
>   1914, Dec. 1917, Dec. 1918, and July 1919.

*Higgins, John Timothy Donal ;
>   M.B. 1912 ; Surg. R.N., Oct. 1912 ; Surg.-Lt. Cr. 1918.

Higgins, William Albert ;
>   M.B. 1897 ; M.D. 1898 ; Lt. R.A.M.C., Nov. 1915.

*Higginson, Guy St. George ;
>   Ent. 1909 ; 2 Lt. I.A. Res., Dec. 1914 ; attchd. 98 Inf. ; France ;
>   Egypt ; attchd. 69 Punjabis ; Aden, 1916.

*Hill, Frederick Charles ;
>   Ent. 1911 ; 2 Lt. 7 Dorset R., Feb. 1915 ; resigned, ill-health,
>   1915.

Hill, James Herbert ;
>   B.A.I. 1907 ; 2 Lt. R.E., Aug. 1915 ; Capt. 1918 ; M.C. and
>   bar.

*Hill, Lindsay Arthur;
    B.A.I. 1911; 2 Lt. R.E., Feb. 1915; Capt. 1918; M.C.; Croix
    de Guerre (Belge).

Hill, Lionel George William;
    B.A.I. 1909; 2 Lt. R.E., June 1915; Lt. 1916; Capt.;
    France; Salonika; despatches (twice); Italian Silver Medal.

Hill, Samuel Reginald;
    B.A. 1914; 2 Lt. A.S.C., June 1915; France 1916; Lt. 1916;
    A/Capt. 1917; invalided out, 1917.

Hill, Thomas Edward;
    M.B. 1917; Lt. R.A.M.C., Feb. 1918.

*Hill, Thomas Edward;
    Ent. 1914; Sandhurst, Feb. 1915; 2 Lt. 5 Linc. R. Dec. 1915;
    Lt. 1917; empld. with 25 Durham L.I. 1917; with Labour C.
    1918.

*Hillas, Arthure Benedict Edward;
    B.A. 1897; Lt. 7 Gord. Highrs., March 1915; A/Capt. 1916;
    France; twice wounded; wounded and missing, Battle of Arras,
    reported killed in action, 23 Apr. 1917.

Hillas, Henry Grant;
    B.A. 1906; Egyptian Flying Corps, Jan. 1915; Director,
    Secretariat Ministry of Finance, Cairo.

Hilliard, Francis Maybury;
    Ent. 1916; Surg. Sub-Lt. Aug. 1918; H.M.S. "Myosotis";
    N. Sea.

Hilliard, John Williams;
    M.B. and M.D. 1901; Lt. R.A.M.C., Dec. 1915; Surg. 32 Gen.
    Hosp., E.F., France; Capt. 1917.

Hilliard, Leo Matthew;
    Ent. 1912; 2 Lt. 10 Reg. R. of Cavalry, Oct. 1914; Temp. Lt.
    1915; 5 D. Gds. 1916; I. A. 1917; 2 Lt. I. A. July 1918;
    A/Capt. and Adj. 1918; Capt. 1919; att. 7 Lancers.

*Hilliard, Percy Joseph;
    Ent. 1914; Quetta, Jan. 1917; 2 Lt. I.A. Oct. 1917; Lt. 1918;
    att. 19 Lancers.

*Hilliard, Richard Franklin;
    Ent. 1910; 2 Lt. 8 R. Dub. Fus., Oct. 1915.

*Hillyard, Cecil Albert Charles;
    Ent. 1912; 2 Lt. R.G.A., Oct. 1914; Tempt. Capt. 1916; Lt.
    1917.

Hilton, William;
    Ent. 1910; Pte. 8 Bn. 90 Winnipeg Rifles, 1914.

Hipwell, Rev. Richard Senior ;
>   B.A. 1912 ; B.D. and M.A. 1916; Army Chaplain, 4 Cl., Jan.
>   1915.

Hirschmann, Joseph ;
>   Ent. 1915 ; M.B. 1920 ; Surg. Prob. R.N., Apr. 1918.

Hodder, Gerald Edward ;
>   B.A. 1908 ; 2 Lt. A.S.C., Feb. 1909 ; Capt. 1915 ; Temp. Maj.
>   1915.

*Hodgins, Rev. John James ;
>   B.A. 1913 ; Army Chaplain, Nov. 1915-16.

Hodgins, Robert ;
>   Ent. 1897 ; Capt. Supernumerary List, I.A., March 1910 ; Maj.
>   1916 ; died at Formby, Lancs. 1918.

***Hoey, Frederick Cyril** ;
>   Ent. 1914 ; R. Flying. C. Cadet School, Denham, Nov. 1916 ;
>   2 Lt. R. Flying C. ; accidentally killed, 7 June 1917.

Hoffman, Geoffrey Arthur ;
>   M.B. 1915 ; Lt. R.A.M.C., May 1917.

Hogan, Rev. John Edward ;
>   B.A. 1896 ; M.A. 1903 ; Chaplain R.N., Sept. 1900 ; North
>   Sea Fleet, 1914-5 ; invalided, 1915.

Hogan, Wilfred Laurence ;
>   M.B. 1907 ; Lt. R.A.M.C., 1918.

*Hogg, William Frederick ;
>   Ent. 1914 ; 2 Lt. 3 R. Ir. Rif., Mar. 1915 ; Lt. 1916 ; wounded,
>   July 1916 ; M.C. Oct. 1916 ; wounded, May 1917 ; A/Capt. 1918.

Hogg, Rev. William Matthew Banks ;
>   B.A. 1910 ; Army Chaplain, 4 Cl., Aug. 1914.

Hojel, James Graham ;
>   M.B. 1886 ; Capt. I.M.S., March 1888 ; Lt. Col. 1908 ; C.I.E.
>   Jan. 1917.

Holden, Percy Noel ;
>   Ent. 1911 ; 2 Lt. 7 R. Ir. Rif., Aug. 1915 ; 2 Lt. A.S.C. Jan.
>   1917 ; Tempt. Lt. 1918.

Hollwey, James Bell ;
>   Ent. 1914 ; 2 Lt. R.F.A., June 1914 ; Lt. 1915 ; Capt. 1917 ;
>   M.C. 1917 ; A/Maj. 1917.

Holmes, George ;
>   B.A. 1914 ; 2 Lt. R.F.A., Nov. 1914 ; Lt. 1915 ; A/Capt. and
>   Adjt. 1918.

*Holmes, George William ;
  Ent. 1910; 2 Lt. 10 Ches. R., Nov. 1914 ; wounded, France,
  25 Nov. 1915 ; Lt. 1917 ; Training Res. 1917 ; Wt.-Offr. 1917.

Holmes, Gordon Morgan ;
  M.B. 1898 ; M.D. 1903 ; Lt. Col. R.A.M.C., Aug. 1915, B.E.F. ;
  despatches and C.M.G., Jan. 1917 : C.B.E. 1919 ; despatches,
  1919.

*Holmes, Hugh Oliver ;
  B.A. 1908 ; 2 Lt. R.F.A., Nov. 1914 ; Capt. 1916 ; wounded,
  Oct. 1916 ; Gallipoli ; France ; A/Maj. 1918 ; M.C. Jan. 1918.

Holmes, John ;
  Ent. 1912 ; 2 Lt. 11 York. R., May 1915 ; Lt. 1 Garr. Bn. 1915.

Holmes, John Morgan ;
  M.B. 1903 ; Lt. I.M.S., Jan. 1904 ; Capt. 1907 ; M.O. 19
  Lancers, I.A. ; Maj. 1915.

Holmes, Reginald ;
  M.B. 1907 ; M.D. 1909 ; Lt. R.A.M.C. ; France, 1915.

*Holmes, Robert Charles Elrington ;
  B.A. 1913 ; 2 Lt. 3, 2 R. Innis. Fus., Aug. 1914 ; France, 1915 ;
  Capt. 1915 ; wounded, France, July, 1916 ; A/Maj. 1918.

Homan, Arthur Douglas ;
  Ent. 1900 ; 2 Lt. R. Ir. Regt., Nov. 1905 ; Capt. 1914 ;
  France, 1914 ; Salonika, 1916 ; Temp. Maj. att. Oxf. and Bucks
  L.I. ; died of wounds received in action, 9 May 1917.

Homan, Henry Leslie ;
  Ent. 1897 ; 2 Lt. Middx. R., May 1900 ; Capt. 1909 ; killed,
  Neuve Chapelle, 10 March 1915.

Homan, Thomas Delapere ;
  M.B. 1897 ; M.D. 1901 ; Lt. R.A.M.C. May 1918.

Homan, William Travers ;
  Ent. 1889 ; M.D. ; Capt. R.A.M.C., T.F., Oct. 1915.

Hone, Addison ;
  Ent. 1891 ; Lt. Canadian A.S.C., Horse Transport.

Hone, Joseph Browne ;
  Ent. 1896 ; Lt. 4 R. Ir. Rif., March 1915 ; attchd. R. Sc. Fus. ;
  France ; Capt. 1916.

Hone, William Patrick ;
  B.A.I. 1910 ; 2 Canadian Div. Eng. ; 2 Lt. R.G.A., S.R., Sept.
  1916 ; att. 223 Siege Bty. ; Lt. 1918 ; A/Capt. 1918 ; M.C. Nov.
  1918.

H

Hope, Ralph James ;
    B.A.I. 1903 ; Lt. R.E.; May 1916; General Staff; France;
    Germany ; Capt. 1918 ; Mesopotamia.

*Hopking, Henry Richard ;
    Ent. 1918 ; Sandhurst, Sept. 1918.

Hopkins, Francis Gethin ;
    M.B. 1889 ; M.D. 1903; W. African Service ; Lt. R.A.M.C.,
    Oct. 1915 ; died, Plymouth, 2 Feb. 1916.

Hopkins, William Edward ;
    M.B. 1908 ; Lt. R.A.M.C., Oct. 1914 ; Capt. 1915 ; Egypt,
    1915 ; M.C. Feb. 1918.

Horan, Maurice ;
    Medical School, 1906 ; Lt. R.A.M.C., April 1917 ; Capt. 1918.

*Horne, Andrew John ;
    M.B. 1915 ; M.D. 1921 ; Lt. R.A.M.C., Feb. 1914 ; Gallipoli,
    1915 ; Capt. 1916 ; despatches, Nov. 1916 ; India, 1916 ; Mesopo-
    tamia, 1917-19 ; Afghanistan, 1919-20 ; typhoid and malaria,
    1920.

Houghton, George John ;
    Ent. 1890 ; L.R.C.P.&S.I.; Lt. R.A.M.C., Apr. 1900 ; Maj.
    1912 ; despatches, May 1917 ; Lt.-Col. 1917 ; D.S.O.; Temp.
    Col. 1918 ; A.D.M.S. 1919 ; Croix de Guerre, Oct. 1919.

Houghton, John William Hobart ;
    M.B. 1898 ; Lt. R.A.M.C., Jan. 1899 ; Lt.-Col.1915 ; wounded,
    Oct. 1917 ; despatches, Dec. 1917 ; D.S.O. Jan 1918 ; Col. 1918 ;
    wounded, May, 1918.

Houston, Joseph Wilfred ;
    M.B. 1905 ; Lt. R.A.M.C., Feb. 1908 ; Capt. 1911 ; despatches.
    May 1915 and Jan. 1916 ; D.S.O., Jan. 1916 ; A/Maj. 1918.

Houston, William Mitchell ;
    M.B. 1899 ; Lt. I.M.S., Jan. 1900 ; Maj. 1911 ; Hosp. Ship
    " Goorkha."

*Howard, William Edward Sharpe ;
    Ent. 1910 ; Lt. 4 R. Ir. Rif., June 1914 ; wounded, France, 16
    June, 1915 ; Capt. 1915.

Howe, Ivan Albert ;
    B.A. 1913 ; 2 Lt. R.G.A., Dec. 1915 ; Lt: 1917.

*Howe, Norman David ;
    Lic. Eng. 1914 ; 2 Lt. R.E., Aug. 1914 ; Lt. 1915 ; wounded,
    Dardanelles, Aug. 1915 ; Egypt ; France ; Capt. 1917.

Howe, William Molyneux :
Ent. 1904 ; 2nd A.M., R.F.C., Aug. 1915 ; France, 1915 ; died after an operation, France, 26 Nov. 1918.

*Howes, Charles William ;
B.A. 1913 ; Pte. Leins. R., Nov. 1914 ; 2 Lt. 19 Durh. L.I., July 1915 ; Lt. 1916 ; Capt. ; killed in action, 22 April 1918.

Huggett, Reginald Norman ;
B.A. and LL.B. 1914 ; 2 Lt. A.S.C., Dec. 1914 ; Lt. 1915.

Hughes, George Arthur ;
M.B. 1875 ; Lt. A.M.S., Feb. 1897 ; D.S.O. 1898 ; Col. 1904 ; retd. 1905 ; temp. empld., 1915.

Hughes, Hamilton ;
B.A. 1902 ; Pte. 10 R. Dub. Fus.

Hughes, John Blacker Aickin ;
B.A. 1901 ; M.A. 1917 ; 2 Lt. R.E., Oct. 1914 ; Temp. Capt. A.S.C., Jan. 1915.

Hughes, Thomas ;
B.A. 1908 ; Temp. Capt. 6 Conn. Rangs., Feb. 1915 ; Lt. 1915 ; A/Capt. R. Ir. Regt., 1918.

Hughes, Thomas Arthur ;
M.B. 1909 ; Lt. I.M.S., July 1910 ; Capt. 1913 ; N.W. Frontier, India, 1914–16 ; German E. Africa, 1917–19 ; Afghan War, 1919 ; despatches (E. Africa), July 1918 ; Bt. Lt.-Col. 1920, for services in Afghan War.

Hughes-Hunter, Sir William Bulkeley Hughes, Bart. ;
B.A. 1905 ; M.A. 1908 ; Capt. 6 R. W. Fus., Dec. 1913 ; Brigade Maj. 1915 ; Maj. 1916.

Humpherson, Sydney Frederick ;
Ent. 1916 ; 2 Lt. R.F.A., Jan. 1917 ; Lt. 1918.

*Hungerford, Winspeare Toye ;
Ent. 1915 ; 2 Cav. C.S., July 1917 ; 2 Lt. 1 Res. R. Cav., April 1918 ; 2 Lt. I.A., Jan. 1919 ; Lt. 1920 ; att. 12 Cav.

Hunt, Rochfort Noel ;
M.B. 1900 ; Lt. R.A.M.C., Nov. 1900 ; Maj. 1912 ; Temp. Lt.-Col. 1916 ; despatches, Jan. 1917 ; D.S.O. Jan. 1918 ; Medaille des Epidemies (en Vermeil), 1919.

*Hunt, Robert Oliver ;
B.A. 1913 ; 2 Lt. 10 R. Lanc. R., Jan. 1915 ; invalided, 1915 ; Dardanelles ; Lt. 1917.

*Hunt, William ;
M.B. 1915 ; Lt. R.A.M.C. (S.R.), Aug. 1914; Capt. 1916;
M.C. Dec. 1916; despatches, Dec. 1917 ; Lt. R A.M.C., 1918;
Temp. Capt. 1918 ; Maj. ; wounded, Oct. 1918.

*Hunt, William Victor ;
Ent. 1913 ; 2 Lt. A.S.C., March 1915; Lt. 1915; invalided;
Dardanelles.

Hunter, Duncan Francis ;
M.B. and M.D. 1908 ; Lt. R.A.M.C., Nov. 1915 ; West Lanca-
shire Clearing Station ; Capt. 1916.

Hunter, Henry Hamilton ;
B.A. 1896 ; LL.D. 1901 ; Capt. Uganda Volunteer Rifles, 1915.

Hunter, John Frederick ;
Ent. 1912 ; 2 Lt. 6 R. Innis. Fus., Dec. 1914 ; wounded ; Lt.
1917.

*Hunter, William Adams ;
Ent. 1915; D.U.O.T.C. May 1918 ; volunteered and accepted.

*Hurst, Nicholas ;
Ent. 1915 ; 2 Lt. 5 R. Muns. Fus., Aug. 1915 ; A/Capt. 1917 ;
Lt. I.A., att. 9 Gurkhas, 1918 ; ; M.C. 1918 ; Capt. 1920.

Hutcheson, Robert Barrett ;
B.A. 1907 ; 2 Lt. 2 R. Ir. Rif., Feb. 1909 ; Capt. 1915 ; Lt.-Col.
1918, whilst Com. Musk. School ; Labour C. 1919.

Hutcheson, William ;
M.B. 1906 ; M.D. 1911 ; Lt. R.A.M.C., July 1915 ; Capt. 1916 ;
France.

Hutchinson, Rev. Samuel ;
B.A. 1899 ; M.A. 1902 ; Army Chaplain, 4 Cl., Feb. 1915;
France, 1915 ; M.C. Jan. 1918.

Hyde, Dermot Owen ;
M.B. 1899; Lt. R.A.M.C., Apr. 1900 ; Maj. 1912 ; D.A.D.M.S.
1915 ; despatches, June 1916, Jan. 1917, July 1919 ; D.S.O. Jan.
1917; Lt.-Col. 1918 ; C.B.E. June 1919 ; Temp. Col. ; despatches,
1919.

Hyde, Patrick George ;
M.B. 1899; Lt. R.A.M.C., June 1901 ; Maj. 1913 ; died, Aldershot, 2 March 1915.

I

Ingram, John Kells;
Ent. 1889; Lt. 14 Ches. R., May 1915; Lt. 1 Garr. Bn., Aug. 1915; Gibraltar, 1915; Capt. 1918.

Inman, Arthur Walter Patrick;
M.B. 1878; Lt. R.A.M.C., March 1872; Col. 1905; ret. 1907; temp. emp. 1915.

Irvine, Arthur Edmund Stewart;
Ent. 1898; Lt. R.A.M.C., July 1905; D.S.O.; Maj. 1915; Dep. Assist. Dir. of Med. Services, 1916; A/Lt.-Col. 1919; despatches, Jan. 1917 and Dec. 1917; Officer, Ordre de Mérete Agricole, Oct. 1919.

Irvine, Rev. Frederick Julius;
B.A. 1901; Chaplain R.N., Oct. 1909; H.M.S. "Hannibal," 1914–16; "Royal Arthur," 1916–18; "Bacchante," 1918–19.

*Irvine, John Samuels;
Ent. 1912; 2 Lt. 3,1 R. Innis. Fus., Nov. 1914; typhoid, Gallipoli, Oct. 1915; Lt. 1 R. Innis. Fus., March 1916; wounded, Oct. 1916; wounded, Feb. 1917.

Irvine, Stannus Charles Edward;
Lic. Eng. 1897; Lt. N. Rhodesian Rifles; died of wounds, German East Africa, 17 Apr. 1915.

Irvine, William John;
B.A. 1900; Pte. R. Dub. Fus.

Irwin, Alexander Eric Hardcastle;
Ent. 1898; 2 Lt. 3 R. Dub. Fus., May 1915.

Irwin, Florine Isabel;
Ent. 1916; Gen. Serv. Lab. Assist. V.A.D., R. Victoria Hosp., Netley, Aug. 1917; Nursing, V.A.D., Aug. 1918–Mar. 1919.

Irwin, Herbert Edwardes;
B.A. 1877; M.A. 1894; Lt. 97 R., Jan. 1876; Col. R. War. R. 1900; retd.; Col. commanding Depot R. W. Fus., Dec. 1914.

Irwin, Herbert Quintus;
B.A. 1907; 2 Lt. 1 Conn. Rang. May 1909; Capt. 1915; killed in action, St. Julien, 26 April 1915.

Irwin, James Murray;
M.B. and M.A.O. 1881; Maj. R.A.M.C., Feb. 1894; Col. A.M.S. 1911; D.D.M.S. 1915; Temp. Maj.-Gen. 1916; C.B. June 1917; despatches, Jan. 1917, May 1917, Dec. 1917, Dec. 1918, and July 1919; Croix d'Officier, Legion of Honour; D.M.S., 3rd Army, B.E.F., 1 917; K.C.M.G. Jan. 1918; Hon. Maj.-Gen. A.M.S. 1919.

Irwin, Rev. Percival Doherty ;
    B.A. 1908; M.A. 1911 ; Army Chaplain, 4 Cl., Apr. 1915–18.

Irwin, William James ;
    Ent. 1912 ; 2 Lt. 17 R. Ir. Rif., May 1915 ; wounded, Oct. 1916 ;
    Lt. 1917.

J

*Jackson, Claude Robert ;
    Ent. 1910; 2 Lt. R.F.A., July 1913; Lt. 1915; M.C., 1 Jan.
    1916 ; Capt. 1917 ; A/Maj. 1917.

*Jackson, Cyril Ashworth Lyndon ;
    Ent. 1916; Driver R.A.S.C., M.T., 1918–19 ; France.

*Jackson, Eugene Wentworth Disney ;
    Ent. 1912; 2 Lt. R.E., Sept. 1915; France, 1916, 1917, 1918;
    A/Capt. 1919 ; wounded, June 1917 and June 1918; M.C. Sept.
    1918.

Jackson, Francis ;
    Ent. 1902; D.I. R.I.C. ; Capt. new armies, Oct. 1914 ; Staff
    Capt. 1915.

Jackson, Gordon Alexander ;
    M.B. 1908 ; Surg. R.N., May 1909 ; retired.

*Jackson, Henry Kellett ;
    Ent. 1913 ; 2 Lt. 9 R. Ir. Fus., Oct. 1914 ; Lt. 1915.

*Jackson, James Alfred ;
    B.A. 1904; 2 Lt. R.F.A., Dec. 1915 ; Lt. 1917.

Jackson, John William Edge ;
    Ent. 1898 ; 2 Lt. A.S.C., Oct. 1915.

Jackson, Robert Best ;
    M.B. 1906 ; Lt. R.A.M.C., Dec. 1914 ; Capt. 1916.

Jackson, Robert William Henry ;
    M.B. 1887 ; M.D. 1892 ; Capt. R.A.M.C., July 1890 ; Maj. 1902 ;
    re-empld. 1914–20 ; Dardanelles, Egypt, Mesopotamia, German E.
    Africa.

*Jagoe, James Francis ;
    B.A. 1914; 2 Lt. 16 L'pool R., Jan. 1915; Capt. 1917.

Jagoe, Rev. John Arthur ;
    B.A. 1910 ; M.A. 1913 ; Army Chaplain, 4 Cl., March 1918.

James, Ernest Trevor ;
> B.A. 1914 ; 2 Lt. 10 Welsh R., Feb. 1915 ; A/Lt. 1916, whilst 2nd in command of Trench Mortar Batts. ; Lt. 1917.

James, Henry Hubert ;
> M.B. 1911 ; Lt. R.A.M.C., Sept. 1917 ; Capt. 1918.

Jameson, Charles Edward Eustace ;
> Ent. 1910 ; 2 Lt. 3 R. Dub. Fus., Aug. 1914 ; Capt. 1915 ; Lt. I.A., May 1918.

Jameson, Ernest Tooke ;
> M.B. 1907 ; Lt. R.A.M.C. ; I.E.F., Turkish Arabia ; Capt. Nov. 1916.

*Jameson, Francis Octavius ;
> Ent. 1912 ; E. African Horse.

*Jameson, Harold Gordon ;
> B.A.I. 1912 ; 2 Lt. R.E., Oct. 1914 ; killed in action, Dardanelles, 16 Aug. 1915.

*Jameson, James Edward ;
> Ent. 1909 ; Lt. 5 R. Muns. Fus., Aug. 1914 ; Capt. Jan. 1916 ; 2 Lt. 2 R. Muns. Fus. Jan. 1916 ; Italian Silver Medal for Military Valour, May 1917.

*Jameson, John Francis ;
> Ent. 1902 ; Lt. Motor Machine Gun Serv., Nov. 1914.

Jamieson, Thomas Mitchell ;
> B.A. 1887 ; L.R.C.P. & S. Edin. ; Capt. R.A.M.C., T.F., June 1915.

Jeffreys, Richard Mills ;
> Ent. 1917 ; Cadet Air Service, April 1918 ; demobilised as Hon. 2 Lt. 1919.

Jellett, Henry ;
> M.B. 1894 ; M.D. 1896 ; Master of the Rotunda Hospital ; British Red Cross, France ; despatches, May 1915 ; Croix de Guerre, Nov. 1915 ; Croix de la Couronne (Belg.) 1916 ; C.O. Munro Ambulance Corps.

Jellicoe, Richard Carey ;
> B.A. 1898 ; 2 Lt. A.S.C., May 1900 ; Maj. 1914 ; D.S.O. ; Deputy Asst. Director of War Office, 1915-16 ; Assist. Q.M. Gen. 1916-17 ; Director of Labour, 1917 ; Temp. Brig.-Gen. 1917 ; despatches (twice).

Jencken, Francis John ;
> M.B. 1881 ; Lt. A.M.S., 1882 ; Col. and A.D.M.S., 1911 ; Sur.-Gen. 1915 ; C.B. Jan. 1918 ; commended for services, Feb. 1917 and Feb. 1918 ; Maj.-Gen. from March 1915.

*Jenkins, Cuthbert Esmond ;
> Ent. 1913; Lt. A.S.C., Aug. 1914; Pte. 7 R. Dub. Fus., 1914;
> wounded, Dardanelles, Aug. 1915; 2 Lt. 10 Bn., July 1916; Lt.
> 1918 ; A/Capt. 1918 ; Croix de Guerre, Aug. 1918.

Jennings, Cyril Cuthbert ;
> Ent. 1912; 2 Lt. 14 High. L.I., Apr. 1915; Lt. 1917 ; M.C.

Jewell, Norman Parsons ;
> M.B. 1908; M.D: 1911 ; Hon. Capt. E.Af.M.S., Dec. 1914;
> M.C. Apr. 1917 ; despatches E. A. Campaign, July 1918.

Jobson, Thomas Battersby ;
> M.B. & M.D. 1897 ; Lt. R.A.M.C., Apr. 1915; Capt. 1916.

*John, Samuel Spedding ;
> B.A. 1913; 2 Lt. 9 Ches. R., Nov. 1914; M.C., Festubert, 25
> Sept. 1915; wounded, Nov. 1915; despatches 1 Jan., 1916; Lt.
> 1915; A/Capt. 1917.

Johns, Archibald Tisdall;
> M.B. 1897; M.D. 1898 ; Lt. R.A.M.C., July 1915.

Johns, Harry French ;
> M.B. 1902; M.D. 1904 ; Lt. R.A.M.C., Jan. 1916 ; wounded,
> Oct. 1916 ; Capt. 1917.

Johns, Tyndall Stuart ;
> B.A. 1890; Lt. 12 R. Ir. Rif., Sept, 1914 ; Capt. 1915.

Johnson, Alexander Downing ;
> Ent. 1898 ; 2 Lt. 3 S. Staff. R., Jan. 1915 ; Temp. Capt. att. 2
> Bn.; killed in action, France, 25 Sept. 1915.

Johnson, Benjamin ;
> L.M. & L.Ch. 1905; M.B. 1913; Lt. R.A.M.C., July 1906;
> Capt. 1910 ; France, 1914 ; Prisoner of War, Oct. 1914–June 1915;
> Salonika, 1915; Temp. Maj. 1916; A/Lt.-Col. 1916; despatches
> July 1917 and Oct. 1917 ; D.S.O. June 1918 ; Maj. 1918.

Johnson, Edward Sandwith ;
> M.B. 1913; M.D. 1914 ; Lt. R.A.M.C., Dec. 1914 ; Capt. 1916 ;
> wounded, Sept. 1916; M.C. Sept. 1916.

Johnson, Lionel Stewart ;
> Ent. 1919 ; 2 Lt. R.F.A. Nov. 1914 ; Lt. 1916 ; A/Capt. 1917 ;
> France ; M.C.

*Johnson, Reginald ;
> M.B. 1913; M.D. 1915 ; Lt. R.A.M.C., Jan. 1916 ; Capt. 1917 ;
> gassed, Sept. 1917 ; M.B.E.

Johnson, Thomas William Gerald ;
  M.B. 1915 ; 2 Lt. 5 Conn. Rang., Nov. 1914 ; wounded, Dardanelles, Sept. 1915 ; M.C. Oct. 1915 ; Lt. R.A.M.C., Feb. 1916 ; Capt. 1917.

Johnson-Smyth, Rev. Edward ;
  B.A. 1893 ; M.A. 1898 ; Army Chaplain, 4 Cl., Aug. 1916 ; died, Rouen, 10 Feb. 1917.

*Johnston, Champagné L'Estrange ;
  Ent. 1915 ; 2 Lt. 16 R. Ir. Rif., Jan. 1915 ; 2 Lt. Army Cyclist Corps, Feb. 1915 ; Lt. 1917 ; A/Capt. 1917.

*Johnston, Edward Daniel ;
  Ent. 1911 ; Pte. R.E. June 1915.

Johnston, George Cooper ;
  Ent. 1910 ; Pte. A.S.C., Nov. 1915.

Johnston, George Jameson ;
  Med. School, 1887 ; M.B., R.U.I. ; Surg., Dublin Castle Red Cross Hospital ; Lt.-Col. R.A.M.C., Jan. 1918.

Johnston, Herbert Augustus ;
  Ent. 1907 ; Pte. new armies, Aug. 1914 ; 2 Lt. R. Flying Corps, Aug. 1915 ; killed, France, 4 March 1916.

Johnston, James Ernest ;
  M.B. 1902 ; Staff. Surg. R.N. Nov. 1911 ; Surg.-Comdr. 1917.

Johnston, Kathleen Elizabeth ;
  Ent. 1904 ; No. 4 Gen. Hosp., Versailles ; despatches, June 1915 ; Royal Red Cross decoration.

*Johnston, John Alexander Weir ;
  B.A.I. 1904 ; Lt. Ordnance Dept., Dec. 1914 ; Capt. 1915 ; Maj. 1918.

*Johnston, Meredith St. George Corbet ;
  B.A. 1915 ; Pte. A.S.C., Nov. 1915 ; Lt. A.S.C. (M.T.), Dec. 1915 ; A/Capt. and Adj. (T.F.) 1919.

*Johnston, Samuel Ralph Christopher St. George ;
  Ent. 1908 ; 2 Lt. 3 R. Ir. Regt., Jan. 1916 ; wounded, 22 Feb. 1917 ; Lt. 1917.

Johnston, Terence Greer ;
  Ent. 1916 ; 2 Lt. New Armies.

Johnston, Thomas Ernest ;
  Ent. 1914 ; 2 Lt. 6 R. Innis. Fus., Aug. 1915 ; France, Somme Battle, Guillemont, 1916 ; wounded and invalided, Oct. 1916 ; Ry. Trans. Offr. 1917 ; Lt. 1917 ; France, Messines, Ypres, 1917 ; wounded, gas-poisoned, and invalided, Aug. 1917.

106 WAR LIST, TRINITY COLLEGE, DUBLIN.

*Johnston, Wilfrid ;
Ent. 1911 ; 2 Lt. R.F.A., Nov. 1915 ; Lt. 1917 ; M.C. ; Capt.
1918, whilst Ed. Offr.

Johnston, William Walter Cuthbert ;
Ent. 1911 ; Pte., B Co., 5 Hamps. R., India.

*Jolley, John Edward ;
B.A. 1914 ; 2 Lt. 3 R. Ir. Regt., Aug. 1914 ; Lt. 1915 ; M.C. ;
A/Capt. 1917.

Joly, John Swift ;
M.B. and M.D. 1902 ; Capt. R.A.M.C., July 1917 ; Palestine,
1918.

*Jones, Alexander Thomas ;
Ent. 1914 ; Cadet, R.E., May 1916 ; 2 Lt. R.E. Aug. 1916 ;
France.

Jones, Arthur Edward Booth ;
M.B. 1901 ; M.D. 1902 ; Lt. R.A.M.C., July 1907 ; Capt. 1911 ;
A/Maj. 1918.

Jones, Cecil Vernon Hope ;
Ent. 1915 ; Pte. 3 East Anglian Field Amb., May 1915 ; L.-Cpl.
Aug. 1915.

Jones, Charles Booth ;
M.B. 1910 ; Lt. R.A.M.C., Jan. 1916 ; Capt. 1916.

*Jones, Harold Paget Evans ;
Ent. 1914 ; 2 Lt. 1 D. of Corn. L.I., Sept. 1915 ; wounded,
Sept. 1916 ; Lt. 1917 ; A/Capt. 1918 ; wounded and gassed, France,
Apr. 1918.

*Jones, Harold Richard ;
Ent. 1914 ; Sandhurst, Feb. 1915.

Jones, Julian Babington ;
M.B. 1907 ; Lt. R.A.M.C., Aug. 1908 ; Capt. 1912 ; despatches,
Feb. 1915, June 1915 ; M.C. June 1915.

Jones, Kingsmill Williams ;
M.B. 1901 ; M.D. 1903 ; Lt. R.A.M.C., T.F., Feb. 1912 ; France
1914 ; Capt. 1914 ; Capt. 3 E. Lan. Fld. Amb., 1915 ; wounded,
Hooge, 1915 ; D.S.O., Sept. 1915 ; despatches, Jan. 1916 ; wounded,
Sept. 1916 ; D.A.D.M.S. 1917 ; resigned and att. 1 Buffs. ; gassed,
May 1918 ; killed in action, Flanders, 2 Aug. 1918.

*Jones, Lewis Arthur ;
Ent. 1916 ; B.A. 1919 ; volunteered and accepted May 1918.

*Jones, Reginald Hastings ;
M.B. 1913 ; Lt. R.A.M.C., Aug. 1914 ; Capt. 1915 ; wounded,
Nov. 1918.

Jones, Theophilus Percy ;
M.B. 1890 ; Capt. R.A.M.C., July 1895 ; Lt.-Col. 1915 ; Dardanelles ; C.M.G., Jan. 1916 ; despatches, July 1916, Dec. 1917,
Dec. 1918 ; Col. 1917 ; D.D.M.S., 1918 ; C.B. Jan. 1919.

*Jordan, Percy Thomas ;
Ent. 1911 ; 2 Lt. 3, 1 R. Innis. Fus., Oct. 1914 ; killed, Dardanelles, 21 Aug. 1915.

*Jordi, Pedro Ricardo ;
B.A.I. 1907 ; Lt. R.E., Oct. 1914 ; Capt. 1915 ; A/Maj. 1918 ;
France ; Salonika.

Joughin, George ;
M.B. 1915 ; Lt. R.A.M.C., July 1915 ; Capt. 1916.

*Joule, Arthur ;
Ent. 1915 ; 2 Lt. 6 R. Ir. Fus., Jan. 1916 ; wounded, France,
Apr. 1917 ; Lt. 1917 ; prisoner of war, March 1918.

*Joy, Frederick Charles Patrick ;
B.A. 1912 ; 2 Lt. 3, 2 R. Ir. Rif., Aug. 1914 ; Lt. 1915 ; killed
in action, France, 16 June 1915.

Joy, Henry Richard Ludlow ;
M.B. 1896 ; M.D. 1899 ; Capt. R.A.M.C., Aug. 1915.

Joyce, Thomas Michael ;
Ent. 1920 ; Mercantile Marine 1914 ; Sub-Lt. R.N. Div., 1916 ;
France, 1917–18 ; Lt. Tank Corps 1918.

Joynt, Richard Lane ;
M.B. 1890 ; M.D. 1892 ; Temp., Lt.-Col. R.A.M.C., Feb. 1918 ;
O.B.E. March 1920 ; Consultant, Orthopædic Workshops.

*Julian, Ernest Lawrence ;
B.A. 1897 ; Ex-Reid Prof. of Law ; Lt. 7 R. Dub. Fus., Sept.
1914 ; died of wounds, Dardanelles, 8 Aug. 1915.

K

*Kane, Akbar Bailey Alexander ;
Ent. 1912 ; Pte. 16 Middl'x R. (Public Schs. Bn.).

Kane, Francis William ;
Ent. 1881 ; Lt. Australian A.M.C. ; Dardanelles, 1915 ; Capt.
1916.

*Kavanagh, Desmond M'Morrogh ;
>   B.A.I. 1920; Cadet D.U.O.T.C.; volunteered and accepted, 1918.

*Kavanagh, George Charles M'Morrogh ;
>   Ent. 1913; 2 Lt. R.E., May 1916; wounded, 1917; Lt. 1917.

Kaye-Parry, Eric ;
>   B.A.I. 1908; Lt. R.E., Jan. 1914; despatches, 1 Jan. 1916; Capt. 1917 ; A/Maj. 1918 ; Belgian Croix de Guerre, Feb. 1918 ; despatches (twice).

Kaye-Parry, Kenneth ;
>   B.A. 1913; Pte. R. W. Kent R., March 1916.

Kaye-Parry, Stanley ;
>   B.A. 1911; Corp. D Co. 7 R. Dub. Fus. ; 2 Lt. 7 R. Dub. Fus., Sept. 1915 ; Dardanelles ; Lt. 1917.

Keane, Francis James Alphonsus ;
>   M.B. and M.D. 1910 ; Lt. R.A.M.C., Oct. 1915 ; Capt. 191 Bronze Medal for Valour (Italy), 1919.

Keane, Henry Joseph ;
>   M.B. 1907 ; M.D. 1909; Lt. R.A.M.C., Dec. 1915 ; Capt. 1916.

Kearney, Sir Francis Edgar ;
>   B.A. 1890; LL.D. 1894 ; Capt. May 1915 ; empld. recg. duties; Knighted, 1916.

*Keating, Daniel James ;
>   Ent. 1915 ; 2 Lt. 1, 2 Leins. R., Apr. 1916; Lt. 1917; A/Capt. 1918.

*Keatinge, Gerald FitzMaurice ;
>   Ent. 1914; B.A. 1919 ; Surg. Sub.-Lt. R.N.V.R., Nov. 1916 ; H.M.S. "Coppy."

Keatley, John James ;
>   B.A. 1914 ; Surg. Prob. R.N.V.R., June 1915; H. M. S. "Oropesa"; Surg. R.N. 1917; wounded, Nov. 1917 and April 1918.

*Kee, William ;
>   Ent. 1910; Sergt. 7 R. Dub. Fus., Sept. 1914; Lt. Oct. 1915; M.C., Dec. 1916; A/Capt. 1918.

Keegan, Kevin Joseph :
>   Ent. 1912 ; Platoon Sgt. Canadian Contingent.

*Keely, Rodney Edward ;
Ent. 1913 ; 2 Lt. R.E. Aug. 1918; France 1917–19.

Keene, George Henry ;
M.B. 1902 ; M.D. 1905; Capt. R.A.M.C., May 1916.

*Keightley, Philip Charles Russell ;
Ent. 1913 ; 2 Lt. R.G.A., Dec. 1915; Lt. 1918.

Kelly, Augustine Patrick ;
Ent. 1912 ; 2 Lt. A.S.C., Oct. 1914 ; Flying Offr. R.F.C.,
July 1916; wounded, France, Mar. 1918 ; Lt. R.A.F. 1918;
M.C., Nov. 1918.

Kelly, Carlile ;
M.B. 1905 ; M.D. 1912 ; Capt. R.A.M.C., Jan. 1913;
despatches ; M.C., Feb. 1915 ; A/Major 1918.

Kelly, Charles Patrick ;
M.B. 1914 ; Lt. R.A.M.C., Aug. 1915 ; killed in action, 2 July
1916.

Kelly, David Herbert ;
Ent. 1913 ; 2 Lt. 3 R. Innis. Fus., Aug. 1914; Capt. 1915;
attchd. R. Ir. Rif. ; Ed. Instr. 1919.

Kelly, Edward James Gleeson ;
Ent. 1912 ; 2 Lt. 5 Conn. Rang., Nov. 1914 ; Lt. 1915 ; wounded ;
M.C.; A./Capt. 1917.

Kelly, Harry Beatty ;
M.B. 1902 ; Maj. R.A.M.C., Oct. 1914 ; prisoner of war, Sept.
1914–July 1915 ; Temp. Lt.-Col. whilst in command of a Fld.
Amb.; despatches and D.S.O., January 1917 ; Bar to D.S.O., July
1918 ; prisoner of war, July 1918.

*Kelly, Ignatius Joseph ;
Ent. 1913: Sandhurst, Oct. 1916 ; 2 Lt. Conn. Rang., Sept.
1917 ; gassed, March 1918.

Kelly, James Cecil ;
M.B. & M.D. 1913 ; Surg. R.N., Apr. 1914, H.M.S. " Tiger " ;
Surg.-Lt. ; H.M.S. " Vivid," Oct. 1915 ; H.M.S. " Tarantula " ;
despatches, Aug. 1917 ; D.S.C. Sept. 1917 ; Mesopotamia.

*Kelly, James Ignatius ;
B.A. 1908 ; M.Dent.Sc. 1910 ; 2 Lt. O.T.C., T.F., unattached
list, Jan. 1915 ; A/Lt. 1915.

*Kelly, Robert James ;
B.A. 1903 ; Pte. Black Watch, Aug. 1914.

*Kelly, Thomas James;
    M.B. 1913; Lt. R.A.M.C., Sp. Res., May 1913; empld. Aug.
1914; Arnott Medal, 1915; wounded, Aisne, Sept. 1914; Capt.
1916; M.C., Jan. 1917; Lt. R.A.M.C, 1917; wounded, Nov.
1917; Med. de l'Assist. Publique 1917; Capt. 1918; despatches,
June 1918; wounded, Oct. 1918; S. Stanislaus, 3 Cl. with
swords, 1918; D.A.D.M.S., 1918.

Kelly, Thomas William Gordon;
    M.B. 1887; M.D. 1888; Capt. Northern Command, York Co.,
R.A.M.C. (Militia), Nov. 1897; Maj. R.A.M.C., 1909; Sanitary
Offr.; Hon. Capt. in Army.

Kelly, William Davenport Crawley;
    M.B. 1901; Lt. R.A.M.C., Sept. 1902; Maj. 1914; Temp.
Lt.-Col. 1915; despatches, June 1916 and May 1917; D.S.O.,
June 1917; Médaille d'Honneur avec glaives.

Kempston, Noel Chester;
    Ent. 1911; 2 Lt. 4 Conn. Rang., June 1915; killed in action,
12 Oct. 1916.

Kendall, George William;
    M.B. 1893; M.D. 1895; Lt. R.A.M.C., Aug. 1914; Capt. 1915.

*Kennedy, Cecil Frederick;
    Ent. 1910; 2 Lt. 6 R. Ir. Fus., Sept. 1914; wounded, Dar-
danelles, Aug. 1915.

Kennedy, Frederick Alexander;
    B.A. 1901; Pte. A.S.C. (M.T.), Apr. 1915.

Kennedy, Henry Brew;
    B.A. 1911; Lt. A.S.C., Oct. 1914; Capt. and Adjt., Dec. 1914;
despatches, Jan. 1917; M.C., June 1917.

Kennedy, Henry Edward;
    Ent. 1900; Lt. A.S.C., June 1915; Suez, 1916; Capt. 1916.

Kennedy, William Howard;
    Ent. 1900; 2 Lt. 4 Leins. R., Oct. 1914; Lt. 1915.

Kenny, Austin;
    Ent. 1891; Pte. 7 R. Innis. Fus., Aug. 1915; France, 1916;
L.-Cpl.; killed in action, 9 Sept. 1916.

Kenny, Cecil Stacpoole;
    B.A. 1912; 2 Lt. 9 Shrops. L.I., Aug. 1915; drowned at sea,
11 Nov. 1915.

*Kenny, Foley Joseph;
    Ent. 1912; 2 Lt. 5 R. W. Fus., Aug. 1914; 2 Lt. R. Innis.
Fus., 1915; Capt. 1916.

Kenny, William Wallace ;
>M.B. 1876; Lt. A.M.S., Aug. 1877; Surg.-Gen. A.M.S., Dec. 1914 ; D.D.M.S., Northern Command ; C.B. and despatches, Jan. 1917.

Keogh, Sir Alfred ;
>M.D. (*honoris causa*) 1909; K.C.B. 1906; Surg.-Gen. A.M.S., Oct. 1914 ; Director General A.M.S ; Lt.-Gen. 1913; G.C.B., Jan. 1917; G.C.V.O.; C.H.; Grand Officer Ordre de la Couronne (Belge), Sept. 1917; Grand Officer, Legion of Honour, France, Sept. 1917; Order of White Eagle, 2 Cl., Serbia.

Kerr, Arthur Francis George ;
>M.B.1901 ; M.D. 1908 ; Lt. R.A.M.C., Sept. 1915 ; Capt. 1916.

Kerr, Rev. Frederick Hugh Woodhams ;
>B.A. 1907 ; Army Chaplain, 4 Cl., April 1918-19.

Kerr, Rev. George William ;
>B.A. 1896 ; Army Chaplain, 4 Cl., March, 1915-16.

Kerr, Henry Goldfrap Sheppard;
>Ent. 1906 ; 2 Lt. R.G.A., Oct. 1915 ; Lt. 1917.

*Kerr, Henry Forrest ;
>B.A.I. 1900; Pte. London Elec. Eng., Feb. 1916.

*Kerr, Robert Goodman ;
>B A. 1911 ; 2 Lt. 7 Innis. Fus. Sept. 1914 ; Capt. 1914 ; M.C., Jan. 1917; A/Lt.-Col. att. 9 R. Ir. Fus.; killed in action, 11 July, 1918.

Kerr, Rev. Walsingham Cook ;
>B.A. 1895 ; Army Chaplain, 4 Cl., Aug. 1915-19.

Keys, William David Acheson ;
>M.B. & M.D. 1898 ; Lt. I.M.S., June 1900; Maj. 1911 ; Persia, 1916 ; despatches, Mesopotamia, Aug. 1917 ; C.I.E., June 1919.

Kidd, Charles Roland ;
>L. Dent. Sc. 1906 ; Lt. R.A.M.C., Aug. 1918 ; Persian Gulf.

*Kidd, George Montgomery ;
>B.A. 1910 ; 2 Lt. 5 R. Ir. Fus., March 1915 ; Capt. 1915 ; Adjt.; M.C. 1915 ; Dardanelles, 1915 ; Salonika, 1916 ; Serbia ; Palestine ; France ; A/Major 1918 ; gassed and wounded, Oct. 1918.

*Kidd, Gerald Ralph ;
>Ent. 1911 ; 2 Lt. unatt., Jan. 1914 ; Lt. I.A. Sept. 1915 ; A/Capt. 1916-17 ; A/Major 1917 ; Capt. 1918.

*Kidd, John Armstrong Crozier ;
>M.B. 1916 ; Lt. (on prob.) R.A.M.C., Aug. 1914 ; Lt. Sept. 1916 ; Egypt 1917 ; Capt. 1917.

Kidd, Leonard ;
> M.B. & M.D. 1888 ; Maj. R.A.M.C., Jan. 1918.

*Kidd, William Sydney ;
> Ent. 1912 ; 2 Lt. 6 R. Muns. Fus., Sept. 1914 ; Lt. 1914 ;
> France, 1916 ; wounded and missing, reported killed in action,
> 21 March, 1918.

Kiddle, Frederick ;
> M.B. 1892 ; Lt. R.A.M.C., Jan. 1895 ; Lt.-Col. 1915 ; de-
> spatches, Feb. 1915, Jan. 1916 ; C.M.G., Jan. 1916 ; Col. A.M.S.
> 1917.

Kieran, Edward Austin ;
> Ent. 1920 ; Sapper R.E., Aug. 1914 ; France, 1916-18.

Kilbride, Patrick Joseph ;
> B.A. 1886 ; Pte. E. Af. Frontiersmen ; died of pneumonia while
> training.

Kilkelly, Charles Randolph ;
> M.B. 1883 ; Maj. A.M.S., May 1897 ; Lt.-Col. 1901 ; C.M.G.;
> M.V.O.; O.C. Convalescent Hosp., Woodcote Park, Epsom, 1916 ;
> Surg. R.M. Coll., Sandhurst, 1917.

Kilkelly, Patrick Percy :
> M.B. 1891 ; Lt. I.M.S., July 1893 ; Lt.-Col., 1913 ; India,
> 1916.

King, Charles Hume ;
> Ent. 1910 ; 2 Lt. 4 R. Ir. Fus., Oct. 1914 ; wounded, France,
> June, 1915 ; Lt. 1915 ; Salonika, 1916 ; Egypt and Palestine,
> 1917.

*King, Edward Joseph ;
> Ent. 1913 ; Temp. 2 Lt. 6 R. Innis. Fus., Sept. 1914 ;
> Dardanelles, 1915 ; Temp. Capt. 1915 ; wounded, Balkans, Nov.
> 1915 ; 2 Lt. 1916 ; Lt. 1916 ; M.C., March 1918 ; A/Capt. 1918.

*King, Francis Joseph Ord ;
> M.B. 1914 ; Lt. R.A.M.C., Dec. 1914 ; Capt. 1915 ; wounded,
> Aug. 1916 ; A/Major 1918.

*King, Gordon Ulick ;
> Ent. 1911 ; 2 Lt. 8 Ches. R., Nov. 1914 ; killed in action,
> 9 April, 1916.

*King, Maurice Baylis ;
> M.B. 1915 : Lt. R.A.M.C., S.R., Aug. 1914 ; Capt. 1916 ; M.C.,
> Jan. 1917 ; Bar to M.C., July 1917 ; A/Maj. ; despatches, 1919.

King, Rev. Richard George Salmon ;
> B.A. 1893 ; M.A. 1913 ; Army Chaplain, 4 Cl., Nov. 1914 ;
> despatches, Jan. 1917.

King, Rev. Samuel Waldron ;
B.A. 1909 ; Army Chaplain, July 1915.

King, William Ernest ;
Ent. 1904 ; Sergt. 2 Bn. Australian Inf., 1914; killed in action,
Gallipoli, 12-14 Aug. 1915.

King-Edwards, Thomas Ramsay ;
M.B. 1907; M.D. 1908 ; Surg. in charge, Red Cross Hospital,
Swyncombe House, Oxford.

*Kinghan, Robert William ;
Ent. 1911 ; 2 Lt. 8 R. Ir. Fus., Sept. 1914; Adjt. 1914 ; Capt.
1916 ; France ; despatches, Jan. 1917; New Armies, 1917 ;
wounded, March 1918; M.C., Sept. 1918.

Kingston, William Young ;
L. Dent. Sc. 1913 ; Dental Surg. Lt. R.A.M.C., March
1916 ; Capt. 1917.

*Kinsey, Edward Digby ;
Ent. 1909 ; L.R.C.P.& S.I.; Pte. R.A.M.C.; Lt. R.A.M.C., Feb.
1918 ; M.C., Nov. 1918 ; Capt.

Kirk, Rev. Paul Thomas Radford-Rowe ;
B.A. 1903 ; M.A. 1906 ; Army Chaplain, 4 Class, Oct.1915-18 ;
Egypt, 1916.

*Kirker, James Alastair ;
Ent. 1914 ; 2 Lt. R.F.C., Apr. 1916 ; France ; Lt. R.A.F. 1918.

Kirkpatrick, Henry ;
M.B. 1894 ; Lt. I.M.S., Jan. 1898 ; Maj. 1910 ; Lt.-Col. 1918.

Kirkpatrick, Robert FitzGerald ;
Ent. 1904 ; Comm. 1918.

Kirkpatrick, William ;
M.B. and M.D. 1889 ; Maj. R.A.M.C., June 1915 ; in command
1 Southern Gen. Hosp., Stourbridge, 1915 ; Commended for Services
Sept. 1917 and Feb. 1920 ; A/Lt.-Col. 1918.

Knaggs, Henry Thomas ;
M.B. 1893; Capt. R.A.M.C., July 1886 ; Col. A.M.S.
1915 ; C.B.; C.M.G., Jan. 1917 ; A.D.M.S. 1919.

Knapp, Arthur Edward ;
L.M. & L. Ch. 1907 ; R.A.M.C., June 1917 ; Capt. 1918.

Knapp, William ;
B.A.I. 1898 ; M.B. 1908 ; Lt. R.A.M.C., Oct. 1918 ; France.

*Knowles, Henry Forbes Lancelot ;
Ent. 1913 ; 2 Lt. R.F.A., Dec. 1915; Lt. 1917; France,
Flanders.

I

*Knox, Alexander Edmund ;
> B.A.I. 1912; 2 Lt. I.A. Res. of Offrs. 1st Sappers and Miners,
> Aug. 1916; Lt. 1917; Mesopotamia.

Knox, Hercules John ;
> M.B. 1906; M.D. 1907; Lt. R.A.M.C., March 1918.

Knox, Ernest Blake ;
> M.B. 1898; M.D. 1901; Lt. R.A.M.C., Nov. 1899; Maj.
> 1911; Temp. Lt.-Col., 1916; despatches, Jan. 1917; Lt.-Col.
> 1918.

Knox, Samuel Wright;
> B.A. 1896; LL.B. 1904: Capt. 16 R. Ir. Rif., Nov. 1914.

*Kyle, David Logan ;
> B.A.I. 1914; 2 Lt. R.E., Jan. 1915; killed in action near Ypres
> 19 May 1915.

Kyle, Victor Blacker ;
> M.B. 1909; M.D. 1910; Lt. R.A.M.C., June 1915; Salonika,
> 1916; Capt. 1916.

Kyrke, Rev. Vernon ;
> M.A. 1917; Army Chaplain, Aug. 1918

L

*Laidlow, Robert ;
> Ent. 1915; 2 Lt. 2 D. Gds., Jan. 1916 ; Lt. 1917.

*Laidlaw, William Allison ;
> Ent. 1916; 2 Lt. Lab. C., Feb. 1918; France 1918-19.

Laing, John Joseph ;
> Ent. 1919; Pte. R.F.A.; 2 Lt. March 1915; Lt. 1916 ; wounded,
> France, 1916; 2 Lt. R.A.F. March 1918; wounded Sept. 1918.

Laird, Arthur Hill ;
> M.B. 1909 ; Lt. R.A.M.C., May 1915 ; Capt. 1916.

Laird, Francis Morrow ;
> B.A. 1916; Pte. D. Co. 7 R. Dub. Fus., Dec. 1914; wounded,
> Suvla Bay, 9 Aug. 1915; L.-Cpl. 10 R. Dub. Fus.; 2 Lt. 8 R.
> Dub. Fus., Oct. 1916; wounded, Aug. 1917; wounded and a
> prisoner of war, March 1918.

Lamb, John ;
> B.A. 1912; M.A. 1915; 2 Lt. 11 W. Rid. R., June 1915; 2 Lt.
> M.G.C., Jan. 1916; Lt. 1917.

Lambkin, Douglas Raymond;
Ent. 1908; Inns of Court O.T.C., Sept. 1915; 2 Lt. 5 R. Dub.
Fus., Oct. 1916; Lt. 1918; M.C.

Lambkin, Ernest Charles;
M.B. 1908; Capt. R.A.M.C., July 1912; despatches, Aug. 1915,
June 1916; A/Major 1918; D.S.O. June 1918; despatches,
Gen. Allenby, Oct. 1918.

La Nauze, William;
Ent. 1912; Lt. 4 R. Ir. Rif., Jan. 1915; killed near Yyres,
16 May 1915.

Landy, Charles Herbert;
Ent. 1899; 2 Lt. R. Mun. Fus., 1904; resigned, 1910; joined
2 Inf. Bgde. S. African Force, 1915; East Africa, 1916.

Lane, George William Baillie;
Ent. 1906; Pte. R.E. Sept. 1914; 2 Lt. A.S.C., July 1915;
Lt. 1916; Inspr. of M.T. 1918.

Lane, John William;
M.B. and M.D. 1907; Capt. R.A.M.C., Feb. 1912; despatches,
May 1915, June 1915.

*Lane, Philip Armstrong;
Ent. 1912; 2 Lt. A.S.C., Sept. 1914; Temp. Lt. 1915; Lt. att.
Sco. Rif., Oct. 1918.

Lane, Samuel Armstrong;
M.B. 1912; M.D. 1913; Lt. R.A.M.C., Sept. 1914; Capt. 1915.

Lane, William Aubrey;
B.A. 1907; 2 Lt. A.S.C. (M.T.), June 1915; France, 1915;
Lt. 1916; despatches, Jan. 1917; M.C. June 1917; A/Capt. and
Adjt. 1918.

*Lane-Joynt, William Stephen Russell;
Ent. 1904; 2 Lt. 4 R. Innis. Fus., Aug. 1914; wounded, France,
13 May 1915; Lt. 1915; Capt. 1915; Record Off. 1917; Capt.
R.A.S.C. (S.R.), 1917.

Langrishe, John du Plessis;
M.B. 1906; Capt. R.A.M.C., July 1910; A/Lt.-Col. 1917;
despatches and D.S.O. Dec. 1917; Major 1919.

*Larkin, Alfred Sloan;
Ent. 1913; 2 Lt. A.S.C., Aug. 1914; Lt. 1915; Capt. 1918;
I. A. Res. of Offrs. 1918.

Latham, Donald Victor;
Ent. 1917; Surg. Sub-Lt. R.N.V.R., July 1917; Mediterranean.

116 WAR LIST, TRINITY COLLEGE, DUBLIN.

Latham, Reginald Ormsby ;
    B.A. 1893 ; Capt. Ordnance Dept., Oct. 1914 ; Major Res. of Offrs. 1917.

Lavery, John Perry ;
    B.A. 1913 ; 2 Lt. R.G.A., Jan. 1915 ; Temp. Lt. 1916 ; M.C. ; Lt. 1917.

Law, Alexander Henry ;
    B.A.I. 1899 ; Lt. R.F.A. (T.F.), Aug. 1910 ; A/Capt. 1914 ; Capt. 1916 ; France ; despatches ; wounded, 1916 ; Min. of Munitions, 1917.

Law, Samuel Horace ;
    M.B. & M.D. 1896 ; Temp. Major R.A.M.C., Oct. 1917.

Law, Thomas Pakenham ;
    B.A. 1899 ; 2 Lt. I. Gds., (S.R.), June 1915 ; att. 2 Bn. ; killed in action, Loos, 27 Aug. 1915.

Law, William Francis ;
    M.B. 1882 ; M.D. 1885 ; Lt. R.A.M.C., June 1915 ; Capt. 1916 ; A/Major 1918.

Law, William John ;
    Ent. 1902 ; 2 Lt. 7 Lan. Fus., Aug. 1910 ; Maj. 1914 ; Temp. Lt.-Col. ; killed in action, Gallipoli, 19 Dec. 1915 ; despatches ; French decoration.

Lawder, George William Dance ;
    B.A. 1909 ; Pte. Canadian E.F. ; at Front 1916 ; Canadian Light Trench Mortar Battery ; killed in action, 27 Sept. 1918.

*Lawder, Trevor Abbott ;
    M.B. 1914 ; Lt. R.A.M.C., Aug. 1914 ; Capt. 1915 ; despatches, Jan. 1916 ; Croix de Guerre, with Star, Dec. 1918 ; A/Major 1918.

*Lawler, Robert Edward ;
    Ent. 1911 ; 2 Lt. 7 R. Muns. Fus., Sept. 1914 ; Lt. 1915 ; wounded, Dardanelles, 15 Aug. 1915 ; Temp. Capt., Ry. Transport Offr. 1917.

Lawrence, George Russell ;
    Ent. 1914 ; French Red Cross, Dec. 1915 ; France 1916 ; 2 Lt. A.S.C., March 1917 ; wounded ; Staff Capt. Peace Conference, 1918 ; A/Major, War Office, 1919.

Lawrenson, Reginald Robert ;
    Ent. 1889 ; Lt.-Col. 11 High. L. I., Aug. 1915 ; France ; despatches (three times) ; D.S.O. ; Bar to D.S.O. 1918 ; died of wounds, 27 April 1918.

Lawson, Edmund Fallowes ;
>M.B. 1911 ; Lt. R.A.M.C., Nov. 1917; Capt. 1918 ; att. Chinese Lab. C., France.

*Lawther, James Murphy ;
>Ent. 1915 ; 2 Lt. M.G.C., Feb. 1917 ; wounded ; Lt. 1918.

*Layng, Arthur Edward ;
>B.A. 1915 ; LL.D. 1913 ; 2 Lt. 8 R. Dub. Fus., Aug. 1915 ; wounded, June 1916.

*Leader, Leonard William Leader ;
>Ent. 1912 ; 2 Lt. 4 Conn. Rang., Nov. 1914 ; Lt. 1916 ; France, 1916 ; wounded, Sept. 1916 ; despatches, Jan. 1917 ; 2 Lt. 2 Conn. Rang. 1917 ; att. 8 R. Innis. Fus., 1917 ; prisoner of war, Apr. 1918.

Leahy, Eugene ;
>B.A.I. 1905 ; Cadet R.G.A., March 1916 ; 2 Lt. R.G.A., Sept. 1916 ; Lt. 1918.

*Leahy, James Daly ;
>Ent. 1911 ; 2 Lt. 4 R. Ir. Fus., Aug. 1914 ; Capt. 1916 ; M.C. Oct. 1918 ; France ; Salonika ; Palestine.

Leahy, Michael Patrick ;
>M.B. 1906 ; Lt. R.A.M.C., Jan. 1907 ; Capt. 1910 ; wounded, Flanders, Sept. 1914 ; prisoner of war, Sept. 1914-July 1915 ; Major 1919.

*Leared, Donald Ivan ;
>Ent. 1917 ; Cadet R.A.F., Aug. 1918.

*Lecky, Hugh ;
>B.A. 1902 ; M.A. 1907 ; 2 Lt. 7 R. Dub. Fus. March 1915 ; Lt. 1915 ; Capt. 1916.

*Lee, Alfred Tennyson ;
>Ent. 1913 ; 2 Lt. 6 R. Muns. Fus., Sept. 1914 ; Lt. 1915 ; wounded, Suvla, Aug. 1915 ; A/Capt. 1917 ; Italy 1918 ; demobilised Sept. 1919.

*Lee, Joseph Bagnall ;
>B.A. 1908 ; LL.D. 1914 ; 2 Lt. 6 R. Muns. Fus., Sept. 1914 ; Lt. 1915 ; killed in action, Dardanelles, 8 Aug. 1915.

Lee, Reginald Henry ;
>M.B. 1903 ; Capt. I.M.S., Feb. 1909 ; Major 1917.

Lee, Robert Ernest.
>M.B. 1910 ; M.D. 1911 ; Lt. R.A.M.C., Aug. 1914 ; Capt. 1915 ; France, 1915-18 ; drowned in " Leinster," 10 Oct. 1918.

Leech, John Frederick Wolseley ;
M.B. 1904 ; M.D. 1908 ; Temp. Lt. R.A.M.C., July, 1915 ;
Capt. 1916 ; Salonika ; despatches, July 1917.

*Leeman, Percival Garmany ;
M.B. 1913 ; Lt. R.A.M.C., Jan. 1916 ; wounded, Oct. 1916 ;
Capt. 1917 ; wounded, Nov. 1918 ; M.C. Apr. 1919.

Leeper, Rev. Arthur Lindsay;
B.A. 1905 ; M.A. 1908 ; Army Chap. 4 Cl., July 1918.

Leeper, Rev. Cyril Frederick ;
B.A. 1911 ; M.A. 1919 ; Army Chap. 4 Cl., May 1918.

Leggett, William ;
M.B. 1902 ; M.D. 1910 ; Lt. R.A.M.C., Apr. 1915 ; Malta, 1915 ;
Capt. 1916.

Leland, Francis William George ;
B.A. 1899 ; 2 Lt. A.S.C., May 1900 ; Maj. 1914 ; D.S.O.;
C.B.E. ; Temp. Col. 1918 ; A/Lt.-Col. 1919 ; I.E.F. Mesopotamia
1916-1918.

*Leland, John Henry Frederick ;
B.A. 1907 ; 2 Lt. R. W. Fus., Aug. 1914 ; killed in action,
Dardanelles, 10 Aug., 1915.

Leland, Lionel Thomas Hillier ;
Ent. 1899 ; Lt. Res. of Offrs., Aug. 1914 ; Temp. Capt. 9 Worc.
R., Sept. 1914 ; Capt. 1915 ; Staff Adjt. 1918.

*Lemass, Edwin Stephen ;
B.A. 1912 : 2 Lt. A.S.C., Sept. 1915 ; France ; Capt.

*Lemass, Herbert Justin ;
Ent. 1913 ; 2 Lt. 1, 2 R. Dub. Fus., Dec. 1915 ; killed, 23 Oct.
1916.

Lemass, Peter Henry ;
M.B. 1909 ; Surg. R.N., Jan. 1915 ; Surg.-Lt.

Lemon, Robert Ernest ;
B.A.I. 1907 ; 2 Lt. 1 K.G.O. Sappers and Miners, Oct. 1917 ;
Lt. 1918.

Lenehan, Thomas Joseph ;
Med. School, 1888 ; M.B., R.U.I. ; Capt. R.A.M.C., July 1891 ;
Maj. 1903 ; Res. of Offrs., Aug. 1914-1919.

Lennon, William Sherlock ;
LL.B. 1908 ; D.I., R.I.C. ; Capt. 6 R. Dub. Fus., Nov. 1914 ;
Major 1916 ; att. Egyptian Army.

*Le Peton, Desmond Alexandre;
Ent. 1915; 2 Lt. 3 Som. L.I., Sept. 1915; killed in action, 8-9 Aug. 1916.

*Lepper, Rev. Alfred William;
B.A. 1907; M.A. 1914; 2 Lt. 1, 2 Shrops. L. I., Apr. 1917; France; prisoner of war, 21 March 1918.

*Leslie, Lionel David;
Ent. 1916; Pte. R.F.A., Jan. 1917.

*L'Estrange, Francis Albert;
M.B. 1915; Lt. R.A.M.C., March 1915; France; Capt. 1916; wounded, Sept. 1917; mentioned for service (Gen. Allenby), June 1918.

Leventon, Asher;
Med. School, 1891; F.R.C.S.I.; Capt. I.M.S., July 1898; Lt.-Col. 1915.

Levinge, George Tenison;
B.A.I. 1910; 9 Australian Lt. Horse; wounded Gaba Tepe, July 1915; Lt.

Levingston, John Learmouth;
Ent. 1913; Pte. R. Dub. Fus.; Temp. 2 Lt. 1, 2 R. Dub. Fus., Oct. 1917; France, 1916; wounded.

*Levis, Francis Arthur;
Ent. 1913; Temp. 2 Lt. 3 Lein. R., Sept. 1914; Capt. 1915; 2 Lt. Lein. R. 1915; Lt. 1916; A/Capt. 1918.

*Levis, George John Francis;
Ent. 1912; Pte. 5 Lein. R., Nov. 1914; L.-Corp.; killed in action, France, 5 Nov. 1915.

Levis, James Henry Bruce;
Ent. 1913; 2 Lt. 6 R. Ir. Rif., Nov. 1914; killed, Dardanelles, 12 Aug. 1915.

*Lewis, Henry William;
B.A.I. 1916; Cadet R.E., Oct. 1916; 2 Lt. R.E., Nov. 1917; killed in action, near St. Quentin, 12 Oct. 1918.

*Lewis, Richard George;
Ent. 1913; Temp. 2 Lt. 6 Leins. R., Aug. 1914; Temp. Lt. 1915; 2 Lt. Lein. R., 1915; Lt. 1916; Temp. Capt. 1917-18; A/Capt. 1918.

Liddy, Joseph Francis Frederick;
Ent. 1921; Staff Sergt. A.S.C., 1916; 2 Lt. R.F.C., Nov. 1917; Flying Offr. E. Coast Defences, R.A.F., 1918; Russia, 1919; 2 Cl. Order of St. Anne with swords.

Lidwell, John George Frederick ;
>Ent. 1887 ; Pte. 7 B.S.A.R. ; wounded, S. Africa.

Lidwill, Robert Arthur ;
>B.A. 1899 ; Lt.-Col. 3 R. Ir. Fus., Jan. 1912; Bt.-Col. 1918.

Lillis, Martin Michael Arthur ;
>B.A. 1913 ; Ll.B. 1914 ; 2 Lt. 1, 2 R. Ir. Regt., Sept. 1915;
>attchd. R. Flying Corps, Feb. 1916 ; killed in action, 11 Apr. 1917.

*Linden, Samuel M'Cullagh ;
>B.A. 1912; Pte. N. Irish Horse, Feb. 1916; 2 Lt. R.G.A.,
>Jan. 1917 ; 90 H. A. G. ; killed in action, 31 July 1917.

Lindsay, Andrew Watson ;
>Ent. 1916 ; 2 Lt. 7 Shrops L. I., Dec. 1917 ; M.C

*Lindsay-Young, Evelyn ;
>B.A. 1914 ; 2 Lt. unattchd. Sept. 1918; 2 Lt. I.A., Aug. 1915 ;
>attchd. 19 Punjabis ; Lt. 1915 ; Capt. 1917 ; A/Major 1917-18 ;
>Egyptian E.F., 1918-19 ; Baluchistan Fd. F., 1919-20.

*Lindsay-Young, Laurence Hingston ;
>B.A. 1913 ; T.F. India, Aug. 1914-Jan. 1915 ; 2 Lt. A.S.C.,
>Jan. 1915 ; 2 Lt. R. Sc. Fus., March 1915 ; att. 1 Bn. ; wounded,
>June, 1915 ; Lt. 1916 ; att. 1 Bn. ; Pilot R. Flying C., Oct. 1916 ;
>Capt. 1918 ; died of wounds, France, 25 Dec. 1918.

Line, Conrad William H. ;
>Ent. 1911 ; 2 Lt. A.S.C., Oct. 1914 ; France, 1915 ; Lt. 1915 ;
>Capt. 1917.

Linehan, Hugh ;
>Ent. 1916 ; 2 Lt. Labour Corps, Dec. 1917.

Lipman, Edward ;
>M.B. 1916 ; Lt. R.A.M.C. Sept. 1916 ; Capt. 1917.

Lipsett, Lewis Richard ;
>B.A. 1899 ; LL.D. 1902 ; Lt. A.S.C., Jan. 1915 ; Capt. 1915 ;
>Major 1916.

Lipsett, William Alfred ;
>B.A. 1908 ; Grenadier, 10 Bn. 1 Canadian Inf. Div. ; killed in
>action, Ypres, 23 Apr. 1915.

Little, Eric Archibald ;
>B.A. 1900 ; LL.D. 1903 ; Pte. R.A.M.C.

Little, Frederick ;
>Ent. 1919 ; A/Capt., General List ; France ; German East Africa ;
>Mesopotamia ; India.

*Little, Joseph James;
Ent. 1911; 2 Lt. 1, 2 R. Ir. Regt., Nov. 1915; Lt. 1917.

*Little, Otway Henry;
B.A. 1912; Lt. R.E., Jan. 1915; att. Survey Dept., Egypt; prisoner of war, Sinai, 1916; Capt. 1919.

Little, Richard Dermod W.;
Ent.1912; Pte. 1 Div. Australian A.M.C., Aug. 1914; wounded; Gallipoli.

*Littledale, Cyril Richard Evelyn;
Ent. 1911; 2 Lt. 3 R. Dub. Fus.; Aug. 1914; wounded, France, April 1915; Dardanelles, 1915; Capt. 1915; France; M.T., R.A.S.C., 1917; Germany, 1919.

Litton, Francis Henry;
B.A.I. 1897; 2 Lt. R.E., July, 1916; Lt. 1917; A/Capt. 1917.

*Livingston, Henry Gerald;
B.A. 1909; 2 Lt. 6 R. Muns. Fus., Oct. 1914; Capt. 1915; wounded, Dardanelles, Aug. 1915.

Lloyd, Owen Acheson;
Ent. 1920; L.-Corp. L'pool R.; France.

Lloyd, Richard Averill;
B.A. 1913; 2 Lt. 10 L'pool R., Nov. 1914; Lt. 1914; wounded, France, June 1915; Capt. 1916; att. R. Mil. Coll. 1919.

*Lloyd, Wilfrid Lewis;
Ent. 1913; Temp. 2 Lt. 7 Shrop. L.I., Sept. 1914; Temp. Lt. 1915; Temp. Capt. 1916; M.C. Oct. 1916; Lt. I.A., 1916; A/Capt. 1918; Lt. Shrop. L. I., Jan. 1917; Capt. I.A., 1919.

*Lloyd-Blood, Lancelot Ivan Neptune;
Ent. 1913; Pte. Inns of Court Bn., Aug. 1915; 2 Lt. 5 R. Dub. Fus., Jan. 1916; wounded, France, 1916; Lt. 1917; A/Capt. 1918; M.C. Dec. 1918.

Lloyd-Dodd, Alfred Ernest;
Ent. 1907; 2 Lt. 17, 10 R. Ir. Rif., Aug. 1915; New Armies, 1916; Trench Mortar Batts.

*Long, Bertram Raymond;
B.A. 1911; 2 Lt. 5 R. Ir. Regt., Oct., 1915; wounded, Sept. 1916; Lt. 1916; Lt. R.E., 1918.

Long, George Barklie;
Ent. 1903; Capt. 2, 4 R. Dub. Fus., Nov. 1914; att. 2 R. Ir. Rif. 1918.

Long, Henry William;
M.B. 1900; Lt. R.A.M.C., June 1901; Maj. 1913; prisoner of war, Sept. 1914–July 1915; Temp. Lt.-Col. 1916.

*Longworth, Ernest Victor;
Ent. 1894 ; 2 Lt. 17 R. Ir. Rif., Jan. 1916; Capt. 1916 ; New
Armies, 1916 ; Staff, Courts Martial Offr., 1918.

*Loveridge, Claude Warren ;
Ent. 1920; 2 Lt. 7 York and Lan. R., Nov. 1914 ; Lt. 1915;
A/Capt. 1916; Lt. R.E., Dec. 1917 ; France ; wounded.

Lovett, Samuel Henry Wesley ;
B.A. 1894 ; M.A. 1895 ; Chaplain R.N., May 1901 ; H.M.S.
"Vengeance," 1914–15 ; "China," 1915–16 ; R. N. Air Station,
1916–17 ; ret. 1917.

*Low, Gavin ;
B.A.I. 1913 ; Lt. R.E., Jan. 1915 ; France, 1915 ; Capt. 1916 ;
France ; A/Maj. 1918.

*Lowe, Rupert Cecil ;
M.B. 1914 ; Lt. R.A.M.C., Dec. 1915 ; Capt. 1916 ; France.

Lucas, Thomas John Rashleigh ;
M.B. 1880 ; Maj. R.A.M.C., Feb. 1893 : C.B. 1900 ; Col. A.M.S.,
1910 ; A.D.M.S. Jan. 1914; ret. 1914; re-empld. 1914 ; Officer
in charge of R. Vict. Hosp., Netley ; reward for distinguished
and meritorious service, June 1916 ; despatches, Feb. 1917 and
Sept. 1917.

*Luce, Rev. Arthur Aston, F.T.C.D. ;
B.A. 1905; D.D. 1920 ; Fellow, 1912 ; 2 Lt. O.T.C., T. F.
Unattached List, Jan. 1915 ; Lt. 12 R. Ir. Rif., June 1915 ;
France and Flanders, 1915–18 ; Capt. 1916 ; M.C. Jan. 1918.

*Lumley, Eric Alfred ;
M.B. 1914 ; Lt. R.A.M.C., Dec. 1914; France, 1914; Capt.,
Jan. 1916 ; wounded, Oct. 1917 ; M.C. June 1918.

Lumsden, John ;
M.B. 1894 ; M.D. 1895 ; Deputy Comr. of St.J.A.B. 1904 ;
Physician, Castle Red Cross Hosp., Dublin ; Maj. R.A.M.C. 1917 ;
France, 1917 ; K.B.E. May 1918.

*Lunn, James Stewart ;
B.A. 1913 ; 2 Lt. 4 R. Dub. Fus., July 1913 ; Capt. 1915.

Luther, Anthony John ;
Med. School, 1881 ; L.R.C.P. & S.I.; Capt. R.A.M.C., July
1887 ; Col. 1915; despatches, Feb. 1915, Jan. 1917, and Dec.
1918 ; A.D.M.S., B.E.F., 1915 ; A.D.M.S., France, 1915–17 ;
D.D.M.S., France, 1917–18 ; C.B. 1918 ; A.D.M.S., France,
1919.

Luther, Guy Fitzmaurice John ;
Med. School, 1888 ; L.R.C.P. & S.I.; Surg. Capt. Australian
A.M.C. ; killed, Dardanelles, Sept. 1915.

*Lyle, Arthur Nevin ;
> B.A.I. 1914; 2 Lt. R.E., Oct. 1914; Lt. 1915; Capt. 1917;
> A/Maj. 1919; Gallipoli; Serbia; Macedonia; Turkey; O.B.E.;
> despatches (three times).

*Lynch, Francis William ;
> Ent. 1913; 2 Lt. 4, 1 Conn. Rang., Aug. 1914; att. 1 Bn.;
> killed in action, Ypres, 27 Apr. 1915.

*Lynch, James Stewart ;
> Ent. 1915 ; 2 Lt. 16 L'pool R., Sept. 1915 ; 2 Lt. 1 R. Guernsey
> L.I., Mar. 1917 ; wounded and missing, 30 Nov. 1917.

Lynch, Joseph Edward ;
> Ent. 1898 ; 2 Lt. R. Ir. Fus., May 1905; Lt. 10 York R., Sept.
> 1914 ; Capt. 1915 ; killed in action, France, 26 Sept. 1915.

Lynch, Stephen Hugh ;
> Ent. 1910 ; 2 Lt. 7 London Bgde. R.F.A., Dec. 1915 ; Lt. 1917.

*Lyndon, Charles Cecil ;
> Ent. 1909 ; Cpl., Motor Despatch Rider R.E., Sept. 1914 ; 2 Lt.
> A.S.C. (M.T.) Jan. 1915 ; Capt. 1916.

Lyndon, Rev. Charles Henry Preston ;
> B.A. 1912 ; Army Chaplain, 4 Cl., March 1916 ; Egypt, 1916 ;
> Macedonia, 1916-18 ; despatches, Mar. 1918 ; Sen. Chap. 27 Div.
> Nov. 1918 ; South Russia, 1918–19 ; Military O.B E. 1919 ; Sen.
> Chap. of the Army of the Black Sea, 1919.

*Lynn-Grant, Charles James ;
> Ent. 1916 ; Garr. O.C.B., July 1917 ; 2 Lt. Serv. Bns. R. Ir.
> Fus., Sept. 1917.

*Lyons, Alex. Cuthbertson ;
> Ent. 1910 ; 2 Lt. 2 R. Innis. Fus., Aug. 1914; Lt. 1914 ; Adjt.
> 1918 ; A/Capt. 1918.

*Lyons, Robert Henry Cummins ;
> M.B. 1912; Lt. R.A.M.C., Aug. 1914 ; Capt. 1915.

Lyster, Charles George ;
> Ent. 1895 ; Pte. R.G.A.

Lyster, Philip Graves ;
> B.A. 1898 ; 2 Lt. R.A., May 1900; Maj. R.F.A., Oct. 1914.

M

Macafee, William ;
> B.A. 1903 ; Lt. A.S.C., Aug. 1915 ; Egypt, 1916.

Macan, Arthur Vernon ;
> Ent. 1899 ; 2 Lt. 88 Victoria Fusiliers, Oct. 1915 ; wounded, April 1917.

*M'Ardle, Robert ;
> Ent. 1916 ; 2 Cav. C.S., July 1917 ; 2 Lt. 1 Res. Cav. R., April 1918.

Macartney-Filgate, Edward John Patrick ;
> Ent. 1883 ; Lt.-Col. Oct. 1914 : in command 12 Lan. Fus., Sept. 1914 ; Col. 1916 ; Staff, 1917.

*Macassey, Donald Melville Livingston ;
> Ent. 1913 ; 2 Lt. A.S.C., June 1915.

*Macassey, Stephen Edgar L. ;
> B.A. 1913 ; 2 Lt. A.S.C., May 1915 ; Capt. 1915 ; Inst. R.A.S.C. Training Establishment, 1916 ; Maj. 1918.

Macbeth, Ivan Robert ;
> Ent. 1910 ; Lt. A.S.C., Sept. 1914 ; Capt. 1915.

MacCabe, Frederick Faber ;
> M.B. 1894 ; Surg. Maj. S. Irish Horse, Aug. 1914 ; despatches, Sept. 1917 ; Bt. Lt.-Col. 1919.

MacCabe, John Francis ;
> B.A.I. 1901 ; M.A. 1904 ; Lt. R.N.V.R., Aug. 1915 ; A/Lt. Comdr., 1918 ; D.S.O. ; despatches.

*M'Cahon, Robert ;
> B.A.I. 1914 ; 2 Lt. R.E., Aug. 1915 ; wounded, Feb. 1916 ; died of wounds received in action at Bonzincourt, near Arras, 30 Mar. 1918.

*M'Calden, Joseph Crawford Alfred ;
> M.B. 1914 ; Lt. R.A.M.C., Sept. 1914 : Capt. 1915.

*M'Cann, Thomas Stanislaus Michael ;
> Ent. 1914 ; Woolwich, June 1916.

*M'Carter, Frederick Buick ;
> M.B. 1912 ; Lt. R.A.M.C., Sept. 1914 ; Capt. 1915 ; France ; M.C. Feb. 1918 ; bar to M.C. Sept. 1918.

*M'Carter, William Harold Raphael ;
> M.B. 1914 ; Lt. R.A.M.C., Sept. 1914 ; Capt. 1915 ; India ; despatches, May 1917 ; wounded, July 1917 ; prisoner of war, 1918 ; mentioned for services while a prisoner of war, May 1919.

M'Carthy, Gerald Florence ;
B.A. 1917; 2 Lt. A.S.C., Nov. 1914 ; Dardanelles, 1915 ;
Lt. 1915 ; Salonika, 1916.

M'Carthy, Justin Shine ;
Ent. 1908 ; Pte. R. Fus. ; killed, 20 July, 1916.

M'Carthy, Thomas Paul ;
Ent. 1904 ; 2 Lt. A.S.C., June 1915; France, 1915; Lt.
M.G.C. July 1917.

M'Carthy, William Hilgrove Leslie ;
M.B. 1909 ; M.D. 1911 ; Capt. R.A.M.C. May 1913 ; M.O.,
Ir. Gds., France, 1914 ; wounded, 1915; despatches, June 1915,
Jan. 1916 ; M.C. Jan. 1916 ; A/Lt.-Col. 1916 ; wounded, July
1917 ; bar to M.C. Sept. 1918 ; D.S.O. Mar. 1919.

MacCartney, Henry Frederick Tucker ;
Ent. 1894 ; 2 Lt. York R., Jan. 1879 ; I.A. 1880 ; Lt.-Col.
1906 ; Recruiting Staff, Dublin 1916.

M'Caughey, William ;
Ent. 1919 ; 2 Lt. R.G.A., Nov. 1916 ; Lt. 1918 ; France;
Flanders.

M'Caul, George Barton ;
M.B. 1904 ; M.D. 1905 ; Lt. R.A.M.C., June 1915 ; France;
Capt. 1916 ; France ; Egypt ; Mesopotamia ; Macedonia ; M.C.
Nov. 1918.

M'Caul, Rev. Matthew Wilson ;
B.A. 1905 ; Indian Army Chaplain, Calcutta; Chap. to 1 High.
L.I., Mesopotamia, 1916 ; Army Chaplain, 4 Cl., April 1916.

M'Causland, Charles Edward ;
Ent. 1920 ; 2 Lt. 3 I. Gds., April 1918 ; B.E.F., France; Lt. 1919.

M'Causland, James Edward ;
M.B. 1908 ; M.D. 1909 ; Surg. R.N., Jan. 1915; H.M.S.
" Ophir " ; Surg.-Lt.

M'Caw, George Tyrrell ;
B.A.I. 1893 ; M.A., 1903 ; Lt. Depot Field Survey Bn., R.E.,
May 1918 ; France ; Capt. G.S.O. 3, War Office, att. as expert
in Survey and Geodesy to Geographical Section, General Staff.

M'Cay, James Frederick Daniel ;
Ent. 1912 ; 2 Lt. 15 R. I. Rif., June 1915 ; Lt. 1916 ; killed in
action, 27 Mar. 1918.

M'Clean, Canon Richard Arthur ;
B.A. 1891 ; LL.D. 1894 ; Army Chaplain, 4 Cl., Feb. 1915–17 ;
despatches, Feb. 1916 ; C.B.E.

M'Clelland, John ;
Ent. 1910; Lt. 6 R. Ir. Fus., Nov. 1914 ; resigned comn.; Pte.
R. Marine L.I.; wounded, Achi Baba, July 1915; Lt. R. Innis.
Fus., Aug. 1917 : wounded, Marcoign, Dec. 1917; wounded,
Villers Brelonneux, Apr. 1918.

*M'Clelland, William Erskine ;
B.A. 1912; Lt. 6 R. Muns. Fus., Dec. 1914; Lt. 1915;
wounded, Dardanelles, Aug. 1915 ; Capt. 1916 ; employed Records,
1919.

M'Clenaghan, Herbert Eric St. George ;
Ent. 1915; 2 Lt. 3 R. Ir. Fus., Jan. 1916 ; France, 1916-18 ;
wounded, Sept. 1916; Lt. 1917; I.A. Nov. 1918; India, 1918-20 ;
A/Capt. 1919 ; Capt. 1920.

M'Clintock, William James ;
Ent. 1911; Surg. Prob. R.N.V.R., 1917; H.M.S. " Hardy " ;
Surg.-Lt. R.N., July 1918.

M'Combe, Robert ;
B.A. 1907; 2 Lt. I.A. Res. of Officers, June, 1915 ; Mesopotamia, 1915, 1916 ; wounded, April, 1916; 2/103 Mahrattas,
1916; 101 Grenadiers ; Egypt, Palestine, Arabia ; Capt. 1917;
M.C. ; despatches, 1918.

M'Combe, Rev. William John ;
B.A. 1901 ; Army Chaplain, 4 Cl., Oct. 1914-17.

*M'Conkey, Alan Ivor Grey ;
Ent. 1911 ; 2 Lt. I.A., Jan. 1914 ; atthd. 4 L'pool R.; wounded,
Flanders, Apr. 1915 ; 2 Lt. 58 Vaughan's Rif. I.A., 1915; Lt. 1916 ;
Capt. 1918.

*M'Conkey, George Sydney ;
M.B. 1914 ; Lt. R.A.M.C., Aug. 1914 ; Capt. 1915.

*McConnell, Alfred ;
Ent. 1904 ; 2 Lt. R.G.A., Dec. 1916 ; Lt. 1917 ; gassed, July
1917.

*M'Cormick, Francis Joseph Harpur ;
Ent. 1910 ; 2 Lt. 8, 3 R. Dub. Fus., Sept. 1914 ; Lt., att.
1 Garr. Bn. R. Ir. Regt., 1915 ; Capt. 1917.

*M'Cormick, Hilgrove ;
B.A. 1910; 2 Lt. 3 Leins. R., Aug. 1914 ; despatches ; Temp.
Capt., Brig. Mach. Gun Offr., 1915 ; 2 Lt. 1 Leins. R., June
1915 ; M.C. July 1915 ; Instructor, Mach. G.C. 1916-18 ; Temp.
Maj. 1918 ; despatches, Mesopotamia, Aug. 1918 ; Political,
Baghdad, 1918.

*M'Cormick, Ian Campbell ;
Ent. 1914 ; Sub-Lt. Hood Bn. R.N.R., Aug. 1915; killed in
action, Jan. 1917.

*M'Cormick, John Eric ;
Ent. 1913 ; 2 Lt. 3 Leins. R., Aug. 1914 ; Lt. 1915 ; Salonika ; Capt. 1917 ; despatches.

M'Cormick, Rev. Thomas Eaton ;
B.A. 1897 ; M.A. 1905; Army Chaplain, 4 Cl., Feb. 1916–17; France.

*M'Cormick, Victor Ormsby ;
Ent. 1915 ; 2 Lt. 3 Leins. R., Nov. 1915.

M'Crea, Edward D'Arcy ;
M.B. 1917 ; Lt. R.A.M.C., July 1917 ; Capt. 1918.

M'Crea, Thomas ;
B.A. 1915; 2 Lt. 12, 11 R. Innis. Fus., Apr. 1915 ; M.C.

M'Cready, Rev. David Frederick ;
B.A. 1897 ; M.A. 1902 ; Army Chaplain, 4 Cl., Jan. 1915.

M'Cready, Henry Ernest ;
M.B. 1905 ; M.D. 1907; Capt. R.A.M.C., Apr. 1915 ; France ; despatches, May 1917 ; M.C., Jan, 1918 ; A/Lt.-Col. 1918.

M'Cready, Rev. John Davidson ;
B.A. 1893 ; M.A. 1898 ; Army Chaplain, 4 Cl., Sept. 1914–19.

M'Cready, Rev. Maurice Percy ;
B.A. 1906 ; M.A. 1912 ; Army Chaplain, Oct. 1912 ; 3rd Cl. 1915 ; B.E.F. 1915–17 ; despatches, 1915, 1916, and 1918 ; Shorncliffe 1917–19.

M'Cready, Wiclif ;
B.A. 1902 ; M.B., R.U.I.; Capt. 10 R. Ir. Rif., Nov. 1914 ; Capt. R.A.M.C., May 1916.

M'Creery, Albert Thomas James ;
M.B. 1907 ; Lt. R.A.M.C., Aug. 1908 ; Capt. 1912 ; I.E.F. to Turkish Arabia; despatches ; prisoner of war, Kut el Amara, May 1916 ; released, Nov. 1916 ; M.C., Oct. 1916 ; despatches, Oct. 1919 ; A/Major, 1918 ; died at Bombay, Sept. 1921.

M'Creery, Benjamin Thomas ;
M.B. 1879 ; R.A.M.C.

M'Cullagh, John Thomas ;
M.B. 1914 ; Lt. R.A.M.C., Nov. 1914 ; wounded and typhoid, Gallipoli ; Capt. 1916 ; severely wounded, Dublin, Apr. 1916 ; commended for services, Sept. 1917.

M'Cullagh, William Lennox ;
Ent. 1918 ; Gunner R.H.A. and R.F.A.

*M'Culloch, Robert Maxwell ;
Ent. 1913 ; 2 Lt. R.F.A., Dec. 1914 ; Lt. 1916 ; killed in action, 19 Apr. 1917.

MacCulloch, Robert Ross;
Ent. 1908; Pte. Black Watch, Sept. 1914; Motor Machine Gun Service, Sergt. No. 1 Battery, 1915; France, 1915.

McCullough, Mary Gill Caskey;
M.B. 1911; Area Medical Controller, Q.M.A.A.C., Western Command, 1918.

M'Cutcheon, James;
M.B. 1903; Staff Surg. R.N., May 1912; Surg. Cr. 1916 despatches, Apr. 1918.

Macdermott, Alfred Tudor;
B.A.I. 1893; Major R. Dub. Fus., Sept. 1917; served 1916-19.

McDermott, Samuel;
B.A. 1914; 2 Lt. R.G.A., Jan. 1916; Lt. 1917; A/Capt. 1917; B.E.F.; despatches; M.C.

M'Donald, Mark;
M.B. 1892; Lt. Comdr R.N.V.R., May 1915.

*M'Donald, Mark William;
Ent. 1914; 2 Lt. 4 R. Innis. Fus., June 1915; accidentally drowned Clonmany, Co. Donegal, 2 Aug. 1915.

MacDonnell, Lucius Gerald Armstrong;
M.B. 1890; M.D. 1900; Capt. 2 Light Horse Field Amb. Australian Imp. Force.

MacDonnell, Richard Graves;
Ent. 1881; Lt. R. Berks. R., May 1885; Capt. 1894; retd 1904; re-empld. Aug. 1914; Military Intelligence Offr., attache Naval Centre, Queenstown.

*M'Donogh, Charles Lewers;
M.B. 1916; Lt. R.A.M.C., Oct. 1916; Capt. 1917; Capt R.A.F. Med. S. 1918.

MacDowell, Francis Lewis Hartwell;
B.A. 1913; Surg.-Lt. R.N., Nov. 1917.

M'Dowell, Lawrence FitzHenry;
M.B. 1895; M.D. 1903; Lt. R.A.M.C., Jan 1916; France 1916.

M'Elwaine, Eric James Dalby;
B.A. 1909; 2 Lt. I.A., 76 Punjabis, Nov. 1911; Lt. 1913 wounded, Mesopotamia, 1915; Capt. 1915; A/Major 1918.

M'Elwaine, Percy Alexander;
B.A. and LL.B. 1907; 2 Lt. 14 R. Ir. Rif. 1916; Lt. 1918.

M'Entire, Dorothy Alexandra ;
>Ent. 1920 ; Motor Driver, A.S.C. ; France 1917-18.

M'Entire, James Thomas ;
>M.B. 1903 ; Lt. R.A.M.C., Aug. 1903 ; France, Aug. 1914 ; despatches, Oct. 1914 ; Mons Star ; Legion of Honour, Croix de Chevalier, Nov. 1914 ; Maj. 1915 ; despatches, Jan. 1916 ; Salonika 1917 ; A/Lt.-Col.; died on active service, 29 Oct. 1918.

M'Entire, Ronald Gordon John ;
>M.B. 1912 ; Lt. R.A.M.C., Sept. 1914 ; Capt. 1915 ; resigned, ill-health, May 1916.

MacFadden, Richard Read ;
>B.A.I. 1907 ; Sappers and Miners ; Mohmund ; Waziristan ; Mesopotamia ; despatches ; served 1915-19 ; Capt., July 1918, whilst with Ry. Dept.

M'Farland, Francis John Elliott ;
>B.A.I. 1909 ; Trooper, N. Ir. Horse, June 1916 ; Lt. 4 R. Ir. Fus., Aug. 1917 ; Egypt, Palestine, France ; M.C.; missing after raid near Bailleul, 22 July, 1918.

M'Farland, Rev. Edward William ;
>B.A. 1899 ; M.A. 1915 ; Army Chaplain, 4 Cl., Apr. 1916-19 ; M.C. 1917.

MacFarlane, James Erskine ;
>M.B. 1907 ; Lt. R.A.M.C., Apr. 1917 ; Capt. 1918.

*M'Ferran, Thomas Malcolm ;
>Ent. 1914 ; Cadet 7 Bn., May 1916 ; 2 Lt. R. Dub. Fus. Sept. 1916 ; empld. with R.F.C. ; reported missing 21 June 1917 ; afterwards reported killed on that date in an air fight near Bicelaere.

*M'Ferran, William Robert ;
>Ent. 1913 ; Pte. " D " Co. 7 R. Dub. Fus., Sept. 1914 ; 2 Lt. 7 Bn., Sept. 1915 ; Lt. 1917.

M'Fetridge, William Christopher ;
>M.B. 1905 ; M.D. 1907 ; Lt. R.A.M.C., Oct. 1915 ; Capt. 1916 ; Egypt.

*M'Garry, John Vernon Leslie ;
>Ent. 1913 ; 2 Lt. 6 R. Ir. Fus., Nov. 1915.

M'Garvey, George Edward ;
>Ent. 1914 ; Cpl. Motor Despatch Rider, R.E. ; 2 Lt. Serv. Bns. R. Ir. Rif., Feb. 1918.

M'Gee, William Richard Arundel ;
>Ent. 1910 ; 2 Lt. R.F.A., S.R., 1910 ; 2 Lt. R.F.A., May 1915 ; wounded, Loos, 26 Sept. 1915 ; accidentally wounded, 29 Dec. 1915 ; M.C.; Lt. 1917 ; A/Major 1918.

K

M'Gibney, Francis George;
Ent. 1909 ; Cadet, 28 Lond. R., Feb. 1916 ; 2 Lt. 4 R. Ir. Fus.,
Oct. 1916 ; Front 1917 ; att. 1 Bn.; killed in action, Roeux, 3 May
1917.

M'Gonigal, Robert William;
Ent. 1909 ; 2 Lt. R.G.A., Nov. 1914 ; M.C., Jan. 1916 ; Serbia :
Capt. 1917.

McGranahan, John Benson;
M.B. 1918 ; Lt. R.A.M.C., May 1918.

M'Ivor, William John;
M.B. 1904 ; Lt. R.A.M.C., March 1916 ; Capt. 1917.

*Mack, Gordon Sylvester Bradshaw;
Ent. 1916 ; O.T.C., Apr. 1918 ; volunteered and accepted.

Mack, Rev. Gwynn Seton Bradshaw;
B.A. 1915 ; Army Chaplain, 4 Cl., Nov. 1917.

*Mack, William Henry Bradshaw;
Ent. 1913 ; Pte. R.F.A., Feb. 1916 ; 2 Lt. R.G.A., June 1916 ;
Lt. 1917 ; A/Capt. 1917, and until demobilised, Jan. 1919 ; service
overseas with 188 Siege Battery, R.G.A., Oct. 1916 to Jan. 1919.

M'Kane, Robert William;
B.A. 1906 ; 2 Lt. R.G.A., Dec. 1916 ; Lt. 1918.

Mackay, Charles Joseph;
Ent. 1912 ; 2 Lt. 5 Leins. R., Jan. 1913 ; Capt. 1915 ; att. R.
Flying C., 1916 ; France ; M.C., Dec. 1916.

*M'Keag, Hugh Theodore Alexander;
Ent. 1910 ; B.Dent.Sc. 1915 ; 2 Lt. 3 R. Ir. Rif., Mar. 1915 ;
1 Gen. Bn. R. Ir. Fus., Sept. 1915 ; Lt. 1916 ; Capt. 1/6 Gurkha
Rif., March 1919.

*M'Keag, Philip Wolfe;
M.B. 1914 ; Lt. R.A.M.C., Feb. 1915 ; Capt. 1916 ; wounded.

M'Kee, Harry;
Ent. 1914 ; Pte. 19 R. Ir. Rif., Nov. 1915 ; 7 O. Cadet Bn.,
June 1916 ; 2 Lt. 20 R. Ir. Rif., Sept. 1916 ; joined 12 R. Ir. Rif.
in France, March 1917 ; wounded, Mouevres, 23 Nov. 1917 ; in
hospital to Sept. 1918 ; Lt. 1918 ; att. O.U.T.C. at Trinity College
to Aug. 1919.

McKenna, Francis Hector J.;
Ent. 1914 ; 2 Lt. 3 R. Dub. Fus., Aug. 1914 ; invalided out
Jan. 1915 ; Pte. 10 R. Dub. Fus., May 1916 ; France ; wounded,
1918 ; Lt. R. Dub. Fus. 1918 ; demob. 1919.

*M'Kenney, Charles Noel ;
Ent. 1915; 2 Lt. 1,2 R. Ir. Rif., Oct. 1916 ; Lt. 1918; prisoner
of war, May 1918.

MacKenzie, Kenneth Fitzgerald ;
Ent. 1919 ; 2 Lt. R.G.A., Dec. 1917 ; France ; Germany.

MacKenzie, Rev. Marcus ;
B.A. 1892 ; M A. 1912 ; M.B. Edin. ; Lt. R.A.M.C., Nov.
1915 ; Mediterranean E. F.; Capt. 1916.

*M'Keon, Michael Aloysius Vincent ;
B.A. 1914; 2 Lt. R.G.A., Oct. 1914 ; R. Flying Corps, Dec. 1915 ;
Lt. 1916.

Mackeon, Rev. Robert Church ;
B.A. 1908 ; Army Chaplain, 4 Cl., Dec. 1915–19.

M'Kew, Rev. Joseph Henry ;
B.A. 1910 ; Army Chaplain, 4 Cl., Aug. 1915 ; M.C. 1917.

M'Kew, Rev. Robert ;
B.A. 1898 ; B.D. 1902 ; Chaplain R.N., Dec. 1902 ; H.M.S.
" Cornwall," 1914-17 ; H.M.S. " Collingwood," 1917-19 ; Instr.
Comdr. 1917 ; C.B.E.

*M'Kiernan, Thomas Hugh Robinson ;
Ent. 1912 ; L.M.&L.Ch., 1918 ; Surg. Prob. R.N.V.R., H.M.S.
" Ness " ; Surg. Lt. Apr. 1918.

*M'Kinley, Rev. Harold Creighton ;
B.A. 1911 : Army Chaplain, 4 Cl., Dec. 1915–19.

M'Knight, Matthew ;
M.B. 1911 ; M.D. 1912 ; Lt. R.A.M.C., Oct. 1914 ; Capt. 1915.

*Macky, Whiteside ;
Ent. 1913 ; 2 Lt. 17 R. Ir. Rif., Jan. 1915 ; Lt. 3 King's Af.
Rif. 1917.

MacLaughlin, Arthur Maunsell ;
M.B. 1897 ; Lt. R.A.M.C., Dec. 1899 ; Maj. 1911. ; Lt.-Col.
1917 ; A/Col., A.D.M.S., France 1918 ; C.B.E., June 1919 ;
despatches 1919.

*McLean, Alexander Dewar ;
Ent. 1913 ; Pte. A.S.C., M.T., Oct. 1916 ; India, July 1917–
Dec. 1919 ; 2 Lt. 1/5 R. W. Surr. R., March 1918 ; Lt. 1919.

M'Lean, Robert Edward ;
B.A. 1880 ; M.A. 1883 ; Maj. 13 R. Ir. Rif., Feb. 1915 ; Major,
Staff, 1918.

K 2

MacLulich, John Peers ;
> M.B. 1896 ; M.D. 1899 ; Capt. R.A.M.C., May 1915 ; retired, ill-health, Oct. 1915.

MacMahon, George Robert ;
> M.B. 1890 ; Fleet Surg. R.N., May 1910 ; Surg.-Comdr.

MacMahon, Henry Herbert ;
> B.A. 1915 ; Pte. 10 R. Dub. Fus., March 1916 ; killed in action, Beaumont Hamel, France, 13 Nov. 1916.

MacMahon, James Francis ;
> Ent. 1920 ; R.F.C. Wireless Operator, Oct. 1917 ; France ; Cadet R.A.F. 1918.

MacMahon, John Aquila ;
> M.B. 1913 ; Lt. R.A.M.C., Sept. 1914 ; attchd. 1 Som. L.I. ; died of wounds received at Ypres, 12 May 1915.

McMahon, William John Alexander ;
> Ent. 1920 ; 2 Lt. M.G.C., March 1917 ; Lt. 1918 ; France ; Belgium ; Germany.

*MacManaway, James Godfrey ;
> Ent. 1916 ; Cadet, R.A.F. Cadet Wing, Stanley Camp, Kent, Aug. 1918.

MacManaway, Rev. John James ;
> B.A. 1888 ; M.A. 1918 ; Army Chaplain, 4 Cl., May 1917 ; B.E.F.

Macmanaway, Richard Thomas Ringwood ;
> Ent. 1914 ; 2 Lt. A.S.C., March 1915 ; Lt. 1917 ; R.A.F., 1918.

M'Murtrie, James ;
> Mus.B. 1902 ; Pte., No. 12617, 14 Arg. and Suth'd Highrs., July 1915.

M'Murtrie, John Malcolm ;
> Mus.D. 1915 ; No. 97764 1st, Pte. R.A.F.

MacNamara, Henry Charles ;
> B.A. and LL.B. 1910 ; 2 Lt. R.F.A., May 1914 ; Lt. 1914 ; Capt. 1918.

*Macnamara, John Philip ;
> Ent. 1911 ; M.B. 1916 ; Lt. R.A.M.C. (on prob.), Aug. 1914 ; Capt. 1917 ; N.W. Frontier, Afghanistan.

M'Naught, Kenneth Cresdee ;
> Lt. Dent. Sc. 1914 ; Surg. Dent. Lt. R.A.M.C., Nov. 1915 ; Capt. 1916 ; Mesopotamia.

M'Neight, Arthur Anderson ;
M.B. 1904 ; Lt. R.A.M.C., Jan. 1905 ; Capt. 1908 ; Capt. I.M.S. 1910 : Major 1916 ; Med. Off., 18 Inf., I.A.

M'Neight, William Robert Percy ;
M.B. and M.D. 1903; Lt. R.A.M.C., Nov. 1915; Capt. 1916 ; despatches, Nov. 1917 ; A/Maj. 1918 ; 135 Fld. Amb., France and Belgium.

MacNeile-Dixon, Francis Harold ;
B.A. 1915 ; 2 Lt. A.S.C., Jan. 1914 ; Temp. Capt. 1915 ; Capt. 1917 ; A/Maj. 1918.

MacNicol, Robert Heuston ;
M.B. 1902 ; Lt. R.A.M.C., Aug. 1903 ; Maj. 1915.

Macnie, John ;
Ent. 1892 ; Capt. and Adj. Bedf. Yeo., May, 1915 ; 2 Lt. R.F.A., Jan. 1917 ; A/Capt. 1917 ; Lt. 1918.

Macnie, William Randolph ;
Ent. 1915 ; Surg. Prob. R.N.V.R., 1917.

M'Ninch, James Watt ;
B.A. 1914 ; Pte., Motor Despatch Rider, R.E., Dec. 1915.

*Maconchy, John King ;
B.A.I. 1912 ; 2 Lt. O.T.C., T.F., unattch. list, Nov. 1911 ; Lt. 1914 ; Lt. R.E., Oct. 1918 ; Egypt.

*M'Quade, Cecil Enrys ;
Ent. 1914 ; Surg. Sub-Lt. R.N.V.R., Aug. 1916 ; H.M.S. " Arlanza."

McQuade, Rev. Frederick ;
B.A. 1391 ; Chaplain, R.N., 1899 ; H.M. Dyd., Bermuda, 1913–19.

Macraith, Hawtrey Andrews ;
B.A. 1902 ; 2 Lt. A.S.C., Sept. 1914 ; France, 1914, 1915, 1916 ; Lt. 1915 ; Capt. 1916.

*M'Swiney, Bryan Austin ;
Ent. 1912 ; Surg. Sub-Lt. R.N.V.R., Sept. 1915 ; H.M.S. " Staunch."

M'Swiney, Eugene John ;
M.B. 1915 ; Lt. R.A.M.C., July 1915 ; Capt. 1916 ; died of pneumonia on service, 26 Dec. 1919.

M'Walter, James Charles ;
M.B. 1913 ; Lt. R.A.M.C., June 1915 ; Malta ; Capt. 1916.

McWilliam, William ;
Ent. 1898 ; 2 Lt. 4 Conn. Rang., July 1915 ; A/Capt. 1917, whilst Courts Martial Offr. ; Staff, 1918.

*McWilliam, William Nicholson ;
Ent. 1914 ; 7 Cadet Bn. Jan. 1917; 2 Lt. R.G.A., March 1917;
Lt. 1918 ; France; Flanders.

*Madden, John Eusebius ;
Ent. 1913; 2 Lt. A.S.C., Nov. 1915 ; Lt. 1917.

*Madden, Robert John Bowman ;
M.B. 1914; Lt. R.A.M.C., Aug. 1914 ; Capt. 1915 ; France;
wounded, Aug. 1916; despatches, April 1917; M.C. May 1917;
A/Maj. 1918.

Madden, William Henry ;
B.A. 1909 ; 2 Lt 16 R. Ir. Rif., Feb. 1915 ; France, 1915 ; Capt.
1917 ; killed in action, 24 Mar. 1918.

*Madill, Thomas ;
Ent. 1913 ; Surg. Prob. R.N.V.R.,Sept. 1916 ; H.M.S. " North
Star."

*Magee, Albert William Darnley ;
Ent. 1907 ; M.B. 1919; Lt. (on prob.) R.A.M.C., Aug. 1914.

Magill, Robert ;
M.B. 1905 ; Capt. R.A.M.C., Dec. 1912 ; Temp. Maj. Comdg.
Field Amb. 1915 ; A/Lt.-Col. Comdg. Field Amb. 1917; despatches,
Jan. 1917 and May 1917 ; D.S.O. June 1917; Croix de Chevalier,
Legion of Honour, July 1917.

*Magill, Rupert ;
Ent. 1901 ; 2 Lt. 3 R. Dub. Fus., June 1914; Capt. 1915 ;
atthd. R. Ir. Regt.; wounded and gassed, 24 May 1915 ; Offr.
Cadet Bn. 1916 ; empld. Recg. Duties, 1917; despatches, Jan.
1917.

Magill, Rev. Waller ;
B.A. 1901 ; M.A. 1909; Acting Army Chaplain.

Magnier, William Joseph ;
B.A. 1913 ; 2 Lt. 7 R. Muns. Fus., Jan. 1915; wounded. Dardanelles, Aug. 1915 ; Lt. 1916 ; A/Capt. 1918 ; M.C.

*Magowan, John Hall ;
Ent. 1911 ; 2 Lt. R.F.A., Nov. 1915. ; wounded, Sept. 1916;
Lt. 1917 ; Staff, 1917.

Magowan, Samuel Edgar ;
Ent. 1919 ; 2 Lt. R. Ir. Rif.

Magowan, William ;
Ent. 1920 ; Pte. R.A.F., May 1918; Wireless Operator, 1919;
Home.

*Maguire, James Joseph ;
> Ent. 1914 ; 2 Lt. A.S.C., April 1915; Lt. 1917; with I.A. 1917.

*Maguire, Robert Augustine ;
> Ent. 1915 ; 3 B. Res. Bde., R.H.A., Jan. 1917 ; Lt. R.F.A., Dec. 1918.

Maguire, William Henderson ;
> Ent. 1915; Pte. 12 R. Innis. Fus., May 1917 ; France, Jan. 1918 ; 2 Lt. R. Innis. Fus., June 1918.

*Mahony, James Francis ;
> Ent. 1916 ; Cadet D.U.O.T.C., 1918 ; volunteered and accepted.

*Maitland, Walter ;
> Ent. 1910; 2 Lt. 10 S. Lan. R., July 1915; Lt. 1917.

Mallins, John Robert ;
> M.B. 1895 ; Lt. R.A.M.C., Aug. 1884; Lt.-Col. Aug. 1914 ; O.B.E.

*Mallins, Sackville O'Connor ;
> Ent. 1913 ; Sandhurst, Oct. 1916 ; 2 Lt. 1, 2 Conn. Rang., Sept. 1917 ; Lt. 1919.

Malone, Albert Edward ;
> M.B. 1911; Surg. R.N., Oct. 1912 ; China.; Persian Gulf, E. Medit. ; Red Sea ; R.N. Hospital, Pembroke Dock ; Surg.-Lt.-Cr. 1918.

Malone, Edmond Mortimer ;
> B.A. 1911; 2 Lt. unatt. Jan. 1911 ; I.A., 1913 ; Capt. 1915.

Malone, Francis Laurence Gerard ;
> Ent. 1919 ; Pte., Inns of Court O.T.C. 1918.

*Malone, George ;
> Ent. 1913 ; 2 Lt. 2 R. Ir. Regt., May 1915; Lt. 1915 ; severely wounded, Dublin, Easter, 1916 ; empld. Prisoners' of War Camp, 1917-19.

*Malone, Joseph James ;
> Ent. 1915 ; Cadet 7 Bn., May 1916 ; 2 Lt. 11 R. Dub. Fus., Sept. 1916 ; killed in action, 16 Aug. 1917.

Mander, Alfred Ernest ;
> B.A. 1914; 2 Lt. 4 W. Rid. R , Nov. 1914 ; Lt. 1916 ; Capt. 1917; killed in action, 9 Oct. 1917.

Manders, Richard ;
> B.A. 1877 ; K.C. ; C.B. 1903 ; Lt. R.N.V.R., Sept. 1915.

Manley, John Abraham ;
Ent. 1920; Temp. 2 Lt. 1, 2 R. Muns. Fus., June 1917 ;
att. 2 R. Ir. Regt. ; Lt. 1918 ; France ; wounded.

Manning, Rev. Charles Campbell ;
B.A. 1896 ; M.A. 1901 ; Army Chaplain, 4 Cl., Nov. 1914–18 ;
despatches, 1917 ; M.C. 1918.

Manning, Fitzmaurice ;
Med. School, 1884 ; L.R.C.P. & S.I. ; W. African M.S. 1897 ;
B.E.F. in Cameroons, 1914–15.

Manning, George Frederick ;
B.A. 1898 ; Lt. King's Af. Rif. ; killed, Kawriga, 9 Sept. 1914.

*****Manning, Robert Charles** ;
B.A.I. 1912; Lance-Corp. Canadian Contgt., Aug. 1914 ; 2 Lt.
R.E. April 1915; wounded, Ypres, 21 Sept. 1915 ; despatches,
3 Jan. 1916; M.C., 14 Jan. 1916 ; Capt. and Adjt. 1916 ; despatches,
Jan. 1917; D.S.O. 1917; Legion of Honour, Jan. 1918; Maj.
1918 ; 170 Tunn. Co. ; died of wounds, 6 Sept. 1918.

Manning, Thomas Edward ffrench ;
M.B. 1903 ; Capt. S. Af. Med. Corps ; invalided ; died from
exposure whilst discharging medical duties in Africa.

Manning, William Wybrants ;
B.A. 1908 ; 2 Lt. 3 Wilts. R., Mar. 1915 ; France with 2 Bn.,
1915–17, until severely wounded, 31 July 1917 ; Lt. 1917 ;
seconded to 1 King's African Rifles, 1918 ; served with it 1918–19.

*****Mannix, Edward John** ;
M.B. 1915 ; Lt. R.A.M.C., May, 1916 ; Capt. 1917.

Marks, Alexander Hammett ;
M.B. 1903 ; M.D. 1905 ; Capt. Australian A.M.C. ; attchd.
3 Austral. Fld. Artillery, July 1912 ; Gallipoli ; Lt.-Col. 1916 ;
despatches; D.S.O. Jan. 1917 ; Croix de Guerre, Nov. 1918 ;
C.B.E. 1919.

Marks, Edward Oswald ;
B.A.I. 1905 ; M.B. 1916 ; Lt. R.A.M.C. Aug. 1916 ; France ;
Capt. 1917.

Marrable, Francis Arthur ;
Ent. 1905 ; Sergt., Machine Gun Section, 7 R. Dub. Fus. ;
died 18 Aug. 1915, of wounds received at Suvla Bay.

Marrable, Harold Trevor ;
M.B. 1904 ; M.D. 1913 ; Lt. R.A.M.C., Sept. 1915.

*****Marriott, Charles Stowell** ;
Ent. 1913 ; 2 Lt. 21 Lan. Fus. Oct. 1915 ; Lt. 1916.

Marshall, George Archibald ;
M.B. 1882 ; Lt.-Col. Australian A.M.C. ; wounded, Gaba Tepe, Gallipoli, May 1915 ; D.A.D.M.S. Aug. 1915.

Marshall, Gilbert ;
M.B. 1917 ; Temp. Lt. R.A.M.C , Jan. 1918.

*Martin, Charles Andrew ;
Ent. 1912 ; 2 Lt. 6 R. Dub. Fus., Sept. 1914 ; Lt. 1915 ; wounded, Dardanelles, Aug. 1915 ; wounded and missing, reported killed in action, Serbia, 6 Dec. 1915 ; Order of White Eagle, 5th Cl., Mar. 1917.

Martin, Charles James ;
M.B. 1895 ; Maj. R.A.M.C., Sept. 1914 ; D.A.D.M.S., 2 Lond. Div., B.E.F., 1915 ; despatches, Dec. 1916 and Jan. 1917 ; O.B.E. 1919.

Martin, Charles James ;
Sc.D. (*honoris causâ*) 1912 ; Lt.-Col. Australian A.M.C., Sept. 1917 ; C.M.G. Jan. 1919.

*Martin, David Stanley ;
M.B. 1914 ; Lt. R.A.M.C., Aug. 1914 ; Capt. 1915 ; A/Maj. 1918.

*Martin, Edward Henry ;
Lic. Eng. 1914 ; 2 Lt. R.G.A., Oct. 1914 ; Lt. 1916 ; France ; Assist. Inspector, Ministry of Munitions.

*Martin, Ernest Burdsall ;
B.A. 1911 ; 2 Lt. I.A., Supply and Transport Serv., Apr. 1915 ; Capt. 1919.

Martin, Henry Graham ;
Med. School, 1890 ; L.R.C.P. & S.I. ; Lt. R.A.M.C., Jan 1889 ; Lt.-Col. 1915 ; Temp. Col. 1918 ; A.D.M.S. 1919 ; C.M.G.

*Martin, Richard Ross ;
Ent. 1913 ; 2 Lt. 5 Conn. Rang., Sept. 1914 ; Capt. 1915 ; Salonika ; Capt. M.G.C. 1917 ; R. Ir. Rif. 1918 ; Staff Capt. 1918 ; Maj. 1918 ; despatches, Feb. 1919 ; Mesopotamia.

*Martin, Thomas Shannon Patrick ;
B.A.I. 1912 , 2 Lt. 5 Conn. Rang., Sept. 1914 ; wounded, Dardanelles, Aug. 1915 ; Capt. 1916 ; Gallipoli ; Salonika ; Palestine ; France.

Martin, Thomas Stanhope Gildea ;
Med. School, 1891 ; Lt. R.A.M.C., Nov. 1914 ; Capt. 1915 ; France ; Egypt.

Martin, William Robert ;
Ent. 1915 ; B.A. 1919 ; Pte. R. Ir. Rif., April 1916 ; 2 Lt. 5 R. Ir. Rif. (S.R.), Dec. 1916 ; France, 1917 ; wounded, Cambrai, Nov. 1917 ; Lt. 1918.

*Mason, John Isaac ;
Ent. 1914 ; 2 Lt. 3 R. Suss. R., Aug. 1914 ; Lt. 1916 ; A/Capt. 1917 ; M.C.

*Mason, Thomas Godfrey ;
B.A. 1913 ; Despatch Rider, Sept. 1914 ; 2 Lt. 3 R. Ir. Rif. June 1915 ; Lt. 1916 ; wounded July, 1916.

Massy, Hugh Hammond de Moleyns ;
Ent. 1913 ; 2 Lt. 6 R. Innis. Fus., Nov. 1914 ; 2 Lt. R. Innis. Fus., Aug. 1916 ; Lt. 1916.

*Mather, Robert William ;
Ent. 1916 ; Quetta, July 1917 ; 2 Lt. I.A., Aug. 1918.

*Mathews, Richard Henry ;
M.B. and M.D. 1911 ; Civil Surgeon ; Eye Specialist ; King George V Hosp., Dublin.

Matson, John Agar ;
M.B. 1888 ; M.D. 1889 ; Lt. R.A.M.C., Jan. 1916 ; Capt. 1916.

Maunsell, Archibald John Stephens ;
B.A. 1886 ; M.A. 1889 ; 2 Lt. R. War. R., Aug. 1886 ; Maj. 1901 ; retd. 1904 ; Maj. 4 R. War. R. 1909–1918.

Maunsell, George Wyndham ;
B.A.I. 1911 ; 2 Lt. I.A. Res. of Offs. ; 2 Lt. Queen Victoria's Own Sappers and Miners ; killed in action on the Tigris, 23 Feb. 1917.

Maunsell, Richard Lucius Dixie ;
Ent. 1919 ; Cadet R.A F., 1918.

*Maunsell, Richard John Caswell ;
B.A. 1907 ; 2 Lt. 5 R. Innis. Fus., Dec. 1914 ; temp. Capt. 1915 ; Staff Capt. 1917.

Maunsell, Robert Charles Butler ;
M.B. 1894 ; Surg. Castle Red Cross Hosp., Dublin ; Temp. Maj. R.A.M.C., 83 (Dub.) Gen. Hosp., France, Apr. 1917.

*Maver, Alexander Maxwell ;
Ent. 1913 ; 2 Lt. 10 N. Staff. R., Mar. 1915 ; Lt. 1917.

Maxwell, Euphan Montgomerie ;
M.B. 1910 ; M. O. St. George's Hospital, Malta.

*Maxwell, Henry ;
Ent. 1912 ; 2 Lt. 8 Ches. R., Nov. 1914 ; Adjt. ; Temp. Capt. ; killed in action, 10 Oct. 1916.

Maxwell, Joseph Archibald ;
M.B. 1912; Surg. R.N., Apr. 1914 ; Surg. Lt.

*Maxwell, Thomas ;
Ent. 1914 ; 2 Lt. 8 R. Dub. Fus., Sept. 1914 ; France, 1915;
killed in action, 9 Sept. 1916.

May, Aylmer William ;
M.B. and M.D. 1898 ; Maj. N. Rhodesia Med. Corps, 1914–1915 ;
Maj. R.A.M.C. 1916 ; B.E.F., France.

May, Harold Gostwyck ;
B.A. 1911 ; 2 Lt. 3 Dorset R., Aug. 1914 ; died of wounds
received at St. Eloi 27 Mar. 1915.

May, Henry O'Hara Hovenden ;
M.B. and M.D. 1903; Temp. Lt. R.A.M.C., Nov. 1916 ; Capt.
1917 ; Mesopotamia ; India ; Russia.

*May, Thomas William ;
Ent. 1914; 2 Lt. 10 R. Innis. Fus., Jan. 1915 ; Lt. 1917 ;
despatches, 1917 ; M.C., 1917 ; wounded, 1918 ; A/Capt. 1918 ;
Bar to M.C., March 1919.

Mayberry, George Mahony ;
B.A. 1908 ; L.A.H., Dub. ; Lt. R.A.M.C., Feb. 1915 ; Capt.
1916.

Mayne, Rev. Howard Bertram ;
B.A. 1904 ; M.A. 1908 ; Chaplain R.N. Sept. 1908 ; H.M.S.
"Shannon" 1914-17, "Africa" 1917–18, "Vivid" 1918.

Mayne, Joseph Herbert ;
Ent. 1903 ; 2 Lt. 1 Bedf. R., May 1908 ; Capt. 1914 ; wounded,
Aisne, Sept. 1914 ; Adjt. 1916.

*Meade, Joseph Michael ;
B.A. 1912 ; 2 Lt. 15, 11 Manch. R., Nov. 1914 ; Gallipoli 1915 ;
Egypt ; Lt. 1916 ; Capt. 1917 ; wounded, Aug. 1917.

*Meade, Michael ;
Ent. 1914; 2 Lt. 5 L'pool Regt., Aug. 1914; France, 1915,
1916, 1917, 1918 ; M.C. 1915; Capt. 1916 ; despatches (twice) ;
reported missing, and afterwards killed, 9 April 1918.

*Meade, Mayo Francis ;
Ent. 1914 ; Pte. R.A.M.C., Nov. 1915 ; Mesopotamia.

*Mecredy, Cedric Cowan ;
M.B. 1916; Lt. I.M.S., Aug. 1916 ; Capt. 1917 ; retired, ill-
health, 1919.

Mecredy, Gerald Gordon ;
M.B. 1908 ; Lt. R.A.M.C., Aug. 1916 ; France ; Capt. 1917.

Mecredy, Ralph John Richard ;
> M.B. 1913 ; Lt. R.A.M.C., T.F., Nov. 1915 ; Capt. 1916.

*Medcalf, Norman Hall ;
> Ent. 1910 ; 2 Lt. 9 Ches. R., Nov. 1914 ; A. Cyclist C. 1915 ;
> Lt. 1916 ; Spl. Appt. 1917 ; Staff Capt., Provost Marshall's Branch,
> Ches. R.; France.

*Mein, Charles Benjamin ;
> Ent. 1915 ; 7 Cadet Bn., July 1916 ; 2 Lt. 11 R. Scots, Mar. 1917 ;
> Lt. 1918.

Meldon, George Edgar Pugin ;
> M.B. 1897 ; M.D. 1898 ; Temp. Capt. R.A.M.C., July 1917.

*Meldon, George James ;
> M.B. and M.D. 1912 ; Lt. R.A.M.C., Oct. 1916 ; Capt. 3 Cav.
> Field Amb.. 1 Div., B.E.F., 1917.

Meldon, James Bernard ;
> M.B. 1900 ; Lt. R.A.M.C., Jan. 1903 ; Maj. 1915 ; France.

Meldon, Philip Albert ;
> B.A. 1899 ; 2 Lt. R.A., March 1900 ; Maj. R.F.A., 1914 ;
> wounded in France, and at Gallipoli, and again in May 1918 ;
> D.S.O. ; Cmdt.'s, Assist., R.F.A. Cadet Sch., Brighton, graded
> Brig.-Maj., 1917.

Meredith, Dermot Owen ;
> B.A.I. 1914 ; 2 Lt. 4 R. Dub. Fus., Aug. 1915 ; 2 Lt. R.E., S.R.,
> Oct. 1916 ; France ; wounded.

Meredith, Edmund Richard ;
> B.A. 1906 ; British Red Cross, Italy, 1917 ; died of dysentery,
> Italy, 20 Aug. 1917.

*Meredith, Frederick William ;
> Ent. 1912 ; 2 Lt. R.G.A., Oct. 1915 ; Lt. 1917.

Mermagen, Rev. Carl Frederick ;
> B.A. 1895 ; M.A. 1899 ; Chaplain, Red Cross Hospital.

*Merrick, Thomas Barker ;
> B.A. 1914 ; 2 Lt. 11 N. Staff. R., July 1915 ; trsf. M.G.C.,
> 1916 ; M.C., June 1917 ; Capt. 1918 ; missing near Eterpigny, and
> afterwards reported killed, 2 Sept. 1918.

*Merrin, Benjamin Damer ;
> Ent. 1911 ; M.B. 1918 ; R.E., 34 Sig. Co. ; 2 Lt. 6 R. Ir. Rif.
> Oct. 1915 ; wounded, Sept. 1916 ; Lt. R.A.M.C., July 1918.

Mervyn, John Frederick Audley ;
> Ent. 1907 ; 2 Lt. 2 Worc. R., Dec. 1913 ; wounded, Gallipoli,
> 28 Apr. and 8 Aug. 1915 ; Capt. 1916 ; Staff 1918.

Metcalfe, Edward Dudley;
> B.A. 1907; 2 Lt. I.A., 3 Skinner's Horse, Aug. 1908; France, 1915-16; Capt. 1916; Mesopotamia, despatches; M.C., Aug. 1917.

Metcalfe, Hugh Sutherland;
> M.B. and M.D. 1910; Lt. R.A.M.C., Nov. 1917; Capt. 1918.

Methven, Colin Thomas;
> Ent. 1918; Air Mechanic, R.F.C., Oct. 1915; France, 1916; wounded, losing right eye and some fingers of left hand, May 1917; training recruits, 1917; discharged, owing to wounds, 1918.

*Middleton, Alfred Henry;
> B.A. 1911; 2 Lt. A.S.C., Nov. 1914; 2 Lt. 2 R. Muns. Fus., Oct. 1915; Lt. 1917.

*Millar, Edward Chaytor;
> Ent. 1906; Pte. R. Dub. Fus.; Sergt. D Co.; killed, Dardanelles, 9 Aug. 1915.

Millar, George McGregor;
> M.B. 1905; Lt. I.M.S., Sept. 1906; Capt. 1909; Med. Off. 24 Sikhs; wounded, July 1917; Major 1918; E. A. Campaign; O.B.E. Feb. 1919.

Millar, Howard Steen;
> M.B. 1910; M.D. 1911; Lt. R.A.M.C., May 1915; France; Capt. 1916.

Millar, Richard Gerald;
> Ent. 1919; 2 Lt. R.A.F., 1918.

Miller, Conolly Stouppe;
> M.B. 1901; Lt. R.A.M.C., July 1915; Capt. 1916.

Miller, David Joseph;
> M.B. and M.D. 1909; Lt. R.A.M.C., May 1915,

*Miller, Edward Albert;
> Ent. 1912; 2 Lt. A.S.C., Sept. 1914; Lt. 1915; Capt. 1916.

Miller, Henry Cecil Douglas;
> M.B. 1914; Lt. R.A.M.C., Sept. 1914; Capt. 1915; wounded, Jan. 1917; despatches, May 1917; M.C.

Miller, John Stewart;
> Ent. 1900; L. Cpl. D Co. 20 R. Fus., Transport Section.

Miller, Richard;
> M.B. 1883; Fleet Surgeon R.N., Feb. 1903; Surg. Capt., retired, 1917.

Miller, Rev. William Herbert Latimer;
> B.A. 1902; Army Chaplain, 4 Cl., Oct. 1907; D.S.O. 1917; 3 Cl. 1918; Temp. 2 Cl. 1918; France, 1914-19.

*Miller, William Verner ;
> Ent. 1912; 2 Lt. 14 Ches. R., May 1915.

*Milligan, Frank Joynt ;
> Ent. 1916 ; R. Flying C., Farnborough, Apr. 1917 ; 2 Lt., July 1917; Flying Offr., Oct. 1917 ; died of wounds, France, 13 March 1918.

Mills, John ;
> Med. School, 1880 ; M.B., R.U.I., 1890 ; Lt. R.A.M.C., June 1915 ; Capt. 1916.

*Milmo, Dermod Hubert Francis ;
> Ent. 1916 ; 2 Lt. 3 R. Muns. Fus., Sept. 1918.

*Minch, William ;
> Ent. 1912; 2 Lt. 3 Conn. Rang., March 1915 ; Lt. 1916 ; Capt. 1918 ; Mesopotamia ; Palestine.

Miscampbell, Thomas Pennell ;
> B.A.I. 1908 ; 2 Lt. R.E., T.F., Dec. 1915 ; Lt. 1917 ; Macedonia.

*Mitchell, Charles Hoffe ;
> B.A. 1897; Lt. 8 R. Ir. Fus., Dec. 1914 ; Lt. 7 R. Innis. Fus., 1916.

*Mitchell, Francis Sidney ;
> M.B. 1915 ; Lt. R.A.M.C., Apr. 1915 ; killed in action, France, 15 Feb. 1916.

Mitchell, Henry Blayney Owen ;
> Ent. 1913 ; 2 Lt. 7 R. Innis. Fus., Sept. 1914 ; attd. Observer R. Flying C. ; prisoner of war, Nov. 1916 ; Lt. 1917 ; M.C.

*Mitchell, Herbert ;
> M.B. 1915 ; Lt. R.A.M.C., Oct. 1915 ; wounded, Sept. 1916 ; Capt. 1916.

Mitchell, John Samuel ;
> Ent. 1907 ; Pte. N. Irish Horse ; France, 1915.

Mitchell, Lionel Arthur ;
> M.B. 1890; Capt. R.A.M.C., Jan. 1895; Lt.-Col. 1914 ; despatches, Sept. 1917.

*Mitchell, Stanley Cyril ;
> B.A. 1915 ; Surg. Prob. R. N. V. R., Oct. 1915 ; H. M. S. "Express." ; Surg.-Lt. R. N., July 1918, H. M. S. "Stoke."

Mitchell, Stuart Jocelyn ;
> B.A. 1909; Pte. R. Canadian Dragoons, Sept. 1914 ; France, 1915.

Mitchell, Wright ;
> M.B. 1904 ; Lt. R.A.M.C., July 1906 ; Capt. 1910 ; prisoner of war, Sept. 1914–July 1915 ; despatches, March 1918, Aug. 1918 ; Major 1918 ; O.B.E. Jan. 1920.

Moeran, Rev. Francis Meredith ;
> B.A. 1888 ; M.A. 1891 ; Temp. Army Chaplain, 1914.

Moeran, Robert Warner ;
> Ent. 1886 ; 7 Canadian E.F.

Moffatt, Douglas Macleod ;
> M.B. 1909 ; M.D. 1911 ; Lt. R.A.M.C., Jan. 1916 ; M.C. Nov. 1916 ; Capt. 1918.

*Moffatt, William James ;
> B.A.I. 1915 ; 2 Lt. R.E., Sept. 1915 ; wounded, July, 1916 ; Lt. 1917 ; France ; Palestine ; Egypt.

Moffatt, William James ;
> B.A.I. 1911 ; 2 Lt. R.E., Nov. 1918.

*Mollan, Robert Augustine ;
> Ent. 1913 ; B.A. 1919 ; 7 Cadet Bn., Aug. 1916.

*Molloy, Hastings Harley ;
> Ent. 1912 ; M.B. 1917 ; Surg. Prob. R.N.V.R. ; Lt. R.A.M.C., July 1917 ; Capt. 1918.

Molloy, Leonard Greenham Star ;
> M.B. and M.D. 1889 ; Capt. Duke of Lancaster's Own Yeomanry, Apr. 1904 ; Maj. 1913 ; second in command of Regt., 1915 ; France 1915–17 ; Battle of Somme ; despatches, Jan. 1917 and Apr. 1917 ; Messines Ridge ; D.S.O. June 1917 ; Staff 1917.

Molony, James Gorges Massy ;
> L.M. and L.Ch. 1907 ; M.B. 1921 ; Lt. R.A.M.C., Jan. 1916 ; Capt. 1917 ; France and Belgium, 1916–18 ; gassed, 1918 ; Prisoner of War, March 1918 ; despatches, 1918.

*Montgomery, Arthur Henry ;
> Ent. 1915 ; 2 Lt. 3 R. Ir. Regt., Jan. 1916 ; att. 12 R. Ir. Rif., 1916 ; wounded, March 1917 ; Lt. 1917 ; empld. Min. of Lab., 1919.

Montgomery, Arthur Samuel ;
> B.A. 1899 ; 2 Lt. 5 R. Innis. Fus., Feb. 1915 ; Salonika, 1916 ; Lt. 1916 ; died at Salonika, 21 June 1916.

Montgomery, Edward George ;
> Ent. 1919 ; Pte. R.A.M.C., Sept. 1914 ; Staff-Sergt. 1915 ; Salonika ; 2 Lt. R.F.A., Oct. 1917 ; France 1917.

Montgomery, Edward Henry ;
Ent. 1914 ; 2 Lt. R.F.A., Jan. 1916 ; killed in action, Eaucort, L'Abbey, France, 16 Oct. 1916.

Montgomery, Edward Hugh ;
M.B. 1893 ; M.D. 1895 ; Lt. R.A.M.C., June 1916 ; H. M. S. "Aquitania" ; Capt. 1917.

Montgomery, Richard Nathaniel ;
B.A.I. 1904 ; Pte. R.A.M.C., Oct. 1915 ; 2 Lt. R.E., July 1916 ; France ; Lt. 1918.

Mooney, Arthur Barclay ;
B.A. 1903 ; Pte. Cadet Corps, 7 Leins. R., 1915 ; France, 1916.

Mooney, Cecil Douglas ;
B.A. 1914 ; 2 Lt. A.S.C., Sept. 1914 ; M.C. Dec. 1916 ; Lt. 1917.

Mooney, Gerald Kingston ;
Ent. 1909 ; 2 Lt. 6 D. Gds., June 1915.

Mooney, Herbert Francis ;
Ent. 1915 ; Cadet, Cavalry ; 2 Lt. 1 Lan. Reserve, May 1917 , I.A. 1918.

Moore, Alexander ;
Ent. 1885 ; 2 Lt. Conn. Rang., July 1898 ; Lt.-Col. Commanding 66 Punjabis, I.E.F., Turkish Arabia, 1915 ; wounded.

•Moore, Arthur Robert ;
B.A. 1904 ; M.A. 1907 ; 2 Lt. 4 London R., Aug. 1914 ; Capt. 1915 ; wounded, France, March 1915 ; despatches, May 1915 ; M.C., June 1915 ; missing, believed killed, 1 July 1916.

Moore, Brindly Hone ;
M.B. 1916 ; Temp. Lt. R.A.M.C., Nov. 1916 ; Capt. 1917 ; Major 1918 whilst Embarcation M.O., Malta.

•Moore, Dacre William ;
Ent. 1911 ; 2 Lt. 15 R. Ir. Rif., Oct. 1914 ; Lt. M.G.C. 1915 ; killed in action, 11 June, 1916.

Moore, David Lucius Henry ;
Ent. 1912 ; 2 Lt. A.S.C., Sept. 1914 ; Lt. 1916 ; Flying Offr., R.F.C., 1917 ; Lt. 1918.

Moore, Rev. David Keys ;
B.A. 1877 ; M.A. 1881 ; English Chaplain, Lille, 1913–20 ; M.B.E. 1920.

Moore, Edward Cecil Frederick ;
B.A.I. 1905 ; 2 Lt. I.A. Res. Cavalry, Aug. 1915 ; Intelligence Dept. ; Mesopotamia, 1915 ; Staff 1916 ; M.C.

*Moore, Edward Dawson ;
Ent. 1913 ; 2 Lt. R.E., Jan. 1915; wounded, Dardanelles, Aug.
1915 ; M.C. ; Major; despatches.

*Moore, Frank Malcolm ;
Ent. 1914 ; 2 Lt. 3 R. Ir. Rif., April 1915 : wounded, France,
July 1916 ; Lt. 1916 ; Lt. I.A. 1917 ; Capt. 1920.

Moore, George Abraham ;
M.B. 1891 ; M.D. 1898 ; Capt. R.A.M.C., July 1895 ; France
1914 ; Lt.-Col. 1915 ; despatches, Dec. 1914, Jan. 1916 ; C.M.G.,
Jan. 1916 ; Col. 1917 ; despatches, Dec. 1917 ; D.S.O., Jan.
1918 ; D.D.M.S., 1918.

*Moore, Henry Geoffrey Hamilton ;
Ent. 1911 ; 2 Lt. 2 R. Ir. Regt., Aug. 1914 ; killed in action,
France, 19 May 1915.

Moore, Henry John ;
B.A. 1903 ; LL.B. 1905 ; 2 Lt. 12 Welsh R., July 1915 ;
att. 2 Bn. ; killed in action, 15 July 1916.

Moore, James ;
B.A. 1901 ; 2 Lt. R.E., May 1916 ; Lt. 1917.

*Moore, Maurice Sydney ;
M.B. 1911 : M.D. 1912 ; Surg. R.N., April 1914 ; Surg.
Lt.-Cmdr.

Moore, Robert ;
M.B. and M.D. 1905 ; Lt. R.A.M.C., April 1915 ; Capt. 1916.

Moore, Robert Henry ;
B.A. 1891 ; M.A. 1897 ; late 5 R. Ir. Regt. ; Lt. T.F. Res.,
Nov. 1914 ; Capt. attchd. 5 R.W. Kent R. ; Dental Surg. R.A.F.,
1919.

Moore, Robert Reginald Heber ;
L.M. and L.Ch. 1881 ; M.B. and M.D. 1890 ; Lt. R.A.M.C.,
Aug. 1883 : Lt.-Col., 1914 ; Deputy Asst. Director Med. Services,
Eastern Command ; Bt.-Col. 1917 ; despatches, Feb. 1917 ; A/Col.
1919.

Moore, Theodore Conyngham Kingsmill ;
B.A. 1917 ; R.F.C., May 1917 ; 2 Lt. July 1917 ; invalided,
Feb. 1918.

Moore, William Edward Armstrong ;
B.A. 1903 ; M.A. 1907 ; Pte. 7 R. Dub. Fus., 1914 ; dischd.
medically unfit, 1915.

*Moore, William Edward Cuming ;
Ent. 1912 ; 2 Lt. 1 Lowland Brig., R.F.A., Feb. 1915 ; Lt. 1916.

L

*Moore, William Michael ;
    Ent. 1913 ; 2 Lt. 7 R. Ir. Fus., Sept. 1914 ; Lt. 1917.

Moorhead, Ernest Samuel ;
    M.B. 1901; Lt. R.A.M.C., Nov. 1915; Capt. 1916.

Moorhead, George Augustine ;
    Ent. 1910 ; Motor Despatch Rider, R.E.

Moorhead, Thomas Gillman ;
    M.B. 1901 ; M.D. 1902 ; Capt. R.A.M.C., Nov. 1915 ; Con-
sulting Physician, Alexandria ; relinquished Com. 1916 ; Hon. Maj.
1917 ; Lt.-Col. 83 (Dub.) Gen. Hosp., France, July 1917.

Monroe, James Harvey ;
    B.A. 1905 ; Lt. R.N.V.R., June 1917.

•Moran, Francis ;
    Ent. 1911 ; 2 Lt. 9 Muns. Fus., Nov. 1914 ; Lt. 1915 ; killed
in action, 22 Aug. 1916.

Moran, Gerald Charles ;
    Ent. 1908 ; Lt. 5 R. Dub. Fus., Apr. 1913 ; died of gas poisoning,
France, 26 May 1915.

Moran, George Septimus ;
    Ent. 1916 ; Surg. Sub-Lt. R.N.V.R., 1918.

*Moran, John William ;
    Ent. 1907 ; 2 Lt. A.S.C., S.R., Apr. 1912 ; empld. Aug. 1914 ;
France, Dec. 1915 to July 1919 ; Temp. Capt. 1916 ; despatches,
1918 and July 1919 ; O.B.E. June 1919 ; disembodied, July 1919.

Moran, Thomas Whitley ;
    Ent. 1916 ; 2 Lt. R.G.A., Jan. 1918 ; France ; Belgium.

Morgan, Arthur Eustace ;
    B.A. 1910 ; 2 Lt. R.F.A., June 1915 ; Lt. 1917 ; A/Major,
1918.

Morgan, Eric Basil ;
    B.A.I. 1913 ; 2 Lt. A.S.C. Nov. 1914 ; 2 Lt. R.F.A., Feb. 1915 ;
Lt. A.S.C., 1918.

Morgan, Rev. Henry Richard Bertram ;
    B.A. 1892 ; Army Chaplain, 4 Cl., May 1915-16.

Morgan-Owen, Llewelyn Isaac Gethin ;
    Ent. 1898 ; 2 Lt. South Wales Bord., 1900 ; Capt. 1909 ;
Major 1915 ; Brig.-Major 40 Inf. Brig., 1915 ; Gen. Staff Offr.
1916 ; Gallipoli ; Mesopotamia ; despatches ; Bt. Lt.-Col. 1917 ;
G.S.O., Lt.-Col. 1917 ; D.S.O. ; C.M.G.

Morgan, Thomas Frederick Poole;
B,A. 1899 ; 2 Lt. R.G.A., May 1900 ; Capt. 1913; retd. 1913;
Gen. Staff Offr. 1914 ; Maj. Res. of Offrs. 1917.

*Morgan, William John;
B.A.I. 1919 ; Cadet D.U.O.T.C. ; volunteered and accepted:

Morgan, William Pringle;
M.B. 1885; Lt. R.A.M.C., Nov. 1916; Capt. 1918; Malta;
Salonika.

*Moriarty, Gerald Ruadh O'Neil;
Ent. 1918 ; R.M.C., Camberley, Dec. 1918.

Morphy, Arthur Albert;
Ent. 1913 ; 2 Lt. A.S.C., Sept. 1914; wounded near Neuve
Chapelle ; Lt. 1915 ; died of wounds, 29 Nov. 1917.

*Morphy, Edward MacGillicuddy;
B.A.I. 1908 ; 2 Lt. R.G.A., Oct. 1914 ; Lt. 1915 ; Capt. 1917;
M.C.; A/Maj. 1918 ; France.

*Morphy, George Newcomen;
B.A. 1907 ; 2 Lt. A.S.C., Aug. 1914 ; Lt. 1916; Capt. 1917.

Morris, Charles Reade Monroe;
M.B. 1905 ; Lt. R.A.M.C.. Jan. 1906 ; Capt. 1909 ; despatches,
Jan. 1917; A/Lt.-Col. Jan. 1917; D.S.O. June 1917; bar to D.S.O.

Morris, Francis John;
Med. School, 1901; Lt. R.A.M.C., Nov. 1914; Temp. Maj. 1916;
M.C. Jan. 1916.

Morris, Rev. William Frederick;
B.A. 1914 ; Army Chaplain, 4 Cl., Sept. 1915–19 ; M.C. 1917;
prisoner of war, May 1918.

•Morrison, Douglas St. George;
B.A. 1913 ; 2 Lt. R.F.A., July 1912 ; France 1914 ; Lt. 1915 ;
accidentally killed, 3 Sept. 1917.

*Morrison, Howard St. John William R.;
Ent. 1912 ; Pte. D Co. 7 R. Dub. Fus., Sept. 1914 ; 2 Lt. Dec.
1915 ; Capt. 12 R. Ir. Rif. June 1917 ; prisoner of war, March
1918.

Morrow, Robert;
M.B. 1884 ; M.D. 1912 ; Military Med. Work, London.

Morrow, Rev. Robert Moore;
B.A. 1887 ; M.A. 1893 ; Army Chaplain, 4 Cl., March 1916–20.

*Morton, David Hamill;
B.A.I. 1914 ; 2 Lt. 7 Innis. Fus., Sept. 1914 ; Lt. 1915 ; Capt.
1916; wounded, Oct. 1916; prisoner of war.

Morton, Nathaniel ;
> B.A. 1909 ; 2 Lt. I.A., 8 Cavalry, Aug. 1910 ; Lt. 1910 ; Capt. 1915 ; War Office, 1914-15.

Moses, Marcus Alwynne ;
> • Ent. 1906 ; Capt. and Adjt. 2 Rhodesian Regt. ; died in hospital, Salisbury, S. Rhodesia, 24 Dec. 1914.

'Moss, Arnold Wilson ;
> Ent. 1914 ; Pte. D Co. 7 R. Dub. Fus., Aug. 1914 ; L-Cpl. ; missing, Gallipoli, 15 Aug. 1915 ; recommended for D.C.M.

Moss, Richard Cecil ;
> B.A.I. 1900 ; R.E. 1917-19 ; Maj. ; Deputy Assist. Director, Mesopotamian Rys.

*Mostyn, William Roger Stanley ;
> Ent. 1909 ; 2 Lt. 6 R. Fus., Nov. 1912 ; Capt. and Adjt., 1915 ; War Office, 1918.

Mouillot, Augustus de Thierry ;
> Ent. 1899 ; 2 Lt. Bedf. R., July 1903 ; Lt. I.A. 1906 ; Capt. 1912 ; died of wounds, Mesopotamia, 12 Jan. 1916.

Mounsey, John Milburn ;
> Ent. 1915 ; Pte. R.A.M.C., 1915 ; Italy.

Moyers, William Arthur ;
> B.A.I. 1902 ; 2 Lt. R.E., Ry. Transport, Jan. 1916 ; Capt. 1918 ; A/Maj. 1918 ; France ; Belgium ; despatches.

Mulcahy-Morgan, William Edmund Victor ;
> Ent. 1906 ; 2 Lt. A.S.C., Apr. 1916 ; Lt. 1917.

*Mullan, Charles Seymour ;
> B.A. 1914 ; 2 Lt. R G.A. Nov. 1915 ; wounded ; Lt. 1917.

*Mullett, Hugh Aloysius ;
> Ent. 1911 ; 7 Cadet Bn., July 1916 ; 2 Lt. 10 R. Dub. Fus., Jan. 1917 ; wounded, Arras, April 1917 ; Lt. 1918.

Mullock, Richard Wilson ;
> M.B. 1900 ; M.D. 1902 ; Civil Surg. R. Sussex Regt.

Munn, Lionel Oulton Moore ;
> B.A. 1912 ; 2 Lt. 11 R. Innis. Fus., Oct.1914 ; France ; Lt. 1916 ; A/Capt., Bomb. Offr. 1918.

*Murdock, Frederick Victor ;
> Ent. 1917 ; Cadet D.U.O.T.C., 1918 ; volunteered and accepted.

Murdoch, John ;
> M.B. and M.D. 1905 ; Surg. Croydon War Hospital.

Murphy, Charles Edward;
>Med School, 1881; F.R C.S.I.; Capt. R.A.M.C., Apr. 1915;
Lord Derby's War Hospital, Warrington.

Murphy, Christopher Fowler;
>Ent. 1907; 2 Lt. Oxf. and Bucks L.I., 1910; Lt. 1914; killed in action, Ypres, 21 Oct. 1914.

*Murphy, Dermott;
>B.A. 1915; 2 Lt. R.E., Nov. 1915; Lt. 1917; A/Capt. 1917; France.

*Murphy, Frederick John;
>M.B. 1916; Lt. R.A.M.C., 1916; Capt. 1917.

Murphy, Geraldine;
>M.B. 1916; Hospital Staff, Malta, 1916; att. R.A.M.C., Jerusalem.

Murphy, Grosvenor Fitzell Leybourne;
>M.B. 1915; Lt. R.A.M.C., Jan. 1916; Capt. 1917; died of pneumonia, Norwich, 22 Nov. 1918.

*Murphy, Henry James Leopold;
>Ent. 1914; 2 Lt. R.G.A., Feb. 1916; wounded, Sept. 1916; Lt. 1917; Capt.

*Murphy, James Kennedy;
>Ent. 1914; 2 Lt. 6 Linc. R., Nov. 1914; Lt. 1915; Capt. 1917; M.C.

Murphy, James Neville Herbert;
>Ent. 1911; 2 Lt. 5 R. Dub. Fus., Aug. 1914; killed in action, France, 10 May 1915.

Murphy, John Howard Blackwood;
>Ent. 1913; Pte. R.A.M.C.; Egypt; Lt. New Armies, Feb. 1917; empld. Egyptian Labour C.

*Murphy, Johnston;
>B.A. 1914; 2 Lt. 6 R. Ir. Rif., Dec. 1914; wounded, Dardanelles, Aug. 1915; Lt. 1916; wounded, France, July 1916.

Murphy, Patrick Kennedy;
>M.B. 1912; Lt. R.A.M.C., Oct. 1914; Surgeon R.N., Oct. 1915.

Murphy, Robert Walpole;
>M.B. 1911; M.D. 1912; Lt. R.A.M.C., Jan. 1915; Capt. 1916; wounded, May, 1916; O.B E.

Murphy, William Allen;
>Ent. 1916; Surg. Prob. R.N.V.R., H.M.S. " Hornet," 1917; Mediterranean; Surg. Sub-Lt. July 1918.

*Murphy, William Haughton ;
> B.A. 1913 ; 2 Lt. 4 R. Dub. Fus., June 1915; wounded, France, Sept. 1916; despatches, Jan. 1917; Lt. 1917; Lt. 2 King's Af. Rif. 1917.

*Murray, Cyril Albert ;
> Ent. 1911 ; 2 Lt. 5 R. Ir. Fus., Sept. 1914 ; Lt. 1915 ; 2 Lt. 1 2 R. Ir. Fus., 1917 ; Lt. 1917 ; att. R.E. for Signal Service, 1917 ; A/Capt. 1918–19.

*Murray, Eric Richard ;
> Ent. 1914 ; Surg. Sub-Lt. Aug. 1917 ; H.M.S. "Poppy," N. Patrol.

Murray, Henry Walker ;
> M.B 1878 ; Lt. R.A.M.C., July 1880 ; Col. A.M.S., 1914 ; Asst. Director Med. Services, Eastern Command.

*Murray, Herbert Edward ;
> M.B. 1913 ; Lt. R.A.M.C., Oct. 1914; attchd. 16 London R.; Flanders ; Lt. I.M.S., Dec. 1915 ; Capt. 1916.

Murray, John ;
> M.B. 1886 ; Capt. R.A.M.C., T.F., Dec. 1908 ; Surg. Wandsworth Base Hosp. ; Maj. R.A.M.C. Sanitary Service, 1915.

*Murray, Menzies ;
> B.A. 1914; 2 Lt. 10 R. W. Fus., Jan. 1915 ; Lt. 1915 ; wounded, France, 1916 ; Capt. 1916 ; M.C.

·Murray, Randolph Noel Churchill ;
> Ent. 1912 ; 2 Lt. 7 R. Innis. Fus., Sept. 1914 ; Lt. 1914 ; France ; Capt. 1916 ; died of wounds in German Field Hospital, 28 Apr. 1916.

*Murray, Ronald Leslie ;
> Ent. 1912 ; Sapper R.E., Jan. 1916 ; 2 Lt. R.G.A., Nov. 1916 ; Lt. 1918 ; M.C. ; bar to M.C. Feb. 1919.

Murray, Walter Harold E. B. ;
> B.A.I. 1907 ; 2 Lt. R.E., Aug. 1915 ; Lt. 1917.

*Musgrave, Arthur Stanley Gordon ;
> B.A.I. 1912 ; Sapper, 4 Fld. Co., 2 Div., Canadian Contgt. ; wounded, Flanders, Oct. 1915; 2 Lt. R.E., May 1916; Lt. 1917; Temp. Capt. 1917 ; Gen. Staff Off. 1917 ; Palestine ; M.B.E.

*Musgrave, Christopher Norman ;
> B.A.I. 1914 : 2 Lt. R.E., Oct. 1914; Lt. 1915 ; wounded; France, Sept. 1915 ; Temp. Capt. 1917 ; Staff 1918 ; despatches (twice).

*Musgrave, Francis Edward ;
> B.A.I. 1915 ; 2 Lt. R.E., Sept. 1915 ; Lt. 1916 ; France ; M.C. Aug. 1917 ; bar to M.C. ; despatches (twice) ; Capt. 1918 ; A/Maj. 1919.

Mussen, Arthur Augustus ;
>   M.B. 1892 ; M.D. 1895 ; Maj. R.A.M.C.,. T.F., Jan. 1909 ;
>   Liverpool Merchants' Mobile Hospital, 1915 ; France, 1915 ;
>   Sanitary Services, 1919.

*Myles, Charles William Chester ;
>   M.B. 1912 ; Lt. R.A.M.C., Jan. 1914 ; Capt. 2 Welsh Field
>   Amb., 1915 ; Dardanelles ; A/Maj. 1918 ; despatches, Jan. 1918 ;
>   M.C. Jan. 1918 ; died on active service, 19 Oct. 1918.

Myles, Charles Duncan ;
>   M.B. 1900 ; Lt. R.A.M.C., Nov. 1900 ; Maj. 1912 ; despatches,
>   Oct. 1914 ; Temp. Lt.-Col., 1916 ; A.D.M.S., Egyptian, E.F.,
>   1916 ; A/Lt.-Col. 1917 ; Lt.-Col. 1918 ; O.B.E. 1918.

Myles, Edmund Henry ;
>   M.B. 1878 ; Lt. R.A.M.C., Mar. 1880 ; Maj. 1892 ; ret. 1902 ;
>   re-empld. 1914 ; commended for services, Feb. 1917.

Myles, Sir Thomas ;
>   M.B. 1881 ; M.D. 1888 ; Lt.-Col. R.A.M.C., Nov. 1914 ;
>   despatches and C.B. Jan. 1917 ; Temp. Col. 1917.

Myles, Thomas William ;
>   M.B. 1901 ; M.D. 1910 ; Staff Surg. R.N., Feb. 1910 ; Surg.-
>   Cr. ; O.B.E. ; Crown of Italy, 1916 ; **Greek Medal of Mil.
>   Merit (2 Cl.)** ; Officer of the Order of St. George by King of
>   Hellenes, Aug. 1919.

Myles, William Saunders ;
>   M.B. 1899 ; Capt. Australian A.M.C., Apr. 1917.

N

Naish, Rev. Walter ;
>   M.A. 1886 ; Lt.-Col. 4 Hamps. R., Dec. 1913 ; served first half
>   of the war and was invalided out.

Napper, William Henry ;
>   B.A.I. 1908 ; 2 Lt. A.S.C., Oct. 1914 ; Capt. 1914 ; France, 1915 ;
>   Maj. 1916 ; M.C. ; Salonika ; Caucasus ; Constantinople.

*Nash, Edgar Llewellyn Foot ;
>   M.B. 1914 ; Lt. R.A.M.C., Aug. 1914 ; Capt. 1915 ; M.C.
>   1919.

Neale, Arthur Hill ;
>   B.A. 1910 ; 2 Lt. I.A., 1 Brahmins, Feb. 1912 ; killed in action,
>   Mesopotamia, 22 Jan. 1916.

Neale, Charles Addison ;
> B.A.I. 1915 ; 2 Lt. R.E. (Inland and Water T.) June 1917 ;
> Mesopotamia.

Neilson, William Hardcastle ;
> B.A.I. 1897 ; Capt. Assam-Bengal Ry. Volunteer Rifles.

Neligan, Maurice Victor ;
> Ent. 1919 ; 2 Lt. R.F.A., Nov. 1916 ; Lt. 1918 ; France ;
> despatches.

*Nelis, James Edward Thornhill ;
> Ent. 1912 ; Lt. 5 R. Innis. Fus., Nov. 1914 ; killed, Suvla
> Bay, Gallipoli, 15 Aug. 1915.

Nelson, Francis West ;
> B.A. 1914 ; 2 Lt. 5 R Ir. Fus., Aug. 1915 ; A/Lt. 1917, Trench
> Mortar Batt.

*Nesbitt, Alan Thomas Augustine ;
> Ent. 1911 ; 2 Lt. 6 Conn. Rang., Aug. 1914 ; Temp. Lt. 1915 ;
> attchd. R. Flying Corps 1915 ; France, 1915, 1916 ; Lt. 1916.

*Nesbitt, Alexander Ewing ;
> B.A.I. 1910 ; 2 Lt. R.E., Mar. 1915 ; Lt. 1916 ; A/Cap. 1916.

Nesbitt, Francis Albert Slade ;
> Ent. 1917 ; 2 Lt. R.A.F., Sept. 1917 ; France.

Nesbitt, George Edward ;
> M.B. 1905 ; M.D. 1910 ; Acting Sanitary Officer, Dublin District,
> Aug. 1914.

*Nesbitt, Robert Wallace ;
> Ent. 1912 ; L.M. & L.Ch. 1918 ; Pte. R.A.M.C., July 1915 ;
> Surg.-Lt. H.M.S. "Implacable," N. Patrol, 1918.

Neville, Thomas Villiers Tuthill Thacker ;
> Ent. 1898 ; 2 Lt. 3 D. Gds., May 1900 ; Capt. 1909 ; killed,
> Ypres, 13 May 1915.

*Nevin, Harry Millar ;
> Ent. 1919 ; O.C.B. 1918 ; Temp. 2 Lt. Ser. Bns. R. Innis.
> Fus., 1919.

*Newcomen, George Arnold ;
> B.A. 1880 ; LL.B. 1885 ; Pte. Red Cross Motor Amb.

Newell, Frederick Arthur ;
> Ent. 1912 ; Pte. 2 Bn. 31 Inf. Brig., 10 Div. ; wounded,
> Dardanelles, Aug. 1915.

*Newell, John Geoffrey ;
> B.A. 1912 ; 2 Lt 1 W. York R., Feb. 1912 ; Capt. 1914 ; M.C.
> Jan. 1918 ; Recrtg. Staff Offr. 1919.

*Newland, Cecil Dunbar ;
Ent. 1911 ; 2 Lt. 3 Arg. and Suth'd Highrs., Aug. 1914 ;
wounded, July 1915 ; Lt. 1915 ; Capt. 1917 ; Lt. I.A. 1916 ;
Capt. 1918.

Newland, Foster Reuss ;
M.B. 1885 ; Capt. R.A.M.C., July 1886 ; A.D.M.S. 1915-16 ;
Flanders, 1915, 1916 ; D.D.M.S. 1916 ; Temp. Surg.-Gen., 1916 ;
despatches, 15 June 1916 ; C.M.G. Jan. 1917 ; despatches, Jan.
1917 ; despatches, Dec. 1917 ; C.B., Jan. 1918 ; despatches, Nov.
1918 ; Knight of Grace Order of the Hospital of St John of
Jerusalem Dec. 1918 ; D.M.S., Italy, 1918 ; Surg.-Gen. 1918 ;
K.C.M.G. 1919 ; Croce di Guerra (Italy) 1919.

Newton-Brady, Arthur ;
M.B. 1914 ; Lt. R.A.M.C., Jan. 1917 ; Capt. 1917.

Nicholson, Rev. Jaffray Brisbane ;
B.A. 1889 ; Army Chaplain, 4 Cl., July 1915–18.

Nicholson, James Frederick ;
B.A. 1916 ; 2 Lt. M.T., R.A.S.C., March 1917 ; Mesopotamia
and Persia, 1917–19.

Nicholson, John Francis ;
M.B. 1903 ; M.D. 1913 ; Lt. R.A.M.C., March 1916 ; Capt.
1917.

Nicolls, John Michael ;
M.B. 1880 ; Lt. R.A.M.C., May 1885 ; Lt.-Col. 1905 ; ret.
1906 ; re-empld. 1914–19 ; Med. Off., Mil. Detention Barracks
and Prisons.

Nixon, Sir Christopher William, Bart. ;
Ent. 1897 ; 2 Lt. R.A., March 1900 ; Maj. 1914 ; wounded,
Oct. 1916 ; D.S.O.; R.F.A. depot, Athlone, 1919.

Nolan, Alexander Shelley ;
Ent. 1913 ; 2 Lt. 8 R. Ir. Fus., May 1915 ; Lt. 1917.

Nolan, Chaworth Lewis ;
M.B. 1882 ; Fleet Surg. R.N., Aug. 1904 ; retired.

Nolan, James Noel Greene ;
M.B. 1912 ; M.D. 1913 ; Lt. R.A.M.C., June 1917.

*Nolan, Walter Spear ;
Ent. 1910 ; 2 Lt. New Armies, Nov. 1914 ; Brig. Mach. Gun
Offr., 1915 ; France, 1915 ; Capt. 1917.

Nolan, William Anthony Joseph ;
Ent. 1917 ; 2 Lt. 4 R. Muns. Fus., Sept. 1915 ; att. 1 R. Ir.
Fus. 1917 ; Lt. 1917.

Norman, Harold Hugh ;
M.B. 1898; Lt. R.A.M.C., July 1899 ; Lt.-Col. 1915 ; despatches, Jan. 1916, Jan. 1917; Bt.-Col. 1917.

*North, George Cecil ;
Ent. 1913; Cadet, R.F.A., March 1916 ; 2 Lt., June 1916 ; France 1916 ; M.C., Aug. 1917 ; Lt. 1917 ; A/Capt. 1917.

*North, Harry Lonsdale ;
Ent. 1912; 2 Lt. 3 R. Ir. Regt., July 1915 ; Lt. 1917; killed in action, 27 Sept. 1918.

Norway, Frederick Hamilton ;
Ent. 1912; 2 Lt. 2 D. of Corn. L.I., March 1915; died of wounds, France, 4 July 1915.

*Notley, Walter ;
Ent. 1915 ; Pte. I. Gds., March 1915; 2 Lt. New Armies, Aug. 1917; 2 Lt. I.A. 1917 ; M.C.

Noyes, Claud Robert Barton ;
B.A. 1913; 2 Lt. 15 Lan. Fus., Jan. 1915 ; killed in action, July 1916.

*Noyes, Edward Brownrigg ;
Ent. 1908: 2 Lt. 9 R. Berks. R., Dec. 1914 ; Capt. 1915 ; Staff Lt. War Off. 1917.

*Nunan, Manus ;
Ent. 1915; 2 Lt. 7 R. Muns. Fus., Nov. 1915 ; Lt. 1917 ; wounded for second time, Oct. 1918.

Nunan, Patrick Francis ;
M.B. & M.D. 1911 ; E. Af. Protectorate M.S. ; served in German E. Af.

Nunan, William ;
M.B. 1905; M.D. 1906 ; Capt. I.M.S. Sept. 1918 ; Mesopotamia.

*Nunan, William Alexander ;
Ent. 1917 ; Cadet D.U.O.T.C. 1918; volunteered and accepted.

Nunn, Richard ;
M.B. 1883; M.D. 1886 ; Lt. R.A.M.C., May 1915; Capt. 1916.

*Nunn, Richard Narcissus ;
Ent. 1913: 2 Lt. 7 R. Lanc. R., Nov. 1914 ; Lt. 1915 ; gassed, France, Oct. 1915 ; Lt. I.A. 1916 ; M.C.

*Nurock, Max ;
B.A. 1915 ; 2 Lt. A.S.C., Dec. 1915 ; Lt. 1917.

O

*Oakshott, William Albert Neville;
Ent. 1910; 2 Lt. 8 R. Muns. Fus., Oct. 1914; Lt. 1915; wounded,
Apr. 1916; Lt. 7 R. Ir. Rif., Jan. 1917; killed in action, 16 Aug.
1917.

*O'Beirne, John Joseph;
Ent. 1913; 2 Lt. R.F.A., Feb. 1915; wounded, Neuve Chapelle,
May 1915; Lt. 1916.

O'Brien, Charles;
M.B. 1911; M.D. 1914; Temp. Surg. R.N. Aug. 1914; Lt.
R.A.M.C., Feb. 1915; Capt. 1916; Mesopotamia; wounded, March
1917; M.C.

*O'Brien, Edwin Cecil Bray;
Ent. 1912; 2 Lt. A.S.C., Sept. 1914; Lt. 1915; Capt. 1916;
Lt. I.A. 1917; Capt. 1919.

O'Connell, Maurice James;
Ent. 1908; 2 Lt. R.F.A., Mar. 1915; Lt. 1918; 222 Bde.
I.M.B.; killed by premature explosion of a trench mortar, 30 July
1918.

O'Connor, Edwin FitzGerald;
M.B. 1912; Lt. R.A.M.C., Nov. 1914; 2 Welsh Field Amb.,
Mediterranean E.F.; Capt. 1915.

O'Connor, Francis William;
Ent. 1910; French Med. Serv.

*O'Connor, Hubert Michael;
Ent. 1904; 2 Lt. 6 Shrops. L.I., Jan. 1915; M.C., June 1916;
Capt. 1916; died of wounds, 17 Aug. 1917.

O'Connor, Rev. James;
B.A. 1910; M.A. 1913; Army Chaplain, 4 Cl., July 1915.

O'Connor, Rev. John;
B.A. 1901; Army Chaplain, 4 Cl., Jan. 1916.

O'Connor, Michael Anthony;
Ent. 1919; 2 Lt. R.A.F., 1918.

O'Connor, William Moyle;
M.B. 1887; M.D. 1897; Lt.-Col. R.A.M.C., 1913; O. C. 6
Lond. Fld. Amb., Flanders, 1915; despatches, Jan. 1916; invalided
home, Oct. 1915; died 21 Jan. 1916.

*Odbert, Arthur Noël Birchell;
Ent. 1919; 2 Lt. R.A.F., Nov. 1918.

Odlum, William Julian ;
>B.A. 1910; 2 Lt. R.F.A., 1910; Lt. Sp. Res. 1913 ; Adjt. 1915 ;
>France ; Italy; despatches (twice) ; Capt. 1916 ; M.C. Feb. 1919.

O'Donel, William James ;
>Ent. 1917 ; 2 Lt. R.E., May 1918 ; France ; Belgium.

O'Donnell, Godfrey Cathbar ;
>Ent. 1912 ; 2 Lt. 6 Leins. R., Sept. 1914 ; Gallipoli ; Serbia ;
>Lt. 1915 ; Flying Offr. R.F.C., July 1915 ; Lt. R.A.F. 1918 ;
>A/Capt. 1918.

O'Donnell, Rev. Henry Gresson Beatty ;
>B.A. 1912 ; Army Chaplain, 4 Cl., Aug. 1916–19 ; France, 1916.

*O'Donoghue, Richard John Langford ;
>B.A. 1912 ; 2 Lt. A.S.C., Sept. 1914 ; Lt. 1915 ; Maj. 1916 ;
>D.S.O., Jan. 1918.

•O'Duffy, Kevin Emmet ;
>B.A. 1912 ; 2 Lt. R. Muns. Fus., Sept. 1914 ; Lt. 1915 ; killed
>in action, Dardanelles, 15 Aug. 1915.

*Ogilvie, James Carter ;
>Ent. 1909 ; 2 Lt. 5 R. Muns. Fus., Aug. 1914 ; Egypt, 1915 ;
>Capt. 1916 ; France, 1916 ; Lt. R.A.M.C., Sept. 1917 ; M.C.
>Apr. 1918 ; Bar to M.C., Oct. 1918 ; wounded, Oct. 1918 ; French
>Croix de Guerre, Oct. 1918 ; Capt. 1918.

O'Grady, de Courcy Stamer ;
>B.A. 1909 ; 2 Lt. 5 Conn. Rang., Sept. 1914 ; died Mar. 1915.

O'Grady, Guillamore ;
>B.A. 1902 ; M.A. 1908 ; Capt. S. Ir. Horse, Aug. 1914 ; Maj.
>1916 ; Staff Capt. 1918.

O'Grady, Hugh Hammond Massy ;
>Ent. 1876 ; 2 Lt. Feb. 1881 ; Maj. 1899 ; retd. from R. Suss. R.
>1901 ; re-empld. 1914.

*O'Grady, James Joseph ;
>Ent. 1912 ; 2 Lt. R.G.A., Nov. 1915 ; France, 1916 ; wounded,
>1916 ; Lt. 1917 ; M.C., March 1919.

O'Grady, Standish Conn ;
>B.A.I. 1910 ; 2 Lt. R. Flying Corps, July 1916 ; Flight Comdr.,
>1917 ; Temp. Capt., 1917 ; France ; M.C.; despatches.

O'Grady, Standish de Courcy ;
>M.B 1896; Lt. R.A.M.C., Jan. 1898 ; Lt.-Col. 1915 ; Temp. Col.
>1916 ; despatches. Feb. 1915, May 1917, Dec. 1918 ; D.S.O., June
>1917 ; D.A.D.M.S. 1918 ; C.M.G., Jan. 1919 ; A.D.M.S. 1919.

O'Grady, William Hugh Art ;
B.A. 1908 ; Pte. 6 Middlesex.

O'Keeffe, Charles Fitzgerald ;
B.A.I. 1912 ; 2 Lt. New Armies, July 1915 ; empld. Egyptian Labour Corps, 1915 ; A/Capt. 1916 ; Lt. 1917 ; despatches (twice).

*O'Keeffe, Joseph Richard ;
Ent. 1905 ; 2 Lt. 11 N. Lan. R., Apr. 1915 ; France, 1915 ; killed in action, 4 May 1916.

O'Keeffe, Raymond Patrick ;
Ent. 1920; Cadet, 8 Hertfordshire Cadet Bn., 1918.

*O'Kelly, Harry Kane ;
Ent. 1911 ; W. Rid. R. ; 2 Lt. A.S.C., Dec. 1914 ; despatches, Oct. 1914 ; wounded, Nov. 1914 ; D.S.O., Dec. 1914 ; Temp. Capt. 1916 ; Adjt. 1916.

*O'Kelly, Richard ;
B.A. 1913 ; L.A.H. ; Lt. R.A.M.C., Aug. 1914 ; wounded, Flanders, June 1915 ; wounded, France, Oct. 1915 ; Capt. 1915 ; Palestine 1918 ; A/Lt.-Col. 1919 ; died, Cairo, 27 Dec. 1919.

*Olden, George Frederick Clifton ;
Ent. 1912 ; 2 Lt. 6 R. Dub. Fus., Jan. 1915.

Oldham, Ralph Stransham ;
M.B. and M.D. 1906 ; Lt. R.A.M.C., Oct. 1914 ; Capt. 1915.

*Oldham, Thomas Vicars ;
M.B. 1914 ; Lt. R.A.M.C., Oct. 1914 ; Capt. 1915.

Oliver, John Dudgeon ;
M.B. 1914 Lt. R.A.M.C., June 1917 ; Cambridge Hosp. Aldershot, 1917 ; Middlesex Gen. Hosp. for Overseas, 1917 ; Capt. 1918.

Oliver, Rev. Richard John Deane ;
B.A. 1886 ; M.A. 1889 ; Army Chaplain, Jan. 1893 ; 1 Cl. 1910 ; Assist. Chaplain Gen. Centr. Force and E. Command, 1916-20 ; despatches (twice) ; C.B.E. 1919.

*Oliver-Thompson, John Herbert :
Ent. 1914 ; 2 Lt. 11 S. Staff. R., May 1915 ; 2 Lt. M.G.C., Feb. 1916 ; Lt. 1916 ; A/Capt. 1916 ; A/Maj. 1918 ; killed in action, 21 March 1918.

O'Loughlin, Rev. Bryan ;
B.A. 1911 ; Army Chaplain, 4 Cl., Oct. 1916–18.

O'Malley, Rev. John James Evans ;
B.A. 1907 ; Temp. Army Chaplain, Aug. 1914 ; Army Chaplain, 4 Cl., Feb. 1915 ; Temp. 3 Cl., 1916.

O'Meara, Harold John :
>B.A.I. 1912 ; 2 Lt. R.F.A., May 1916 ; Lt. 1918.

*O'Morchoe, Arthur Donel ;
>Ent. 1910 ; 2 Lt. 5 Leins. R., Aug. 1914 ; wounded, France, July, 1915 ; Capt. 1915 ; A.D.C. 1917.

*O'Morchoe, Kenneth Gibbon ;
>Ent. 1911 ; Lt. 5, 2 Leins. R., Aug. 1913 ; wounded, France, 12 March 1915 ; Capt. 1915 ; 2 Lt. 1, 2 R. Dub. Fus., May 1915 ; Lt. 1916 ; Temp. Capt. 1916 ; empld. with W. Afr. Frontier Force 1917 ; Temp. Capt. 1917.

Oram, Walter Charles ;
>M.B. 1900 ; M.D. 1905 ; Capt. R.A.M.C., Apr. 1915 ; Radiologist 1 West Gen. Hosp.

O'Reilly, Charles Joseph ;
>M.B. 1913 ; Temp. Lt. R.A.M.C., Aug. 1914 ; Capt. 1915 ; M.C., Nov. 1915 ; despatches, Jan. 1916, June 1919 (Italy) ; Lt. R.A.M.C., Jan. 1917 ; Bar to M.C., Nov. 1917 ; Capt. 1918 ; D.S.O., June 1919.

O'Reilly, Rev. Charles Temple Meyrick Mandeville ;
>B.A. 1914 ; M.A. 1917 ; Army Chaplain, 4 Cl., Nov. 1918.

*O'Reilly, Keith Wilfred Robert ;
>Ent. 1910 ; 2 Lt. I. A. Res. of Officers 1914 ; attchd. 87 Punjabis ; N.W. Indian Frontier 1914 ; attchd. 89 Punjabis ; Flanders, 1915 ; Mesopotamia, 1915.

Ormsby, Gilbert John Anthony ;
>M.B. and M.D. 1898 ; Lt. R.A.M.C., Jan. 1899 ; Lt.-Col. 1915 ; despatches, Feb. 1915 ; D.S.O., Feb. 1915 ; A.D.M.S. 1917–18 ; A.D.M.S. 34 Div. British Armies in France, 1918 ; Bt. Col. 1918 ; A/Col. 1918 ; wounded, 27 May 1918 ; despatches (four times).

Ormsby, Henry Houston ;
>M.B. 1909 ; Surg. R.N., Nov. 1910 ; Surg. Lt.-Cmdr., Nov. 1916.

Ormsby, Sir Lambert Hepenstal ;
>M.B. 1874 ; M.D. 1877 ; Hon. Lt.-Col. New Zealand M.S., Feb. 1915.

Ormsby, William Edwin :
>M.B. 1902 ; Lt. R.A.M.C. Sept. 1914 ; wounded, Flanders, 1915 ; Capt. 1916.

Ormsby-Scott, Richard Deane-Freeman ;
>Ent. 1919 ; 2 Lt. 3 Conn. Rang. Oct. 1918.

O'Rorke, Charles Hyacinth ;
>M.B. 1907 ; Lt. R.A.M.C., Aug. 1908 ; Capt. 1912.

O'Rorke, George M'Kenzie ;
> B.A.I. 1904; 2 Lt. R.E., Jan. 1915; l.t. 1916; Capt. 1918;
> A/Major 1918; Lt.-Col. R. E., Port Directorate I. W. & D. ;
> M.B.E. Nov. 1918; despatches, Aug. 1919; Mesopotamia.

O'Rorke, John Marcus William ;
> B.A. 1906; 2 Lt. I.A., Jan. 1907; Capt. 25 Cav., 1914; Staff
> Capt. B.E.F., 1915; Brig.-Major B.E.F., 1916; Gen. Staff Offr.
> 1917; Temp. Major 1919; D.S.O.

Orr, Alexander William Burrell ;
> Ent. 1914: Pte. 20 R. Fus.; killed in action, France, 14 Feb.
> 1916.

Orr, Robert Gerald ;
> B.A.I. 1908; Lt. 11 R. Innis. Fus., Dec. 1914 ; Staff Lt. 1916 ;
> France; Lt. R.E. 1917–19.

*Orr, Thomas Alfred Hazlett ;
> Ent. 1913; 2 Lt. 14, 8 W. York. R., Apr. 1915 ; Lt. 1916 ;
> wounded, Nov. 1917; A/Capt. 1918.

Orr, Walter Leslie ;
> Ent. 1908 ; 2 Lt. 4 R. Ir. Rif., Nov. 1914 ; att. 2 Bn.; killed
> in action, Flanders, 25 Sept. 1915.

Osborne, William Henderson ;
> Ent. 1920 ; 2 Lt. 4 Leins. R., June 1915 ; att. 8 R. Ir. Rif.;
> Lt. 1917; B.E.F.; wounded ; M.C.

Osler, Sir William, Bart., F.R.S. ;
> Sc.D. (hon. causa) 1912 ; Hon. Col. R.A.M.C., Sept. 1908.

Ost, John ;
> Ent. 1913; Temp. 2 Lt. 10 Devon. R., Nov. 1914 ; 2 Lt. 1,
> 2 Devon R., Nov. 1916 ; Lt. 1918 ; empld. Min. of Lab., 1919.

O'Sullivan, Alexander Charles, F.T.C.D. ;
> B.A. 1882 ; M.A. 1885: Fellow, 1886 ; M.B. 1894 ; Lecturer in
> Pathology, 1895 ; M.D. 1899; Maj. R.A.M.C., Dec. 1915 ; Malta,
> 1915–1916 ; Lt.-Col. 1915 ; despatches, March 1917 ; Consulting
> Pathologist, Irish Command.

O'Sullivan-Beare, Daniel Robert ;
> M.B. 1883 ; Temp. Lt.-Col. R.A.M.C., Jan. 1916 ; Home ;
> died 1921.

O'Sullivan-Beare, Donald Barry ;
> Ent. 1920 ; Pte. 1 R. Dgs., 1918 ; Sgt. 1918 ; att. 5 Sq. M.G.C.,
> Cav. ; India and Rhine.

O'Sullivan, Muriel Eleanor ;
> B.A. 1911 ; Military Hospital, France.

O'Sullivan, Timothy Adolphus ;
    Ent. 1912; Sandhurst June 1915; Inns of Court O.T.C. 1915;
    2 Lt. R.G.A., Sept. 1916; Lt. 1918; France; Germany.

O'Sullivan, William Bradley ;
    Ent. 1914; Lt. R.G.A., Aug. 1918; France; Flanders.

O'Toole, Michael Joseph ;
    Ent. 1915; Cadet R.A.F., 1918.

Otway, Alexander Loftus ;
    M.B. 1903; Lt. R.A.M.C., 1904; Maj. 1915; despatches, Oct.
    1914.

*Otway, Herbert Francis ;
    B.A. 1911; 2 Lt. 1, 2 Leins. R., 1912; Lt. 1913; attchd. A.
    Cyclist Corps, 1914; M.C. July 1915; Capt. 1915; Off. C. of
    Gent. Cadets, R.M. Coll. 1917–18.

*Oulton, Charles Cameron Courtenay ;
    Ent. 1910; 2 Lt. 4 R. Dub. Fus., Aug. 1914; Lt. 1915;
    wounded, Flanders, May 1915; Capt. 1916.

*Overend, George Acheson ;
    B.A. and Ll..B. 1906; 2 Lt. R.G.A. (S.R.), Oct. 1917; A/Capt.
    and Adjt. 1918.

*Owens, Percival Hurst ;
    Ent. 1912; 2 Lt. R.E., Aug. 1916.

*Owens, Ruben Hirst ;
    Ent. 1915; Pte. 3 Res. Bgde. R.F.A., Feb. 1916; 2 Lt. R.G.A.,
    July 1916; Fly. Off. R.A.F.; Lt. R.A.F. 1918; France; Cologne.

*Owens, William Brabazon ;
    Ent. 1913; 2 Lt. R.E., Oct. 1915; wounded, March 1916;
    died of wounds received in action, France, 25 June 1916.

P

Palmer, Arthur ;
    B.A.I. 1902; Platoon Sergt. Malay States V. M., 1915; 2 Lt.
    1916.

*Panter, George William ;
    Ent. 1912; 2 Lt. 2 R. Ir. Rif., Dec. 1914; Lt. 1915; Flanders;
    despatches, Jan. 1916; attchd. R. Flying Corps 1916–18; wounded,
    France, July 1916; Temp. Capt. and Adjt. 1917; empld. Air
    Min., 1918; M.B.E.

Panter, Thomas Whelan ;
    Ent. 1918; Surg. Prob. R.N.V.R., Oct. 1917.

Panton, Arthur William;
B.A.I. 1909; M.A. 1911; 2 Lt. R.E., Jan. 1916; missing at Hamel, 3 Sept. 1916; presumed to have died on or since that date.

*Panton, Herbert Samuel Caleb;
B.A.I. 1912; Lt. 5 R. Ir. Fus., Jan. 1915; M.C. 1915; Capt. 1915; Lt. R.E., Jan. 1917; A/Capt. 1918; Gallipoli; Macedonia; despatches (twice);

*Panton, Robert Claude;
B.A.I. 1910; 2 Lt. 4, 2 R. Dub. Fus., Sept. 1914; wounded, France, May 1915; Lt. 1915; Capt. 1917; empld. Min. of Munitions, 1916-19.

*Papprill, Frederick Ernest;
Ent. 1909; 2 Lt. 9 Leic. R., Feb. 1915; att. E. Lancs.; killed in action, 3 June 1917.

Parke, James Cecil;
B.A. 1904; LL.B. 1906; Capt. 6 Leins. R., Jan. 1915; wounded; Capt. 6 Essex R., June 1916; Major 10 Bn. 1918.

Parker, Cyril Brien Denis;
Ent. 1919; Gunner R.F.A., 1915-19; France.

Parker, Edward;
M.B. 1916; Lt. R.A.M.C., Feb. 1917; M.C.; Capt. 1918; Permanent; N.-W. Frontier, India.

Parkes, Edward Ernest;
M.B. 1899; Lt. R.A.M.C., Jan. 1901; Maj. 1912.

*Parkes, Fitzwilliam Cecil;
Ent. 1912; Pte., D Co., 7 R. Dub. Fus., Nov. 1914; wounded, Gallipoli, Aug. 1915; Salonika.

Parkinson-Cumine, Benjamin Deane;
Ent. 1910; 2 Lt. 7 R. Ir. Fus., Aug. 1914; Adjt. 1914; Capt., Bgde. Machine Gun Offr. 1915; M.C. Feb. 1918; Major 1918.

*Parr, Charles William;
Ent. 1913; Y.M.C.A., Salonika, 1916.

*Parr, Percy Crowe;
M.B. 1918; Lt. R.A.F., M.S. Oct. 1918; Capt. 1919; malaria, Sth. Russia, 1919.

Parr, William Burleigh;
B. Dent. Sc. 1916; Surg. Prob. R.N.V.R., March 1917; Surg.-Lt. R.N., July 1917; H.M.S. "Gibraltar."

M

Parr, Victor Henry;
B.A. 1912 ; Capt. 7 R. Innis. Fus., Nov. 1914 ; M.C.; D.S.O.; Major 1917 ; despatches ; wounded three times ; prisoner of war, 1918.

Parsons, Alfred Robert;
M.B. 1888; M.D. 1897; Lt.-Col. R.A.M.C., 83 (Dub.) Gen. Hosp., France, May 1917.

Paterson, Thomas George Ferguson;
M.B. 1901 ; Lt. I.M.S., Jan 1902 ; Maj. 1915 ; 37 Lancers, I.A.; I. E. F. to Turkish Arabia ; wounded, Persian Gulf, Dec. 1914 ; D.S.O. Aug. 1917; despatches, Aug. 1917, March 1918 ; Bt. Lt.-Col. 1919.

Patrick, Rev. Thomas Joseph ;
Ent. 1906; 2 Lt. R.A.S.C., Dec. 1917-19.

Patrickson, Eric Colquhoun ;
B.A.I. 1907 ; 2 Lt. R.E., March 1915 ; Lt. 1915 ; Capt. 1919, whilst Div. Offr. R.E.

Patterson, Arthur Henry ;
B.A.I. 1909 ; Pte. A. Co. R.F.A., 1915 ; killed in action, Oct. 1916.

*Patterson, Roney Moore ;
Ent. 1912; 2 Lt. 4, 2 R. Dub. Fus., Sept. 1914 ; Lt. 1915 ; Capt. 1917 ; M.C.

Patterson, William Reginald Lambert ;
Ent. 1911 ; 2 Lt. R. Sc. Fus., S.R., Apr. 1912 ; Capt. R. Ir. Fus. 1914 ; wounded, France, 1914 ; Comm. Depot, 1914.

*Patton, John Henry Alexander ;
Ent. 1910 ; 2 Lt. 5 R. Ir. Rif., Aug. 1914 ; Capt. 1915 ; France ; Flanders ; Rhine ; att. R.E. for Army Sig. Ser. 1918 ; M.C. and Bar.

Patton, Thomas Walters ;
B.A. 1909 ; 2 Lt. 5 R. Ir. Fus., Aug. 1915.

Peake, Robert Harding ;
Ent. 1902 ; Pte. R.A.M.C., Dispenser; Sergt. Mil. Station Hospital, Calcutta.

*Pearsall, Richard Montague Stack ;
B.A. 1914 ; 2 Lt. 16 L'pool R., Jan. 1915 ; Staff Lt. (Spl. appt.) 1916-19.

Pearson, Rev. James Alexander ;
B.A. 1912 ; Army Chaplain, 4 Cl., Aug. 1915-19.

Pearson, Mortimer Henry ;
M.B. 1893 ; Lt. R.A.M.C., Dec. 1914 ; Malta, 1915 ; Capt. 1915.

Pearson, William ;
M.B. and M.D. 1907 ; Maj. R.A.M.C., Apr. 1915 ; Graylongwell War Hospital, Chichester.

Pearson, Rev. William Thomas Kingston ;
B.A. 1911 ; Army Chaplain, 4 Cl., May 1915-20.

*Pedlow, William ;
Ent. 1913 ; 2 Lt. 1, 2 R. Dub. Fus., Aug. 1915 ; France 1917 ; Capt. 1917 ; despatches, 1917 ; M.C. Feb. 1918 ; killed in action, 12 Oct. 1918.

*Pemberton, Frederick ;
B.A.I. 1913 ; Pte. R.E., Inland Water Transport, March 1916 ; Coy. Sergt.-Major ; Mesopotamia ; mentioned.

Pendered, Richard Dudley ;
B.A. 1910 ; Capt. 4 North'n R., Oct. 1914.

Pentland, Alexander ;
M.B. 1878 ; M.A. 1890 ; Maj., Australian A.M.C.

Pentland, Charles James ;
M.B. and M.D. 1910 ; Lt. R.A.M.C., Dec. 1915.

*Pepper, John Gerald Wellington ;
Ent. 1908 ; 2 Lt. R.G.A., Sp. Res., Jan. 1912 ; empld. Aug. 1914 ; Lt. 1915 ; Capt. 1916.

Perdue, Cecil Graham ;
Ent. 1909 ; 2 Lt. I.A. Res. 1916.

*Perdue, Rev. John George ;
B.A. 1889 ; M.A. 1907 : 2 Lt. A.S.C., Jan. 1916 ; Lt. 1917 ; empld. Min of Munitions.

*Perrin, George Wilmot ;
B.A. 1913 ; 2 Lt. A.S.C., Nov. 1914 ; Lt. 1915 ; A/Capt. 1917.

Perry, James Felix ;
Ent. 1900 ; Sergt. 53 Canadians, 1915.

Perry, Samuel James Chatterton Prittie ;
Med. School, 1888 ; Lt.-Col. R.A.M.C., Mar. 1915.

Perry, William Millar ;
B.A. 1914 ; 2 Lt. R.F.A., S.R., July, 1915 ; France, 1916 ; Lt. 1917.

Persse, Geoffrey ;
B.A. 1905 ; LL.B. 1906 ; Corp. 9 Wellington R., New Zealand ; killed, Gallipoli, 7 Aug. 1915.

*Persse, Reginald Barry Louvain ;
    Ent. 1913 ; 2 Lt. 3, 2 Shrops. L.I., Dec. 1914 ; Lt. 1916 ;
    Lt. R.A.F., Apr. 1918 ; A/Capt. 1918.

Peyton, Thomas Henry ;
    M.B. 1906 ; M.D. 1907 ; Capt. R.A.M.C., Sept. 1914 ; A/Major
    1915 ; 1 Home Cos. Fld. Amb. ; France, 1915 ; despatches, Jan.
    1916 ; despatches, Salonika, Dec. 1916 ; D.S.O. Jan. 1917.

Peyton, William de Malet ;
    M.B. 1913 ; Lt. R.A.M.C., Dec. 1914 ; Capt. 1915 ; A/Major
    1918.

Phelan, Ernest Cyril ;
    M.B. 1906 ; Capt. R.A.M.C., Jan. 1910 ; despatches ; M.C.
    Feb. 1915 ; A/Lt.-Col. 1917 ; D.S.O. Jan. 1918 ; despatches,
    Dec. 1918 ; Major 1918.

Phibbs, John Lynch ;
    M.B. 1908 ; M.D. 1911 ; Lt. R.A.M.C., July 1918.

Phillips, Albert Edward ;
    Ent. 1916 ; Surg. Sub-Lt. R.N.V.R., 1917.

*Phillips, John Skelton ;
    Ent. 1914 ; 2 Lt. 3 Leins. R., June 1915 ; 2 Lt. Machine Gun,
    Corps, Nov. 1915 ; France, 1915 ; Lt. 1916 ; Belgium ; Italy.

*Phillipson, Roland Burton ;
    Ent. 1914 ; 2 Lt. 1, 2 Conn. Rang., Sept. 1915 ; Lt. 1917-19.

Phipps, Rev. Charles Benjamin ;
    B.A. 1898 ; LL.D. 1903 ; Off. Minister, R.N. Aux. Patrol,
    June, 1915 ; Kingstown.

*Phipps, John Peddar ;
    Ent. 1916 ; Quetta, April 1917 ; 2 Lt. I.A., Jan. 1918.

Piel, Paul Douglas ;
    Ent. 1919 ; Pte. R. Innis. Fus., Nov. 1914 ; France ; wounded
    five times.

Pierce, William Henry ;
    Ent. 1908 ; 2 Lt. R.G.A., Oct. 1914 ; Egypt ; Salonika ;
    Observer R. Flying C., June 1916.

*Pierson, Henry Alfred De Esterre ;
    Ent. 1912 ; 2 Lt. A.S.C. (M.T.), Nov. 1915.

*Pigot, David Richard ;
    Ent. 1917 ; R.G.A., Brighton, Nov. 1918.

*Pigot, Walter Thomas ;
    B.A.I. 1912 ; 2 Lt. I.A. 83 Wallagahbad L.I., 1914 ; attchd. 63
    Palamcottah L.I. ; E. Africa 1916 ; Capt. ; Palestine, 1918.

*Pile, Charles Devereux ;
> M.B. 1915 ; Lt. R.A.M.C., July 1915 ; Egypt 1915 ; Capt. 1916 ;
> Salonika, 1916 ; France, 1917 ; wounded, March 1918 ; invalided,
> April 1918.

Pile, William Devereux ;
> Ent. 1908 ; Petty Offr. R.N.A.S. ; Mudros 1917 ; E. Med. Sq.

*Pim, Douglas Chetham ;
> M.B. 1915 ; Lt. R.A.M.C., Aug. 1914 ; Capt. 1915 ; despatches,
> Aug. 1917 ; Mesopotamia ; D.S.O. Sept. 1917.

Pim, George Adrian ;
> B.A. 1908 ; 2 Lt. I.A., Feb. 1909 ; East Africa, 1915–16 ;
> Capt. 130 Baluchis, 1916 ; Capt. 1915 ; A/Maj. 1918.

*Pim, Hugh Maxwell ;
> B.A. 1913 ; 2 Lt. I.A., 24 Punjabis, Jan. 1914 ; Lt. 1914 ;
> Egypt 1914–15 ; Mesopotamia 1915 ; Capt. 1915 ; despatches,
> Apr. 1916 ; M.C. Apr. 1916.

Pim, Rev. John Bernard ;
> B.A. 1908 ; M.A. 1913 ; Chaplain R.N., Aug. 1914 ; H.M.S.
> "Sutlez," 1914–15 ; "Victory," 1915–16 ; "Commonwealth,"
> 1916–17 ; " Dido," 1917–19.

*Place, Charles Godfrey Morris;
> B.A. and LL.B., 1908 ; Pte. 7 R. Dub. Fus. ; Capt. 8 E. Surr.
> R., Jan. 1915 ; France, 1915 ; M.C. Dec. 1916 ; Temp. Maj. 1917 ;
> wounded, Oct. 1917 ; D.S.O., Nov. 1917.

Place, Edmond Byrne;
> Ent. 1898 ; late Capt. Limerick City Militia ; Transport Offr.,
> E. African Force, 1915.

Place, Hugh Llewellyn ;
> Ent. 1909: 2 Lt. 5 R. Muns. Fus. 1910 ; 2 Lt. A.S.C. Aug. 1914 ;
> Temp. Capt. 1916 ; Capt. 1917.

Place, Norbert Dumayne ;
> Ent. 1899 ; 2 Lt. Bedf. R., Jan. 1904 ; Capt. I.A. 8 Rajputs,
> Jan. 1913 ; Maj. 1919.

Plant, Leslie Horrocks ;
> B.A. 1911 ; 2 Lt. R.F.A., Dec. 1914 ; Lt. 1916 ; R.F.C. 1917 ;
> Lt. R.A.F., Apr. 1918.

Plumer, Arthur Murray ;
> Ent. 1916 ; B.A.I. 1921 ; O.T.C. May 1918 ; volunteered and
> accepted.

Poë, John ;
> M.B. 1896 ; Lt. R.A.M.C., July 1897 ; Lt.-Col. R.A.M.C., 1915;
> despatches, D.S.O., June 1915 ; A.D.M.S., France, 1916–19;
> despatches, Jan. 1917 and Dec. 1917 ; Bt. Col. 1918 ; Col. 1918 ;
> C.M.G. 1918 ; D.D.M.S., France, 1919.

Pollard, Frederick William ;
> L.M. and L.Ch. 1901 ; Lt. R.A.M.C., June 1917 ; Capt. 1918.

Pollard, James William ;
> Ent. 1911 ; Pte. R.A.M.C., May 1915 ; France, 1915–18;
> invalided, 1918.

Pollard, Richard Payne ;
> M.B. 1910 ; Capt. R.A.M.C., Oct. 1915 ; A/Maj. 1918 ; M.C.
> April 1919 ; Croix de Guerre.

Pollock, Charles Frederick ;
> M.B. 1867 ; Col. R.A.M.C., Aug. 1898.

Pollock, Henry Brodhurst ;
> Ent. 1901 ; Sub. Lt. R.N.V.R. Nov. 1914 ; Lt. Comdr.
> 1915 ; Gallipoli, 1915–16 ; France, 1916–19 ; wounded, July 1916 ;
> Comdr. " Drake" and " Hood" Bns., Nov. 1917 ; D.S.O., Dec.
> 1917 ; gassed, March 1918 : Bar to D.S.O., Sept. 1918 ; despatches
> (four times).

Ponton, John Alfred William ;
> M.B. 1908 ; M.D. 1913 : Temp. Lt. R.A.M.C., July 1917 ; Capt.
> 1918.

Poole, John Hewitt Jellett ;
> B.A.I. 1916 ; Draughtsman, Civilian Ry. Co. ; France.

Poole, Walter Croker ;
> M.B. 1883 ; Lt. R.A.M.C., Feb. 1887 ; Maj. Res. of Offrs.
> 1914–19.

*Pope, Richard Alexander Deniston ;
> Ent. 1917 : Pte. A.S.C. (M.T.), July 1917.

Popham, Francis Stewart ;
> B.A. 1907 ; 2 Lt. R. Muns. Fus., Nov. 1901 ; Capt. 5 R. Dub.
> Fus. June 1909 ; Railway Transport Offr., Dublin, 1914 ; de-
> spatches, Jan. 1917 ; Bt. Maj. 1918.

Popham, Robert Stewart ;
> Ent. 1894 ; 2 Lt. Notts and Derby R., Feb. 1897 ; D.S.O. ;
> wounded, Aisne, 20 Sept. 1914 ; Maj. 1915 ; Bt. Lt.-Col. 1918;
> Gen. Staff Offr., France, 1916–18 ; Salonika, 1918.

Porter, Harold William ;
> B.A.I. 1908 ; 2 Lt. R.E., S.R., 1908 ; Lt., empld. Aug. 1914 ;
> Capt. 1917 ; Temp. Maj. 1918 ; France ; Dep. Assist. Dir. Eng.
> Stores, 1918.

Porter, Robert Kerr ;
>B.A. 1914 ; 2 Lt. 3 R. Scots, Apr. 1915 ; empld. recruiting
duties, 1917.

Potter, John Crampton ;
>Ent. 1893 ; 2 Lt. 3 R. Ir. Regt., Jan. 1916 ; Lt. 1917.

*Potterton, **William Hubert** ;
>B.A.I. 1914 ; Lt. R.E., May 1915 ; wounded ; killed in action,
battle of Somme, 23-24 July 1916.

Pounden, John Colley ;
>M.B. 1899 ; M.D. 1900 ; Lt. R.A.M.C., Oct. 1915 ; Maj. 1918 ;
S.M.O. Inf. Depot, Catterick, Yorks.

Powell, Ashley ;
>B.A. 1909 ; Intelligence Offr., Egyptian Forces, ; wounded,
1918.

Powell, Blacker Castles ;
>M.B. 1913 ; Lt. R.A.M.C., Aug. 1915 ; Salonika : Capt. 1916.

*Powell, Charles George ;
>B.A. 1911 ; 2 Lt. 15 Durh. L.I., Apr. 1915 ; Lt. 5 Bn. 1916 ;
A/Capt. 1918.

Powell, **Edward Darley** ;
>B.A.I. 1898 ; Lt. R.E., May 1915 ; Capt. R.E., Nov. 1915 ;
despatches (twice) ; M.C. 1917 ; Maj. 1918 ; D.S.O. 1918 ;
wounded and missing, afterwards believed killed, 1 Sept. 1918.

*Powell, Edward Hawkshaw ;
>Ent. 1911 ; B.A. 1920 ; Corp. Canadian A. Med. Serv. Jan.
1915 ; 2 Lt. 10 R. Ir. Fus., Mar. 1917 ; France, 1917–18 ; wounded,
Aug. 1917 ; 84 Punjabis, India, 1918–20.

Powell, Harold Thomas ;
>Ent. 1912 ; 2 Lt. 7 Leic. R., Aug. 1915 ; Lt. M.G.C. Nov. 1916.

Powell, Ievan Herbert ;
>M.B. 1913 ; Lt. R.A.M.C., Sept. 1914.

Powell, John Allman ;
>M.B. 1907 ; M.D. 1910 ; Lt. R.A.M.C. June, 1917 ; Capt. 1918.

Powell, John Lowry ;
>M.B. 1899 ; Maj. R.A.M.C., Jan. 1912.

Powell, William Jackson ;
>M.B. 1905 ; Lt. I.M.S., Sept. 1905 ; Capt. 1908 ; I.E.F., Turkish
Arabia ; wounded, Ctesiphon, Dec. 1915 ; Maj. 1917 ; Persia,
1919.

*Power, Kenneth William ;
> Ent. 1909 ; 2 Lt. R.F.A., Aug. 1914 ; prisoner, Loos, Sept.
> 1915 ; Capt. 1917.

*Power, Richard Wood ;
> Ent. 1914 ; 2 Lt. 3 R. Ir. Rif., Nov. 1915 ; Surg. Prob.
> R.N.V.R., July, 1916 ; H.M.S. "Norseman"; H M.S. "Violent,"
> 1916-18.

*Power, Thomas Declan ;
> M.B. 1914 ; Temp. Surg. R.N., Dec. 1914 ; Temp. Surg. Lt.

Praia, Duarte ;
> Ent. 1917 ; Pte. 5 R. Portuguese Infantry, 1917-19.

*Pratt, Francis Young ;
> Ent. 1912 ; 2 Lt. A.S.C., Nov. 1914 ; Lt. 1915 ; B.E.F.

Pratt, Joseph Dallas ;
> M.B. 1879 ; M.D. 1882 ; M.O. 4 Lond. R., 1890 ; Maj. 1902 ;
> R.A.M.C., T.F. 1908 ; M.O. in charge South Staff and Depts.,
> Dublin.

*Pratt, Mervyn Palles;
> Ent. 1911 ; 2 Lt. I.A., Jan. 1914 ; Capt. attchd. 5 R. Ir. Regt. ;
> Dardanelles, 1915 ; 121 Pioneers, I.A., 1915 ; wounded, Mesopo-
> tamia, 22 Feb. 1917 ; died, 13 April 1920, N. W. Frontier, India.
> Death due to wounds received in 1917.

Prentice, David Shields ;
> B.A. 1915 ; Surg. Prob. R.N.V.R., Dec. 1914 ; H.M.S. "Stag."

Prentice, Herbert John ;
> B.A.I. 1908 ; 2 Lt. R.E., Aug. 1915 ; Lt. 1917 ; M.C.

Preston, Charles Alexander ;
> B.A. 1906 ; M.A. 1912 ; 2 Lt., Unattchd. list, T.F. 1910 ; Lt.
> O.T.C., T.F., 1914.

*Preston, George Elystan ;
> Ent. 1917 ; O.T.C. May 1918 ; volunteered and accepted.

Price, Alfred Henry ;
> M.B. 1916 ; Surg. Prob. R.N.V.R., June 1914 ; H.M.S.
> "Nemesis "; Temp. Surg. Lt. R.N., July 1916.

*Price, Ernest Dickinson ;
> Ent. 1912 ; 2 Lt. 3 R. Ir. Regt., Aug. 1914 ; died of wounds,
> France, 19 March, 1916.

*Price, Harold Robert ;
> B.A.I. 1914 ; 2 Lt. R.F.A., Oct. 1914 ; wounded, France, Aug.
> 1915 ; wounded, France, Sept., 1916 ; Lt. 1916 ; despatches, Jan.
> 1917.

Price, Ivan Henry ;
B.A. 1887 ; LL.D. 1890 ; D.I., R.I.C. ; attchd. General Staff,
Irish Command ; Maj., Aug. 1914 ; despatches, D.S.O. Jan. 1917 ;
Bt. Lt.-Col. 1919.

*Price, Ivon Kinahan ;
Ent. 1911 ; 2 Temp. Lt. A.S.C., Oct. 1914 ; wounded, Flanders,
Aug. 1915 ; Temp. Lt. 1915 ; 2 Lt. A.S.C., 1916 ; Lt. 1917 ;
A/Capt. 1918.

Price, James Chernside ;
Ent. 1916 ; Sandhurst, July 1917 ; 2 Lt. I.A., Aug. 1918.

Price, William Robert ;
Ent. 1888 ; Pte. R.A.M.C., King George V. Hosp., Dublin.

Priestley, Dyker Stanton ;
Ent. 1913 ; M.A. (Oxon.) ; 2 Lt. 11 R. Ir. Rif., Jan. 1915 ; 2 Lt.
M.G.C., Jan. 1915 ; died of wounds, 8 Oct. 1917.

*Priestman, Harold Eddey ;
Ent. 1913 ; 2 Lt. 16 L'pool R., Dec. 1914 ; Lt. 1915 ; Capt.
1916 ; Dep. Asst. Mil. Sec., H.-Qs. Staff, India, 1918.

Pringle, George Alexander ;
M.B. 1896 ; M.D. 1902 ; Lt. R.A.M.C., June 1915 ; Malta and
Hosp. ship " Karapara " ; Capt. 1916.

Pringle, Harold ;
M.B. 1899 ; M.D. 1902 ; Lt. R.A.M.C., Aug. 1915 ; Capt. 1916 ;
Maj. 1918 ; France.

Pringle, John Alexander ;
M.B. 1905 ; M.D. 1908 ; Lt. R.A.M.C., Oct. 1914 ; Capt. 1915 ;
France.

Pringle, Seton ;
M.B. 1903 ; Surg. Dublin Castle Red Cross Hosp. ; Anglo-French
Red Cross, Bar le Duc, Jan. 1916 ; Hon. Lt.-Col. R.A.M.C. June
1917 ; O.B.E. 1919.

*Pritchard, Robert William ;
M.B. 1916 ; Surg. R.N., Jan. 1917.

Proctor, Edwin Vere ;
B.A. 1910 ; Hd. Qrs. Signaller, 21 Bn. Australian Force ;
(twice wounded) Gallipoli, 1915 ; R.F.C.

Proctor, George Norman ;
B.A. 1907 ; 2 Lt. I.A., 83 Wallajahbad L.I., Aug. 1907 ; Capt.
1915 ; I.E.F. British East Africa ; invalided home, Dec. 1916 ;
A/Maj. 1918.

Proctor, James Claude Beauchamp ;
B.A. 1907; LL.D. 1910; Capt. 10 R. Innis. Fus., Sept. 1914;
France, 1915 ; killed in action, France, 1 July 1916.

Proctor, Richard Louis Gibbon ;
Ent. 1916 ; Cadet I. A., Quetta, 1918 ; invalided, 1919.

*Prost, Arthur Grieveldinger ;
Ent. 1917 ; Cadet R.A.F., 1918.

*Pulling, Oswald Langley ;
Ent. 1910 ; 2 Lt. R.G.A., March 1915.

Purcell, Frederick Michael ;
Ent. 1919 ; 2 Lt. R.A.F. Nov. 1918.

*Purcell, Herbert Kevin ;
B.A. 1914 ; 2 Lt. 7 Leins. R., Sept. 1914; Lt. 1914.

Purcell, Noël Mary Joseph ;
Ent. 1910 ; 2 Lt. 7 Leins. R., Sept. 1914 ; Lt. 1914.

*Purefoy, Thomas Amyrald Wray ;
Ent. 1912 ; 2 Lt. A.S.C., May 1915 ; Lt. 1917 ; empld. Min. of
Lab.

Purser, Francis Carmichael ;
M.B. 1899; M.D. 1901; Maj. R.A.M.C., Sept. 1915; despatches,
Sept. 1917 ; O.B.E. 1919.

*Purser, Frederick Gerald ;
Ent. 1912 ; 5 Canadian Bn., Aug. 1914 ; wounded, Festubert,
March 1915.

Purser, John ;
B.A.I. 1907 ; R.N.V.R. March 1915 ; Sub. Lt. R.N.V.R., Sept.
1915 : appointed to H.M.S. " Vernon " for service in the Paravane
Dept., 1916 ; Experimental Officer, 1917 ; left the service, Apr.
1919.

Purser, Lydmar Moline ;
M.B. 1899 ; Maj. R.A.M.C., Apr. 1912 ; despatches, Feb. 1915
and Jan. 1916 ; wounded, Sept. 1916 ; despatches and D.S.O. Jan.
1916 ; Lt.-Col. 1917.

'Purser, Philip Addison ;
Ent. 1913 ; Pte. Middlesex Hussars, Aug. 1914 ; 2 Lt. A.S.C.,
Nov. 1914 ; France, 1915 ; invalided, Apr.1915 ; Lt. 1916 ; killed
in civil disturbances, Dublin, 30 April 1916.

Q

Quekett, John ;
> M.A. 1912; 2 Lt. 5 R. Highrs., July 1916 ; killed, 3rd battle of Ypres, 31 July 1917.

*Quigley, John ;
> Ent. 1915 ; Pte. Ulster Div., Nov. 1915 ; 2 Lt. R. Ir. Rif. Oct. 1916.

Quill, Richard Henry ;
> M.B. 1871 ; M.D. 1877 ; Surg. Gen. A.M.S.; ret. : commended for services, July 1917 ; C.B. Aug. 1917.

*Quin, James Sinclair ;
> Ent. 1914 ; Surg. Prob. R.N.V.R., July 1916 ; H.M.S. "Raider."

*Quin, Joseph Archibald ;
> M.B. 1914 ; Lt. R.A.M.C., Aug. 1914 ; Capt. 1915.

Quin, Walter William McGregor ;
> Ent. 1915 ; Pte. 11 R. Dub. Fus., Jan. 1917.

*Quinlan, Harold Daniel ;
> Ent. 1914 ; 2 Lt. 4 Hussars, June 1915 ; Lt. 1917 ; killed in action, 26 March 1918.

Quinn, John Peter ;
> Ent. 1919 ; 2 Lt. 6 R. Muns. Fus., Oct. 1915 ; Lt. 1917 ; France ; Flanders.

Quinn, Rev. Joseph ;
> B.A. 1886 ; M.A. 1892 ; Army Chaplain, 4 Cl., July 1915.

*Quinn, Joseph Patrick ;
> M.B. 1914 ; Lt. R.A.M.C., S.R., Aug. 1914 ; Capt. 1915 ; despatches, Jan. 1917 ; M.C. June 1917 ; Capt. R.A.M.C., 1918.

R

*Rainsbury, Finn Barre Prendergast ;
> Ent. 1914 ; Pte. 21 U. P. S. Royal Fusiliers, Jan. 1916 ; killed in action, Bazentin-le-Petit, 22 July 1916.

Rainsford, Arthur Fitzpatrick ;
> Ent. 1890 ; 101 Bn. Winnipeg, Jan. 1916.

Rainsford, Henry Monserrat ;
> Ent. 1879 ; Lt. R.A.M.C., June 1915 ; Capt. 1916.

*Ramsay, Robert Clement Burke ;
> M.B. 1916 ; Lt. R.A.M.C. (on prob.), Aug. 1914 ; Lt. R.A.M.C.,
> Sept. 1916 ; Capt. 1917.

*Ramsden, William Cecil ;
> Ent. 1909 ; Assist. to the Prof. of Chemistry ; Capt. unattached
> list, T.F., Feb. 1913 ; Capt. R.E., Oct. 1914 ; France and Flanders,
> 1915–19.

*Rankin, Robert William Roy ;
> Ent. 1912 : 2 Lt. R.E., Oct. 1915 ; France ; despatches, Jan.
> 1917.

Ratcliffe, Cecil Wentworth Godon ;
> Ent. 1914 ; Pte. 13 R. Suss. R., Apr. 1916 ; France, Somme,
> Thiepval, Beaumont Hamel, 1916 ; 2 O. Cadet Bn., 1916 ; 2 Lt.
> 3 W. York R. Apr. 1917 ; Ypres, 1917 ; wounded Oct. 1917 ;
> invalided out, Dec. 1918.

*Rathborne, Joseph William Lombard ;
> Ent. 1913 ; Temp. 2 Lt. 6 R. Muns. Fus., Nov. 1914 ; wounded,
> Dardanelles, Aug. 1915 ; 2 Lt. 1 R. Muns. Fus. Oct. 1916 ; Lt.
> 1916.

*Rattray, Melville John ;
> B.A.I. 1911 ; 2 Lt. R.E., Aug. 1915 ; Lt. ; Macedonia.

Raymer, Robert Richmond ;
> B.A. 1905 ; Hon. Lt. in Army, Sept. 1902 ; Maj. 2 Bn. Royal
> Jersey Militia, 1910 ; in command of 1/5 Bn. Sth. Staffs R., Feb.
> 1915, in France ; wounded, July 1916 ; despatches (4 times) ; D.S.O.
> June 1916 ; C.M.G. June 1919 ; Lt.-Col. S. Wales Borderers,
> 1918.

*Rea, Horace James Anderson ;
> Ent. 1916 ; Sandhurst, April 1916 ; 2 Lt. 4 Hussars, May 1917.

Rea, Vivian Trevor Tighe ;
> Ent. 1912 ; B.A., Q.U.B. ; Lt. 2 R. Ir. Rif., Feb. 1913 ; killed
> in action, France, 25 Oct. 1914.

Read, George Averill ;
> B.A. 1908 ; 2 Lt. 3 Leins. R., Aug. 1914 ; Capt. 1915 ; France,
> May 1915 ; invalided, Nov. 1915 ; France, Oct. 1916 ; killed in
> action, 8 March 1917.

*Read, Henry Marvelle ;
> B.A. 1912 ; 2 Lt. 2 Life Gds., June 1915 ; France, 1916 ; Lt.
> Gds. M.G.R. 1917.

ʻRead, Thomas Frederick Henry ;
> Ent. 1913 ; 2 Lt. R.F.A., Oct. 1914 ; Lt. 1916.

Reade, Rev. Guy Gregory Harper;
Ent. 1898; Lt. 97 R. Canadian Militia; Lt. 3 Glouc. R., Aug. 1914; attchd. 1 Bn.; France, 1916; Capt. 1916.

Reade, John Henry Loftus;
Ent. 1899; 2 Lt. 2 Manch. R.; despatches; killed, France, 28 Oct. 1914.

*Redding, John Edward ;
Ent. 1912; 2 Lt. 7 L'pool R., Aug. 1914; France, 1915; wounded, Givinchy, Oct. 1915; Capt. 1916; Assist. Adjt. 1916; Lt. I.A., May 1916; A/Capt. 1918.

Rees, Rev. Frederick Ivon Lewis ;
B.A. 1911; Army Chaplain, 4 Cl. Apr. 1917–19.

Reeves, Robert Clanmalier ;
B.A. 1900; 2 Lt. R.F.A., May 1900; Maj. 1914; D.S.O.; A/Lt.-Col. 1918.

Reid, Alexander William Douglas Coote ;
B.A. 1904: Lt. 13 Durh. L.I., Oct. 1914; Capt. 1915; Adjt. 1916; A/Maj. 1918.

Reid, Robert D. M'Minn ;
Ent. 1914; 2 Lt. 14 High. L.I., April 1915.

Reid, William Andrew Bether ;
Ent. 1918; R.M. C. Camberly, Dec. 1918.

Reilly, Alexander Maxwell;
B.A.I. 1909; 2 Lt. 9 R. Innis. Fus., Oct. 1915; A/Capt.; died of wounds, 26 Nov. 1916.

Reilly, Rev. John Curtis ;
B.A. 1913; M.A. 1919; Army Chaplain, 4 Cl., Jan. 1916–19 ; despatches, 1917.

Rennison, Arthur John ;
B.A. 1899; 2 Lt. A.S.C., May 1900 ; Capt. I.A., 1909 ; Dardanelles ; Mediterranean E.F. ; despatches; Maj. 1915; D.S.O.

Rennison, Rev. Eric David Robert ;
B.A. 1912; Army Chaplain, 4 Cl., Nov. 1915 ; Mediterranean E.F., 1916 ; Palestine, 1916–19.

Rennison, Walter Martyn ;
Ent. 1912 ; 2 Lt. 3 R. Ir. Regt., Jan. 1915 ; wounded, May 1916 ; killed in action, 30 Dec. 1916.

Renton, Harold ;
Ent. 1919; Pte. S.A.M.C.

Revell, Robert Arthur;
B.A. 1912; 2 Lt. Essex R., Aug. 1912 ; Lt. 1913 ; Capt. ; died of wounds, Dardanelles, 13 June, 1915.

Rhodes, Arthur ;
    M.B. 1894 ; M.D. 1901 ; Capt. R.A.M.C., Jan. 1916 ; Australian
    Imp. F. ; Egypt, 1916.

Rice, Henry James ;
    M.B. 1917; Lt. R.A.M.C., Sept., 1917; Capt. 1918; M.C.
    June 1919.

*Rice, William Hector ;
    Ent. 1917 ; O.T.C., Apr. 1918; R.A.F., June 1918 ; wounded.

Richards, William Reeves ;
    Ent. 1908 ; Lt. 6 R. Dub. Fus., Nov. 1914 ; Capt. and Adjt.
    1915 ; despatches ; killed in action, Dardanelles, 15 Aug. 1915.

Richardson, Albert Victor John ;
    M.B. 1908 ; Surg. R.N., Nov. 1908 ; Surg. Lt. Cr. Nov. 1914 ;
    Maj. R.A.F. Med. S., 1918 ; A/Lt.-Col. 1919.

*Richardson, Cecil Arthur ;
    Ent. 1916 ; 7 O. Cadet Bn., Jan. 1918; 2 Lt. 5 R. Ir. Regt.,
    July 1918.

Richardson, David Alexander ;
    B.A. 1899 ; Pte. 10 Canadians, Aug. 1914 ; wounded, Ypres,
    22 Apr. 1915 ; invalided home, March 1916.

Richardson, Rev. Jonathan Oswald Airth ;
    B.A. 1892 ; M.A. 1895 ; Army Chaplain, 4 Cl., Nov. 1915.

Richardson, Samuel Robert ;
    M.B. 1910 ; M.D. 1911 ; Lt. R.A.M.C., Dec. 1914 ; Capt.
    1915.

*Richey, Henry Alexander ;
    B.A. 1887 ; Capt. 12 R. Innis. Fus., May 1915.

Richey, James Ernest ;
    B.A.I. 1909 ; 2 Lt. R.E., Oct. 1914 ; wounded, France, Oct.
    1915 ; Lt. 1916 ; M.C. ; Capt. 1917.

Ridgeway, Joseph Chamney Atkinson ;
    M.B. 1907 : M.D. 1910 ; Uganda Medical Service; Lt. R.A.M.C.,
    Dec. 1915 ; Capt. 1916.

Riggs, Arthur Francis M'Causland ;
    Ent. 1914 ; Temp. 2 Lt. 7 Yorks. L.I., Nov. 1914 : Temp. Lt.
    1915 ; 2 Lt. Mar. 1916 ; M.C. ; Lt. 1917.

*Robb, George Cecil ;
    Ent. 1912 : 2 Lt. 3 R. Ir. Rif., Aug. 1914 ; Lt. 1915 ; Capt.
    1917 ; wounded, Sept. 1917 ; wounded, Dec. 1917.

Roberts, Arthur Hamilton Stewart ;
    M.B. 1893 ; M.D. 1903 ; M.O. in charge Troops, Horses, and
    Fort, Spithead.

*Roberts, David;
    Ent. 1911 ; 2 Lt. 7 Linc. R., Nov. 1914; Lt. 1915; M.C.
Mar. 1916 ; Capt. 1916 ; died of wounds, 23 April 1917.

Roberts, Gerald Stewart ;
    Ent. 1905; Australian Contingent ; invalided from Dardanelles,
1915.

*Robertson, Charles Wyndham ;
    Ent. 1909 ; 2 Lt. R.E., Aug. 1914 ; France 1914; Gallipoli 1915 ;
Lt. 1915 ; Capt. 1917 ; Egypt; Palestine; despatches.

Robertson, Clement ;
    B.A.I. 1910 ; Pte. Univ. & Public Schools Bn. Jan. 1915; 2 Lt.
3 R.W. Surr. R., Jan. 1915 ; France, 1915 ; attch. R.E. 1915 ; Lt.
M.G.C. Jan. 1917; A/Capt. 1917 ; Tank Corps, 1917 ; killed in
action at Paschendaele, 4 Oct. 1917 ; V.C. Dec. 1917.

*Robertson, Frederick William ;
    Ent. 1914; Surg. Sub. Lt. R.N.V.R., Nov. 1916; H.M.S.
" Medea."

Robertson, Herbert Rennie ;
    M.B. and M.D. 1895 ; Lt. R.A.M.C.; Capt. ; died on service
after an operation, 29 July, 1916.

Robertson, James Robert ;
    B.A. 1901 ; 2 Lt. R. Berks R., May 1905; Capt. 1913 ; Adjt.
Machine Gun Section ; invalided from Cameroons ; M.C. ; D.S.O. ;
A/Lt.-Col. 1917-19 ; Off. Co. of Genl. Cadets R. Mill. Col. 1919 ;
Brig.-Maj. Sch. of trng. Instrs., 1919.

Robertson, John ;
    B.A.I. 1899 ; Capt. R.E., May 1916; Temp. Col. 1918 ; Dep.
Dir. Eng. Stores, 1918 ; Bt. Maj. 1919 ; France ; despatches (3
times) ; C.B.E.

Robertson, Rev. Michael William ;
    B.A. 1907 ; M.A. 1911; Army Chaplain, 4 Cl., Sept. 1915–
1919 ; Mediterranean E. F.

Robinson, Archibald Louis ;
    M.B. 1907 ; B.Sc. 1915 ; Bacteriologist, Western Command,
Liverpool, 1916.

*Robinson, Arthur Joseph Herbert ;
    Ent. 1916 ; 2 Lt. Ser. Bns. Leins. R., May 1918 ; att. 2 Bn. ;
France ; wounded.

Robinson, David Lubbock ;
    B.A. 1904 ; Trooper, Canadian Contingent, 1914 ; 2 Lt. Royal
Marines, May 1915 ; Lt. Tank Corps May 1916 ; Capt. 1917 ;
D.S.O. ; Croix de Guerre (with palms) ; wounded.

Robinson, Edmond;
> M.B. 1915; Lt. R.A.M.C., Aug. 1914; Capt. 1915; despatches, Jan. 1916; att. 8 Seaforth Highrs.; killed in action, France, 20 March 1917.

*Robinson, George;
> Ent. 1904; 2 Lt. unatthd. List, Mar. 1914: Capt. 7 R. Ir. Fus., Nov. 1914; France, 1916; wounded, Sept. 1916; empld. Bd. of Agriculture, 1918; M.C.

*Robinson, James Salmond;
> M.B. 1915; Lt. R.A.M.C., Sept. 1914: Capt. 1915; India, 1916.

Robinson, Rev. John Lubbock;
> B.A. 1901; Temp. Chap. R.N., Feb. 1918.

Robinson, John Thomas;
> B.A. 1915; 7 Cadet Bn., Aug. 1916.

Robinson, Norman Lubbock;
> Ent. 1907; Trooper, Canadian Contingent, 1914; 2 Lt. R.F.A., June 1915; Lt. 1917; M.C.

Robinson, Oliver Long;
> Med. School 1885; M.R.C.S., L.R.C.P.; Lt. R.A.M.C., July 1891; Lt.-Col. 1913: Professor of Tropical Medicine, R. A. Med. College; E.E.F.; despatches, July 1917; C.B. 1919.

Robinson, Thomas Trevor Hull;
> M.B. 1905; Lt. R.A.M.C., Jan. 1906; Capt. 1909: despatches, May 1915; Maj. 1916: despatches, Jan. 1917; A/Lt.-Col. whilst in comd. of Fid. Amb., 1917; Maj. 1918: D.S.O. Jan. 1919.

Robson, Richard Ivan;
> Ent. 1912; 2 Lt. 15 R. Ir. Rif., Oct. 1914; Capt. 1916; M.C. 1916; died of wounds, near Ypres, 6 Aug. 1917.

*Roche, Christopher Augustus;
> B.A. 1899; Lt. Army Ordnance, July 1915.

Roche, Rev. Francis Cavendish;
> B.A. 1908; M.A. 1913; Army Chaplain, Sept. 1914; died of enteric, Alexandria, 14 Nov. 1915.

Roche, James Dillon Knight;
> M.B. 1907; Lt. R.A.M.C., Jan. 1909; Capt. 1912.

*Roche, Stamford Hearn;
> Ent. 1914; British Red Cross, Nov. 1916.

*Roche, Thomas Allen;
> Ent. 1912; 2 Lt. 5 R. Ir. Regt., Jan. 1916.

Roche, Thomas Galvin ;
> M.B. 1916; Lt. R.A.M.C., March 1917 ; Capt. 1918.

*Roche-Kelly, James ;
> B.A.I. 1912; Lt. South Ir. Horse, May 1914 ; Capt. 1915; M.C.

*Roddy, Francis Augustus ;
> M.B. 1914; Lt. R.A.M.C., Oct. 1914; Capt. 1915; wounded, France, July 1916.

Roe, John Windsor ;
> B.A. 1900: 2 Lt. R.A., Aug. 1900 ; Capt. 1912 ; Staff Capt.
> .1914; Maj. 1915; Mesopotamia; invalided home; R.A. Bde.,
> I.E.F. ; died of wounds received in action, France, 7 Aug. 1916.

Roe, Samuel George ;
> Ent. 1894 ; 2 Lt. R. Innis. Fus., 1898 ; Capt. 1904 ; killed in action, France, 26 Oct. 1914.

Roe, William Edward ;
> B.A. 1903 ; 2 Lt. Dorset R., March 1900 ; 2 Lt. A.S.C., 1902 ;
> France, 1914 ; Maj. 1914 ; despatches, Dec. 1914 ; Egypt. 1915 ;
> Dep. Assist. Qr. Master Gen., 1915 ; Bt. Lt.-Col. 1918; Dep.
> Asst. Dir. of Supply and Transport, Ireland, 1918.

*Roe, Wray Palliser Hickman ;
> B.A.I. 1911 ; 2 Lt. R.E., Sept. 1915; France ; wounded ;
> despatches, Jan. 1917 ; Lt. 1917 ; empld. Min. of Lab. 1918.

*Rogers, Francis Lyttleton Lloyd ;
> Ent. 1912 ; 2 Lt. R.F.A., Nov. 1914 ; killed in action, France,
> 7 Jan. 1916.

Rogers, George Herbert Beechy ;
> B.A. 1910 ; Pte. Australian Contgt.

Rogers, Henry ;
> M.B. 1899; Lt. R.A.M.C., June 1901 ; Maj. 1913 ; despatches,
> May 1915; Temp. Lt.-Col., 1914–19 ; despatches, June 1915,
> May 1917 ; D.S.O., June 1917.

Rogers, Rev. Louis ;
> B.A. 1915 ; M.A. 1918 ; Army Chap., 4 Cl. June 1918–19 ;
> M.C. 1919.

Rogers, Rev. Travers Guy ;
> B.D. 1901; Temp. Army Chaplain 4 Cl., Dec. 1915 ; M.C.
> 1916 ; Army Chaplain, 4 Cl., Feb. 1918.

Rolleston, Charles Ffrench ;
> M.B. 1903 ; Temp. Major R.A.M.C., May 1918; serving wit
> the Manor (Co. of London) War Hosp., 1918.

Rolleston, Francis Leslie ;
Ent. 1910 ; 2 Lt. A.S.C., Oct. 1914 ; Capt. 1915.

Rollins, Ernest Edward ;
M.B. 1918; Lt. R.A.F. Med. S., Sept. 1918.

Rollins, Herbert ;
Ent. 1917 ; R.A.F. 1918 ; Hon. 2 Lt., Jan. 1919.

Ronaldson, John Gray ;
M.B. 1911 ; Lt. R.A.M.C., Feb. 1914 ; Capt. 1915 ; France ;
M.C. 1918 ; Bar to M.C. 1918 ; A/Maj. 1918.

Ronaldson, William Pollock ;
Ent. 1907 ; Lt. 1 King's African Rifles, Dec. 1916 ; German E.
Africa ; wounded, Jan. 1917.

Ronan, John Galway ;
B.A. and LL.B. 1911 ; Lt. Motor Machine Gun Ser., 5 Leins. R.,
June 1915 ; Capt. 1917 ; M.C.

*Ronan, Walter Joseph ;
M.B. 1914; Lt. R.A.M.C., Dec. 1914 ; Capt. 1915 ; O.B.E.
1919.

Ronayne, Charles Richard Louis ;
M.B. 1900; Lt. R.A.M.C., June 1900 ; Temp. Lt.-Col. 1915.

*Ronayne, James Andrew ;
Ent. 1910 ; 2 Lt. 5 R. Muns. Fus., Aug. 1914; killed, France,
25 Sept. 1915.

Ronayne, Rev. Robert William ;
B.A. 1895 ; M.A. 1898 ; Army Chaplain, 4 Cl., Nov. 1914–19.

Roper-Caldbeck, William Roper ;
B.A. 1876 ; Maj. Special List, March 1915 ; attchd. 3 Bedf. R.;
Staff, 1918.

Ross, Rev. Arthur Edwin ;
B.A. 1891 ; B.D. 1895 ; Army Chaplain, 4 Cl., Jan. 1916 ;
3 Cl. 1916 ; despatches, Jan. 1917 ; M.C. and Bar, 1918 ; Bishop
of Tuam, 1920.

Ross, George Charles Cumberland ;
M.B. 1899 ; Staff Surgeon R. N. ; Lost in H.M.S. "Hawker,"
Oct. 1914.

*Ross, Harold Aemilius ;
Ent. 1915 ; 2 Lt. 1, 2 R. Ir. Regt., Apr. 1916 ; Lt. 1917 ;
empld. Min. of Lab. 1919.

Ross, Major Sir Ronald;
Sc.D. (Hon. Causâ) 1904; K.C.B.; late I.M.S.; Temp.
Lt.-Col. 1917; K.C.M.G. 1918.

Rothwell, William Edward;
B.A. 1901; 2 Lt. R. Garr. R., Sept. 1902; Lt. R. Innis. Fus.,
1905; Capt. 1912; A.D.C. to G.O.C. 2 Div. B.E.F., 1914;
wounded, Aisne, Sept. 1914; Adjt. 1915–16; Maj. 1916;
Comdt. Musk. Camp, 2nd Army, Brit. Armies in France; Temp.
Lt.-Col. 1917; D.S.O.

Rowan, Rev. Benjamin William;
B.A. 1898; Army Chaplain, 4 Cl., May 1906; 3 Cl. 1916;
B.E.F. 1914–16; despatches, 1915 and 1916.

Rowan, Rev. Reginald Percy;
B.A. 1909; M.A. 1911; Army Chaplain, 4 Cl., March 1917.

Rowlette, Robert James;
M.B. 1898; M.D. 1899; Physician, Castle Hospital, Dublin;
Temp. Capt. R.A.M.C., July 1917; Lt.-Col. 83 (Dub.) Gen. Hosp.,
France, 1918.

Royse, Rev. Thomas Henry Foorde Russell Buckworth;
B.A. 1905; M.A. 1908; Army Chaplain, 4 Cl., Sept. 1914;
France, 1915; 3 Cl. 1916; despatches, 1916; M.C.

*Ruby, James Henry;
Ent. 1914; 2 Lt. 17 Durh. L.I., Feb. 1916; Lt. 1917; R.F.C.
1918.

Russell, George Blakely;
M.B. 1882; Lt. R.A.M.C., Aug. 1884; Maj. 1896; retd. 1904;
re-empld. 1914.

Russell, John Joshua;
M.B. 1885; Capt. R.A.M.C., July 1886: Col. A.M.S., 1915;
A.D.M.S., B.E.F., 1914–15; despatches, Oct. 1914, Jan. 1916;
D.D.M.S. 1916–18; C.B. Jan. 1916; despatches, May 1917;
D.D.M.S., B.E.F., 1916–18; D.D.M.S. (Ireland) 1918–19;
Surg.-Gen. 1918.

*Russell, Joshua Forbes;
B.A.I. 1915; 2 Lt. R.E., Sept. 1915; Lt. 1916; France; A/Capt.
1918.

•Russell, Marcus Ralph;
B.A. 1910; Cavalry Cadet Squadron, March 1916; 2 Lt. 2 Cav.
Res. July 1916; att. 8 Hussars; killed in action, 22 March 1918.

*Russell, Mortimer M'Gee;
M.B. 1916; Lt. (on prob.) R.A.M.C., Aug. 1914; Lt. R.A.M.C.,
Sept. 1916; Mesopotamia, 1917–19; Capt. 1917; N.-W. Frontier,
India, 1919–20.

Russell, Robert Edwin ;
> B.A. 1911 ; 2 Lt. I.A. 31 Lancers, Oct. 1915 ; Lt. 1916.

*Russell, Samuel Wilfrid ;
> Ent. 1913 ; 2 Lt. 7 Welsh R., Sept. 1914 ; Lt. 1916 ; Capt. 1916.

*Russell, Thomas Wallace ;
> Ent. 1915 ; 2 Lt. 10 R. Dub. Fus., Nov. 1915 ; killed in action, 13 Nov. 1916.

Russell, William James Alexander ;
> Ent. 1915 ; B.A. 1918 ; Temp. Surg. Sub-Lt. R.N.V.R., July 1918, H.M.S. "Mastiff."

Russell, William Robert ;
> B.A. 1905 ; 2 Lt. Canadian Army, 1907 ; Maj. Lord Strathcona's Horse, June 1915 ; France, 1916.

Rutherfoord, Harold Edward ;
> M.B. and M.D. 1897 ; Surg. War Hospital, Chiswick.

Rutherford, Cecil ;
> M.B. 1911 ; Lt. R.A.M.C., May 1915 ; Mediterranean E. F., 1915 ; Egypt 1916 ; Capt. 1916.

Rutherford, Henry Ireland Gascoyne ;
> M.B. 1915 ; Lt. R.A.M.C., Sept. 1915 ; France, 1916.

Rutherford, Nathaniel John Crawford ;
> M.B. 1896 ; Lt. R.A.M.C., Jan. 1899 ; Lt.-Col. 1915 ; D.A.D.M.S., 1915 ; D.S.O., Feb. 1915 ; wounded, Dec. 1916.

Rutledge, Laurence Hugh Nesbitt ;
> Ent. 1908 ; 2 Lt. 11 R. Innis. Fus., Apr. 1915 ; Lt. I.A., Supply and Trans. Corps, Jan. 1917.

Ruttle, Rev. Richard Noël ;
> B.A. 1905 ; Army Chaplain, 4 Cl., Dec. 1915–18.

Ruttledge, Victor John ;
> M.B. 1891 ; Lt. R.A.M.C., May 1915 ; Capt. 1916 ; died on service, 3 Nov. 1916.

Ryall, Rev. Charles Richard ;
> Ent. 1915 ; Chaplain, I.A., Jan. 1915 ; I.E.F., France, 1915 ; with Exped. Force, 1915–18.

*Ryall, George ;
> Ent. 1913 ; Pte., Feb. 1915 ; 2 Lt. 15 Manch. R., March 1915 ; severely wounded, Somme offensive, 1916 ; Lt. 1917 ; Capt. and Adjt. R.A.F.

*Ryan, John Milo ;
M.B. 1915; Temp. Lt. R.A.M.C., Nov. 1915; Temp. Capt.
1916 ; Capt. R.A.M.C., May 1919.

Ryan, Joseph Ernest Noel ;
M.B. 1909; M.D. 1910; Capt. R.A.M.C., T.F., Aug. 1914 ;
France.

Ryan, Perceval Cecil Hardinge ;
M.B. 1887 ; M.D. 1891 ; Lt. R.A.M.C., Nov. 1915.

Ryan, Thomas ;
M.B. 1908 ; Colonial M.S.; drowned at sea, 24 Apr. 1917.

*Ryan, William Aloysius ;
M.B. 1914; Lt. R.A.M.C., Aug. 1914 ; Capt. 1915.

S

Sadleir, Rev. Ralph Granby ;
B.A. 1894 ; Chaplain R.N., Jan. 1900 ; R.N. Hosp. and Dyd.,
Portland, 1913-18 ; R.N. Hosp. Haslar, 1918-19.

St. Clair, John ;
Ent. 1920; Pte. Highland Cyclist Bn. 1916 ; Sgt. in Gas School,
Dublin, 1918.

Samuels, Arthur Purefoy Irwin ;
B.A. 1909 ; M.A. 1912; Lt., Unattchd. List, T.F., June 1914 ;
Capt. 11 R. Ir. Rif., Feb. 1915 ; wounded, June 1916 ; killed in
action, France, 24 Sept. 1916.

Samuels, George Ernest ;
B.A.I. 1908 ; 2 Lt. R.F.A., Dec. 1915 ; France; Lt. 1916 ;
A/Maj. 1917.

Sandes, John Drummond ;
M.B. 1906; Lt. I.M.S., Feb. 1907 ; Capt. 1910 ; S.M.O.,
H.M.S. " Harding," 1914 ; France 1915 ; Kitchener Hosp.,
Brighton, 1915–16 ; India 1916 : Maj. 1918.

Sands, Thomas Lewis ;
M.B. 1903 ; M.A. and M.D. 1906 ; Surg. Capt. Cape Mounted
Rif., 1915; Maj. S. A. Med. Corps, Aug. 1915.

Sansom, Alfred John ;
M.A. 1898 ; Capt., June 1915 ; A/Lt.-Col. Cmdg. 7 R. Sussex R.,
May 1915 ; killed near Arras, 5 July 1917.

*Sargent, Alma Kingsley ;
Ent. 1912 ; Pte. 5 R. Dub. Fus., Nov. 1915 ; France ; Sergt.;
Staff Sergt. Instr., A.G.S.

Satchwell, Ralph William ;
Ent. 1915 ; 2 Lt. R.G.A., Dec. 1915 : 76 S.B.; killed in action,
31 Jan. 1917.

Satchwell, Robert Henry ;
Ent. 1916 ; Surg. Sub-Lt. R.N.V.R., Dec. 1918.

Saunders, Rev. Arthur James Neville ;
B.A. 1900 ; M.A. 1916 ; Temp. Chaplain to R.A.F. 1918-19.

Saunders, Charles Howard ;
M.B. 1892 ; Capt. R.A.M.C., T.F., July 1908 ; A/Maj. 1919.

*Saunders, George Francis Thomas ;
Ent. 1914 ; Pte. R.A.M.C., 1915 ; Sapper, S.R. Section, R.E.;
B.E.F.

Savage-Armstrong, John Raymond Savage ;
Ent. 1900 ; Capt. 4 Leins. R., July 1908 ; attchd. 1 Devon R. ;
wounded, France, Apr. 1915 ; Adjt. 1916.

Sawyer, Richard Henry Stewart ;
M.B. 1879 ; Maj. R.A.M.C., Aug. 1893 ; Major-General 1915 ;
C.M.G., Feb. 1915 ; despatches, June 1916 ; D.D.M.S. 1916 ;
despatches, May 1917 and Dec. 1917 ; C.B., Jan. 1917

Scaife, Cecil ;
M.B. 1905 ; M.D. 1906 ; Lt. R.A.M.C., July 1906 ; Capt. 1910 ;
A/Lt.-Col. 1917 ; Maj. 1918.

Scaife, Leicester C. P.
Ent. 1914 ; 2 Lt. 3 North'd Fus., Nov. 1914 ; wounded.
France, Apr. 1915 ; Lt. 1916 ; Temp. Capt. and Assist. Sup. of
Phys. Training, 1918.

Scanlen, Rev. William Alexander ;
B.A. 1912 ; Army Chaplain, 4 Cl., May 1917-19.

Scharff, John William ;
Ent. 1913 ; Surg. Prob. R.N.V.R., July 1915 ; H. M. S.
" Digby " ; H.M.S. " Mons."

Scholefield, Richard John ;
B.A. 1904 ; 2 Lt. A.S.C., Feb. 1915 ; invalided.

Scholefield, Robert Shelton ;
B.A. 1910 ; 2 Lt. Conn. Rang., 1912 ; Lt. 5 R. Fus., Dec. 1913 ;
Capt. 1915 ; wounded, Armentières, Oct. 1914 ; wounded and taken
prisoner, Loos, Sept. 1915 ; Capt. 1915.

*Schute, Frederick Geoffrey ;
     Ent. 1908 ; 2 Lt. 4 R. Ir. Fus., Aug. 1914 ; Capt. 1916.

*Schute, John Hartley ;
     B.A. 1913 ; Lt. 6 R. Ir. Fus., Nov. 1914 ; killed in action,
     Dardanelles, 15 Aug. 1915.

Scott, Charles Edward ;
     Ent. 1909 ; 2 Lt. 9 Notts and Derby R., Oct. 1914 ; wounded,
     Suvla Bay, 21 Aug. 1915; Capt. 1916 ; M.C.

Scott, Charles Victor George ;
     B.A.I. 1898 ; I. Defence Force, 3 Punjab Rif. 1917–20.

Scott, Horatio Frederick Ninian ;
     M.B. 1888 ; M.D. 1892 ; Capt. R.A.M.C., Aug. 1915 ; B.E.F. ;
     wounded, May 1916 ; A/Maj. 1918.

Scott, Thomas Douglas ;
     B.A.I. 1905 ; Lt. R.E., Jan. 1915 ; Suez Canal, 1915 ; Gallipoli,
     1915 ; Sinai, 1916 ; M.C.; Temp. Capt. 1916 ; Palestine and
     Syria, 1917–19 ; Temp. Maj. 1918 ; Assist. Polit. Off. E.E.F.,
     1918–19 ; despatches (twice).

Scovell, Rowland Hill ;
     M.B. 1884 ; Lt. R.A.M.C., March 1915 ; Embarkation Officer,
     Dublin ; Capt. 1916.

Scroope, Charles Frederick ;
     B.A. 1908 ; 2 Lt. I.A., 66 Punjabis, Feb. 1911 ; Lt. 1911 ;
     I.E.F.; Capt. 1915.

Seale, Edward Albert ;
     M.B. 1890 ; M.D. 1893 ; Lt. R.A.M.C., Nov. 1915.

Searancke, Francis Kenyon ;
     B.A.I. 1909 ; Sap. Ry. Constr. Troops, R.E., 1918 ; 2 Lt. R. Ir.
     Fus., 1918.

Seeds, Arthur Atkinson ;
     M.B. and M.D. 1898 ; Lt. R.A.M.C., July 1899 ; Lt.-Col. 1915 ;
     France, 1915.

*Semple, John Mervyn ;
     Ent. 1912 ; 2 Lt. 1, 2 R. Ir. Rif., Jan. 1916 ; Lt. 1917.

Semple, Rev. Samuel Hanna ;
     B.A. 1902 ; M.A. 1915 ; Army Chaplain, att. Scottish Division.

Seon, Sidney Osborne ;
     Ent. 1921 ; 2 Cl. Mech. Wireless Section, R.A.F., att. R.F.A.,
     66 B., Nov. 1915 ; Mesopotamia, May 1916–June 1918 ; Leading
     Air Craftsman, 1917.

Seymour, Charles Richard Foster ;
B.A. 1899 ; 2 Lt. Hamps. R., Feb. 1900 ; Lt. I.A. 1902 ; Capt.
13 Rajputs, 1909 ; Maj. 1915.

Seymour, Frank Robert ;
M.B. and M.D. 1907 ; Capt. R.A.M.C., Dec. 1915 ; Maj. 1917 ;
despatches, Aug. 1917.

Seymour, William Henry ;
B.A. 1913 ; 2 Lt. A.S.C., May 1915 ; France, 1915.

Shanks, Walter ;
M.B. 1899 ; M.D. 1909 ; Lt. R.A.M.C., Sept. 1915 ; Capt.
1916.

*Shanley, Harmon John ;
Ent. 1914 ; 2 Lt. 5 Conn. Rang., Dec. 1914 ; Lt. 1917.

*Sharkie, Joseph Henry Faussett ;
Ent. 1914 ; 2 Lt. 4 R. Ir. Rif., July 1915 ; wounded, May 1916,
and March 1917 ; Lt. 1917 ; France ; Salonika.

Sharpe, Rev. Thomas Gordon ;
B.A. 1906 ; M.A. 1909 ; Army Chaplain, 4th Cl., Aug. 1918–19.

*Sharpe, William M'Cormick ;
Ent. 1912 ; 2 Lt. R.G.A., Oct. 1914 ; Lt. 1915 ; wounded, July
1916 ; Temp. Capt. 1916 ; D.S.O. ; Maj. 1918 ; Italian E.F.

*Shaw, Arthur Frederick Bernard ;
M.B. 1911 ; M.D. 1913 ; Lt.R.A.M.C., Dec. 1913 ; Capt. 1915 ;
2 Welsh Fld. Amb., Mediterranean E.F. ; despatches, July 1917.

*Shaw, Douglas Gordon ;
Ent. 1906 ; 2 Lt. A.S.C., May 1912 ; France ; Lt. 1914 ; Temp.
Capt. 1916 ; Capt. 1917.

*Shaw, Frederick Roland Studdert ;
M.B. 1915 ; Temp. Lt. R.A.M.C., Aug. 1914 ; Capt. 1916 ;
M.C. Jan. 1917 ; Lt. R.A.M.C., Jan. 1917 ; A/Maj. 1918 ; Capt.
1919.

Shaw, George William Bernard ;
M.B. 1917 ; Lt. R.A.M.C., July 1917 ; Capt. 1918.

*Shaw, James Hunter ;
B.A. 1913 ; 2 Lt. A.S.C., Nov. 1914 ; Lt. 1915 ; Capt. 1917,
transferred to Tank Corps, Dec. 1917 ; wounded, Aug. 1918.

*Shaw, James Rowan ;
B.A. 1904 ; 2. Lt. 9 Ches. R., Apr. 1915 ; killed, France, 22 Feb-
1916.

Shaw, John de Burgh ;
Ent. 1912 ; Pte. 7 R. Dub. Fus., Sept. 1914.

Shaw, Richard James Herbert ;
B.A. 1907 ; Lt. 5 Conn. Rang., Feb. 1915 ; Capt. 1915 ; Capt. New Armies, 1916 (spec. empld.)

Shaw, Robert Hill ;
M.B. 1892; M.D. 1898; Lt. R.A.M.C., T.F., May 1911 ; Capt. 1914 ; M.O., Newhaven Fort, 1914-15 ; M.O. in charge Military Hospital, Brighton, 1915-17 ; M.O., Shoreham, Sussex, 1917-18.

Shaw-Hamilton, Robert Cope Hardy ;
Ent. 1896 ; 2 Lt. 4 D. Gds., May 1900 ; Res. of Offrs., Dec. 1914 ; Adjt. and Temp. Capt. 21 Lancers, Oct. 1915 ; Capt. 1916 ; Bt. Maj. 1918.

*Shee, John Robert Lloyd ;
B.A.I. 1913 ; 2 Lt. 1 Duke of York's Own Lancers, 1915.

*Shee, William Cecil Lloyd ;
Ent. 1908 ; Temp. 2 Lt. 3 R. Ir. Regt., Oct. 1914 ; 2 Lt. 1, 2 Bns. 1915 ; wounded, France, Oct. 1915 ; Lt. 1915 ; A/Capt. 1918.

Sheehan, Edmond Houston ;
M.B. 1909 ; Lt. R.A.M.C., Sept. 1915 ; Capt. 1916.

Shegog, Richard Wellington ;
M.B. 1915 ; Lt. R.A.M.C., Sept. 1915 ; Capt. 1916 ; att. 1/4 N. Lancs. R. ; died of wounds, 1 Aug. 1917.

*Shegog, Wellington ;
B.A.I. 1910 ; 2 Lt. R.E., June 1916 ; Lt. 1917.

Sheil, Leonard James ;
M.B. and M.D. 1912 ; Lt. R.A.M.C., Sept. 1914 ; Capt. 1915 ; Salonika, 1916 ; despatches, Oct. 1917 ; A/Maj. 1918 ; M.C. Jan. 1919.

Shekleton, Richard Auchmuty ;
M.B. 1893 : M.D. 1894 ; Lt. R.A.M.C., July 1916 ; torpedoed in H.M.S. "Britannia," 1916 ; Capt. 1917.

*Shepherd, Joseph Mackay ;
Ent 1914 ; 2 Lt. 15 L'pool R., July 1915 ; Machine Gun Corps, 1916 ; Lt. 1917 ; Capt. 1918 ; Maj. 1919 ; France, Belgium, and Egypt; wounded.

*Sheridan, Bertrand Cecil Owens ;
M.B. 1914; Lt. R.A.M.C., Aug. 1914 ; Capt. 1915 ; despatches, Jan. 1917 ; M.C. May 1917.

*Sheridan, Leonard ;
Ent. 1912 ; 2 Lt. 8 R. Dub. Fus., Jan. 1915 ; Capt. 1917 ; killed in action near Moncourt, 27 March 1918.

Sherlock, Charles Gregg ;
>   M.B. and M.D. 1907 ; Lt. R.A.M.C., Aug. 1908 ; Capt. 1912 ;
>   Bagdad ; died of wounds, 14 Nov. 1918.

*Sherlock, David Thomas Joseph ;
>   B.A. 1904 ; 2 Lt. 3 R. Ir. Regt., Dec. 1914 ; Temp. Capt. 1
>   Garr. Bn. 1915 ; Lt. 1916 ; Adjt. 1917.

Sherowitz, Cecil Guedalla ;
>   M.B. 1915 ; Lt. R.A.M.C., Jan. 1916 ; resigned, ill health.

*Sherrard, Henry Erskine ;
>   B.A. 1912 ; 2 Lt. 5 R. Ir. Fus., Dec. 1914 ; Lt. 1915 ; A/Capt.
>   1918.

Shirley, Paul ;
>   Ent. 1910 ; 2 Lt. 3 R. Innis. Fus., Aug. 1914 ; Capt. 1915 ;
>   attchd. 2 Welsh R., 1915 ; France, Egypt, Salonika, 1915–16 ;
>   Musketry Instr., 3 Bn. 1916 : att. Lab. Corps, 1917.

Shirley, Rev. Paul William Nassau ;
>   B.D. 1909 ; Army Chaplain, 4 Cl., Feb. 1916-19.

*Shoritt, Cecil de Lisle ;
>   Ent. 1913 ; 2 Lt. R.G.A., Sept. 1915 : Flying Offr. R.F.C.
>   1917.

*Shortt, Charles John de Vere ;
>   B.A. 1917 ; Temp. Surg. Sub-Lt. R.N.V.R., Mar. 1918.

*Sidwell, Arthur Geoffrey Ledger ;
>   Ent. 1915 ; Sandhurst, Apr. 1916 ; 3 Lt. 1, 2 R. Dub. Fus.,
>   May 1917 ; Lt. 1918 ; 2 Lt. R.A.F., June 1918.

*Simms, Alfred George Francis ;
>   Ent. 1906 ; Lt. Army Cyclist Corps, Dec. 1914 ; Lt. 6 Conn.
>   Rang., Aug. 1917 ; France ; Certif. for gallant conduct and devo-
>   tion to duty : missing, believed drowned, 30 Dec. 1917.

Simon, Frank ;
>   Ent. 1911 ; 2 Lt. 9 R. Dub. Fus., Sept. 1914 ; Lt. 1916 ; Capt.
>   Otago R., May 1917 ; killed in action, Flanders, 10 Jan. 1918.

Simpson, Irwin Edward Paget ;
>   Ent. 1920 ; R.N. Res. before the war ; Sub-Lt. R.N. Res., Mar.
>   1915 ; Lt. 1917 ; Armed Merchant Cruiser and 20th Mine-laying
>   Destroyer Flotilla, Medit. and N. Sea.

Simps n, Cswald Givan Ewart ;
>   B.Dent.Sc. 1913 ; Pte. R.A.M.C., Jan. 1916 ; Lt. Dent. Surg.
>   R.A.M.C., June 1916 ; Capt. 1917.

Sinclair, Wilfred ;
>Ent. 1917; Pte. R.A.F. 1918; Sgt. 1918; B.E.F.; N.C.O..
Pilot.

*Small, Hugh Alexander ;
>Ent. 1913; 2 Lt. 16 L'pool R., Jan. 1915; killed in action,
10 July 1916.

Small, James Alexander ;
>M.B. 1913 ; French Red Cross, 1916.

*Smartt, Robert Bevan Nangle ;
>Ent. 1911; B.A. 1917; 2 Lt. 6 Leins. R., Nov. 1914.

Smeeth, Henry George ;
>M.B. 1887, M.D. 1888; Maj. R.A.M.C., 18th Field Amb.,
Aug. 1914; France, 1914; Temp. Lt.-Col., 1915; despatches,
June 1916, Jan. 1917 ; A/Lt.-Col. 1919.

Smith, Alfred Hayes ;
>M.B. 1908 ; Lt. R.A.M.C., April 1916 ; Capt. 1917.

Smith, Arthur Alexander ;
>B.A. 1908; L. Dent. Sc. 1911; Temp. Lt., Dental Surgeon,
Nov. 1915; France, 1915; Capt. 1916.

*Smith, Ernest Frederick William ;
>Ent. 1913; 2 Lt. 7 Leins. R., Sept. 1914 ; att. R.F.C. ; died
27 Dec. 1916, from injuries received in flying action.

Smith, Ernest St. George ;
>Ent. 1896 ; 2 Lt. 5 R. Dub. Fus., March 1900; Capt. 1910 ;
Adjt. 1912; Maj. 1915 ; Temp. Lt.-Col. 1917.

Smith, George Henry ;
>B.A.I. 1883 ; served in ranks of Volunteers.

Smith, Henry St. George ;
>Ent. 1917 ; R.A.F.

*Smith, James Frederick ;
>Ent. 1909 ; Sergt. 7 R. Dub. Fus., 1914 ; killed in action, Dar-
danelles, Sept. 1915.

Smith, Joseph Vincent ;
>Ent. 1916 ; Pte. R. Dub. Fus., ; 2 Lt. M.G.C. Dec. 1917.

*Smith, Lawder Benjamin Sandys ;
>B.A.I. 1913 ; Lt. A.S.C., Sept. 1914; Capt. 1915 ; att. R. Ir.
Fus. and R. Ir. Regt; France ; M.C. ; Lt. I.A. Mar. 1918 ;
Capt. 1/119 Infantry, I.A. 1919.

Smith, Lionel Fergus ;
>M.B. 1894 : Lt. R.A.M.C., July 1895 ; Lt.-Col., 1915 ;
despatches, Aden, July 1916 ; despatches, Salonika, Dec. 1916 ;
C.M.G. Jan. 1917 : despatches, Nov. 1917 ; A.D.M.S. Salonika,
1918–19.

Smith, Michael Joseph ;
M.B. 1894 ; M.D. 1901 ; Fleet Surg. R.N., Nov. 1911 ; H.M.S.
"Magnificent" ; Surg. Capt. 1919 ; retired.

*Smith, Paul Herbert Shelley ;
Ent. 1911 ; Surg. Prob. R.N.V.R., Dec. 1914 ; H.M.S.
"Vigilant."

*Smith, Philip Norbert ;
Ent. 1914 ; 2 Lt. S. Ir. Horse, Nov. 1915 ; Lt. 1916 ; empld.
7 R. Ir. Regt. 1918.

Smith, Ralph Henry Tottenham ;
Ent. 1911 ; Lt. A.S.C., Sept. 1914 ; Capt. 1916 ; att. W. York
R. 1917.

Smith, Richard Travers ;
M.B. 1894 ; M.D. 1896 ; Capt. R.A.M.C., July 1916 ; Temp.
Maj. 1918.

*Smith, Robert John ;
B.A. 1909 ; 2 Lt. 15 Lan. Fus., Oct. 1914 ; Capt. 1915 ; 15 York
and Lanc. R., 1915 ; killed in action, 6 May 1916.

Smith, Samuel Boyland ;
M.B. and M.D. 1898 ; Lt. R.A.M.C., Nov. 1900 ; Major 1912 ;
D.A.D.M.S, 1915 ; despatches, May 1917 ; D.S.O. June 1917 ;
wounded, Aug. 1917 ; Lt.-Col. 1918 ; A.D.M.S. France, 1918–19 ;
O.B.E. 1919.

*Smith, Vivian Fielding ;
Ent. 1914 ; 2 Lt. 13, 2, 7 Lan. Fus., Apr. 1915 ; Lt. 1915.

*Smith, William ;
B.A.I. 1919 ; Cadet D.U.O.T.C. 1918 ; volunteered and accepted.

Smith, William Brownlow Ashe ;
M.B. 1897 ; M.D. 1898 ; Lt. R.A.M.C., Jan. 1916.

Smith, William Harden ;
Ent. 1916 ; Temp. Surg. Sub-Lt. R.N.V.R., H.M.S. "Redoubt,"
1917.

*Smith, William Leslie Winslow ;
Ent. 1912 ; 2 Lt. R.G.A., Dec. 1915 ; Lt. 1917 ; A/Capt. and
Adjt. 1918 ; M.C. Jan. 1919.

Smith, William Perceval ;
Ent. 1910 ; 3rd. Writer, R.N. Dec. 1912 ; 2nd Writer, 1916 ;
H.M.S. "Warrior," Mediterranean and N.Sea, 1914–15 ; R.N.
depot, Devonport, 1915-6 ; invalided out 1917.

Smith, William Richard Hugh ;
M.B. and M.D. 1902 ; Lt. R.A.M.C., Jan. 1916 ; Capt. 1917.

Smithwick, Rev. Frederick Falkiner Standish ;
    B.A. 1901; Army Chaplain, June 1904 ; 4 Class, 1906 ; B.E.F.
    1914-18 ; despatches 1915, 1916, and 1917.

Smyly, Phyllis Claudia ;
    B.A. 1915 : Military Hospital, Malta.

Smyth, Andrew Ralph ;
    Ent. 1920; 2 Lt. 18 Lond. R. (Lond. Ir. Rif.), May 1918 ;
    Flanders and France ; Lt. att. R. Ir. Rif., 1919.

*Smyth, Donald Seymour ;
    Ent. 1911 ; 2 Lt. 3 R. Ir. Regt., Aug. 1914 ; prisoner of war,
    Oct. 1914 ; killed in action, 19 Oct. 1914.

*Smyth, George Bestal Jenkinson :
    Ent. 1908 ; 2 Lt. 6 R. Ir. Rif., Aug. 1914 ; wounded, Dar-
    danelles, Aug. 1915 ; Lt. 1915 ; A/Capt. : killed in action,
    22 Oct. 1918.

*Smyth, George Richard Gore ;
    Ent. 1913 ; 2 Lt. 7 L'pool R., Sept. 1914 ; wounded, France,
    March 1915 ; Lt. 1915 ; 2 Lt. 1, 2 L'pool R., Sept. 1916 ; A/Capt.
    1916-17 ; Lt. 1916 ; M.C.

Smyth, Herbert ;
    Ent. 1914 : Lt. 3 R. Ir. Fus., Oct. 1915 ; France ; Retired List,
    1917.

*Smyth, Irvine Johnston ;
    Ent. 1912 ; Pte. 6 Black Watch, Aug. 1914 ; 2 Lt. 6 R. Innis.
    Fus., Dec. 1914 ; killed, Dardanelles, 3 Sept. 1915.

*Smyth, John Hawkins ;
    Ent. 1912 ; 2 Lt. 6 Leins. R., Nov. 1915 ; killed in action, Vimy
    Ridge, 12 April 1917.

*Smyth, Louis Bouvier ;
    B.A. 1906 ; Sc.B. 1914 ; 2 Lt. O.T.C., T.F., Unattchd. List,
    Jan. 1915 ; Lt. 1916.

Smyth, Reginald Osborne ;
    M.B. 1912 ; M.D. 1914 ; Lt. R.A.M.C., June 1917 ; Capt. 1918.

*Smyth, Robinson Stewart ;
    M.B. and M.D. 1904 ; Lt. R.A.M C., July 1905 ; despatches,
    1 Jan. 1915 ; France, 1914, 1915; Major 1915 ; died in hospital.
    5 Apr. 1916, having been invalided home.

*Smyth, William ;
    B.A. 1914 ; Lt. R.E., Feb. 1915 ; Capt. 1917 ; A/Maj. 1918 ;
    M.C.

*Snell, Philip Sidney;
Ent. 1912; 2 Lt. 6 R. Ir. Fus., Sept. 1914; killed, Dardanelles, 9 Aug. 1915.

*Snodgrass, William M'Elrea ;
M.B. 1915; Lt. R.A.M.C., S.R., May 1915; Capt. 1915; wounded, Aug. 1916; M.C. Jan. 1917; Capt. R.A.M.C., 1919.

Somers, Frederick William ;
B.A. 1902; Pte. R.A.M.C. ; France 1917.

*Somerville, Richard Newman ;
B.A.I. 1914; 2 Lt. R.E., Oct. 1914; 94 Fld. Co.; killed in action, France, 9 Oct. 1915.

Spaight, Henry William ;
Med. School 189-; L.R.C.P. & S.I.; Lt. R.A.M.C., Sept. 1914; Capt. 1915; 2 Wessex Field Amb., France.

*Sparling, John William ;
Ent. 1911; 2 Lt. R.G.A., Oct. 1914; Malta; Lt. 1916.

*Speares, John ;
M.B. 1915; M.D. 1919; Lt. R.A.M.C., Nov. 1915; Capt. 1916; Mediterranean E. F., 1916-17; invalided, dysentery, 1917.

*Speedy, William Dunwoodie ;
Ent. 1916; Cadet B. Res. Bde. R.H.A. Nov. 1916; 2 Lt. 33 Batt. 6 A Res. Bde. R.F.A., Apr. 1917; France 1917; wounded, Feb. 1918; gassed 1918; Lt. 1918; 2 Lt. R.H. and R.F.A., March 1918.

*Spence, Rev. Alexander ;
B.A. 1912; Army Chaplain, May 1916; France, 1916; M.C. ; prisoner of war, March 1918; died of wounds, 31 March 1918; buried in Ham.

*Spencer, Frederick Albert ;
B.A. 1911; 2 Lt. A.S.C., Feb. 1911; Temp. Capt. 1914; Adjt. 1914; Capt. 1917; Capt. M.G.C., 1917; A/Maj. 1918.

Spickernell, Geoffrey ;
Ent. 1913; 2 Lt. 4 E. Kent R., Nov. 1914; Temp. Capt. 1915, Bgde. M. G. Offr; Lt. 1917.

Spong, William Arthur Roseberry ;
M.B. 1907; Lt. R.A.M.C., July 1907; Capt. 1911.

Spratt, Rev. John Hilton ;
B.A. 1911; Army Chaplain, 4 Cl., Apr. 1916.

Stack, George Hall ;
B.A. 1903; 2 Lt. R.E., June 1898; Maj. 1915; France, 1915; despatches, Nov. 1915; D.S.O. Feb. 1916; Mesopotamia, 1916; A/Lt.-Col. 1916; Bt. Lt.-Col. 1917.

Stack, George Hall ;
  M.B. 1907; Lt. R.A.M.C., Aug, 1908 ; Capt. 1912 ; wounded, Flanders, Sept. 1914; A/Lt.-Col. 1918–19.

Stack, Henry Thompson ;
  M.B. 1902; Lt. R.A.M.C., Jan. 1905 ; Major 1915.

Stanistreet, Arthur Handel ;
  Ent. 1886; Temp. Army Chap. 1916–19.

Stanistreet, George Bradshaw ;
  M.B. 1889 ; Capt. R.A.M.C., July 1891 ; Lt.-Col. 1913 ; D.A.D.-Gen. A.M.S., 1913; despatches and C.M.G., Jan., 1917 ; Col. 1917; D.D. Gen. A.M.S. 1918; Temp. Maj.-Gen. 1918 ; C.B. June 1918 ; despatches, July 1918; Order of the Crown of Italy, Apr. 1919 ; K.B.E. June 1919.

Stanley, Herbert Vernon ;
  M.B. 1908 ; Lt. R.A.M.C., July 1909 ; Capt. 1913 ; M.C. Jan. 1917 ; M.B.E. ; A/Maj. 1919.

*Stanton, Geoffrey Reeves ;
  B.A 1910; 2 Lt. A.S.C., June 1915 ; Lt. 1917.

Stanton, George ;
  M.B. 1915 ; Lt. R.A.M.C., Sept. 1914; Capt. 1916 ; died 16 Aug. 1916 of wounds received in action on 1 July 1916.

Stanton, Rev. James Henry;
  B.A. 1907 ; served in British Red Cross Hosp. 1916–18.

Stanton, Robert ;
  B.A. 1907 ; 2 Lt. 6 R. Dub. Fus., Sept. 1914 ; missing, believed killed, Dardanelles, 7 Aug. 1915.

Stanton, Thomas ;
  M.B. 1916 ; Lt. R.A.M.C., Jan. 1917 ; Capt. 1918 ; wounded, Somme.

Staples, Robert George Alexander ;
  Ent. 1913 ; Pte. Motor Transport, 1915.

Starkie, Walter Fitzwilliam ;
  B.A. 1917 ; Y.M.C.A., and Teacher in Active Service Army Schools, B.E.F. Italy, 1918–19.

Starling, Ernest Henry ;
  Sc.D. (Hon. Causâ) 1912; F.R.S. ; Maj. R.A.M.C., Nov. 1915 ; Lt.-Col. 1916 ; Salonika ; despatches, Oct. 1917 ; C.M.G. 1918.

Starr, Arthur James;
  Ent. 1913 ; 2 Lt. 11 R. Innis. Fus., Aug. 1915 ; Lt. 1917 ; att. 9 Bn. ; killed in action, 22 March 1918.

Steel, Edwin Bedford ;
  M.B. 1893 ; Capt. R.A.M.C., Jan. 1898 ; Maj., Oct. 1906 ; died of wounds, France, 23 Nov. 1914.

Steel, Richard Francis;
M.B. 1902: Lt. I.M.S., Aug. 1903; Maj. 1915: Indian Gen. Hosp., E.F.

Steele. William Henry;
M.B. 1866; M.D. 1871; Lt. R.A.M.C., Oct. 1866: Lt.-Col.; ret. 1897 ; temp. empld. ; commended for services, Feb. 1917.

*Stephens, George John William ;
B.A. 1904 ; 2 Lt. 7 R. Muns. Fus., Jan. 1916: Lt. Lab. Corps, 1917.

Stephens, John ;
B.A.I. 1906 ; Lt. Canadian Siege Artillery, Aug. 1916 ; France ; A/Capt.

Stephenson, Claudius;
Ent. 1911: 2 Lt. 12 Ches. R., Sept. 1914; Lt. 1915; **Capt.** 1916; died of wounds, 2 Nov. 1916.

*Stevens, William Pearson ;
Ent. 1913 ; 2 Lt. 7 L'pool R., Sept. 1914 ; Lt. 1915; Capt. 1917 ; Capt. M.G.C., 1917.

Stevenson, Archibald M'Corkell ;
Ent. 1915 ; 2 Lt. R.A.S.C., March 1918.

Stevenson, Frederick ;
M.B. 1907; Lt. I.M.S., Feb. 1908; Capt. 1911; M.O. King George's Own Central India Horse; Egypt, 1915.

*Stevenson, George ;
B.A.I. 1914 ; Trooper, Behar Light Horse, Patna District ; Lt. I.A. Res. of Offrs ; att. 3 Sappers and Miners.

Stevenson, Leonard William Hugh ;
Ent. 1914 ; 2 Lt. 9 R. Innis. Fus., Oct. 1914 ; M.C. ; killed in action, France, 1 July 1916.

Stevenson, Maurice MacCaw ;
B.A. 1911 ; 2 Lt. I.A., 1 Lancers, Aug. 1911; Lt. 1912; attchd. 18 Lancers; France, 1915; Capt. 1915.

Stevenson, Walter Clegg ;*
M.B. 1900 ; M.D. 1902; Capt. R.A.M.C., Home Hosp. Res., Aug. 1914; King George V Hosp., Dublin; France, Fld. Amb., 1918.

Stevenson, William Flack ;
M.B. 1865 ; C.B.; Col. July 1896 ; Hon. Surg. to the King, 1904 ; Hon. Maj.-Gen. 1913.

Stewart, Alan Darnby Huston ;
Ent. 1919 ; Pte. R.A.M.C.

Stewart, Charles Frederick ;
 Ent. 1889 ; late 5 R. Innis. Fus.; Capt. 9 York R., Sept. 1914 ;
 retired, ill health.

Stewart, Herbert St. George ;
 Ent. 1906 ; 2 Lt. 6 R. Innis. Fus., Nov. 1914 ; Lt. 1916.

Stewart, Hugh ;
 M.B. 1904 ; Lt. R.A.M.C., 1905 ; France 1914 ; Egypt ; France ;
 Major 1915 ; M.C. 1915 ; despatches, Jan. 1916 ; Temp. Lt.-
 Col., 1916 ; despatches Jan. 1917 ; D.S.O. June 1917 ; despatches
 (4 times) ; killed on active service, 12 Apr. 1918.

*Stewart, John Frederick ;
 Ent. 1913 ; 2 Lt. A.S.C., Nov. 1914 ; Lt. 1915.

Stewart, Philip Smyly :
 M.B. 1903 ; Lt. R.A.M.C., Jan. 1906 ; Capt. 1909 ; wounded,
 Mons retreat, Oct. 1914 ; Maj. 1918.

Stewart, Richard Arthur ;
 M.B. 1913 ; Lt. R.A.M.C., Aug.1914 ; Capt. 1915 ; France, 1914 ;
 M.C. July 1916.

*Stewart, Samuel George, F.T.C.D. ;
 B.A. 1908 ; Fellow, M.A. 1911 ; 2 Lt. O.T.C., T.F., Jan. 1915 ;
 2 Lt. R.F.A., May 1915 ; France, 1915 ; Lt. 1917 ; M.C. 1917 ;
 wounded, 1917 ; Maj. R.H. and R.F.A., Oct. 1917 ; bar to M.C.
 1917 ; killed in action, 27 Oct. 1918.

Stewart, Rev. Thomas Francis ;
 B.A. 1896 ; M.A. 1905 ; Chaplain R.N., Aug. 1914 ; H.M.S.
 " Commonwealth " ; killed, motor cycle accident, 15 March, 1916.

*Stewart, William John ;
 M.B. 1913 ; Lt. R.A.M.C., Aug. 1914 ; Capt. 1915.

Stewart-Moore, Charles Francis ;
 B.A. 1900 ; 2 Lt. 3 Leins. R., July 1915 ; wounded, July 1916 ;
 Lt. 1916.

Stewart-Moore, Henry ;
 B.A.I. 1907 ; Lt. 6 R. Innis. Fus., Jan. 1915 ; att. 7 Bn. ;
 killed in action, Macedonia, 10 Sept. 1916.

*Stewart-Moore, John Leslie ;
 B.A. 1913 ; 2 Lt. 15 R. Ir. Rif., Oct. 1914 : Lt. 1915 ; France,
 1915, 1916 ; wounded, Oct. 1916 ; Lt. New Armies, 1916 ; Trench
 Mortar Batts., 1916 ; despatches, Jan. 1917.

Still, Rev. John Henry Pellatt ;
 B.A. 1911 ; Army Chaplain, 4 Cl., May 1915-18 ; France, 1915 ;
 invalided, 1917 ; Chap. R.A.F., Nov. 1918.

o

Stoker, Edward Alexander Graves ;
Ent. 1906 ; Lt. A.S.C., Feb. 1915 ; Lt. M.G.C., Cavalry, Feb. 1915.

Stoker, Henry ;
Ent. 1880 ; L.R.C.P. & S.I. ; Maj. Australian A.M.C., July 1915 ; No. 2 Australian Gen. Hosp., Cairo.

Stokes, Adrian D. ;
M.B. 1910 ; M.D. 1911 ; Lt. R.A.M.C., Aug. 1914 ; France, 1914 ; Capt. 1915 ; despatches, June 1916 and Dec. 1917 ; D.S.O. Jan. 1918 ; Chevalier de l'Ordre de Couronne (Belge), Apr. 1918.

Stokes, Denis Jeffcott ;
M.B. 1909 ; Lt. R.A.M.C., Oct. 1914 ; Capt. 1915 ; M.C. Nov. 1918 ; A/Maj. 1918 ; Croix de Guerre, Nov. 1919.

Stokes, Harold William Puzey ;
B.A. 1899 ; 2 Lt. A.S.C., May 1900 ; Maj. 1914 ; Dep. Assist. Dir. of Supplies, 1915 ; D A.Q.M.G. 1916 ; Assist. Dir. of Supplies & Transport, Brit. Armies in France, 1918 ; Temp. Lt.-Col. 1918 ; Legion of Honour ; D.S.O.

Stokes, Henry ;
M.B. 1903 ; M.D. 1905 ; Civil Surgeon King George V Hospital, Dublin ; Capt. R.A.M.C., Sept. 1916 ; A/Lt.-Col. 1918 ; O.B.E. 1919.

*Stokes, Henry Albany ;
Ent. 1913 ; 2 Lt. 5 Conn. Rang., Aug. 1915 ; empld. R. Innis. Fus. ; Lt. 1917 ; Lt. I.A. 1917 ; Capt. 1920.

Stokes, Henry James Dudgeon ;
B.A. 1908 ; 2 Lt. A.S.C., Nov. 1914 ; Lt. 1915 ; Temp. Capt. & Adjt. 1918.

Stokes, Thomas George Nesbitt ;
M.B. 1898 ; Lt. I.M.S., Jan. 1900 ; Major 1911.

Stone, Herbert ;
M.B. 1904 ; R.N.

*Stone, William Henry Copeland ;
B.A.I. 1916 ; Cadet R.E., Oct. 1916 ; 2 Lt. June 1918 ; France, despatches.

Stoney, Edward Crawford ;
M.B. 1907 ; Lt. R.A.M.C., July 1909 ; Capt. 1913.

Stoney, Rev. Edwin Fazakerley ;
B.A. 1896 ; M.A. 1901 ; Army Chap. 4 Cl., Feb. 1918-19.

Stoney, Franc Aubrey Sadleir ;
B.A. 1896 ; 2 Lt. A.S.C., March 1915.

Stoney, Johnstone Percy Lipyeatt;
Ent. 1899; 2 Lt. 2 Worc. R., May 1901; wounded, Aisne, Sept 1914; Maj. 1916.

Stoney, Richard Atkinson;
M.B. 1901; French Red Cross, Base Hosp., Villeneuve, Dec. 1914 to June 1915; Medicin Maj. 2 Classe, French Army; Chevalier, Legion of Honour, 1920.

Stoney, Robert Thomas;
Ent. 1911; L.R.C.P. & S.I. 1917; Surg. Prob. R.N.V.R., Nov. 1914-19; Temp. Surg. Sub-Lt. 1914.

Story, William George Theaker;
M.B. 1888: Lt. R.A.M.C., Aug. 1915; H.M. Hospital S. "Nevasa."

*Stringer, Albert Edward;
B.A.I. 1914; 2 Lt. 7 R. Dub. Fus., Oct. 1915; 2 Lt. R.E. Aug. 1916; Lt. 1917; A/Capt. 1918; France; despatches.

Stritch, George Seymour Russell;
Med. School. 189-; L.R.C.P. & S., Edin.; Capt. 5 Durh. L. I., Sept. 1914; Capt. 6 Conn. Rang., May 1915; killed in action, Flanders, 7 Feb. 1916.

Stronach, John Clark;
B.A.I. 1909; Cpl. Punjab Light Horse.

Strong, Charles Eric;
Ent. 1919; 2 Lt. R.G.A., June 1918; France.

Strong, Herbert William;
Ent. 1915; Pte. Mech. Transport S., Oct. 1916; 2 Lt. R.A.S.C. Nov. 1918.

Stuart, Alexander George;
M.A. 1896; Lt.-Col. I.A.; killed in action, Sept. 1915.

*Stuart, John Henry James;
B. Dent. Sc. 1917; Temp. Dent. Surg. Sub-Lt. R.N.V.R., June 1917; R.N. Hosp., Plymouth.

Stuart, John Matthew Blackwood;
B.A.I. 1904; Pte. Ir. Yeo. Rhodesian Field F., Jan. 1900-1901; I.A. Res. of Officers; 2 Lt. attchd. 3 Sappers and Miners, May 1915; Mesopotamia 1915; Indian Frontier; Afghanistan; Capt. 1919.

*Stubbs, John William Cotter;
M.B. 1913; Lt. R.A.M.C., Jan. 1914; Capt. 1915; despatches, May 1915; M.C. June 1915; D.A.D.M.S. 1916; D.S.O. June 1919; A/Lt.-Col. 1918.

Stubbs, Thomas Troubridge;
Ent. 1894; 2 Lt. R. Muns. Fus., Nov. 1900; Maj. 1915; Temp.
Lt.-Col. commanding 2 R. Muns. Fus., 1915; France, 1915.

Studdert, Reginald Hallam;
B.A. 1915 : 2 Lt. R.F.A., July 1913; Capt. 1915; Bt. Major
1917; A/Major 1917, 1919; wounded, Oct. 1917; M.C.; D.S.O.

Sugars, Harold Saunderson;
M.B. 1908; Lt. R.A.M.C., March 1915; Capt. 1916; wounded,
May 1917; M.C. June 1917; D.S.O. July 1917; despatches,
Dec. 1917; Arnott Medal 1918.

Sugars, John Charles :
B.A. 1898; 2 Lt. R.F.A., T.F., May 1915.

Sullivan, Fleetwood William Porter;
M.B. 1917; Lt. R.A.M.C., May 1918.

*Sullivan, Launcelot Lucian Adey;
Ent. 1913; R.G.A. School, Aug. 1918.

*Sullivan, Robert Ievers;
M.B. 1914; M.D. 1916; Lt. R.A.M.C., S.R., Nov. 1914; Capt.
1915; Lt. R.A.M.C., Jan. 1917; M.C. Nov. 1917; despatches,
Dec. 1917; wounded, April 1918; Capt. 1918.

*Sullivan, William John;
Ent. 1913; 2 Lt. A.S.C., June 1915; Lt. 1918.

Supple, William Hamilton;
Ent. 1896; 2 Lt. 2 R. Dub. Fus., Feb. 1900; Capt. 1908;
Major 1915; Ord. Off. 1915–19.

Sutcliffe, Paul;
B.A. 1909; Petty Offr., R.N. Air Service, Feb. 1915.

Sutcliffe, William Henry;
M.B. 1908; Lt. R.A.M.C., Sept. 1914; Capt. 1915; Gallipoli;
Salonika; France; M.C. Sept. 1918.

*Sutherland, Thomas Gerrard;
Ent. 1915; Sandhurst, Dec. 1916; 2 Lt. 1, 2 R. Muns. Fus.,
Jan. 1918; wounded, Oct. 1918.

Sutton, Rev. Frederick Olynthus;
B.A. and LL.B. 1882; Army Chaplain, 4 Cl., Oct. 1914;
despatches, Jan. 1917.

Swan, James Graham Goodenough;
M.B. 1899; Lt. I.M.S., Jan. 1901; Major 1912; Flanders;
C.I.E.

Swan, William Travers ;
    M.B. 1884 ; Maj. R.A.M.C., May 1897 ; Col. A.M.S., 1914 ;
    A.D.M.S., B.E.F., France, 1915–18 ; despatches, Feb. 1915,
    June 1915, June 1916, Dec. 1917 (Salonika) ; C.B. June 1915 ;
    Major-Gen. 1917 ; D.M.S., Egyptian E.F., 1918.

Swanepoel, Petrus Johannes ;
    M.B. 1917 ; Temp. Surg. R.N., Dec. 1917 ; North Sea ; Cape
    Station.

Sweetnam, Thomas Charles Augustus ;
    M.B. 1904 ; M.D. 1905 ; Lt. R.A.M.C., May 1918.

*Sweetnam, Thomas William ;
    M.B. 1915 ; Lt. R.A.M.C., Oct. 1915 ; wounded, France, Sept.
    1916 ; Capt. 1916.

Swifte, Ernest Godwin Meade ;
    Ent. 1889 ; Capt. Army Motor Res. of Officers, July 1906 ; Capt.
    R.G.A. (Head Quarter Staff), 2 Cav. Brig., Sept. 1914 ; I.E.F.
    France, 1915 ; Major Tank Corps, 1916.

Switzer, Ernest Vivian ;
    Ent. 1917 ; Cadet D.U.O.T.C., 1918 ; volunteered and accepted.

Switzer, Kenneth Walker ;
    Ent. 1916 ; Pte. Apr. 1917 ; 2 Lt. R.F.C., Aug. 1917 ; Lt.
    Aeroplane Offr. 1918.

*Synge, Victor Millington ;
    Ent. 1912 ; Surg. Prob. R.N.V.R., March, 1916 ; North Sea,
    1916.

*Synnott, Frederick William ;
    Ent. 1912 ; 2 Lt. 3 R. Dub. Fus., Nov. 1914 ; attchd. 1 I. R. Ir.
    Fus., 1914 ; France, 1915 ; Lt. 1915 ; Capt. 1916 ; M.C.

T

Tabuteau, Thomas Bousfield Herrick ;
    M.B. 1917 ; Lt. R.A.M.C., Nov. 1917 ; Capt. 1918.

Tacchella, Carl Frederick Hollinshed ;
    B.A. 1910 ; M.A. 1913 ; 2 Lt. Bangalore Rif. Vol.

Tandy, Oswald Cornwallis Stratford ;
    M.B. 1912 ; Lt. R.A.M.C., S.R., Aug. 1914 ; France, 1915 ;
    Capt. 1915.

Tarrant, Hugh Sherrard ;
> M.B. 1900 ; M.O. Haulbowline Military Hosp., Queenstown.

Tate, Gerrard William ;
> M.B. 1889 ; Lt. R.A.M.C., July 1891 ; Lt.-Col. 1913 ; A.D.M.S.
> E. Afr. Force, 1916 ; D.D.M.S., 1917–19 ; D.S.O. Feb. 1917 ;
> despatches, Oct. 1917 and Sept. 1918 ; Col. A.M.S., 1918 ; C.M.G.
> 1918.

Tate, Godfrey ;
> M.B. 1896 ; Lt. I.M.S., Jan. 1898 ; Maj. 1909 ; M.O.
> 22 Sam Browne's Cavalry ; Lt.-Col. 1917.

Tate, Robert George Hetherington ;
> M.B. 1902 ; M.D. 1903 ; Lt. R.A.M.C., Jan. 1906 ; Capt. 1909 ;
> wounded ; despatches, 1 Jan. 1916 ; Brevet Maj. 1916 ; Maj. 1918 ;
> A/Lt.-Col. 1918.

*Tate, Robert William, F.T.C.D. ;
> M.A. 1903 ; Fellow, 1908 ; Maj. D.U.O.T.C., Unattached List,
> T.F., Oct. 1912 ; K.B.E.

Tate, Thomas Marshall ;
> M.B. 1889 ; M.D. 1890 ; 2 Lt. 5 R. Ir. Rif., Aug. 1914 ;
> France ; 2 Lt. 1, 2 R. Ir. Rif., May 1916 ; Lt. 1916.

Tatlow, Robert Evelyn Tissington ;
> M.B. and M.D. 1911 ; Lt. R.A.M.C., T.F., Oct. 1914 ; France,
> 1915 ; Capt. 1915 ; despatches, Jan. 1916 ; Major 1918.

*Taylor, Charles ;
> Ent. 1912 ; 2 Lt. A.S.C., March 1915 ; Lt. 1916 ; att. Conn.
> Rang., Oct. 1917.

Taylor, Daniel Brumhall ;
> Ent. 1901 ; 2 Lt. 17 R. Ir. Rif., Apr. 1915 ; Lt. 1917 ;
> prisoner of war, March 1918.

Taylor, Edward Henry ;
> M.B. 1890 ; M.D. 1896 ; Professor of Surgery, Trinity College ;
> Surg. Dublin Castle Red Cross Hosp ; Lt.-Col. R.A.M.C., 83 (Dub.)
> Gen. Hosp., France, May 1917.

Taylor, Edward ;
> B.A.1. 1921 ; Pte. M.T., R.A.S.C.

Taylor, George ;
> M.B. 1899 ; M.O. Princess Patricia Hosp. Bray ; Temp. Lt.
> R.A.M.C., July 1917 ; drowned, Mesopotamia, 30 Oct. 1917.

Taylor, Godfrey ;
> M.B. 1897 ; Fleet Surg. R.N., Nov. 1913 ; lost in H. M. S.
> " Formidable," Jan. 1915.

Taylor, Hugh Neville Adam ;
M.B. 1897 ; M.D. 1899 ; Maj. R.A.M.C., T.F., May 1912.

Taylor, James Benjamin ;
L.M. 1917 ; Lt. R.A.M.C., Jan. 1918 ; wounded, France, Apr. 1918 ; Capt. 1919.

Taylor, James Braid ;
I.C.S. Student, T.C.D. 1913-14 ; 2 Lt. att. E. Kent R.

*Taylor, John Arthur Harold ;
Ent. 1909 ; 2 Lt. 3, 1 R. Dub. Fus., July 1912 ; killed in action, Dardanelles, 24 Sept. 1915.

Taylor, William Alfred ;
M.B. 1911; Temp. Lt. R.A.M.C., Jan. 1915; despatches, June 1916 ; Capt. 1916 ; wounded, Aug. 1916.

Taylor, William ;
M.B. 1902 ; Surg. Dublin Castle Red Cross Hosp ; Temp. Lt.-Col. R.A.M.C., 1916 ; despatches, Sept. 1917 ; Temp. Col. 1917 ; C.B. June 1919.

Taylor, William Hamilton Hepburn ;
Ent. 1919 ; Flight Cadet R.A.F., 1918.

Teeling, Samuel George ;
B.A. 1898 ; Pte. 3 R. Muns. Fus., Jan. 1916.

Teeling, Theodore Francis P. J. B. ;
Ent. 1909 : 2 Lt. K. O. Sco. Bord., March 1914; Lt. 1914 ; Capt. 1915.

Tench, Charles Gerald ;
M.B. 1893 ; Capt. R.A.M.C., T.F., Nov. 1914.

Ternan, Alfred William Maunsell ;
Ent. 1919; Pte. Artists' Rif. (28 London R.), 1918.

Thacker, James Henry Joseph ;
B.A. 1910; D.I., R.I.C.; Lt. A.S.C., Oct. 1915; France, 1915.

Thacker, William Stuart ;
M.B. 1908 ; M.D. 1909 ; F.S.C.S. Edin. ; Temp. Lt. R.A.M.C., June 1915 ; Malta ; Capt. 1916.

Thom, Rev. John ;
B.A. 1908 ; M.A. 1914 : Army Chaplain, 4 Cl., Dec. 1915 ; 3 Cl. 1918 ; M.C. 1916 ; two bars to M.C. 1917 ; Belgian Croix de Guerre, 1918.

*Thomas, Francis Stephen ;
B.A. 1914 ; Sub. Lt. R.N.V.R.

Thomas, Rev. John Henry ;
B.A. 1897 ; M.A. 1904 ; Chaplain, 77 Canadian R., Nov. 1915 ;
France, with 78 Canadian R., 1916 ; Canadian E.F. 1916-19.

*Thomas, Robert Alexander Hastings ;
Ent. 1911; Temp. 2 Lt. A.S.C. (M.T.), May 1915; Mudros,
1915 ; Salonika, 1915, 1916, 1917, 1918 ; 2 Lt. A.S.C., June 1916 ;
M.C. June 1917 ; Lt. 1917.

Thompson, Charles Herbert ;
M.B. 1893 : Lt. R.A.M.C., Oct. 1914 ; Capt. 1915.

Thompson, Croasdaile Miller ;
M.B. 1879 ; Lt.-Col. I.M.S., March 1900 ; retd. ; temp. empld.
March 1915 ; died, 3 Sept. 1916.

Thompson, Edward Charles ;
M.B. 1871 ; Maj. R.A.M.C., S.R. ; Commandant, Belgian Field
Hosp., Flanders.

Thompson, Ernest St. Clair ;
Ent. 1917 ; Pte. A.S.C (M.T.), 1917.

Thompson, Rev. Frederic Basil Kerr ;
B.A. 1900 ; M.A. 1912 ; Army Chaplain, 4 Cl., May 1915.

Thompson, Harold Francis ;
B.A. 1903 : Capt. O.T.C., T.F., Unattached List, Sept. 1913 ;
Capt. 9 Rif. Brig. March 1915 ; wounded, Flanders, Aug. 1915 ;
killed in action, France, 12 July, 1916.

Thompson, Harry Neville ;
M.B. 1883 ; D S.O. ; Maj. R.A.M.C., Aug. 1896 ; Col. A.M.S.,
1913 ; D.D.M.S., Sco. Comd. ; prisoner of war, Sept. 1914-1915 ;
C.M.G. June 1916 ; A.D.M.S. 2 and 48 Divs., 1915 ; D.D.M.S.
6 Corps, 1915-17 ; D.M.S. 1 Army, 1917 ; despatches, Jan. 1916,
June 1916, Dec. 1917, May 1918, Dec. 1918, and July 1919 ;
American D.S.M. ; French War Cross, with palms; Mil. Order of
Avis, 2 Cl. ; C.B. 1918 ; K.C.M.G. 1918.

Thompson, James Arthur ;
M.B. 1901 ; Staff Surg. R.N., June 1910 ; Surg. Cr. 1916.

Thompson, James Harloe Christopher ;
M.B. 1904 ; M.D. 1913 : Temp. Lt. R.A.M.C., Aug. 1916 ; att.
6 King's O.Y.L.I.; S.M.O., 18 C. R. Depot, B.E.F., 1917.

Thompson, John Alexander ;
Ent. 1914 ; Pte. 5 R. Dub. Fus., Oct. 1915 ; killed in Dublin,
Easter Monday, 24 Apr. 1916.

Thompson, John Douglas ;
Ent. 1916 ; Surg. Sub-Lt. R.N.V.R., Aug. 1918 ; H.M.S.
" Marksman," Northern Patrol.

Thompson, John Knox Stafford ;
Ent. 1917; Pte. 9 R. Ir. Rif., 1917; Cpl. 1918; 2 Lt. 1919.

*Thompson, John Webster ;
B.A.I. 1913; Capt. R.F.A., T.F., Oct. 1914 ; Lt. R.N.A.S. and R.A.F. ; France.

Thompson, Robert Gordon ffolliott ;
Ent. 1919; Pte. 19 R. Ir. Rif., 1917; Temp. 2 Lt. 1, 2 York and Lan. R., May 1918; Salonika 1918.

Thompson, Rev. Sidney Lyle ;
B.A. 1900 ; Army Chaplain, 4 Cl., Oct. 1915–19 ; Mediterranean E.F.

*Thompson, Thomas James Logan ;
M.B. 1914; Temp. Lt. R.A.M.C., Dec. 1914; Dardanelles ; Temp. Capt. 1915; France ; M.C. Sept. 1917 ; Capt. R.A.M.C., June 1918 ; A/Major 1918.

Thompson, William Henry Ffolliott ;
B.A.I. 1909 ; M.M., 1 Co., U.S. Naval Aviation Forces.

Thompson, William Irwin ;
M.B. 1905 ; Lt. R.A.M.C., July 1906; Capt. 1910 ; prisoner of war, Sept. 1914–July 1915 ; Temp. Lt.-Col. 1917 ; Major 1918 ; D.S.O. Jan. 1918 ; despatches, Jan. 1920.

Thomson, Douglas Stoker Brownlee ;
M.B. 1903 ; Lt. R.A.M.C., Jan. 1904; Capt. 1907; Maj. 1915; empld. with Egyptian Army.

Thorpe, Arthur Aylmer ;
Ent. 1912 ; 2 Lt. A.S.C., Jan. 1915; Capt. 1917.

*Thrift, William Henry ;
Ent. 1917 ; Eng. Cadet Sch., May 1918.

*Thunder, Patrick Adair ;
Ent. 1909 : Bombardier, 1 Batt. Can. Artillery ; wounded.

Thunder, Wilfred Michael ;
M.B. 1904 ; Lt. R.A.M.C., May 1915 ; Capt. 1916.

Tibbs, Dudley Muriel ;
Ent. 1905 ; Pte. Malay Rif. Volunteers.

Tibbs, Rev. Geoffrey Wilberforce ;
B.A. 1904 ; M.A. 1909 : Chaplain, R.N., Sept. 1913 ; H.M.S. "Jupiter" 1915–16 ; " Minotaur," 1917–19.

Tibbs, Rev. Philip Graydon ;
B.A. 1894 ; M.A. 1911 ; Army Chaplain, I.E.F., Mesopotamia.

Tichborne, Rev. Edward Alan ;
B.A. 1892 ; Army Chap. 4 Cl. Nov. 1915–17.

Tichborne, Rev. Forde ;
B.A. 1885 ; M.A. 1899 ; Temp. Army Chap. 1914–19.

Tichborne, Rev. George Morrow ;
B.A. 1892 ; Chaplain, R.N., June 1898 ; H.M.S. " Triumph "
1914 ; " Tamar " 1914–16 ; " Vernon " 1917 : R.N.A.S. 1917–19.

Tichborne, John ;
M.B. 1897 ; M.D. 1901 ; Temp. Lt. R A.M.C., Oct. 1914 ;
Capt. 1915.

Tidmarsh, Gerald David ;
B.A. 1911 ; 2 Lt. R.F.A., Dec. 1911 ; wounded, Aisne, 14 Sept.
1914 ; Lt. 1914 ; Temp. Capt. 1915 ; Capt. 1916 ; M.C.

Tighe, Augustus Blakely ;
M.B. 1903 ; W. African M.S.; died at Lorne, Togoland, 20
March 1919.

*Tipping, Nathaniel Drew ;
Ent. 1916 ; Cadet D.U.O.T.C. 1918 ; volunteered and accepted.

*Tittle, John Moore ;
Ent. 1913 ; 2 Lt. 6 R. Dub. Fus., Aug. 1914 ; Capt. 1915 ;
wounded, Gallipoli, Aug. 1915.

Tivy, Robert Edward Forrest ;
Ent. 1906 ; 2 Lt. Canadian R.F.C.

Tobias, Rev. John ;
B.A. 1908 ; B.D. 1912 ; Army Chaplain, 4 Cl., Apr. 1916 ;
France.

Tobias, Rev. Matthew ;
B.A. 1902 ; Army Chaplain, Nov. 1906 ; 4 Cl., 1908 ; Malta,
1912–16 ; France, 1916–18 ; 3 Cl. 1918.

*Tobias, William Oliver ;
M.B. 1914 : Lt. R.A.M.C., S.R., Aug. 1914 ; Capt. 1915 ; despatches, Jan. 1916 ; A/Major 1918.

*Tobin, Richard Patrick ;
Ent. 1912 ; 2 Lt. 7 R. Dub. Fus., Aug. 1914 ; Capt. 1915 ;
killed, Dardanelles, 15 Aug. 1915 ; despatches, 29 Jan. 1916.

*Todd, Andrew William Palethorpe ;
M.B. 1915 ; Temp. Lt. R.A.M.C., Aug. 1915 ; Temp. Capt. 1916 ;
M.C. Sept. 1918 ; A/Major 1918 ; Capt. R.A.M.C., Feb. 1919.

Todd-Thornton, James Henry Brooke ;
Ent. 1874 ; Major 13 Notts and Derby Regt. Oct. 1914 ; Major
3 North'd. Fus. 1916 ; died of illness contracted on service, 12 Jan.
1918.

*Tolerton, Samuel Lee;
Ent. 1909 ; 2 Lt. 6 R. Innis. Fus., Aug. 1914 ; killed, Dardanelles, 15 Aug. 1915.

Tomlinson, Thomas ;
B.A.I. 1883 ; Asst. Divisional Offr., R.E., South Dublin, June 1915.

*Tomlinson, William George Philip ;
B.A.1. 1913 ; 2 Lt. R.E., 1918.

Tonkin, Rev. Hugh Frederick ;
B.A. 1908 ; Army Chaplain, 4 Cl., June 1916–19

*Toomey, Archbald Roche;
Ent. 1908 : 2 Lt. 6 Leins. R., Aug. 1914 ; killed, Dardanelles, 10 Aug. 1915.

Toomey, Mark Anthony ;
Ent. 1888 ; Pte. A.S.C., May 1915 ; 2 Lt., May 1915 ; Capt. 1916

Tippin, Henry ;
Ent. 1886 ; Maj. 3 R. Ir R., Mar. 1917.

Torrens, Dudley Francis ;
M.B. 1906 ; Lt. R.A.M.C., July 1916 ; Capt. 1917 ; France ; prisoner of war, March 1918, and M.O. allied prisoners of war till Armistice.

Tottenham, Richard Edward ;
M.B. 1912 ; M.D. 1914 ; Temp. Surg. Lt. R.N., Sept. 1915–19.

Townsend, Rev. Horace Crawford ;
B.A. 1892 ; Army Chaplain, 4 Cl., Dec. 1915 ; M.C. 1917.

Townshend, Edward Hume Steele ;
B.A.I. 1893 ; Executive Engineer, Civil Ry. Co., France, 1917.

Townshend, Horace Montague Dimock ;
M.B. 1902 ; M.D. 1903 ; Temp. Lt. R.A.M.C., Nov. 1915.

Townshend, Robert Ponsonby Loftus ;
B.A.I. 1888 ; Capt. I. Defence F.

*Traill, Anthony O'Brien ;
Ent. 1914 ; 2 Lt. 3 W. Rid. R., Dec. 1914 ; 2 Lt. R.F.C., Oct. 1916 ; Lt. 1917 ; Tank Corps 1918 ; A/Capt. 1918 ; Temp. Capt. 1918.

Traill, Edmund Francis Tarleton ;
Ent. 1896 ; 2 Lt. R. Innis. Fus., Jan. 1900 ; 2 Lt. A.S.C., May 1901 ; Maj. 1914 ; Temp. Lt.-Col. 1916 ; D.S.O.

Traill, Henry Edward O'Brien ;
B.A. 1898 ; M.A. 1903 ; 2 Lt. R.F.A., Mar. 1900 ; Maj. 1915 ; despatches, Jan. 1917 ; D.S.O.; A/Lt.-Col 1917.

Traill, William Stewart ;
B.A.I. 1889 ; 2 Lt. R.E., March 1890 ; Maj. 1910 ; Lt.-Col. 1918 ; D.S.O.; Croix de Guerre (French) ; despatches (3 times).

Trant, Hope ;
Ent. 1920 ; V.A.D., No. 6 Stationary Hosp. and No. 2 Gen. Hosp., France, June 1915–Dec. 1916 ; Brit. Red Cross Motor Convoy July 1917–June 1918 ; 47 Aux. Amb. Car Co., Abbeville, June 1918–Oct. 1919 ; despatches ; M.B.E.

Travers, Spencer Robert Valentine ;
Ent. 1913 ; 2 Lt. 7 R. Muns. Fus., Sept. 1914 ; Lt. 1915 ; killed, Dardanelles, 9 Aug. 1915.

*Trayer, Benjamin Langer ;**
B.A.I. 1920 ; Cadet D.U.O.T.C., 1918 ; volunteered and accepted.

*Trayer, Hugh George ;**
M.B. 1912 ; Lt. R.A.M.C., S.R., Aug. 1914 ; Capt. 1915 ; Gallipoli ; Egypt ; France ; Order of White Eagle, 5th Class, Feb. 1917 ; Capt. R.A.M.C., March 1918 ; A/Major 1918 ; despatches, May 1918.

Treanor, Robert Seymour Stanley ;
B.A.I. 1913 ; 2 Lt. Indian Ord. Dept. ; despatches.

*Tree, Francis Thomas ;**
B.A. 1909 ; 2 Lt. R.G.A., Nov. 1915 ; Lt. 1917 ; empld. Min. of Munitions, 1918.

Treves, Sir Frederick, Bart.;
. M.D. (Hon. Causâ) 1904 ; G.C.V.O. 1905 ; Hon. Col. R.A.M.C., .Sept. 1908.

Trimble, Ailwyn Egerton Copeland ;
Ent. 1919 ; Capt. 7 R. Innis. Fus. 1914–18 ; France ; Flanders ; despatches.

*Trimble, Noch Desmond ;
Ent. 1913 ; 2 Lt. 12 R. Innis. Fus., June 1915 ; killed, France, 29 April 1916.

*Troughton, John Herbert Watson ;
Ent. 1914 ; 2 Lt. 4 R. Ir. Regt., July 1915 ; attchd. 5 T. F. Artillery Training School, 1916 ; Lt. 1917 ; Lt. Tank Corps, 1917 ; France ; empld. Min. of Lab., 1919.

Trouton, Gardiner William ;
M.B. 1885 ; M.D. 1894 ; Surg. Maj. T.F., Oct. 1914 : Dardanelles.

*Tucker, Frederick Charles ;
B. Dent. Sc. 1915 ; Surg. Dent. Lt. R.A.M.C., Oct. 1915 ; Capt. 1916.

Tuckey, Helena Frances ;
B.A. 1909 ; M.A. 1913 ; Military Hospital, France.

*Tully, James Kivas ;
B.A. 1909 ; 2 Lt. 7 Midd'x R., Sept. 1912 ; Capt. 1914 ;
wounded, France, May 1915 ; died of wounds received in action,
16 Sept. 1916.

*Tully, William Lee ;
B.A.I. 1912 ; 2 Lt. R.G.A.. Sept, 1914 ; Lt. 1917.

Tunwell, John William ;
Ent. 1914 ; Temp. 2 Lt. 12 E. Surrey R., Sept. 1915 ; Capt.
1916 ; spl. empld. 1917.

*Turnly, John Francis ;
Ent. 1916 ; 2 Lt. M.G.C., Oct. 1917 ; killed in action, Flanders,
16 April 1918.

*Tweedy, Cecil Mahon John ;
Ent. 1911, 2 Lt. 3 R. Dub. Fus., Aug. 1914 ; wounded, Dardanelles, Sept. 1915 ; Lt. 1916 ; killed in action, 28 Feb. 1917.

*Tyndall, William Ernest ;
M.B. 1914 ; Lt. R.A.M.C., S.R., Sept. 1914 ; Capt. 1915 ;
M.C., Sept. 1918 ; A Maj. 1918 ; Capt. R.A M.C. 1918.

Tyrrell, Garrett William Giffard ;
B.A.I. 1898 ; Lt. R.E., 1915–18 ; France ; despatches (twice).

*Tyrrell, Guy Yelverton ;
Ent. 1911 ; 2 Lt. 3, 2 E. Kent R., Aug. 1914 ; wounded,
France, Feb. 1916 ; Capt. 1916 ; att. R.F.C. 1918 ; M.C.

Tyrrell, Jasper Robert Joly ;
M.B. 1901 ; Lt. I.M.S., Jan. 1902 ; Maj. 1913.

Tyrrell, Reginald Bramley ;
B.A.I. 1897 ; 2 Lt. R.A., March 1900 ; Maj. 1914 ; Ordnance
Offr., 3 Cl., 1914 ; 2 Cl. 1918 ; Assist. Dir. of Ord. Servs. 1918 ;
A/Lt.-Col. 1918 ; O.B.E.

*Tyrrell, William Upton ;
Ent. 1913 ; 2 Lt. 3, 1 R. Ir. Rif., Aug. 1915 ; Lt. 1916 ; att.
R.F.C. 1918.

Tyson, Rev. John George ;
B.A. 1912 ; LL.B. 1914 ; Army Chaplain, 4 Cl., Apr. 1916 ;
France 1916.

U

*Usher, Isaac William ;
Ent. 1914 : 2 Lt. 2 R. Ir. Regt., June 1915 ; Lt. 1915 ; killed
in action, 4 July, 1916.

V

Valentine, John Archibald;
M.B. and M.D. 1902; Temp. Lt. R.A.M.C., June 1917; Capt. 1918.

Valentine, William Arthur;
M.B. 1891 : M.D. 1894; Lt. R A.M.C., T.F., May 1912 : Capt. 1915; Serbian Order of St. Sava, Jan. 1918; Salonika, 1918.

*Vance, Robert Lancelot;
B.A. 1913; M.B. 1915; 2 Lt. 4 R. Ir. Fus., Aug. 1914; Capt. 1915; wounded, Flanders, June 1915; Capt. I.M.S., July 1916.

Varian, Amos George;
M.B. 1914; Temp. Lt. R.A.M.C., May 1915; Capt. 1916, France; Mesopotamia.

Varian, Hilda Maud;
M.B. 1915; Chief Medical Recruiting Controller, Wales, Q.M.A.A.C., 1918.

*Varian, Walter Osborne;
Ent. 1911; 7 Cadet Bn., Oct. 1916; 2 Lt. 5 R. Muns. Fus., Apr. 1917; killed in action, 30 March 1918.

Vaughan, Leslie Reginald;
B.A.I. 1914; 2 Lt. R.E., T.F., May 1915; Lt. 1916; M.C., June 1918.

Vaughan, Reginald Tate;
M.B. 1910; M.D. 1913; Temp. Capt. S. African A.M.C.; German S. W. Africa.

Verschoyle, Francis Stuart;
Ent. 1914; 2 Lt. R.E., Aug. 1914; killed in action, Ypres, 25 Apr. 1915.

*Vickery, Edward Percival Hadden;
M.B. 1914; Temp. Lt. R.A.M.C., Dec. 1914; Capt. 1915; Gallipoli; Egypt; wounded, Sept. 1918.

Vickery, George Gordon;
M.B. 1907; Staff Surg. R.N., May 1915; despatches, Sept. 1917; Surg.-Cmdr. 1919; O.B.E. 1919.

Vickery, Samuel Henry;
M.B. 1903; Staff Surg. R.N., Nov. 1912; Surg.-Cmdr. 1919; died on service, 25 July 1919.

*Vigors, Arthur Cecil;
Ent. 1913 ; 2 Lt. 9 R. Dub. Fus., Aug. 1915 ; France, 1916 ; att. R. Muns. Fus.; killed in action, 9 Sept. 1916.

Vigors, Cliffe Henry ;
Ent. 1883 ; 2 Lt. R. Ir. Regt., Aug. 1885 ; Maj. 1904 ; retd. 1905 ; re-empld. Recg. Duties, 1914 ; empld. Min. of Natl. Serv., 1918 ; O.B.E., Jan. 1919.

Villiers, Arthur William Crips ;
Ent. 1917 ; 2 Lt. R.A.F., Nov. 1918.

Vincent, Rev. John Marshall ;
B.A. 1911 ; M.A. 1914 ; Army Chaplain, 4 Cl., Jan. 1916–19.

W

Waddell, Samuel Gilmore ;
Ent. 1916 ; Lt. R.F.A.

Wade, Ernest Wentworth ;
M.B. 1892 ; M.D. 1895 ; Pte. 5 Vol. Bn. W. Norfolk R., Sept 1914 ; Lt. 2 Vol. Bn. Norfolk R., 1915.

Wade, George Augustus ;
M.B. 1886 ; M.D. 1895 ; Lt. R.A.M.C., Feb. 1887 ; Maj. 1899 ; Maj. Res. of Offs., Aug. 1914 ; died 17 March 1919.

Wade, William Moore ;
M.B. 1904 ; Capt. R.A.M.C., Oct. 1917, whilst with King's African Rifles.

*Wakely, Ion George ;
B.A. 1913 ; 2 Lt. A.S.C., June 1915 ; Lt. 1915 ; 2 Lt. R.G.A., Jan. 1917 ; M.C., Aug. 1917 ; wounded, March 1918 ; Lt. 1918 ; A/Capt. 1918.

Walker, Charles Derwent ;
Ent. 1905 ; M.B. Edin. ; Lt. R.A.M.C., Nov. 1915 ; Capt. 1916.

Walker, Rev. Francis Joseph ;
B.A. 1902 ; M.A. 1905 ; B.D. 1909 ; Army Chaplain, 4 Cl., Apr. 1907 ; despatches, Jan. 1917 ; Assist. to Dep. Chap. Gen. 1917 ; 2 Cl. 1919.

Walker, Francis Spring ;
Med. School 1894, F.R.C.S.I.; Lt. R.A.M.C. Apr. 1900 ; Maj. 1912 ; Lt.-Col. 1917 ; C.B.E.

*Walker, Francis William ;
Ent. 1915; Cadet Corps. R.G.A., Feb. 1916; 2 Lt. R.F.A.,
July 1916; M.C.; Lt. 1918; A/Capt. 1918; France; Belgium ;
despatches.

*Walker, Henry James ;
Ent. 1914 ; 2 Lt. 4 R. Dub. Fus., Mar. 1917 : 2 Lt. Tank Corps,
1917 ; Lt. 1918 ; A/Capt. 1918.

*Walker, Hubert Lawrence ;
Ent. 1913 ; B A. 1919 ; Pte. R.A.M.C., June 1915 ; Sergt. 1915 ;
Salonika, 1915 ; Egypt, 1916 ; The Mediterranean 1917 ; torpedoed
whilst on medical staff of H.M.S. "Dover Castle " ; France 1918 ;
demobilized, Jan. 1919.

*Walker, Joseph Henry Cranston ;
M.B. 1915; Lt. R.A.M.C., S.R., Feb. 1915 ; Capt. 1916 ; Lt.
R.A.M.C. 1918 ; Capt. 1919; M.C.

*Walker, Maurice Cecil ;
Ent. 1915 ; 2 Lt. R.G.A., S.R., Dec. 1915 ; Lt 1917 ; A/Capt.
1918 ; M.C.

*Walker, William Benjamin ;
M.B. 1915; Temp. Lt. R.A.M.C., Oct. 1915 ; Capt. 1916.

Wallace, Arthur William Baillie ;
Ent. 1894 ; 2 Lt. Durh. L. I., May 1898 ; Capt. 1905 ; Dep.
Assist. Adjt. and Qr. Mr. Gen. 1914 ; Maj. 1915 ; France ; Temp.
Lt.-Col. 1916-18 ; Egyptian Army, 1916 ; A.A. and Q.M.G. Home
Forces, 1916-19 ; Bt. Lt.-Col. 1919 ; D.A.A.G., Rhine, 1919.

Wallace, Hill Cecil ;
B.A.I. 1905 ; Capt., Military Rys., Mesopotamia, 1916-19.

Wallace, James Waldo ;
Ent. 1915 ; B.A. 1919 ; Cadet, 19 R. Ir. Rif., Nov. 1915 ; 2 Lt.
10 R. Ir. Rif., Sept. 1916 ; France, 1916 ; wounded, Mar. 1917
and April 1918 ; despatches.

Wallace, John ;
Ent. 1920 ; Cadet R.A.F. 1918.

Wallace, John ;
B.A.I. 1911 ; 2 Lt. 5 Conn. Rang., Feb. 1915 ; Lt. 1915 ;
Gallipoli ; Mesopotamia ; Palestine.

Wallace, Joseph ;
M.B. 1903 ; M.D. 1904 ; Temp. Lt. R.A.M.C., July 1915.

Wallace, Kenneth Moss;
> B.A. 1915; 2 Lt. 8 R. Ir. Fus., Sept. 1914; Lt. 1915; died of wounds, 31 May 1916.

Wallace, Patrick;
> Ent. 1919; Pte. Ir. Gds., 1914; France 1915; wounded, 1918.

*Wallace, Quentin Vaughan Brooke;
> M.B. 1914; Lt. R.A.M.C., S.R., Oct. 1914; Capt. S.R. 1915; despatches, M.C., Jan. 1916; wounded, Aug. 1918; Capt. R.A.M.C. 1918.

*Wallace, Thomas Herbert;
> B.A. and LL.B. 1914; 2 Lt. A.S.C., July 1915; Lt. R.G.A. Apr. 1918; wounded, May 1918; A/Capt. 1918; M.C. and Bar.

*Waller, Bolton Charles;
> B.A. Dec. 1912; 2 Lt. A.S.C., June 1915; Capt. 1918.

Waller, Edmund Standish;
> B.A.I. 1911; Lt. R.F.A., Jan. 1915; Capt. 1918; Gallipoli; Mesopotamia; France; despatches, Feb. 1918; M.C., Feb. 1918; A/Major, 1918.

Waller, Henry;
> B.A.I. 1896; Ambulance Driver in French Army; Croix de Guerre.

Waller, Richard Hope;
> Ent. 1895; 2 Lt. 2 R. Innis. Fus., 1897; I.A., 38 Dogras, 1898; Capt. 1905; attchd. Indian Staff College, 1908; Staff-Capt. with Imp. Serv. Bgde., E. Africa, Oct. 1914; killed, Tonga, E. Africa, Nov. 1914.

Waller, Robert Monsel;
> B.A. 1913; Pte. No. 5 Co., Inns of Court O.T.C., Aug. 1915.

Wallis, Timothy Charles;
> Ent. 1919; 2 Lt. 4 Conn. Rang., Nov. 1916; att. 2 R.Ir. Rif.; France; Lt. 1918; M.C.

Walmsley, George Cecil;
> Ent. 1920; 2 Lt. 1/6 Conn. Rang. Aug. 1917; France; Italy; Palestine.

*Walpole, George Frederick;
> Ent. 1910; 2 Lt. R.F.A., Oct. 1914; Temp. Lt. Nigeria R., Artillery, W. Afr. Frontier Force, 1915–19; France; Cameroons; Nigeria.

Walsh, Finlay Walter;
> Ent. 1904; 2 Lt. 4 R. Dub. Fus.; retired, ill health.

P

*Walsh, Martin Oliver ;
Ent. 1912 ; 2 Lt. 10 Yorks. L.I., April 1915 ; France, 1917 ; killed in action, 3 May 1917.

Ward, Anthony Diver ;
Ent. 1916 ; volunteered and accepted.

*Ward, Basil Jourdain ;
B.A. 1913 ; 2 Lt. R.F.A., Aug. 1915 ; resigned, owing to injury, 1916.

Ward, Egerton John ;
Ent. 1920 ; 2 Lt. 3 R. Ir. Regt., Sept. 1915 ; Lt. 1917 ; France ; Flanders ; Military Order of Aviz (Chevalier), Portugal.

Ward, Espine Montgomery Picton ;
Ent. 1896 ; 2 Lt. Leins. R., Jan. 1902 ; resigned, went to Canada ; 16 Can. Scottish, 1914 ; killed, Festubert Wood, 21 May 1915.

Ward, Henry Rowlands ;
Ent. 1914 ; Pte. R.A.M.C., May 1915 ; France, 1915 (1915 ribbon) ; 2 Lt. R.G.A., May 1917 ; wounded, Oct. 1917 ; trench fever ; gassed several times.

*Ward, Richard Percyvale ;
Ent. 1913 : 2 Lt. 4 R. W. Fus., Aug. 1914 ; wounded, Festubert, 10 March 1915 ; Temp. Capt. 1915 ; wounded, Loos, 30 March 1916 ; att. R.F.C. 1918 ; M.C. ; D.F.C.

*Ward, William Ernest Chadwick ;
Ent. 1914 ; Pte. R.A.M.C. Sept. 1915 ; Mesopotamia, 1916–19.

Warham, Cecil Francis ;
Ent. 1910 ; Pte. 1915 ; 2 Lt. R.A.F., T.F., May 1917.

Warham, Thomas Gerald ;
Ent. 1916 ; Surg. Prob. R.N.V.R., H.M.S. " Speedy," 1917.

Waring, Arthur Durham ;
M.B. 1900 ; Lt. R.A.M.C., Apr. 1900 ; Maj. 1912 ; Lt.-Col. 1917.

Warner, Samuel ;
Ent. 1916 ; 2 Lt. R.F.C., Aug. 1917.

*Warnock, Hector Adolphus Hugh ;
Ent. 1911 ; 2 Lt. 4 R. Ir. Fus., Aug. 1914 ; Lt. 1915 ; died of wounds, Bapaume, France, 16 Aug. 1915.

*Warnock, John Esmond ;
B.A. 1910 ; 2 Lt. R.G.A., S.R., Jan. 1916 ; Lt. 1917 ; A/Capt. 1918.

Warnock, Robert;
Ent. 1914; 2 Lt. 6 R. Ir. Rif., Aug. 1916; Salonika 1916; Palestine, 1917; wounded, 1917; Lt. 1918.

Warren, John Booker Brough;
B.A. 1910; Lt. Bord. R., Oct. 1912; killed, France, 28 Oct. 1914.

Warren, Rev. Robert;
B.A. 1904; M.A. 1907; Army Chaplain, 4 Cl., March 1916.

Warrington, Robert Cecil Ussher;
Ent. 1916; 2 Lt. 4 R. Innis. Fus. Jan. 1918; 36 M.G.C.; France.

*Wassner, William August;
Ent. 1913; 2 Lt. 3 S. Lan. R., Jan. 1915; Lt. 1916; A/Capt. 1917; empld. Min. of Lab., 1919.

Waterfield, Reginald;
Med. School, 1888; L. R. C. P. & S. I.; Staff Surg. R.N., Nov. 1905.

Waterhouse, Arved;
Ent. 1908; 2 Lt. R. Lan. R., Aug. 1914; died on battlefield, Belgium, 13 Oct. 1914.

Waterhouse, Gilbert;
M.A. (Cantab.); Prof. of German, 1915; 2 Lt. O.T.C., T.F., Unattachd. List, Oct. 1914; Lt. 1915; Lt. R.N.V.R., Jan. 1917,

Waterhouse, John Howard;
M.B. 1908; M.D. 1911; Temp. Lt. R.A.M.C., Feb. 1916; Capt. 1917.

*Waters, George Frederick;
Ent. 1912; 2 Lt. R.G.A., S.R., Oct. 1915; Lt. 1917; France; Belgium; despatches.

Waters, William Rickard Lloyd;
M.B. 1914; Temp. Lt. R.A.M.C., Aug. 1915; Salonika, 1916; Capt. 1916.

Watson, Arthur Hubert;
M.B. 1915; Temp. Lt. R.A.M.C., July 1915; Capt. 1916; France, 1917; Egypt, 1917; invalided, 1918.

Watson, Benjamin;
Ent. 1914; 2 Lt. 5 R. Innis. Fus., Jan. 1915; died of wounds, 17 June 1916.

Watson, Charles;
Med. School, 1895; L.S.A.; Capt. R.A.M.C., Nov. 1918.

Watson, Edward John Macartney;
>   M.B. and M.D. 1900; Radiographer Dublin Castle Red Cross
>   Hospital, 1915; Temp. Capt. R.A.M.C., 83 (Dub.) Gen. Hosp.,
>   France, May 1917–18.

*Watson, Evan Philip;
>   Ent. 1913 ; Pte. 17 R. Ir. Rif., Apr. 1915 ; Corp. R.E., Dec. 1915;
>   France; 2 Lt. 12 R. Ir. Rif. 1917; died of wounds received in
>   action, 28 Mar. 1918.

Watson, John Desmond ;
>   Ent. 1913 ; Pte. S. Ir. Horse, Aug. 1916.

Watson, Rev. John Edmund Malone ;
>   B.A. 1908; Army Chaplain, 4 Cl., Dec. 1915; att. Middlesex
>   Regt.; despatches, 1917; M.C. Mar. 1918; killed in action,
>   10 April 1918.

Watson, Rev. Robert;
>   B.A. 1914 ; Army Chaplain, 4th Cl., Feb. 1918.

Watson, Thomas;
>   Ent. 1915; Y.M.C.A., Salonika, 1916.

Watson, Thomas Arnold ;
>   M.B. 1910; Temp. Lt. R.A.M.C. ; Capt. 1916; France; M.C.
>   June 1917.

Watson, William ;
>   B.A.I. 1913 ; Uganda Volunteer Reserve, 1914–17.

Waugh, Rev. Robert Percival ;
>   B.A. 1885 ; M.A. 1893 ; Army Chaplain, 4th Cl., May 1917–19.

Webb, Charles Walsham ;
>   M.B. 1902 ; M.D. 1904 ; Temp. Lt. R.A.M.C., Feb. 1916.

Webb, Samuel Cecil ;
>   B.A. 1907; 2 Lt. 5 R. Muns. Fus., Dec. 1914 ; wounded,
>   Dardanelles, Sept. 1915 ; Capt. 1915; killed in action, Bulgarian
>   Front, 3 Oct. 1916.

Weekes, Charles Alexander;
>   Ent. 1886 ; Pte. R.N.V.R., Anti-Aircraft C., July 1915 ; War
>   Medal and Ribbon; discharged medically unfit, April 1917.

Weir, Crosbie ;
>   M.B. 1916; Lt. R.A.M.C., Sept. 1916.

Weir, John Wybrants Olpherts ;
>   Ent. 1911 ; Canadian Exp. Force ; wounded.

Weir-Johnston, John Alexander ;
>   B.A.I. 1904 ; Lt. Army Ord. Dept. Dec. 1914 ; Maj. 1918;
>   mentioned for services.

Weldon, Arthur Stuart ;
Ent. 1896 ; 2 Lt. 2 N. Staff R., Jan. 1899 ; Maj. 1915 ;
Mesopotamia ; killed in action, 25 Mar. 1917.|

Weldon, Kenneth Charles ;
B.A. 1899 ; 2 Lt. 1, 2 R. Dub. Fus., Feb. 1900 ; Maj. 1915 ;
A/Lt.-Col. Com. R. Innis. Fus. 1916 ; despatches and D.S.O. Jan.
1917 ; Bt. Lt.-Col. 1919.

Weldon, Lewen Barrington ;
Ent. 1894 ; Extra Intelligence offr., Egyptian Army, Hydroplane
ship H.M.S. " Ann " ; Capt. Dec. 1914 ; M.C.

*Wells, Wilfred George Holmes ;
Ent. 1912 ; 2 Lt. A.S.C., Sept. 1915 ; Lt. I.A., June 1917 ;
Capt. 1920.

*West, Arthur Eustace Lockley ;
B.A. 1915 ; 2 Lt. R.G.A., S.R., Nov. 1915 ; A/Capt.: died
of wounds, 28 April 1917.

*West, Cecil M'Laren ;
M.B. 1915 ; Lt. R.A.M.C., S.R., Aug. 1914 ; France ; Capt.
1916 ; Italy 1917 ; M.C. 1918.

West, James Stafford ;
Ent. 1912 ; 2 Lt. R.G.A., Dec. 1915 ; died of wounds received
in action at the battle of the Somme, 20 July 1916.

*West, Reginald Francis ;
B.A. 1913 ; Lt. 8 R. Dub. Fus., Nov. 1914 ; Capt. 1915 ; New
Armies, 1917 ; M.C.

Westby, John Thorp ;
M.B. 1916 ; Lt. R.A.M.C., Jan. 1917 ; Capt. 1918.

Westropp, Hugh Thomas George ;
Ent. 1919 ; Trooper N. Ir. Horse.

Whaite, Thomas Du Bédat :
M.B. 1885 ; Capt. R.A.M.C., July 1886 ; Col. A.M.S., 1915 ;
France, 1915 ; A.D.M.S., France, 1915 ; D.D.M.S., France,
1916–17 ; despatches, Jan. 1916 ; C M.G. and despatches, Jan.
1917 ; Legion of Honour, Croix de Guerre, April 1918 ; Italian
Order of St. Maurice and St. Lazarus, Officer, Sept. 1918 ;
despatches, May 1918 and Jan. 1919 ; C.B., June, 1919, for
services in Italy.

Wheeler, Henry Eliardo de Courcy ;
B.A. 1896 ; M.A. 1903 ; 2 Lt. 8 K. R. Rif. C., Feb. 1897 ;
Capt. 1899 ; Res. of offrs. 1907 ; Offr. in charge of Barracks,
Curragh District, 1914.

Wheeler, Horatio Francis De Courcy ;
B.A. 1910; Lt. A.S.C., Aug. 1915.

Wheeler, Rev. Hugh Trevor ;
B.A. 1896; M.A. 1899; Army Chaplain, 4 Cl., June 1915;
India.

Wheeler, Robert de Courcy ;
M.B. 1908; Lt. R.A.M.C., Nov. 1916.

*Wheeler, Samuel Gerald De Courcy ;
B.A.I. 1898; 2 Lt. 2 R. Dub. Fus., Oct. 1899; Capt. 1908;
Adjt. D.U.O.T.C. 1910-1914; wounded, St. Julien, May 1915;
Maj. 1915; despatches; Staff Capt. 1915; Comdr. Co. of Gent.
Cadets, R. Mil. Coll., 1915; Temp. Lt.-Col. 1918

Wheeler, William Ireland De Courcy ;
M.B. and M.D. 1902; Hon. Major R.A.M.C., March 1916;
Surgeon to Hospital for Officers, Dublin; Temp. Hon. Lt.-Col.
May 1917; despatches, Jan. 1917 and Sept. 1917; knighted, Aug.
1919

*Whelan, Claude Blake ;
Ent. 1911; 2 Lt. K. R. Rif. C., Aug. 1914; wounded. Hooge,
6 July 1915; attchd. R. Flying Corps, 1916: Lt. New Armies,
1916; empld. on Recrg. Duties, 1917.

Whelan, Lawder Thomas ;
Med. School, 1885; F.R.C.S.I.; Capt. R.A.M.C., T.F., Jan.
1909; M.C.; A./Maj. 1919; D.A.D.M.S. 1919.

Whitby, Jonathan Montagu Ferdinand ;
Ent. 1914; 2 Lt. 3 Essex R., April 1915; Lt. 1916; A/Capt.;
wounded.

White, Cecil Godfrey ;
B.A. 1912; 2 Lt. R.F.A., Sept. 1914; Temp. Lt. 1915; Lt.
1916; M.C.; A/Capt. 1917 and 1918; Lt. R.A.F., April 1918.

*White, Charles Thomas Blair ;
B.A., 1912; 2 Lt. 2 L. Gds. Res., March, 1916; Lt. 1917.

White, Francis Westropp Joyner ;
Ent. 1912; 2 Lt. A.S.C., May 1916: A/Capt. 1916; Adj. 1917.

White, George Fawcett ;
M.B. and M.D. 1901; Lt. R.A.M.C., T.F.; Capt. 1915.

*White, Gerald John Davis ;
Ent. 1913; 2 Lt. 2 R. Ir. Regt., Aug., 1915: killed in action,
6 July 1916.

*White, Henry Edwin ;
Ent. 1913; 2 Lt. 17 R. Ir. Rif., Aug. 1916; Lt. 1917.

White, Henry Heathcote ;
>   M.B. and M.D. 1905 ; Temp. Lt. R.A.M.C., Dec. 1914 ; Capt.
>   1915 ; Marseilles, 1916.

*White, Henry Vere ;
>   Ent. 1908 ; 2 Lt. A.S.C., Sept. 1914 ; Capt 1915.

*White, James George ;
>   B.A. 1910 ; 2 Lt. 6 R. Dub. Fus., Dec. 1915.

*White, John Malvern ;
>   B.A. and Ll.B. 1915 ; 2 Lt. A.S.C., Jan. 1916 ; Lt. 1917 ,
>   A/Capt. 1917.

White, Randal Merrick ;
>   Ent. 1912 ; ·2 Lt. 3 Leins. R., Sept. 1915 ; Lt. 1917.

White, Richard ;
>   Ent. 1912 ; 2 Lt. A.S.C., June 1915 ; Lt. 1916 ; Capt. 1918.

*White, Walter Frederick Sydney Bantry Connor ;
>   Ent. 1902 ; 2 Lt. A.S.C., Nov. 1915 ; Capt. 1918 ; M.C.

Whitestone, Charles William Henry ;
>   M.B. 1887 ; Capt. R.A.M.C., Jan. 1891 ; Lt.-Col. 1913 ; de-
>   spatches, Feb. 1917, Sept. 1917.

*Whitsitt, John Reginald ;
>   Ent. 1910 ; 2 Lt. 5 R. Innis. Fus., Sept. 1914 ; Lt. ; died of
>   wounds, Dardanelles, 16 Aug. 1915.

*Whittaker, John Henderson Elrington ;
>   Ent. 1912 ; 2 Lt. 8 R. Innis. Fus., Sept. 1914 ; Lt. 1915.

Whitton, Frederick Ernest ;
>   Ent. 1891 ; 2 Lt. 2 Leins. R., June 1894 ; Capt. 1900 ; wounded,
>   France, Oct. 1914 ; Maj 1915 ; Lt.-Col. 1917 ; Gen. Staff. Off.,
>   War Off., 1916-18 ; Brit. Armies in France, 1918-19 ; C.M.G.

Whyte, Mark Gilchrist ;
>   Ent. 1916 ; Artists' Rifle Corps, April 1917 ; 2 Lt. 20 R. Fus.,
>   Mar. 1917 ; killed in action, 19 Aug. 1918.

Wicht, Johan Frederik ;
>   Ent. 1917 ; M.B. 1920 ; Surg. Prob. H.M.S. " Laertes," Apr.
>   1918.

Wicht, William Frederick ;
>   M.B. 1917 ; Capt. S.A.M.C. 1 Gen. Hosp., Wynberg, Aug. 1917.

Wigham, Joseph Theodore ;·
>   M.B. 1898 ; M.D. 1900 ; Assist. to Lecturer in Pathology ; British
>   Red Cross, Flanders.

*Wigoder, Lionel ;
>   B.A. 1916 ; B. Dent. Sc. 1917 ; R.A.F., M.S., Oct. 1918.

Wilde, Otto Gruber;
> Ent. 1919; Cadet, R.F.C., 1917; Pte. Lab. C., 1918; 2 Lt. R. Muns. Fus. 1919.

Wiley, William;
> M.B. 1903; Lt. R.A.M.C., Jan. 1904 : Temp. Lt.-Col. 1915; despatches, Jan. 1916, Jan. 1917; died on service, 12 Feb. 1917.

Wilkinson, David Stanley;
> Ent. 1908; 2 Lt. 8 Cam'n Highrs., Nov. 1914; R.F.C. 1915; Flying Off. 1917; died of wounds in German prison camp, Limburg, 26 Aug. 1917.

*Wilkinson, Gerrard Napier;
> Ent. 1913; 2 Lt. 7 R. Dub. Fus., Aug. 1914; Capt. and Adjt. 1915; despatches, Jan. 1916; Lt. New Armies, 1917; Lt. I.A. 1918; Capt. 1919; O.B.E.

*Wilkinson, Harold Howard;
> Ent. 1911; 2 Lt. 9 L'pool R., Dec. 1914; Capt. and Adjt., 1916; Maj. and 2nd in Comnd. 1917; Gen. Staff H. Qrs., Western Comnd., 1919; despatches, Aug. 1919; demobilized, Nov. 1919.

*Williams, Arthur Oscar;
> B.A. 1913 ; 2 Lt. 6 Oxf. and Bucks. L.I., Sept. 1914 ; A. Cyclist's Corps, Jan. 1915.

*Williams, Charles Beasley;
> Ent. 1913; 2 Lt. R. Ir. Rif., Aug. 1914; Capt. 1915; killed, Hooge, Flanders, 28 Aug. 1915.

*Williams, Gerald Leopold;
> B.A. and LL.B. 1914; No. 2 Cadet Bn. April 1917 ; 2 Lt. 12 R. Innis. Fus. April 1917; killed in action, 15 Oct. 1918.

Williams, Herbert Armstrong;
> M.B. 1899; Lt. I.M.S., Jan. 1900; D.S.O.; Major 1911; A/Lt.-Col. 1917–19.

Williams, Hugh Emrys;
> M.B. 1912; temp. Lt. R.A.M.C., Jan. 1916; Capt. 1917; wounded, May 1918.

Williams, James Valentine;
> Ent. 1916; Surg. Sub-Lt. R.N.V.R., 1918; H. M. S. ''Spearmint,'' American Convoy.

Williams, Ronald Douglas;
> B.A. 1911 ; 2 Lt. 5 R. Ir. Rif., June 1915 ; Lt. 1917 ; wounded, March 1918; A/Capt. 1918; M.C.

Williamson, Andrew Arnold;
> B.A. 1910 ; 2 Lt. Jan. 1909; I.A., 75 Carnatic Inf., Mar. 1912; Capt. 1915 ; wounded, Dec. 1916.

*Williamson, Edward Benjamin Bickford;
Ent. 1914 ; 2 Lt. 1, 2 Conn. Rang., Aug. 1916 ; att. 6 Bn. ;
killed in action, 19 Feb. 1917.

Williamson, John Francis ;
M.B. 1876 ; Lt. A.M.S., Feb. 1887 ; C.M.G., 1901 ; C.B., 1904 ;
Col. 1903 ; retd., 1908 ; Col. A.M.S., 1910, in list of Offrs. selected
for rewards for distinguished and meritorious service.

*Williamson, John George ;
Ent. 1916 ; Sandhurst, Apr. 1917.

*Williamson, Robert Cecil ;
B.A. 1913 ; LL.B. 1914 ; Quartermaster, ret. pay, late Arg. and
Suth'd High'rs.; re-empld. for recruiting duties.

*Williamson, Usher Arthur Franklin ;
Ent. 1913; 2 Lt. 3 R. Dub. Fus., Aug 1915 ; Lt. 1917 ; Lt.
Lab. Corps, 1917.

Willington, Frederick Francis Clare ;
M.B. 1903 ; M.D. 1905 ; M.O. in charge Officers' Training Centre,
Yelverton ; Lt. R.A.M.C., June 1917 ; Capt. 1918.

*Willis, Samuel William ;
B.A. 1896 ; Capt. 14 R. Ir. Rif., Nov. 1914 ; missing, France,
reported killed in action, 1 July 1916.

Willis, Sandham John ;
Ent. 1917 ; Pte. R.F.A., May 1918.

Willis, Rev. William Ireton ;
B.A. 1907 ; Army Chaplain, 4 Cl., March 1916.

Wills, James Robertson ;
Ent. 1915 ; Temp. Surg. Sub-Lt. R.N.V.R., July 1918 ; H.M.S.
" Marjoram," American Convoy.

*Willson, William Alick Parkinson;
Ent. 1912 ; 2 Lt. 16 R. Ir. Rif., Dec. 1914 ; att. 11/13 ; died of
wounds, France, 1 April, 1918.

Wilmot, Claud Ernest Wellington ;
M.B. 1892 ; M.D. 1894 ; Temp. Lt. R.A.M.C., Apr. 1915 ; Capt.
1916.

*Wilmot, Horace Francis ;
B.A.I. 1913 ; 2 Lt. 7 Leins. R., Sept. 1914 ; 2 Lt. R.E., Feb.
1915 ; Dardanelles, 1915-16 ; invalided, enteric, 1915 ; Egypt,
1916-19 ; Lt. 1917 ; A/Maj. 1918 ; West Frontier Force, 1919 ;
Palestine, 1919 ; despatches (twice), Suvla and Palestine.

*Wilmot, Samuel Howard ;
Ent. 1914 ; Temp. 2 Lt. A.S.C., Dec. 1914 ; Lt. 1916 ; 2 Lt.
R.A.S.C., Jan. 1917 ; Lt. 1918.

Wilmot, Thomas James Townsend ;
> M.B. 1904 ; M.D. 1908 ; Temp. Surg. R.N., Nov. 1914 ; H.M.S. "Pembroke" ; Dardanelles; H. M. S. "Crescent."

Wilson, Alfred Leopold ;
> Ent. 1911 ; Lt. A.S.C., Sept. 1914 ; Capt. 1915.

Wilson, Rev. Arthur Alexander ;
> B.A. 1905 ; Army Chap. 4 Cl., July 1917–20.

*Wilson, Arthur Dominic ;
> Ent. 1913 ; 2 Lt. 3 R. Muns. Fus., July 1915 ; died of wounds, France, 10 Sept. 1916.

*Wilson, Arthur Henry ;
> Ent. 1910 ; Lt. 4 R. Ir. Fus., Aug. 1914 ; Capt. 1916.

*Wilson, Arthur Hone ;
> Ent. 1913 ; 2 Lt. 4 R. Fus., Feb. 1915 ; Lt. 1915 ; att. 8 Bn. ; died of wounds, 18 Nov. 1916.

Wilson, Carmichael ;
> Ent. 1917 ; Pte. Gordon Highrs., 1917 ; France, 1918 ; trench fever, 1918 ; 2 Lt. 1919.

*Wilson, Charles ;
> B.A. 1911 ; 2 Lt. 6 Shrops. L.I.. Feb. 1915 ; Capt. 1916.

Wilson, Crawford Lunham Law ;
> Ent. 1916; B.A. 1921 ; L.R.C.P. & S.I. ; Temp. Surg. Sub-Lt. R.N.V.R., May 1917; Mine Sweeper, May1919.

*Wilson, Cyril Herbert ;
> Ent. 1916 ; Quetta, Dec. 1916.

*Wilson, Daniel Martin ;
> B.A. 1884 ; K.C.: Lt. 9 R. Innis. Fus., Oct. 1914 : Capt. 1915; retired, ill-health, Jan. 1916.

Wilson, Edmund FitzGerald Bannatyne ;
> M.B. 1881; M.D. 1890 ; Maj. S. A. Med. Corps, 1915 ; despatches (Gen. Botha), Sept. 1918 ; killed accidentally, 17 Aug. 1917.

Wilson, Edward Francis ;
> Ent. 1913 ; Lt. R.A.F., Sept. 1918.

Wilson, Rev. Geoffrey Moffat ;
> B.A. 1914 ; Army Chap. 4 Cl., Sept. 1917 ; France, 1917–1920.

Wilson, George Henry ;
> Ent. 1907 ; 2 Lt. R.F.A., T.F., Aug. 1914 : Capt. 1915 ; M.C.; A/Maj. 1917 ; despatches ; killed in action, 4 Nov. 1917.

Wilson, Herbert Vaughan ;
> Ent. 1912 ; 2 Lt. Graves Registration Corps, Apr. 1917.

*Wilson, John Bernard Maxwell ;
> B.A. 1910 ; 2 Lt. 10 Bedf. R., Apr. 1915 ; 2 Lt. 11 Suff. R.,
> May 1915 ; Lt. 1917.

Wilson, John Hugh ;
> Ent. 1906 ; 2 Lt. 4 Linc. R. Oct. 1914 ; 2 Lt. R.F.A., T.F.,
> Feb. 1915 ; A/Capt. 1916 ; Lt. 1916 ; empld. Bd. of Agriculture,
> 1918.

Wilson, John Stevenson ;
> M.B. 1902 ; M.D. 1907 ; Lt. R.A.M.C., June 1917 ; Capt.
> 1918.

*Wilson, Leslie ;
> Ent. 1914 ; 2 Lt. 5 R. Ir. Fus., Oct. 1915 ; France ; invalided,
> 1916.

*Wilson, Logie Weir ;
> Ent. 1912 ; 2 Lt. A.S.C., Oct. 1914 ; Lt. 1915 ; att. R. Ir. Rif.,
> Jan. 1918 ; prisoner of war, 1918.

Wilson, Mark ;
> Ent. 1918 ; Flight Cadet R.A.F., June 1918 ; England, 1918–19.

Wilson, Richard Chapman ;
> M.B. 1900 ; Lt. R.A.M.C., May 1901 ; Maj. 1913 ; A/Lt.-Col.
> 1917-18.

Wilson, Richard Mervyn ;
> M.B. 1886 ; M.D. 1889 ; Capt. R.A.M.C., T.F., March 1914–
> 19 ; France.

Wilson, Thompson Ferris ;
> M.B. 1903 ; Temp. Lt. R.A.M.C., June 1915 ; Lemnos ; Capt.
> 1917 ; Gallipoli ; Egypt ; Salonika ; France ; Germany.

Wilson, Wilfred Claud Stanley ;
> B.A. 1895 ; M.A. 1898 ; Capt. 3 R. Ir. Fus., Nov. 1914 ;
> Temp. Maj. 1916.

Wilson, Sir William Deane ;
> M.B. 1866 ; Lt. A.M.S., Oct. 1867 ; Surg. Gen. 1898 ; K.C.M.G,
> 1901 ; ret. from A. Med. Staff, 1904 ; Surg. Gen. A.M.S., 1907.
> in List of Officers selected for rewards for distinguished and meri-
> torious service.

*Wilson, William Fothergill ;
> M.B. 1915 ; Temp. Lt. R.A.M.C., Oct. 1915 ; Capt. 1916 ; M.C.
> Aug. 1917 ; wounded, Sept. 1917 ; R.A.F., M.S., Nov. 1918.

Winder, Alexander Stuart Monck ;
> M.B. 1908 ; Lt. R.A.M.C., Jan. 1909 ; Capt. 1912 ; Amara,
> Persian Gulf.

Winder, Francis Arthur ;
>M.B. 1895; Temp. Lt. R.A.M.C., Nov. 1915 : Capt. 1916 ;
>O.B.E. June 1919.

Winder, James Herbert Roche ;
>M.B. and M.D. 1899 : Lt. R.A.M.C., Feb. 1901 ; Maj. 1913 ;
>despatches, June 1916 : Maj. 1916 ; Temp. Lt.-Col. 1914–15 : A/Lt.
>Col. 1916 ; D.S.O. Jan. 1918.

Windle, Reginald Joscelyn ;
>M.B. 1884 ; Capt. R.A.M.C., July 1886 ; Col. A.M.S., 1915 ;
>ret. 1917.

Winter, Philip Henry ;
>Ent. 1901 ; Pte. S. Ir. Horse, Sept. 1914 ; 2 Lt. A.S.C., Nov.
>1914 ; Lt. 1915 ; Capt. 1917.

Winter, William Arthur ;
>M.B. 1891 ; M.D. 1895 ; Physician Dublin Castle Red Cross
>Hospital ; Temp. Maj R.A.M.C., 83 (Dub.) Gen. Hosp., France,
>Apr. 1917.

Witherow, Alexander Hunter ;
>Ent. 1914 ; 2 Lt. 17 R. Ir. Rif., Jan. 1915 ; died of wounds,
>3 July 1916.

Witherow, John Thomas ;
>Ent. 1911 ; Cadet 19 R. Ir. Rif. Nov. 1915.

*Witz, Louis Thomas Purser ;
>Med. School 1910 ; Pte. 16 Middlesex R. ; Italy.

*Wood, George Harold ;
>M.B. 1914 ; Temp. Lt. R.A.M.C., April 1915 ; Temp. Capt.
>1916 : Capt. R.A.M.C., Oct. 1918.

*Woodall, Frederick George ;
>Ent. 1912 ; Enlisted as Despatch Rider ; 2 Lt. att. 10 R. Lan. R.,
>Nov. 1914 ; wounded ; 2 Lt. 1 Garr. Bn. Devon R., Sept. 1915 ;
>Lt. 1916 : Lt. Motor M.G.C., Apr. 1916.

*Woodburn, David Barkley ;
>Ent. 1913 ; 2 Lt. R.G.A., Dec. 1915; wounded, Aug. 1917; Lt.
>1917 ; A/Capt. 1918.

Woodcock, Louisa ;
>B.A. and M.A. 1907 ; M.B. (Lond.) ; Physician, Mil. Hosp.,
>Endell St., London ; died of pneumonia, 17 Feb. 1917.

Woodroffe, Harry Lewis Warren ;
>M.B. 1911 ; M.D. 1914 ; Ulster Volunteer Hospital, Pau, France ;
>Lt. R.A.M.C., Nov. 1917 ; Capt. 1918.

Woodroffe, Henry Dobrée ;
   M.B. and M.D. 1907; Temp. Lt. R.A.M.C., Nov. 1915 ; France ; Capt. 1917.

Wood-Martin, Annette Kathleen ;
   Ent. 1912 ; Mil. V.A.D., 2 General, 18 Gen., and 4 Stationary Hospitals, France, 1915–18.

Woods, Arthur ;
   B.A.I. 1903 ; 2 Lt. I.A.Res. of Off., R.E., Aug. 1918–19 ; Afghanistan.

Woods, Charles Rolleston ;
   M.B. 1876 ; M.D. 1879 ; Lt. R.A.M.C., July 1880; Lt.-Col. 1900 ; retd. 1907 ; re-empld. 1914.

Woods, Rev. Frederick William ;
   B.A. 1903 ; M.A. 1909 ; Chaplain R.N., Apr. 1911 ; ret. 1917 ; H.M.S. " Hibernia," 1912–16 ; " Isis," 1915–16 ; " Laurentic," 1916–17.

Woods, Samuel Henry ;
   M.B. 1899 ; M.D. 1903 ; Fleet Surg. R.N., May 1915; Surg.- Cr. ; O.B.E. June 1918.

Woodside, Alfred M'Bride ;
   B.A. 1900 ; 2 Lt. R.F.A., May 1900 ; Maj. 1914 ; A/Lt.- Col. 1916.

Woodward, Rev. Alfred Sadleir ;
   B.A. 1884 ; M.A. 1888 ; Army Chaplain, 4 Cl., Jan. 1916.

Worthington-Eyre, Hedges Eyre ;
   Ent. 1917 ; R.G.A., Brighton, Sept. 1918.

*Worthington-Eyre, Lionel George ;
   Ent. 1912 ; 2 Lt. R.F.A., Apr. 1915 ; despatches, May 1917 ; 78 Bde. ; killed in action, Arras–Cambrai front, 14 July 1917.

*Worthington-Eyre, William Stratford Eyre ;
   B.A.I. 1914 ; 2 Lt. R.E., Apr. 1915 ; Lt. 1916.

Wray, David Witherow ;
   B.A. 1912 ; 2 Lt. 17 R. Ir. Rif., Apr. 1915; Lt. 1 Garr. Bn., 1917.

Wray, Herbert Hans ;
   B.A. 1920 ; Pte. May 1917; 2 Lt. 3 E. Lan. R. March 1918 ; France ; with 2 Bn. May 1918.

*Wright, Alan Glynn ;
   B.A. 1915 ; M.B. 1917 ; 2 Lt. A.S.C., Feb. 1915 ; Lt. 1915 ; Lt. R.A.M.C., Nov. 1917; Capt. 1918.

Wright, Sir Almroth Edward ;
    M.B. 1883 ; M.D. 1889 ; Col. A.M.S., Oct. 1914 ; C.B. 1915;
    despatches, June 1915 ; Ordre de la Couronne (Belge), Apr. 1917 ;
    K.B.E. Jan. 1919.

Wright, Eustace MacDonald ;
    Ent. 1910 ; Pte. A.S.C. (M.T.) ; R. N. Air Serv., Nov. 1914 ;
    Temp-Sub-Lt. R.N.V.R., Nov. 1915.

*Wright, Herbert James ;
    M.B. 1907 ; R.N. Res. List Med. Offrs. ; Staff-Surg. H.M.S.
    " Ophir."

Wright, Herbert James ;
    B.Dent.Sc., 1914; M.B. 1916; Lt. R.A.M.C., Aug. 1916;
    Mesopotamia, 1917–19 ; Capt. 1917 ; Afghanistan. 1919.

Wright, Robert Ernest ;
    M.B. 1907 ; M.D. 1914 ; Capt. I.M.S., July 1910 ; Bt. Maj.,
    Oct. 1915 ; I.E.F., Turkish Arabia ; despatches, Sept. 1915.

Wright, Robert Lancelot G. ;
    Ent. 1912 ; 2 Lt. 8 R. Lanc. R., Nov. 1914 ; Lt. 1917.

Wright, Ruthven Alexanderson ;
    Ent. 1916 ; 2 Lt. R.G.A., March 1917 ; Lt. 1918.

Wright, Samuel Trevor Corry ;
    Ent. 1915 ; Sandhurst, June 1916 ; 2 Lt. 1 K.O. Sco. Bord., May
    1917 ; wounded, France, July 1917 ; Lt. 1918.

Wright, Warren Samuel ;
    B.A. 1905 ; Lt. King's African Rif., Nov. 1915 ; serving with
    Gen. Smuts, 1916.

Wyatt, Cecil John ;
    M.B. 1904 ; Lt. R.A.M.C., July 1905 ; Major 1915 ; A/Lt.-Col.
    1918.

*Wyatt, Claud ;
    Ent. 1906 ; Lt. Dental Surgeon, Nov. 1915 ; Capt. 1916.

Wylie, Francis Verner ;
    B.A. 1913 ; 2 Lt. Sth. Waziristan Militia, July 1916 ; Lt. 1917.

Wylie, John Price ;
    B.A. 1910 ; 2 Lt. I.A. Nov. 1911 ; Lt. Notts and Derby R.,
    March 1914 ; wounded, France, May 1915 ; Capt. 1916 ; A/Maj.
    1916-1918 ; Temp. Maj. 1918 ; D.S.O.

*Wylie, William Evelyn ;
    B.A. 1904 ; 2 Lt. O.T.C., T.F., Unattached List, June 1915 ;
    despatches, Jan. 1917.

Wynne, Albert Edward ;
M.B. and M.D. 1907 ; Lt. R.A.M.C., June 1916 ; Capt. 1917.

Wynne, Frederick Edward ;
M.B. 1894 ; Lt. R.A.M.C., Nov. 1914 ; Dardanelles ; Capt. 1915.

*Wynne, Wilfred Edward Carleton ;
Ent. 1914 ; 2 Lt. R.G.A., S.R., Feb. 1915 ; A/Capt. 1916 ; Lt. 1917 ; A/Capt. 1918 ; despatches, July 1916 ; despatches, 1918.

Y

Yates, Lionel Westropp Peel ;
Ent. 1909 ; D.I., R.I.C. ; Capt. 6 R. Innis. Fus., Oct. 1914 ; Mediterranean E.F., 1915 ; prisoner, March 1918.

*Yeates, Robert Andrew ;
Ent. 1911 ; 2 Lt. 1, 2 R. Dub. Fus., Dec. 1915 ; Lt. 1917.

Young, Charles Grove ;
M.B. 1874 ; M.D. 1880 ; Med. Officer, 12 Suss. R., 1915.

*Young, Charles Owen James ;
M.B., 1916 ; Lt. R.A.M.C., S.R., July 1916 ; Capt. 1916 ; M.C., June 1917.

Young, Ernest William Gilmore ;
M.B. 1910 ; M.D. 1919 ; Temp. Lt. R.A.M.C., Jan. 1916 ; France, 1916 ; wounded, Sept. 1916 ; Capt. 1917 ; Salonika, 1917 ; M C. 1917 ; Palestine, 1917–19 ; O.B.E. 1919.

Young, Guy Owen Lawrence ;
Ent. 1912 ; 2 Lt. 11 R. Ir. Rif., Sept. 1914 ; Lt. 1915.

Young, Rev. James Morogh ;
B.A. 1902 ; Ambulance Driver, French Red Cross, 1915.

Young, Marcus Graham ;
Ent. 1909 ; 2 Lt. 6 S. Staff. R., Aug. 1914 ; Capt. 1916 ; empld. R.A. Hse. Lines, 1919.

Young, Robert Chichester ;
B.A. 1909 ; Lt. R.N.V.R., Oct. 1915 ; 2 Lt. Tank Corps, Jan. 1917 ; A/Maj. 1918 ; M.C., Dec. 1916 ; Bar to M.C.

Young, William Leech ;
M.B. 1918 ; Lt. R.A.M.C., May 1918.

Young, William Matthew O'Grady ;
Ent. 1891 ; Lance Corp. 7 Aust. Lt. Horse ; Sergt. ; three times slightly wounded, Gallipoli ; killed accidentally in Egypt, 28 Dec. 1915.

*Younge, Frederick George Patrick ;
Ent. 1911 ; 2 Lt. 2 Leins. R., Aug. 1914 ; died of wounds Bailleul, 14 Feb. 1915.

Yourell, James Russell ;
M.B. 1907 ; Lt. R.A.M.C., Jan. 1909 ; Capt. 1912 ; despatches, Feb. 1919.

Yourdi, John Robert ;
M.B. 1878 ; Lt. R.A.M.C., July 1881 ; Lt.-Col. 1901 ; retd. 1910 ; re-empld. 1914–19 ; despatches, Aug. 1918 ; O.B.E., 1919.

SUPPLEMENTAL LIST.

Armstrong, John ;
Ent. 1915 ; B.A. 1920 ; Pte. Oct. 1916 ; 2 Lt. 9 R. Ir. Rif. Apr. 1917 ; France, June 1917 ; Lt. 1918 ; prisoner of war, 1918.

MEMBERS OF THE OFFICERS' TRAINING CORPS WHO WERE NOT MEMBERS OF TRINITY COLLEGE.

A

Agnew, Andrew Eric Hamilton ;
2 Lt. 3 R. Dub. Fus., Aug. 1914 ; Capt. 1915 ; died 3 Nov. 1918.

Alexander, David Francis ;
2 Lt. R.G.A., Nov. 1915 ; Lt. 1917.

Alexander, James Richard ;
· 2 Lt. A.S.C., Dec. 1915 ; Lt. 1917.

Alexander, Thomas Jones ;
R.E. Cadet Unit, June 1916.

Allan, Frederick Joshua ;
M.D., R.A.M.C., Sanitary Officer ; Capt. Sept. 1914.

Allen, Frederick Joshua ;
Indian Cavalry Cadet, June 1916 ; 2 Lt. I.A., Jan. 1917 ; Lt. 1918.

Allen, Ivan Wellesly ;
7 O. Cadet. Bn., Jan. 1918 ; 2 Lt. Ser. Bns., R. Innis. Fus., July 1918.

Allingham, John Samuel ;
7 Cadet Bn., May 1917.

Anderson, Walter Thomas ;
B. Res. Bde., R.H.A., Sept. 1916.

Armstrong, Gerald Robert ;
Cav. Cadet Sqdn., Sept. 1917.

Armstrong, John ;
7 Cadet Bn., Jan. 1917.

Q

Ashman, Arthur Thomas ;
7 Cadet Bn., Aug. 1916 ; Lt. Ser. Bns., R. W. Surr. R., June 1918.

Ashton, Horace ;
Garr. Cadet Bn., Cambridge, Feb. 1917.

B

Bailey, Alfred Essex Grahame ;
2 Lt. A.S.C., Jan. 1915 ; Lt. 1915 ; Lt. R.A.F., April 1918.

Barnes, Reginald Victor ;
7 Cadet Bn., July 1916 ; 2 Lt. Ser. Bns., R. Ir. Fus., Oct. 1917.

Barrett, Frederick Robert ;
R.A.F., June 1918 ; 2 Lt. R.A.F., Nov. 1918.

Barrett, Hebron ;
2 Lt. 10 R. Dub. Fus., March 1916 ; Lt. 1918 ; died of wounds 27 March 1918.

Barron, Arthur Sydney ;
R.G.A., Oct. 1918.

Barton, John ;
R.G.A. Cdt Sch., Dec. 1917.

Barton, Vivian Alfred ;
R.F.A. Cadet School, Exeter, Sept. 1916 ; 2 Lt. R.F.A., 1917 ; killed in action, 22 Sept. 1917.

Bateman, Thomas Norman ;
R.A.F. School, Nov. 1917.

Battersby, Francis H. ;
2 Lt. 5 R. Muns. Fus., May 1916.

Beale, Bertram Saxone ;
6 Cadet Bn., Aug. 1916 ; Lt. M.G.C., Nov. 1916 ; Lt. Tank C. 1918 ; A/Capt. 1918.

Beckett, David Duke ;
7 Cadet Bn., Aug. 1916 ; 2 Lt. 4 Conn. Rang., Dec. 1916 ; Lt. 1918.

Beckett, George ;
R.A.F., Tech. Constr., Aug. 1918.

Bennett, L. B. ;
Lt. A.S.C., Feb. 1915.

Beresford, Gervais de la Poer ;
    2 Lt. R.E., Nov. 1915 ; Lt. 1917 ; M.C.

Bernard, John Bullen ;
    7 Cadet Bn., Aug. 1916.

Biggs, George Walter Travers ;
    7 O. Cadet Bn., Nov. 1917.

Bland, John Francis ;
    4 R.G.A., Cadet School, June 1917 ; 2 Lt., Nov. 1917.

Blood, Jeffrey Armstrong ;
    2 Lt. 5 R. Ir. Fus., Sept. 1914 ; wounded, Dardanelles, Aug.
    1915 ; Lt. 1916 ; Lt. I.A., 1916 ; Capt. 1919 ; att. 54 Sikhs.

Blount, Adels Alexander ;
    Rhyll, Sept. 1918.

Bolton, R. ;
    Lt. 10 W. Rid. R., Sept. 1914 ; Capt. 1916 ; M.C.

Booker, Frederick ;
    Cav. Cadet Sqdn., Sept. 1917.

Bourke, Augustus Mary ;
    Cadet School, Oct. 1917 ; 2 Lt. Ser. Bns., Conn. Rang., Feb.
    1918.

Bourke, J. B. ;
    Lt. R.A.M.C., Aug. 1915.

Boyd, Ronald Douglas ;
    7 Cadet Bn., May 1916 ; 2 Lt. R. Muns. Fus., Sept. 1916.

Bradbury, Horace Rees ;
    7 O. Cadet. Bn., July 1917 ; 2 Lt. 3 R. Dub. Fus., Oct. 1917.

Bradford, Alfred ;
    R.G.A. School, Aug. 1918.

Brady, James ;
    2 Cav. Cadet Sq., July 1917.

Brazier-Creagh, Jack Gerard ;
    7 O. Cadet Bn., Nov. 1917.

Bridge, Albert Vincent ;
    7 Cadet Bn., Oct. 1916.

Brindley, Charles Hall ;
    2 Cav. Sch., Oct. 1918.

Brooks, Arthur Cecil ;
    2 Cav. Cdt. Sq., Jan. 1917.

Brown, Ronald Bruce ;
    R.A.F., Aug. 1918.

Browne, George Gilham Tone ;
2 Lt. 6 R. Dub. Fus., Feb. 1916 ; Lt. M.G.C., Aug. 1917.

Browne, Martin Bernard ;
Pte. S. Ir. Horse, May 1917.

Bryers, Richard Beresford Noel ;
R.A.F., Oct. 1918.

Bunyan, William Joseph ;
7 O. Cadet Bn., Jan. 1918 ; 2 Lt. Ser. Bns., R. Muns. Fus., July
1918.

Burgess, Eric Thomas ;
7 O. Cadet Bn., Jan. 1918 ; 2 Lt. Ser. Bns., R. Muns. Fus., July
1918.

Burgess, John Massy ;
O. Cadet Bn., Fermoy, Aug. 1918.

Butler, George Whitwell ;
2 Lt. R.G.A., Nov. 1916.

Butler, Robt. E. ;
7 Cadet Bn., July 1916 ; 2 Lt. 3 Conn. Rang., Oct. 1916 ; att.
R.F.C. ; Lt. R.A.F. Apr. 1918.

Butler, Robert O'Neill ;
7 Cadet Bn., Oct. 1916 ; 2 Lt. 2 Leins. R., March 1917 ; Lt.
I.A., Dec. 1918 ; Temp. Capt. 1919.

Buttanshaw, Cyril ;
2 Lt. R.G.A., Jan. 1916 ; Lt. 1917.

Byrne, Francis ;
3 B. Res. Bde., R.F.A., Aug. 1916.

C

Caldwell, John Foster ;
7 Cadet Bn., July 1917 ; 2 Lt. 4 R. Ir. Fus., Oct. 1917.

Callaghan, James Newcomen ;
7 Cadet Bn., July 1916.

Callear, Herbert ;
2 Lt. 9 R. Dub. Fus., Oct. 1914 ; Capt. 1916 ; killed in action,
16 Aug. 1917.

Campbell, John ;
3 R.G.A. Cadet School, Apr. 1917.

Campsie, Peter Alexander ;
B. Res. Bde. R..H.A, July 1916 ; 2 Lt. R.F.A., Nov. 1916 ; Lt.
1918.

Carey, Falkland Lytton ;
 Sick Berth Attendant, R.N.V.R., Feb. 1916.

Carnegie, J. H. B. ;
 2 Lt. A.S.C., June 1915 ; Capt. 1916.

Carolin, Horace George ;
 Sandhurst, Feb. 1916 ; 2 Lt. Ser. Bns. R. Mans. Fus., Mar. 1917.

Carpenter, Cecil Edward ;
 7 Cadet Bn., Oct. 1916 ; 2 Lt. 11 Devon R., Mar. 1917.

Carrick, Thomas Desmond ;
 Cdt. C. 5 Leinsters, Nov. 1916.

Carroll, Thomas Patrick Joseph ;
 2 Lt. 5 R. Innis. Fus., Aug. 1915 ; Lt. 1917.

Cashel, F. U. ;
 2 Lt. A.S.C., Apr. 1915 ; Capt. 1915.

Cavey, James Daniel ;
 R.F.C., Farnboro', Apr. 1917 ; 2 Lt. R.A.F., Apr. 1918.

Chambers, Thomas Edward ;
 Pte. Black Watch, March 1916, Officers' Cadet Bn. ; 2 Lt. 8 Bn., Sept. 1916 ; Lt. 1918.

Cheeke, William Alexander ;
 Temp. Capt. R.E., May 1916.

Christie, Reginald B. ;
 2 Lt. 15 North'd Fus., July 1915 ; 2 Lt. M.G.C., May 1916 ; Lt. 1917.

Christie, Robert Francis Sanderson ;
 R.F.C., Farnboro', Apr. 1917 ; 2 Lt. R.F.C., 1917 ; killed in action, 15 Oct. 1917.

Coghlan, Frank Xavier ;
 7 O. Cadet Bn., Jan. 1918 ; 2 Lt. Ser. Bns. Conn. Rang., July 1918.

Cole, Harold Gordon ;
 Grove Park School (M.T.), May 1917 ; 2 Lt. R.A.S.C., Jan. 1919.

Collins, John ;
 2 Lt. 8 Ches. R., Sept. 1915.

Conmee, A. W. ;
 2 Lt. 7 Leins. R., Sept. 1914.

Connell, John ;
 Pte. 5 Lancers, Jan. 1916.

Cordner, H. V. ;
Lt. 7 R. Muns. Fus. ; Capt. 1915.

Cox, Ædan ;
B. Res. Bee. R.H.A., July 1916 ; 2 Lt. R.G.A., S.R., Nov. 1916 ; Lt. 1918.

Crawfurd, Francis William ;
4 R.G.A. Cadet School, June 1917 ; 2 Lt. R.G.A., S.R., Nov. 1917.

Crawfurth-Smith, Henry Vaughan ;
Temp. Lt. R.E., 5 Feb. 1916 ; Lt. 1917.

Creed, Charles Frederick Percy ;
A.S.C., H. T., Sept. 1918.

Crichton, Malcolm Nichol ;
Weedon Arty. Sch., Oct. 1917.

Cummins, George Craing ;
Fermoy, Sept. 1918.

Cunningham, James Lawrence ;
2 Lt. 6 R. Muns. Fus., Aug. 1914 ; Lt. 1915.

Cunningham, William Trafford ;
R.G.A. Cadet School, Aug. 1918.

Currall, Norman Frank ;
2 Lt. E. Lan. R., Aug. 1915 ; killed in action, 18 Oct. 1916.

Cusack, Ralph ;
Pte. Red Cross.

Cusack, R. R. ;
Lt. A.S.C., May 1915 ; Capt. 1916 ; A/Maj. 1917 ; D.A. Dir. of Transport, Temp. Maj., June 1918.

D

Dale, Ronald Cecil ;
O. Cadet Bn., Aug. 1918.

Darby, Horatio Gordon ;
Household Bde. Unit, May 1917 ; 2 Lt. Ir. Gds., S.R., Aug. 1917 ; empld. Gds. M.G.R.

Davidovitz, Reuben ;
Trooper S. Ir. Horse, 1916.

Davis, Edlyne Jessop ;
Fermoy, Sept. 1918.

Davis, Vivian Alfred ;
7 Cadet Bn., July 1917; 2 Lt. Leins. R., Oct. 1917.

De Groot, Francis Edward ;
2 Lt. 15 Hussars, Sp. Res., Aug. 1914 ; Lt. 1916 ; Capt. Tank C., Oct. 1918.

De la Cour, Francis R. S. ;
2 Lt. 3 Conn. Rang., Mar. 1914 ; Lt. 1915.

Delmege, Hugh Jocylyn ;
R.A. Cadet School, June 1917 ; 2 Lt. 1 Res. R. of Cav., Nov. 1917.

Deverell, Anthony ;
Fermoy, Sept. 1918.

Dickinson, Page L. ;
2 Lt. A.S.C. (M.T.), Nov. 1915 ; Capt. 1916.

Dickson, Cecil Robert ;
R.G.A., Brighton, Nov. 1918.

Dignan, Cecil Joseph ;
2 Cav. Cadet Sqdn., Aug. 1916 ; Lt. S. Ir. Horse, July 1917.

Dignam, Jack Robert ;
2 Cav. Cadet Sq., Feb. 1917 ; 2 Lt. Sept. 1917 ; I.A., 1918.

Dinsmore, H. ;
2 Lt. 15 W. York R., Apr. 1915 ; Lt. 1918.

Donnelly, Robert ;
Lab. Garr. Bn. 3 R. Ir. Rif., Apr. 1917.

Doyle, John Joseph ;
2 Lt. 6 R. Dub. Fus., Sept. 1914 ; Lt. 1915 ; killed in action, 10 Aug. 1915.

Duke, Alexander Frazer ;
Fermoy, May 1918 ; 2 Lt. Ser. Bns. R. Muns. Fus., Oct. 1918.

Dundon, Sydney Jack ;
2 Lt. L'pool R., Oct. 1916 ; killed in action, 16 Aug. 1916.

Dunn, John Valentine ;
2 Lt. 7 R. Muns, Fus., Nov. 1914 ; Capt. 1915 ; killed in action, 15 Aug. 1915.

Dunne, John Geoffrey David Baird ;
7 Cadet Bn., July 1916 ; 2 Lt. 3 R. Dub. Fus., Oct. 1916 ; died 12 Nov. 1918.

Dunne, John Joseph ;
O.C. Bn., Fermoy, Sept. 1917 ; 2 Lt. 16 R. Ir. Rif., Jan. 1918.

E

Eagleson, Herbert John ;
  Fermoy, Sept. 1918.

Eaton, Guy Wellesley ;
  2 Lt. 8 R. Ir. Fus., Sept. 1914 ; Capt. 1915 ; M.C.; died of wounds, 7 Sept. 1916.

Eland, Reginald George Watton ;
  Trooper R.N.W. Mounted Police.

Elford, Arthur Douglas ;
  2 Lt. 9 York R., Dec. 1915; Lt. 1916 ; killed in action, 13 Nov. 1916.

Elliott, Andrew Francis ;
  7 Cadet Bn., Jan. 1917; Temp. 2 Lt. 1, 2 Conn. Rang., Apr. 1917 ; att. 2 R. Ir. Regt.

Elliott, George Alexander :
  B. Res. Bde., R.H.A., Sept. 1916.

Ennis, Edward Armstrong ;
  7 O. Cadet Bn., July 1917 ; 2 Lt. 3 Leins. R., Oct. 1917 ; died of wounds, 30 Oct. 1918.

Evans, George ;
  Recruiting Staff, Lt. T.F., Nov. 1915.

Evans, Robert Edward ;
  Guards Cadet Bn., July 1917 ; 2 Lt. Ser. Bns. R. Dub. Fus., Oct. 1917.

F

Fagan, George Patrick J. ;
  R.A. Cadet School, June 1917 ; 2 Lt. R.F.A., S.R., Nov. 1917 ; M.C.

Fagan, John J. A. ;
  Cadet R.E., Jan. 1917 ; 2 Lt. R.E., Apr. 1917.

Falkiner, Francis George Stanley ;
  R.G.A., Preston, June 1918.

Fanning, Robert James ;
  2 Lt. 6 R. Innis. Fus., Dec. 1915 ; Lt. 1917 ; M.C.; I.A. 1917 ; A/Capt. 1918.

Farrell, John Henry ;
  2 Cadet Bn., Apr. 1917 ; 2 Lt. Ser. Bns. R. Dub. Fus., Sept. 1917.

Feehan, John ;
Fermoy, Sept. 1918.

Fenelon, Lewis Martin ;
R.F.C., Farnborough, May 1917 ; 2 Lt. R.F.C., Nov. 1917 ;
Lt. R.A.F., Apr. 1918.

Fennell, Richard Joshua Moore ;
R.A.F., Aug. 1918.

Ferguson, Walter James ;
2 Cav. Cadet Sqdn., Aug. 1916 ; Lt. S. Ir. Horse, June 1918.

Fielder, Owen ;
7 Cadet Bn., Oct. 1916.

Fisher, Kenneth Lawrence ;
7 Cadet Bn., July 1916 ; 2 Lt. M.G.C., March 1917 ; Lt. 1918.

FitzGerald, Gerald Eager ;
7 Cadet Bn., July 1916 ; 2 Lt. 4 Leins. R., Aug. 1917.

FitzGerald, John Jellett ;
No. 2 Cadet Bn., Apr. 1917 ; 2 Lt. I.A., Oct. 1917 ; Lt. 1918.

FitzGerald, Lancelot Cecil ;
2 Lt. 5 R. Ir. Fus., Sept. 1914 ; Capt. 1915 ; I.A., 1918 ; Capt.
1919 ; att. 113 Inf.

FitzGerald, Robert William ;
No. 2 Cadet Bn., Apr. 1917 ; 2 Lt. 10 R. Dub. Fus., Aug. 1917 ;
died of wounds, 4 Oct. 1918.

Fitzpatrick, Denis Frank ;
Cav. Cadet School, Apr. 1918.

Flood, Joseph Henry ;
Jesus College, Cambridge, Nov. 1917.

Flood, Owen Anthony ;
Jesus College, Cambridge, Jan. 1918.

Forster, John Cameron ;
2 Lt. R.F.A., May 1917 ; Lt. 1918.

Franks, Alexander Grant ;
A.S.C., Sept. 1917.

Frazer, W. H. ;
2 Lt. R.G.A., Dec. 1915 ; Lt. 1917.

Freeman, Herbert Joseph ;
2 Lt. A.S.C., Oct. 1914 ; Capt. 1915 ; 16 Div. Train ; died of
wounds 29 Oct. 1918.

French, James Anthony ;
7 Cadet Bn., May 1916 ; 2 Lt. 3 R. Ir. Rif., Oct. 1918.

Fudger, Charles Lawrence;
7 Cadet Bn., Aug. 1916; 2 Lt. 6 Leins. R., Dec. 1916; Lt. 1918; M.C.

Furniss, James;
Inns of Court, O.T.C., Jan. 1916.

G

Gailey-White, Albert James;
Cav. Cdt. Sch., Sept. 1917.

Gallagher, Joseph;
Pte. R.G.A., July 1918.

Garner, Charles Johnson;
2 Lt. 18 R. Ir. Rif., March 1915; 2 Lt. R.G.A., Oct. 1915; Lt. 1917.

Gault, Joseph;
2 Lt. 17 R. Ir. Rif., Feb. 1915; Lt. 1916.

Gaynor, George James;
2 Cav. Cadet Sqdn., Aug. 1916; 2 Lt. S. Ir. Horse, Jan. 1917; Lt. 1918; Lt. 7 R. Ir. Regt. 1918.

Gelston, John Epworth Hubbard;
2 Lt. A.S.C., Oct. 1914; Lt. 1915; I.A., Feb. 1919; Capt. 1919; att. 1 Lancers.

Geoghegan, Hugh O'Neill;
7 O. Cadet Bn., Jan, 1918.

Gilmore, Demin Burns;
2 Lt. New Armies, Unattached List, Nov. 1914; Lt. 6 R. Dub. Fus., Aug. 1915; Lt. M.G.C. 1917; Capt. Tank C. 1917.

Goodbody, Jerome Marcus;
Capt. 4 Leins. R:, Feb. 1915.

Goodbody, John Eric;
2 R.F.A. Cadet School, Apr. 1917; 2 Lt. R.F.A., S.R., Nov. 1917.

Gordon, William Jocelyn;
7 O. Cadet Bn., Nov. 1917.

Grant, Charles William;
2 Lt. 7 R. Dub. Fus., Dec. 1915; Lt. 1916.

Graves, Algernon Frederick Charles;
2 Lt. 7 R. Ir. Fus., Aug. 1914; Lt. 1915; Lt. 7 R. Innis. Fus. 1917; Capt. 1917; died of wounds, 26 Aug. 1917.

Green, William;
    7 O. Cadet Bn., Oct. 1916.

Greene, James Wilson;
    7 Cadet Bn., Oct. 1916.

Greene, Terence Kendal;
    2 Cav. Cadet Sq., Feb. 1917; 2 Lt. S. Ir. Horse, July 1917;
    att. Notts Yeo.

Greer, Roderick Denis;
    2 Lt. 7 R. Ir. Fus., Sept. 1914; Lt. I.A., June 1916; Capt.
    1919; att. 7 Gurka Rif.

Gresley, Robert Blackwell;
    Sub. Lt. R. N. Div., Oct. 1915.

Gresson, Richard Arbuthnott Ragnell;
    Rhyll, Sept. 1918.

Griffin, Gerald;
    7 Cadet Bn., July 1916.

Gueret, Paul Joseph;
    7 Cadet Bn., July 1916; 2 Lt. R. Dub. Fus., Oct. 1916; Lt. New
    Armies, 1917; Lt. Labour C. 1918.

Gurney, Samuel;
    7 Cadet Bn., July 1916; 2 Lt. 6 Norf. R., October 1916; Lt.
    1918.

H

Hadden, Addison Barnes P.;
    2 Cav. Cadet Sqdn., Aug. 1916; 2 Lt. S. Ir. Horse, Dec. 1916;
    Lt. 1918.

Haines, Alec C.;
    2 Lt. R. Dub. Fus., Nov. 1914; Lt. 1915; died of wounds, 8
    May 1915.

Hall, Henry Eric;
    7 Cadet Bn., Oct. 1916.

Hall, William Jasper;
    R.A.F., June 1918.

Halpin, James Raymond;
    7 O.C. Bn., Apr. 1918.

Hand, George Francis;
    7 Cadet Bn., Aug. 1916; 2 Lt. 5 R. Muns. Fus., Dec. 1916.

Harberd, Arthur Joseph ;
Rhyll, Sept. 1918.

Harris, David Walter ;
7 Cadet Bn., May 1917 ; 2 Lt. 6 R. Dub. Fus., Aug. 1917.

Harris, John Henry Edward ;
2 Lt. 7 R. Dub. Fus., Feb. 1916 ; Lt. 1917.

Harris, Norman Beamish ;
2 Lt. 6 R. Dub. Fus., Feb. 1916 ; Lt. 1917.

Hartley, Walter John ;
2 Lt. 5 R. Ir. Fus., Sept. 1914 ; Capt. 1915 ; killed in action,
16 Aug. 1915.

Hawtrey, Eric Edmond Harcourt ;
7 O.C. Bn., Dec. 1916 ; 2 Lt. Ser. Bns. R. Dub. Fus., Oct. 1918 ;
M.C.

Hayden, Terence Desmond ;
Pte. S.I.H., July 1918.

Hearne, James Godfrey ;
Horse Transport, June 1918.

Heather, George Johnson ;
7 O.C. Bn., Sept. 1918.

Hemsworth, Dudley de la Warr ;
Pte. R.E., May 1916.

Herlihy, William ;
R.F.A. Cadet School, July 1917.

Hewardine, Albert Edward ;
Pte. N.I.H., Sept. 1918.

Hewitt, Robert Malcolm ;
2 Lt. 15 L'pool R., Dec. 1914 ; Lt. 1916.

Hewson, Maurice George ;
7 O. Cadet Bn., Jan. 1918.

Higgins, Richard ;
Household Bde. Unit, May 1918.

Hilliard, Cyril Henry ;
7 O. Cadet Bn., Jan. 1918.

Hilliard, William Joseph ;
Cav. Cadet Unit, March 1916 ; 2 Lt. Ser. Bns., S. Staff. R., July
1918.

Hodder, Frances Charles Samuel ;
R.A.F., Aug. 1918.

Hodgens, Charles Joseph;
　7 Cadet Bn., July 1916; 2 Lt. Tank C., Jan. 1917 ; Lt. 1918.

Howe, James George ;
　O.C. Bn., Rhyll, Sept. 1918.

Howell, Alfred Henry Redvers ;
　Cadet Sq., 1918.

Howell, Reuben Harrison;
　7 Cadet Bn., May 1917 ; 2 Lt. 11 R. Dub. Fus., Aug. 1917;
　died of wounds, 29 March 1918.

Hughes, John Victor ;
　R.G.A. Cadet Bn., Oct. 1917 ; 2 Lt., Mar. 1918.

Hughes, Stephen Charles Taylor ;
　Lt. A. Ord. Dept., Apr. 1916.

Hume, John Walter ;
　Capt. 7 R. Ir. Fus., Dec. 1914

Hunt, John ;
　O.C. Bn., Brighton, Oct. 1918.

Hurley, William John Brien ;
　2 Lt. A.S.C., June 1915.

Hurley, William Michael ;
　Special War Work, Admiralty, Apr. 1916.

Hutchinson, James ;
　2 Lt. R.F.A., Dec. 1915.

I

Inglis, Harry Flavelle ;
　7 O. Cadet Bn., Nov. 1917; 2 Lt. Ser. Bns., Leins. R., May
　1918.

Irvine, Robert ;
　7 O.C. Bn., July 1917.

Irwin, Joseph Bird ;
　2 Lt. 10 R. Lanc. R., May 1915; Lt. 1917; M.C.; D.S.O.;
　despatches.

J

Jackson, A. R. ;
　Lt. 3 E. Kent R., Feb. 1915; Capt. 1916; Ry. Transport Off.,
　1918.

Jackson, Robert Victor ;
2 Lt. 5 R. Ir. Fus., Feb. 1916 ; Lt. 1917.

Jackson, William Vincent ;
O.C.B. Fermoy, Aug. 1918.

Jepps, Frederick ;
Pte. Black Watch, Dec. 1915.

Johnston, Richard Edward ;
Sandhurst, Aug. 1916 ; 2 Lt. Leins. R., May 1917 ; Lt. 1918.

Johnstone, John Sydney ;
2 Lt. A.S.C., Sept. 1914.

Jones, William Ambrose Colvill ;
Fermoy, June 1918.

Jones-Nowlan, Thomas Chamney ;
7 Cadet Bn., Aug. 1916.

Joyce, John A. ;
7 O.C. Bn., Jan. 1918.

K

Keating, Michael Joseph ;
2 Lt. 13 Lan. Fus., March 1915.

Keating, Thomas James ;
2 Lt. 4 Conn. Rang., Feb. 1916.

Keegan, William ;
7 Cadet Bn., May 1916 ; 2 Lt. 4 Conn. Rang., Sept. 1916.

Kelly, Cecil Grattan ;
2 Lt. A.S.C., Nov. 1914 ; Lt. 1915.

Kelly, John Davis ;
2 Cadet Bn., Apr. 1917 ; 2 Lt. 3 R. Ir. Regt., Jan. 1918.

Kelly, Richard ;
Cav. Cadet Sqdn., Sept. 1917 ; 2 Lt. 10 Hussars, S.R., July 1918.

Kennedy, Herbert Colles ;
R.A.F., Sept. 1918 ; died, 15 Oct. 1918.

Kennedy, Reginald ;
7 O. Cadet Bn., Jan. 1918.

Killeen, Patrick John J. ;
7 Cadet Bn., July 1916.

Kilroy, Alan James Minchin ;
2 Lt. I.A., Feb. 1916 ; Lt. 1918.

Kinnear, Charles Annesley;
  2 Lt. R.F.A., Nov. 1915; killed in action, 16 Oct. 1916.

Kirkland, Gordon C.;
  2 Lt. 7 R. Ir. Fus., Sept. 1914; Lt. 1915; Capt. 1918.

Kirwan, Christopher;
  10 Inf. Cadet Bn., Aug. 1917; 2 Lt. R. Dub. Fus., Dec. 1917.

Knight, George Walker;
  17 O.C. Bn., Apr. 1918.

L

Lannon, Robert James;
  Cadet R.E., Jan. 1917; 2 Lt. Apr. 1917; Lt. 1918.

Lawlor, Anthony;
  R.F.C., Farnboro', Apr. 1917; 2 Lt. R.A.F., Apr. 1918.

Leland, Frederick Wm. Henry;
  2 Lt. 7 Leins. R., Sept. 1914; Lt. 1915; Capt. 1917.

Leonard, John Stanislaw;
  2 Lt. 3 R. Ir. Fus., Aug. 1915; Lt. 1917; King's Afr Rif
  2 R., 1917.

Leslie, Walter E.;
  Pte. A.S.C., June 1916; 2 Lt. Aug. 1916; Lt. 1918.

Levingston, Frank Gerald;
  M.T., A.S.C., Aug. 1918; 2 Lt. Oct. 1918.

Levitt, Nathaniel;
  O. Cadet Bn., Sept. 1917.

Lewis, Francis M.;
  2 Lt. R.G.A., Nov. 1916; Lt. 1918.

Liddle, Lawrence Henry;
  R.F.A. School, March 1918; 2 Lt. Sept. 1918.

Lightburn, Alfred Stuart;
  R.G.A. Cdt. Sch., Apr. 1918.

Lindsay, Albert William Vincent;
  O.C. Bn., Rhyll, Sept. 1918.

Lisney, Harry;
  Eng. Cadet Bn., Aug. 1916.

Lloyd, Robert Courtois;
  7 O. Cadet Bn., Nov. 1916.

Long, Eugene Joseph ;
    2 Cav. Cadet Sqdn., Aug. 1916 ; 2 Lt. S. Ir. Horse, Jan. 1917 ;
Lt. 1918 ; empld. 7 R. Ir. Regt.

Loxton, Alma Seyward George ;
    2 Lt. 9 Black Watch, May 1917 ; Lt. 1918.

Lucas, James Edward ;
    2 Lt. 16 Durham L. I., July 1915 ; A/Capt. ; killed in action,
5 May, 1917.

Lumsden, John Fitzhardinge ;
    2 Lt. 6 R. Ir. Regt., Sept. 1914 ; Lt. 1916.

M

McCaig, Alexander ;
    7 O.C. Bn., Sept. 1918.

M'Caig, Martin Robert ;
    7 Cadet Bn., July 1916.

M'Clean, Alan Joseph Ernest ;
    M.T. Cadet School, March 1917 ; 2 Lt. June 1917 ; Lt. 1918.

M'Cullagh, Leslie Stuart ;
    7 Cadet Bn., July 1916 ; 2 Lt. R.A.F., Apr. 1918.

M'Cullogh, James Blandford ;
    R.A.F., Aug. 1918.

M'Dermott, Roe Charles ;
    7 Officers' Cadet Bn., July 1917.

M Donald, Jan ;
    2 Lt. 11 Gord. Highrs., Dec. 1915.

M'Elroy, Frederick William ;
    7 Cadet Bn., July 1916 ; 2 Lt. Tank C., Nov. 1916 ; Lt. ;
D.S.O. ; died 16 Nov. 1918.

M'Ferran, James Stanley ;
    O. Cadet Bn., Aug. 1918.

MacGuire, Constantine Francis ;
    Rhyll, Sept. 1918.

Mackay, James Ian ;
    Guards' Cadet Bn., July 1917 ; 2 Lt. 4 R. Muns. Fus., Oct.
1917.

MacMahon, Charles Gerald ;
    Cav. Cadet School, Apr. 1918.

M'Nulty, Michael ;
   7 Cadet Bn., Aug. 1916.

Maguire, Harry James ;
   7 O.C. Bn., Apr. 1918.

Malcolmson, Reginald George ;
   Pte. Black Watch, March 1916.

Malcomson, A. ;
   7 Cadet Bn., March 1916 ; 2 Lt. 3 R. Ir. Regt., July, 1916 ; Lt.
1918.

Malone, Antony ;
   2 Lt. R.F.A., Dec. 1915 ; Lt.1917.

Malone, George Ernest ;
   R.A.F., Oct. 1918.

Malone, John Dermott ;
   R.A.F., Oct. 1918.

Manning, Brian O'Donoghue ;
   7 Cadet Bn., Oct. 1916 ; 2 Lt. Ir. Gds., Feb. 1917 ; Lt. 1918.

Manning, Victor Lionel ;
   2 Cadet Bn., M.G. Section ; 2 Lt. M. G. C., May 1917.

Martin, G. J. ;
   2 Lt. 4 R. Ir. Regt, Aug. 1914 ; Capt. 1916.

Martin, Laurence Henry ;
   7 Cadet Bn., Oct. 1916 ; 2 Lt. 10 R. Ir. Fus., Apr. 1917 ;
killed in action, 23 Nov. 1917.

Martin, Lawrence John ;
   Cav. Cdt. Sch., Kildare.

Massy, Hon. Tristram Francis J. L. ;
   2 Lt. R.F.A., Sp. Res., March 1915 ; Lt. 1917.

Mathers, R. C. ;
   Pte. 9 Platoon, Y. Co. 12 W. Rid. R., Aug. 1915 ; France 1916.

Matheson, Robert Nathaniel ;
   Aldershot, Nov. 1917 ; 2 Lt. A.S.C., Jan. 1918 ; A/Capt & Adjt.
1918.

Mathews, Alfred H. ;
   7 Cadet Bn., May 1916 ; 2 Lt. R. Dub. Fus., Sept. 1916.

Mathews, George Jackson ;
   7 Cadet Bn., July 1916.

Mattershed, Percival Charles ;
   2 Cadet Bn., Apr. 1917.

R

Maunsell-Eyre, Richard H. ;
> 7 Cadet Bn., Jan. 1917; 2 Lt. 4 R. Muns. Fus., Apr. 1917;
> Lt. 1918.

Millar, R. M'G. G. ;
> 2 Lt. R.G.A., August 1914; Lt. 1917 ; Lt. Tank C., 1917; Lt.
> 1, 2 Som. L. I., July 1917.

Mitchell, John Mansfield ;
> 2 Lt. O.T.C., T.F., Unattached List, Sept. 1915; Temp. Lt.
> 1917.

Moeran, Francis Douglas Barton ;
> Fermoy, June 1916.

Molyneux, Ernest Thomas ;
> 7 Cadet Bn., May 1916 ; 2 Lt. Sept. 1916; empld. R.F.C. ; Lt.
> R.A.F., Apr. 1918.

Montgomery, C. V. ;
> 2 Lt. R.G.A., Sp. Res., Feb. 1915; Lt. 1917.

Mooney, Desmond ;
> Cadet Co., A.S.C. (M.T.), Dec. 1916 ; 2 Lt. Mar. 1917 ; Lt.
> 1918.

Moore, Frederick Joseph Newton ;
> R.A.F., Aug. 1918.

Moore, Hugh Victor ;
> 7 Cadet Bn., July 1916 ; 2 Lt. 4 Conn. Rang., Oct. 1916 ; killed
> in action, 22 Mar. 1918.

Moore, Thomas Henry ;
> 7 Cadet Bn., July 1917 ; 2 Lt. 12 R. Innis. Fus., Oct. 1917.

Moore, William Robert ;
> Rhyll, Sept. 1918.

Moran, John Ambrose ;
> 7 Cadet Bn., May 1917 ; 2 Lt. Ser. Bns. R. Dub. Fus., Aug.
> 1917.

Moran, William Aloysius R. ;
> B. Res. Brig. R.H.A., July 1916 ; 2 Lt. R.G.A., S.R., Oct.
> 1916; Lt. 1918.

Morgan, Harold Woodman ;
> Eng. Cadet Unit, Sept. 1916 ; 2 Lt. R.E., March 1917; Lt.
> 1917.

Morris, Ernest William ;
> R.A.F., June 1918.

Mouritz, Percival Richards ;
> 7 O.C. Bn., Sept. 1918.

Munro, James Bayne ;
    O.C. Bn., Rhyll, Sept. 1918.
Murphy, Alfred Augustine ;
    Eng. Cadet Sch., May 1918.
Murphy, Arthur W.;
    7 Cadet Bn., July 1916.
Murphy, Bernard Joseph ;
    7 Cadet Bn., Aug. 1916 ; 2 Lt. 5 R. Muns. Fus., Dec. 1916 ;
    died of wounds, 18 Aug. 1917.
Murphy, Denis Michael ;
    Rhyll, Sept. 1918.
Murphy, George Newcom ;
    A.S.C., Aug. 1914.
Murphy, Lawrence William Raymond ;
    7 Cadet Bn., May 1917.; 2 Lt. 5 R. Muns. Fus., Sept. 1917.
Murphy, Norbert ;
    2 Cav. Cadet Sqdn., Aug. 1916 ; 2 Lt. S. Ir. Horse, Dec. 1916 ;
    Lt. 1918.
Murphy, Richard Anthony Joseph ;
    7 O. Cadet Bn., Jan. 1918.
Murphy, R. J.;
    D.P.O.S, Dept., A.S.C., Aug. 1916 ; 2 Lt. R.A.S.C., July
    1917 ; Lt. 1919.
Murphy, William Paul ;
    Fermoy, May 1918 ; 2 Lt. Ser. Bns. R. Ir. Rif., Oct. 1918.
Murray, John Charles ;
    Fermoy, May 1918 ; 2 Lt. 3 R. Ir. Fus., Oct. 1918.
Murray, John Kenneth ;
    2 C.C.S., June 1918.
Murray, Reginald Vivian ;
    2 Lt. 5 R. Ir. Fus., Sept. 1914 ; Lt. 1915 ; Lt. M.G.C., 1916 ;
    Capt. 1917 ; M.C. ; Lt. R. Innis. Fus. 1918 ; A/Major 1918.

N

Narramore, Walter Sydney ;
    2 Cadet Bn., Apr. 1917 ; 2 Lt. Ser. Bns. R. Ir Rif., Aug. 1917.
Nash, F. ;
    Pte. Inf. Unit, July 1916.

Nash, Joseph Francis;
7 Cadet Bn., Aug. 1916 ; 2 Lt. 10 R. Dub. Fus., Dec. 1916.

Neale, James ;
B. Res. Bde. R.H.A., July 1916; 2 Lt. R.F.A., Sept. 1917 ;
M.C.

Nelson, W. J. G. ;
2 Lt. 6 R. Dub. Fus., Nov. 1914 ; R. Def. Force.

Nicholls, Jasper Cecil G. ;
2 Cadet Bn., Apr. 1917 ; 2 Lt 10 R. Ir. Fus., Aug. 1917.

Nixon, Arthur Cecil ;
R.A.F. Sch., Weedon; Lt. R.A.F., Sept. 1918.

Nolan, Thomas Vivian Cairbre ;
Rhyll, Sept. 1918.

North, Norman Frank ;
7 Cadet Bn., May 1917.

O

O'Beirne, Denis Rhoderick ;
7 Cadet Bn., July 1916 ; 2 Lt. 4 R. Ir. Regt., Oct. 1916.

O'Brien, Dermot ;
7 Cadet Bn., Aug. 1916.

O'Brien. John Edmond Noel ;
2 C.C.S., June 1918.

O'Brien, Sydney Joseph ;
7 Cadet Bn., Aug. 1916.

O'Cleary, Daniel Richard ;
2 Lt. R. Dub. Fus., Sept. 1914.

O'Connor, Fergus Lawrence ;
2 Cav. Cadet Sq., Feb. 1917 ; 2 Lt. 8 Hussars, S.R., Sept. 1917.

O'Connor, Robert Aylward ;
2 Lt. A.S.C., Oct. 1915.

O'Connor, William Emmet Taafe ;
Fermoy, June 1918.

O'Conor, Arthur Edmund ;
7 Cadet Bn., Oct. 1916.

O'Conor, Charles William ;
A.S.C., Jan. 1918 ; 2 Lt. R.A.S.C., May 1918.

O'Donnell, Henry Claude ;
R.A.F., June 1918.

O'Donnell, Patrick Gerard ;
7 Cadet Bn., Jan. 1917 ; 2 Lt. 5 R. Muns. Fus., May 1917.

O'Kelly, Edward ;
R.A.V.C., Sept. 1914.

O'Mahony, Gerald John C. T. ;
Fermoy, May 1918 ' 2 Lt. 3 R. Ir. Regt., Oct. 1918.

O'Neill, Aloysius Joseph ;
Pte. A.S.C. (M.T.), Aug. 1915.

O'Neill, James Arthur ;
2 Cav. Cadet Sqdn., Aug. 1916 ; 2 Lt. N. Ir. Horse, Jan. 1917 ;
Lt. 1918.

O'Neill, John Joseph ;
2 Cav. Cadet Sqdn., Sept. 1917.

O'Reilly, Eugene Francis ;
2 Lt. New-Armies, Feb. 1915 ; Lt. Nigeria R., Sept. 1915 ; Lt.
New Armies, 1917.

O'Reilly, James Vincent ;
Inns of Court, Apr. 1917 ; 2 Lt. R.F.A., Jan. 1918.

Ormsby-Scott, Richard D. F. ;
Fermoy, May 1918 ; 2 Lt. 3 Conn. Rang., Oct. 1918.

P

Palmer, John Adnah Jordan ;
20 O.C. Bn., Apr. 1918.

Parker, Cyril B. O. ;
Pte. Inns of Court Bn., Aug. 1915.

Parker, Hugh Lionel ;
Rhyll, Sept. 1918.

Patterson, William Weston ;
O.C. Bn., Gailes, Ayrshire, Jan. 1918.

Paul, Hamilton ;
2 Lt. 5 W. Rid. R., July 1915 ; Temp. Lt. 1915 ; Lt. 1917.

Peard, Harry Holmer ;
Cav. Cadet Unit, March 1916 ; Lt. 3 D. Gds., S.R., Jan. 1918.

Pemberton, Robert Thomas ;
Pte. R.F.A., Sept. 1918.

Phipps, H. C. ;
2 Lt. A.S.C., May 1915 ; A/Capt. 1915.

Pierce, Bernard J. M. ;
    7 Cadet Bn., July 1916; 2 Lt. 5 R. Dub. Fus., Nov. 1916.

Plunkett, Oliver ;
    2 Lt. A.S.C., Dec. 1915 ; A/Capt. 1918.

Poulter, Terence B. ;
    7 Cadet Bn., Oct. 1916; 2 Lt. 5 R. Dub. Fus., March 1917 ; Lt. 1918.

Powell, Frederick William ;
    Inns of Court O.T.C., June 1915.

Power, Henry Richard ;
    2 Lt. 3 R. Ir. Rif., Oct. 1915 ; att. R.F C.; Lt. 1917 ; killed in action, 22 Aug. 1917.

Poynton, Robert Ernest ;
    2 Lt. 6 R. Ir. Fus., Dec. 1915; Lt. 1917.

Pratt, J. E. ;
    2 Lt. R.F.A., Oct. 1914 ; Lt. 1915; M.C.

Pratt, John Hopkins ;
    2 Lt. 3 Innis. Fus., Jan. 1916; Lt. 1917.

Purcell, William ;
    2 Lt. Cadet Sqdn., Aug. 1916 ; 2 Lt. S. Ir. Horse, Dec. 1916.

Q

Quin, Gerard Patrick Columba ;
    Household Bde. Unit, May 1917.

Quinn, James Vincent ;
    7 Cadet Bn., Jan. 1917 ; 2 Lt. 3 Conn. Rang., Apr. 1917 ; Lt. 1918.

R

Ramsay, Alan Livingstone ;
    2 Lt. 3 R. Ir. Regt., Aug. 1914 ; Flanders, 1914 ; wounded, 1915 ; Lt. ; A/Capt. ; killed in action, 24 Apr. 1916.

Ramsay, Cecil Arthur ;
    2 Lt. High. L. I., Dec. 1915.

Ramsay, George Read ;
    2 Lt. 13 W. York R., May 1915.

Ramsay, Robert James ;
    2 Lt. 3 R. Ir. Rif., Aug. 1914.

Revell, John W. ;
  Lt. Royal Marines, Sept. 1914 ; Capt. 1915.

Rice, Victor Hugo Moffatt ;
  Gailes, Ayrshire, Oct. 1917; 2 Lt. Ser. Bns. North'd Fus.,
  Mar. 1918.

Richards, John Henry P. ;
  7 O. Cadet Bn., Jan. 1918 ; 2 Lt. Ser. Bns. Conn. Rang., July
  1918.

Ricketts, William Falkland ;
  7 Cadet Bn., Aug. 1916.

Ritchie, William Hermann ;
  B. Res. Bde., R.H.A., Sept. 1916 ; 2 Lt. R.G.A., S.R., Dec.
  1916.

Robertson, George Edward ;
  R.A.F., Oct. 1918.

Robinson, Cecil Luke ;
  2 Lt. O.T.C., T.F., unattached list, July 1915 ; Local Lt. 1916
  Adjt. D.U.O.T.C., July 1916.

Robinson, David Percy ;
  A.S.C., M.T., Nov. 1918.

Robinson, Thomas John ;
  7 O.C. Bn., Aug. 1916 ; 2 Lt. 5 R. Muns. Fus., Sept. 1916.

Robinson, Thomas Midleton ;
  Pte. A.S.C. (M.T.), Nov. 1916.

Robinson, William S. ;
  2 Lt. A.S.C. (M.T.), May 1915.

Roots, Harold Sydney ;
  2 Cadet Bn., Apr. 1917 ; 2 Lt. Ser. Bns., R. Dub. Fus., Aug.
  1917.

Ross, Ernest Albert ;
  Pte. A.S.C., Sept. 1915.

Rutter, William ;
  10 Inf. C. Bn., Sept. 1916 ; 2 Lt. 3 N. Staff. R., Dec. 1916 ;
  Lt. 1918; A/Capt. and Adj. M.G.C., 1918.

S

Sadeke-Brooks, Arthur Cecil ;
  4 R. F.A. Cadet School, Feb. 1917.

Salazar, Demetrius Sarsfield ;
  2 Cav. Cadet Sqdn., Aug. 1915 ; 2 Lt., Mar. 1917 ; Lt. 1918.

Sampson, Frank Sarsfield :
  7 Cadet Bn., Oct. 1916.

Sandford, Edward Henry ;
  M.G.C., 11 R. Dub. Fus., Apr. 1917.

Sankey, William Filmer ;
  O.C.B. Netheravon, Sept. 1918.

Scales, Victor Watson ;
  Lt., A. Ord. Dept., July 1916 ; A/Capt. 1918.

Scallan, Richard Talbot ;
  B. Res. Brig. R.H.A., July 1916; 2 Lt. R.G.A., S.R., Nov. 1916 ; killed, 31st May 1918.

Shanks, J. A. ;
  Lt. 6 Conn. Rang., Nov. 1914 ; Lt. New Armies, 1917 ; Lab. C , 1918.

Shannon, Ellis James ;
  O.C.B. Fermoy, Aug. 1918; 2 Lt. Ser. Bns., R. Ir. Rif., Mar. 1919.

Shaw, John Frederick Prosser ;
  Eng. Training Centre, Dejanwy, May 1917 ; 2 Lt. R.E., July 1917 ; Lt. 1918.

Shea, Frederick William ;
  Pte. R.F.A., Apr. 1916 ; 2 Lt. R.F.A., S.R., Feb, 1917 ; M.C.; Lt. 1918.

Sibley, John ;
  Pte R.F.A., Aug. 1916.

Simington, Joseph ;
  7 O.C. Bn., Apr. 1918.

Smith, Stanley Herd ;
  2 Cav. Cadet Sq., Feb. 1917.

Smith, Thomas Emmanuel ;
  B. Res. Bde. R.H.A., July 1916 ; 2 Lt. R.G.A. S.R. Nov. 1916; killed in action, 23 Apr. 1917.

Smyth, Sydney ;
  M.M.G. Corps, Sept. 1917.

parrow, Frank Edward ;
  2 Lt. R.E., Dec. 1915 ; Lt. 1916 ; died of wounds, 13 Aug. 1916.

Spence, William N. ;
  2 Lt. R.E., Nov. 1916 ; Lt. 1918.

Stephens, Herbert Stanley ;
  R.H.A., Dec. 1916.

Stewart, Alastair Duncan ;
Pte. 11 R. Dub. Fus., Mar. 1917.

Stewart, William ;
O. Cadet Bn., Fermoy, Sept. 1916.

Stritch, Andrew John Russell ;
Jesus College, Cambridge, Jan. 1918.

Swan, George Edward ;
R.H.A., Dec. 1916 ; 2 Lt. R.G.A., S.R., Sept. 1917 ; Lt. 1919.

Swift, James Hubert ;
2 Cav. C.S., July 1917.

Synnot, Fitzherbert Paget ;
2 Lt. 5 R. W. Fus., Sept. 1914 ; killed in action, Gallipoli,
10 Aug. 1915.

T

Tate, Robert James ;
R.A.F., Aug. 1918.

Taylor, Thomas Connell ;
O.C. Bn., Rhyll, Sept. 1918.

Taylour, Ernest Frederick Noel ;
Pte. 7 Leins. R., June 1915 ; 2 Lt. 4 Conn. Rang., Sept. 1915 ;
Lt. 1917.

Tegart, A. E. ;
2 Lt. A.S.C., Sept. 1914 ; Capt. 1915.

Thompson, William Edward ;
O.C. Bn., Rhyll, Sept. 1918.

Thornton, Ernest Alfred ;
Lt. 6 R. Muns. Fus., Nov 1914 ; wounded, Dardanelles, Aug.
1915 ; I.A. 1918 ; Capt. 1919.

Thunder, Alexander Edmond ;
7 O. Cadet Bn., Jan. 1918 ; 2 Lt. Ser. Bns., R. Ir. Fus., July
1918.

Tighe, Daniel Charles Frederick ;
O.C. Bn., Cambridge, March 1918.

Topping, Frederick Charles ;
2 R.G.A., O.C.B., Uckfield, Sussex, Feb. 1917 ; 2 Lt. R.G.A.,
S.R., July 1917.

Townshend, Frederick William Chisholm Loftus ;
2 Cav. Cadet Sq., May 1917 ; 2 Lt. N. Ir. Horse, Dec. 1917.

Tracy, James ;
R.A.F., Oct. 1918.

Trotter, David William ;
2 C.C.S., June 1918.

Tucker, James Clifford ;
Oct. 1918.

Tulloch, Armstrong Lushington ;
Cav. Cadet School, April 1918.

U

Underwood, Gerald Joseph ;
2 Cav. Cadet Sq., May 1917 ; 2 Lt. 4 Hussars, S.R., Sept. 1917.

Usher, Robert H. ;
2 Cav. Cadet Sq., May 1917 ; 2 Lt. 4 Hussars, S.R., Mar. 1918.

V

Valentine, Robert Lepper ;
2 Lt. 8 R. Dub. Fus., Sept. 1914 ; Lt. 1914 ; died of wounds,
30 Apr. 1916.

W

Walker, John William ;
7 O. Cadet. Bn., Jan. 1918.

Walker, Patrick Joseph ;
7 O. Cadet. Bn., Nov. 1917.

Walker, Reginald Henry ;
2 Lt. 2 Life Gds., March 1916 ; Lt. Gds. M.G.R , 1917.

Wallen, Arthur Wilson ;
Jesus College, Cambridge, Jan. 1918

Wallis, Thomas Gill ;
R.G.A. School, Mar. 1918 ; 2 Lt. R.F.A., Sept. 1918.

Walsh, John Joseph ;
Rhyll, Sept. 1915.

Walsh, Walter Joseph ;
O.C. Bn., Rhyll, Sept. 1918.

Ward, Arthur David ;
2 Lt. 11 R. Ir. Rif., Nov. 1915 ; Lt. 1917.

Ward, Thomas ;
2 Lt. 1, 2 Bord., Aug. 1915 ; Lt. 1917 ; M.G.C. 1917.

Warnock, Geoffrey William ;
7 Cadet Bn., Jan. 1917.

Warren, R. P. ;
2 Lt. A.S.C., Sept. 1914 ; Lt. 1917.

Warren, William John ;
2 Lt. 15 L'pool R., Dec. 1915 ; A/Lt. 1917 ; Training Res.

Watson, Samuel Herbert ;
2 Lt. R.F.A., Oct. 1914 ; M.C. ; Lt. 1917.

Weatherup, Fred. Stephen ;
Household Bde., O.C.B., Aug. 1917.

Webb, Edward ;
2 Cav. Cadet Sq., Nov. 1916 ; 2 Lt. 2 Res. R. of Cav., Jan.
1917 ; Lt. 1918 ; att. 7 Hrs.

Weir, John Horace ;
7 Cadet Bn., July 1916.

West, William John ;
11 Lincs., Aug. 1916.

Westropp, Hugh Massy ;
Pte. N. Ir. Horse, May 1915 ; France, 1916.

Wheeler, R. H. ;
Garr. O.C.B., July 1917 ; 2 Lt. 3 (Res. Garr. Bn.) R. Ir. Fus.,
Oct. 1917.

Whelan, Reginald ;
Household Bde. Unit, May 1917 ; Garr. O.C.B., July 1917.

White, Albert James Gailey ;
Cav. Cadet Sq., Sept. 1917 ; 2 Lt. 2 Res. R. of Cav., Apr. 1918.

White, George ;
Fermoy, June 1918.

White, George Burbidge ;
2 Lt. R.F.A., March 1916.

White, Helenus Martin ;
Rhyll, Sept. 1918.

White, Luke ;
7 Cadet Bn., May 1916.

Whitehead, Walter ;
2 Lt. R. Dub. Fus., Oct. 1915 ; killed in action, 6 Sept. 1916.

Wildman, Jack ;
Cav. Cadet School, April 1918.

Wilkinson, Charles Richard ;
Rhyll, Sept. 1918.

Wilson, Andrew ;
2 R.G.A. Cadet School, May 1917 ; 2 Lt. R.G.A., S.R., Sept. 1917.

Wilson, C. Pilkington ;
General Service Battalion, March 1915.

Wilson, Charles Robert ;
2 Lt. 7 R. Muns. Fus., Dec. 1915 ; Front, 1916 ; M.C. May 1917 ; killed in action, 24 May 1917.

Wilson, David ;
Pte. Black Watch, March 1916 ; Officers' Cadet Bn.

Wilson, Thomas William ;
7 O. Cadet. Bn., Nov. 1917.

Wilson, Victor John Frackleton ;
7 O. Cadet Bn., Nov. 1917.

Wingfield, Richard James Trench ;
2 Lt. R.F.A., Oct. 1914 ; killed in action, Mesopotamia, 27 Apr. 1916.

Woods, William Thornley Stoker ;
2 Lt. R.F.A. Nov. 1915 ; France, 1916 ; killed in action, 27 Oct. 1916.

Wyon, Melville W. ;
Pte. 10 R. Dub. Fus., June 1916.

EMPLOYÉS OF TRINITY COLLEGE.

PORTERS.

Crespin, Claude C.;
    C.S.M., A.S.C., Mar. 1915; attd. to O.T.C.

Keatinge, William ;
    Pte. 12 Lancers. Aug. 1914 ; wounded & gassed.

M'Cann, David ;
    Instructor O.T.C., Aug. 1914; R.Q.M.S., A.S.C., Sept. 1914.

Marsh, George ;
    Sergt. 21 Lancers, May 1915 ; died from shell shock, 6 Mar. 1918.

Mason, Joseph;
    Sergt. 8 R. Dub. Fus., May 1915.

Parrott, Edward John ;
    Instructor O.T.C., Aug. 1914; R.S.M., 8 R. Muns. Fus.,
    Sept. 1914 ; twice wounded, 1916; 2 Lt. & Adjt., Oct. 1916 ;
    despatches, Jan. 1917.

ATTENDANTS.

Carr, John ;
    Pte. R. Ir. Regt., August, 1915 ; gassed ; discharged, 1916.

Holton, James ;
    C.S.M., R. Ir. Fus., Nov. 1915.

Kelly, William ;
    Engine-Room Artificer R.N., Jan. 1915.

Manby, John ;
    Sergt. R.A.M.C., Nov. 1915.

Skerritt, Isaac ;
    Sergt. R.F.A., Dec. 1914 ; discharged ; employed in Woolwich
    Arsenal as clerk.

Skipper, Alfred ;
    Pte. R.N.V.R.

Tonge, Alfred ;
    Pte. 5 Lancers.

SKIPS.

Bateson, William J.;
Sergt. A.S.C., June 1915.

Clements, Robert ;
Pte. R.A.M.C., Aug. 1914.

Jackson, F. J.;
Sergt. R.A.M.C., March 1915.

Roud, Thomas ;
Sergt. 8 R. Muns. Fus., July, 1915 ; shell-shock.

Spinks, John M.;
Pte. 3 D. Gds., March 1914 ; in hospital from debility, Nov.
1916.

Ward, Samuel ;
Pte. 1 L'pool R., Aug. 1914.

LABOURERS.

Boland, Bertie ;
Pte. R.A.F., Sept 1918.

Burleigh, Cecil ;
Pte. R. Innis. Fus., Sept. 1914 ; wounded.

Elkins, George ;
Pte. R.A.M.C., Aug. 1915.

Hickey, William ;
Stoker R.N., Nov. 1915.

Montgomery, James ;
Pte. R.E., Aug, 1915 ; accidentally injured ; discharged 1916.

O'Donnell, William
Pte. R. Ir. Rif., July 1915 ; twice wounded, 1916.

Whelan, Joseph ;
Pte. (M.T.), April 1918.

EMPLOYÉS OF THE TRINITY COLLEGE PRINTING-HOUSE.

Carroll, Owen William;
Pte. R.A.M.C., June 1915; Cpl. Nov. 1915; France, 1916;
Salonika, 1917–18.

Collins, John;
Pte. 10 R. Dub. Fus., Nov. 1915; France, 1916, trench
fever, 1916; killed in action, 21 Nov. 1917.

Connolly, John Joseph;
Pte. 3 R. Dub. Fus., April 1916; France, 1916–18; wounded,
July 1917.

Creely, Joseph;
Pte. 6 R. Ir. Regt., May 1915; France, 1915; wounded (five
times), France, 1915–17; prisoner of war, 1918.

Currey, John James; `
Pte. 10 R. Dub. Fus., Nov. 1915; att. R. Muns. Fus.; France,
1916; died of wounds, 26 Sept. 1918.

Mahon, John Sylvester;
Pte. 7 R. Dub. Fus., Sept. 1914; Suvla Bay, 1915; Sergt. 1915;
Salonika, 1915; frost-bite, 1915; 6 Bn., Salonika, 1916; France.
1917.

Nolan, James;
Trooper S. Ir. Horse, 1915.

Perrin, John Fawcett;
Pte. R.E., 1917–18.

Torkington, Richard;
Pte. R. Dub. Fus., 1915; France, 1916.

Waller, John William;
Pte. R.A.M.C., May 1915; Corp. Nov. 1915; France, 1916–18;
Germany, 1918–19.

Wheelock, Francis;
Pte. 3 R. Ir. Regt., May 1915; Sergt. 1915; Salonika, 1916–18.
mentioned in despatches.

Lightning Source UK Ltd.
Milton Keynes UK
UKOW050025080213

206003UK00001B/12/A